praise for

the six o'clock scramble

"*The Six O'Clock Scramble* has saved our sanity."

—DC Baby

"Fastest and freshest . . . The simple, seasonal recipes pack more flavor with fewer ingredients."

—*Real Simple*

"Aviva Goldfarb's system helps avoid the daily dinner scramble."

—*The Washington Post*

"These recipes are fresh and simple. The meals were easy to make and tasted great—sometimes you don't get both."

—Hybrid Mom

"Let's get one thing straight right away: I don't cook. I avoid it whenever possible. I'm not good at it. I don't enjoy it. But I just may change my mind, thanks to the me-friendly/kid-friendly cookbook, *The Six O'Clock Scramble*, from Aviva Goldfarb."

—Cool Mom Picks

"I absolutely love it! The meals are organized seasonally, so you are buying and cooking produce that is fresh and readily available (and usually affordable). They are all quick and fairly easy. And the kicker? Both of my kids have eaten and enjoyed everything I have made from this cookbook. Do you realize how utterly insane that is? This is a busy mom's lifesaver."

—Val, blogger, "Nothing, Really"

"I am a family physican and my wife is an OB-GYN. We are busy, have four children, and feel strongly about doing as much of our own cooking as possible so we can be home and eating by 6:00 P.M. with our children. The Six O'Clock Scramble Web site and great quick recipes make it possible. And even better is that we are eating low-fat, heart-healthy foods that I can recommend to my patients and friends!"

—Marc Bingham, M.D.,
Boiling Springs, South Carolina

"Aviva accomplishes quite the feat in her cookbooks—providing recipes that are not only quick and healthy, but also taste amazing. I recommend them in my private practice and use them in my own household. They are some of my favorite recipes and practical feeding resources for families."

—Angela Lemond, C.S.P., R.D., L.D., individual and family dietician, www.angelalemond.com

"Your book is awesome! I have made over thirty different recipes in the book and love all of them (that usually never happens when I buy a cookbook). When I put a meal on the table for my family, the first thing that goes through my mind is 'What a masterpiece, I made that!' "

—Kim J.

"I love to serve home-cooked meals, but I loathe deciding what to make for dinner day after day, week after week. So I decided to just 'cook your book'—meaning I'm just cooking every single recipe. I'm finding we save SO much money this way—I just buy all the ingredients on Sunday night, and then don't have to go to the store again. So we're eating out less, avoiding throwing together expensive last-minute meals, etc. And of course I love how quickly these meals get onto the table."

—Kara P., Kirkland, Washington

"Your recipes have been a hit every time with my husband and four girls; they are simple, healthy, and, most important, yummy!"

—Robin D., Cincinnati, Ohio

"I love your cookbook! As a working mother of two very young children, this book has been a lifesaver for me in terms of meal planning and preparation. I literally whip everything up in the midst of getting home from work, picking up the kids, and keeping them occupied until we can sit down. Everything I've made has been delicious."

—Kara H., Olney, Maryland

"Is it possible to fall in love with a cookbook? I've tried a lot of other cookbooks that promise to only take thirty minutes, but this is the first cookbook I've tried that actually delivers on that promise."

—Kari K., Beaverton, Oregon

"This is the best cookbook I have ever tried (and I have tried a lot!). My picky three-year-old eats it, my gourmet-cooking husband loves it, and I do, too. The recipes are healthy, delicious, and easy to prepare. Yes, you can prepare food fast without it being processed, who knew?"

—P.N., North Carolina

SOS!
the six o'clock scramble to the rescue

also by aviva goldfarb

The Six O'Clock Scramble

Peanut Butter Stew and Couscous, Too

(with Lisa Flaxman)

SOS!
the six o'clock scramble to the rescue

earth-friendly, kid-pleasing

dinners for busy families

aviva goldfarb

St. Martin's Griffin ✖ New York

ENVIRONMENTAL WORKING GROUP

A generous portion of the proceeds from this cookbook are donated directly to the Environmental Working Group, www.ewg.org. The Environmental Working Group is a nonprofit policy group that uses the power of public information to protect human health and the environment. EWG specializes in providing useful resources to consumers (such as the Shoppers' Guide to Pesticides in Produce and Skin Deep, a guide to toxins in cosmetics and sunscreens) while simultaneously pushing for national policy change. The Scramble is proud to support the EWG and its vital work.

www.stmartins.com

Library of Congress Cataloging-in-Publication Data

Goldfarb, Aviva.
   SOS! the six o'clock scramble to the rescue : earth-friendly, kid-pleasing dinners for busy families / Aviva Goldfarb.
     p. cm.
ISBN 978-0-312-57811-4
   1. Quick and easy cookery. 2. Dinners and dining. 3. Grocery shopping. I. Title. II. Title: six o'clock scramble to the rescue.
TX833.5.G672   2010
641.5'55—dc22   2009045296

First Edition: April 2010

10 9 8 7 6 5 4 3 2 1

Book design by rlf design

In Memory of Lisa Flaxman,
beloved friend and cooking companion
(1965–2009)
www.lisaflaxmanfund.org

contents

spring

· ·

summer

. . . .

fall

. . . .

winter

acknowledgments

Almost any book, but especially a cookbook, is a group effort. I want to thank the thousands of friends and customers whose recipes, suggestions, ideas, and support have helped The Six O'Clock Scramble thrive since 2003.

For their assistance with this cookbook, I single out for special appreciation my colleagues Jeanne Rossomme, Betsy Goldstein, Kathryn Spindel, Robin Thieme, Lee Unangst, R.D., Rachel Lukawski, and Sarah Chamberlin, Cindy Frank, Stephan Beauchesne, and Mike Bleed for their work on the accompanying Web site. I am also very grateful to my editor at St. Martin's Press, Elizabeth Beier, for her creative insights, epicurean inspiration, and steadfast support, and to her wonderful assistant, Michelle Richter.

I am indebted to The Six O'Clock Scramble recipe testers and contributors, particularly (in alphabetical order): Bev Abrams, Claudia Ades, Kristen Bassick, Anne Berube, Julia Blocksma, Nancy Bolen, Debby Boltman, Vicki Botnick, Koren Bowie, Jennifer Brockett, Debbie Brodsky, Richard Brooks, Sarah Burke, Ann Callison, Alice Clark, Jackie Cohen, Colleen Conners, Valentín Corral, Elizabeth Cullen, Jolynn Childers Dellinger, Jennifer Doig, Katie Ellis, Sara Emley, Sherry Ettleson, Elizabeth Fenimore, Debbie Firestone, Lisa Flaxman, Deb Ford, April Fulton, Jody Gan, Barbara Goldfarb, Mark Goldfarb, Deborah Goldsholl, Jennifer Grosman, Jennifer Gross, Leanne Guido, Michele Houghton, Kim Jackson, Gina Jermakowicz, Vanessa Jones, Melinda Kelley, Greg Kershner, Ilana Knab, Janet Krolman, Debbie Lehrich, Beth Levison, Sheba Lux, Colleen Masse, Margaret Mattocks, Ginny Maycock, Soozy Miller, Diana Molavi, Maria Mullen, Robyn Muncy, Madhavi Naik, Pamela Navarro-Watson, Lisa Newman, Tricia Nudelman, Susan Oliver, Catherine O'Leary, Kelly O'Rourke, Nina Prill, Christina Ramus, Diane Ray, Ruth Robbins, Karen Schachter, Rachel Scherr, Karen Schlesinger, Esther Schrader, Kathryn Schwartz, Heller An Shapiro, Sara Sheldon, Fern Shephard, Evely Laser Shlensky, Lincoln Shlensky, Debi Silber, Maxine Silverman, Sandra Simmons, Suzanne Simon, Lizzy Smith, Monica Smith, Mark Spindel, Bettina Stern, Sandra Swirski, Alexandra Taylor, Kirsten Thistle, Molly Thompson, Kim Tilley, Jessica Tomback, Alyce Traverso, Liz Vangaever, Kevin Warner, Kimberly Wilcox, Nachama Wilker, Linda Willard, Carrie Witkop, Bobbi Woods, Elizabeth Zehner, and Carrie Zisman.

Most important, I thank my nightly dining companions, Andrew, Solomon, and Celia Goldfarb. You fill my heart with love and make the dinner table a joyful place.

SOS!
the six o'clock
scramble to
the rescue

introduction

how to take the chaos out of family dinners and
feel good about what your family is eating

CHANCES ARE that if you've picked up this book, you are familiar with the concept of the Six O'Clock Scramble, maybe even from your own life. The Six O'Clock Scramble is my name for that time of day when we hustle to get dinner on the table for our families, despite the challenges.

For me, 6:00 P.M. used to be stressful because I didn't have any idea what I was going to make for dinner. I'd start scanning the cabinets and refrigerator trying desperately to come up with a dinner plan. At the same time, my kids often needed attention, our pets were agitating for their dinner, my own stomach was growling, and I was starting to get a giant headache from all the pressure! Sound familiar?

In 2003 I developed a solution to that daily stress that, in homage to that busy time of day, I call the Six O'Clock Scramble (www.thescramble.com). I have since shared my golden ticket to calmer cooking with tens of thousands of hungry and stressed-out people, and have gotten great satisfaction from helping them solve their own dinner dilemmas.

The key to this solution is creating a weekly dinner plan and making a grocery list at the beginning of the week (all of which can be found at www.thescramble.com/SOS) so we can shop just once for a whole week of meals, and know that each night we have all the ingredients we need to make healthy and balanced meals for our family.

I am also a strong believer that sitting down as a family to a meal that comes from our own kitchens, not a shrink-wrapped box, helps our children's health and development. So I've tried to stick to recipes that appeal to taste buds of all ages, and that you can tailor to fit your family's needs.

The Scramble takes the "thinking" out of meal planning, saving us time, money, and stress. The system succeeds where others fail because it is sustainable. In other words, it works so easily that we are motivated to keep it up in our own lives and share it with others.

But the Scramble is more than just an organizational aid. Several years ago I realized that the Scramble is also a great way for us to reduce our impact on the environment while also helping ourselves and our families. By shopping with a plan once a week, we use fewer resources because we drive less and waste much less food, and use fewer of those awful plastic or Styrofoam takeout containers that are used once and then thrown away, taking up space in landfills for hundreds or thousands of years, and despoiling our oceans and streams.

The Scramble's recipe collection also features many meatless meals, which reduce our impact on the planet because of the high environmental costs of a meat-heavy diet. What's more, the Scramble's fish recipes use primarily sustainable fish that are also healthier for us to eat.

As someone who treasures both delicious, healthy food and a healthy environment, I have also joined forces with the millions of people across the world who are committed to buying and eating more seasonal and local food. By eating more foods that are in season where (or near where) we live, we can enjoy fresh, flavorful food, support our local farmers and food-related businesses, and reduce our impact on the environment by eating foods that don't have to travel across the world to get to our dinner tables.

Like me, I'm sure you have a very full life, and don't have a lot of time to think about dinner, let alone make it. This book is for people who want to make easy, healthy, and delicious dinners for our families, dinners that we don't even have to think about until six o'clock most days, and dinners that we can feel great about serving to our families because they are true to our own values.

Happy Scrambling!

—Aviva

A note to readers about seasonal menus

This book is organized by seasons so you can plan your menus around what is fresh, locally grown, and in season whenever possible. Of course, this is not an exact science, but rather a guide: Not all produce is available in all regions and climates at the same time, while some fruits and vegetables are available year-round because they do well in cold storage or are imported from tropical climates. I also incorporate healthy and convenient frozen, canned, and shelved ingredients, especially in the cooler months. If you would also like to follow the Six O'Clock Scramble philosophy of planning meals for the week and grocery shopping once a week, I have suggested weekly menus for each season on pages 12, 84, 174 and 248. The grocery lists are available free of charge online for each of the menus at www.thescramble.com/SOS, so you can print them and take them with you to the grocery store on your weekly shopping trip. (Note: To try my online menu planning system, please use the free trial offer on page 322).

the well-stocked kitchen

the scramble staples list

A GOOD LIST OF STAPLES to have on hand can help you in the following ways:

- **Shop Sales:** You can take advantage of local store specials or bulk purchases on these commonly used items.

- **Stock Your Freezer:** Frozen fish, chicken, and vegetables often have the same nutritional value as fresh but are less expensive and can be stored longer with less waste.

- **Shop Faster:** Your grocery trips each week should be even faster if you are well stocked with staples. You should be able to focus your shopping excursions mainly on fresh produce, meats, and dairy.

- **Stretch Your Meals:** With a well-stocked pantry, you can more easily pull together an extra meal or two with unused ingredients in your refrigerator from the week's meals. (The Scramble's recipe database at www.thescramble.com can help!)

Depending on the size of your kitchen and pantry, you can stock up on one or several of the following items. Those items marked with an asterisk (*) are used especially frequently in Scramble recipes and are great candidates for bulk purchase.

Pantry Staples

- oils: olive oil*, vegetable or canola oil*, peanut oil, sesame oil, nonstick cooking spray*, butter, or margarine*

- vinegars: red wine vinegar, rice vinegar, balsamic vinegar*

- vinaigrette salad dressing (or you can make your own)*

- Dijon mustard

- minced garlic (buy in a jar or mince fresh garlic yourself)*

- ketchup and barbecue sauce

- reduced-fat mayonnaise

- Asian sauces: reduced-sodium soy sauce*, hoisin sauce

- wines: rice wine, white cooking wine, red cooking wine, dry sherry

- pitted black and green olives, capers

- bread crumbs, panko, cornmeal, flour

- sweeteners: white and brown sugar, honey, pure maple syrup

- grains: white or brown rice*, quinoa, couscous, wild rice

- pasta (regular or whole grain), variety of shapes*

- cans or boxes of reduced-sodium chicken or vegetable broth*

- 26-ounce jars red pasta sauce*

- 15-ounce cans tomato sauce*

- 28-ounce cans crushed tomatoes

- 28-ounce cans whole tomatoes

- 15-ounce cans diced tomatoes*

- 15-ounce cans naturally sweetened corn kernels (or use frozen kernels)

- canned beans: black*, kidney*, cannellini, and pinto* beans

- salsa*

- nuts: pine nuts, walnuts*, slivered almonds, pecans (store open bags of nuts in freezer)

Spices

- basil

- bay leaves

- black pepper*

- chili powder*

- ground cinnamon

- ground cumin

- curry powder

- dry mustard powder

- garlic powder*

- kosher salt

- oregano

- white pepper

- rosemary

- salt*

- salt-free lemon-pepper seasoning

- thyme

Freezer Staples

- frozen broccoli

- frozen chopped spinach

- frozen peas

- frozen edamame (with or without shells)

- frozen corn

- shredded Cheddar and part-skim mozzarella cheese, divided into 1-pound packages

- salmon (preferably wild), divided into 1- to 1½-pound packages

- firm white fish fillets such as tilapia, cod, and flounder, divided into 1- to 1½-pound packages

- peeled and deveined shrimp, divided into 1-pound packages

- boneless chicken (white or dark meat), divided into 1-pound packages

- ground turkey, chicken, or beef, divided into 1-pound packages

- precooked turkey or chicken sausage, mild or spicy

seasonal guide to fruits and vegetables

A note to readers about this seasonal guide: This chart is a guideline for menu planning purposes. Not all produce is available in all regions and climates at the same time, while some fruits and vegetables are available year-round because they thrive in cold storage or are imported from tropical climates. For more information about what is in season in your region, visit your local farmers markets or see the resources listed at the end of this chart.

SPRING

FRUITS

Bananas (all year)

Honeydew melons (February-October)

Mangoes (April-August)

Oranges (November-June)

Pineapples (February-August)

Tangelos (January-October)

VEGETABLES

Artichokes (March-May)

Asparagus (March-June)

Avocados (all year)

Broccoli (October-May)

Carrots (all year)

Celery (all year)

Green or wax beans (April-October)

Lettuce (all year)

Onions (all year)

Peas (April-July)

Peppers (all year)

Potatoes, white (all year)

Snow peas and sugar snap peas (June-July)

Spinach (March-May)

Tomatoes (May-August)

Zucchini (May-September)

SUMMER

Bananas (all year)

Blueberries (June-August)

Cantaloupes (May-September)

Cherries (May-June)

Crenshaw melons (July-October)

Figs (July-September)

Grapes (June-December)

Honeydew melons (February-October)

Kiwi (June-August)

Mangoes (April-August)

Nectarines and peaches (June-September)

Pineapples (February-August)

Plums (June-September)

Strawberries (June-August)

Watermelons (May-August)

Avocados (all year)

Beets (June-October)

Cabbage (all year)

Carrots (all year)

Celery (all year)

Corn (May-September)

Cucumbers (May-August)

Eggplant (August-September)

Green or wax beans (April-October)

Lettuce (all year)

Onions (all year)

Peas (April-July)

Peppers (all year)

Radishes (May-July)

Potatoes, white (all year)

Snow peas and sugar snap peas (June-July)

Squash, summer (June-August)

Swiss chard (June-August)

Tomatoes (May-August)

Zucchini (May-September)

FALL

FRUITS

Apples (September-May)

Bananas (all year)

Grapefruit (October-June)

Grapes (June-December)

Crenshaw melons (July-October)

Pears (August-May)

Persimmons (November-January)

Pomegranates (September-November)

VEGETABLES

Avocados (all year)

Beets (June-October)

Broccoli (September-May)

Brussels sprouts (October-November)

Cabbage (all year)

Carrots (all year)

Cauliflower (September-November)

Celery (all year)

Green or wax beans (April-October)

Kale (October-February)

Lettuce (all year)

Onions (all year)

Parsnips (October-April)

Peppers (all year)

Potatoes, sweet (September-December)

Potatoes, white (all year)

Squash, winter (September-November)

WINTER

FRUITS

Apples (September-May)

Bananas (all year)

Dates (August-December)

Grapefruit (October-June)

Grapes (June-December)

Honeydew melons (February-October)

Pears (August-May)

Oranges (November-June)

Pineapples (February-August)

Tangerines/Clementines (November-January)

VEGETABLES

Avocados (all year)

Broccoli (October-May)

Cabbage (all year)

Carrots (all year)

Celery (all year)

Kale (October-February)

Lettuce (all year)

Mushrooms (November-April)

Onions (all year)

Parsnips (October-April)

Peppers (all year)

Potatoes, sweet (September-December)

Potatoes, white (all year)

Some of the data for this chart is provided by: Fruits & Veggies—More Matters® courtesy of Produce for Better Health Foundation (PBH), www.fruitsandveggiesmorematters.org, and by Betty P. Greer, Ph.D., R.D., Professor, Family and Consumer Sciences, University of Tennessee Extension.

For more information about what is in season in your region, visit: www.fieldtoplate.com/guide.php.

spring

five weekly spring menus

To help you embrace all the fresh flavors of spring, here are five tasty weekly menus. (You can also make your shopping a breeze by grabbing the accompanying organized grocery list for each of these menus at www.thescramble.com/SOS.)

week 1

Lemon-Oregano Chicken
Grilled Caramelized Ginger Salmon
San Francisco Joes
Ravioli with Spinach and Sun-dried Tomatoes
Mango and Black Bean Salad

week 2

Smokin' Barbecue Meatloaf
Basil-Parmesan Baked Snapper
Chinese Lo Mein Noodles with Asparagus
Crispy Tofu Triangles with Fried Rice
Spinach, Basil, and Red Pepper Wraps

week 3

Lemon-Pepper Pork Chops
Cornmeal-crusted Fish with Black Bean and Corn Salsa
Penne with Prosciutto and Goat Cheese
Chili Potatoes with Sweet Peppers
Earth Day Vegetable Stew with Feta Cheese

week 4

Ginger-Soy Flank Steak
Tilapia Packets with Fresh Herbs and Baby Spinach
Spaghetti Carbonara
Chipotle Bean and Corn Burritos
Mediterranean Quinoa Salad

week 5

Tandoori Chicken
Beef or Turkey Empanadas (Flaky Meat Pies)
Spice-tossed Shrimp with Parmesan Grits
Honey Sesame Spaghetti
Cream of Asparagus Soup with Fresh Croutons

poultry, pork, and beef

Key: (V) = Vegetarian or vegetarian optional;
    * = Scramble Express: 30 minutes or less total;
  (M) = Make-ahead, freeze, or slow-cooker option

sandwiches, wraps, salads, and other lighter fare

Key: (V) = Vegetarian or vegetarian optional;
* = Scramble Express: 30 minutes or less total;
(M) = Make-ahead, freeze, or slow-cooker option

spending our food dollars
where they count—on local food!

SPRING IS IN THE AIR and with it the happy return of all those beautiful, fresh local vegetables. Farmers markets and produce stands reopen (at least those that close for the cool weather). Crisp asparagus and pungent, delicate arugula are as welcome and renewing as bright, blooming daffodils and tulips.

But is buying these locally grown foods an indulgence or a wise use of our food budget? Sometimes buying locally grown foods is more expensive, other times it is not. But for me the overall value is higher. The better quality, taste, and longer shelf life means less food waste and more nutritious fruits and vegetables in the bellies of our loved ones. I've found that I can also freeze in-season fruits and vegetables for an economical and ready source of produce.

I feel good about spending my food dollars to support local farms, where produce is usually grown with fewer, if any, pesticides, livestock is treated more humanely, transportation cost (and pollution) is reduced, and local farmers can support their families rather than having to sell their farm parcels to land developers. Patronizing these local markets also helps our children feel connected to the local community and the wonders of what springs from the earth.

By buying local produce, eggs, meats, and dairy products we make an investment in the health of our families, our communities, and our planet. And I can't think of any other way I'd like to spend my Saturday or Sunday mornings than connecting with the local farmers and their mouth-watering and eye-pleasing bounty.

happy spring!

This simple dish gives you a lot of flavor for just six ingredients and twenty minutes, and is a terrific dinner for a busy night (wait—isn't that every night?). Serve it with couscous, and asparagus (the ideal vegetable to help you celebrate the onset of spring!) with pine nuts.

lemon-oregano chicken

Prep + Cook =
20 minutes

4 servings

Nutritional Information per serving (% based upon daily values): Calories 310, Total Fat 9g, 14%, Saturated Fat 1.5g, 8%, Cholesterol 130mg, 43%, Sodium 360mg, 15%, Total Carbohydrate 1g, 0%, Dietary Fiber 0g, 0%, Sugar 0g, Protein 53g

Nutritional Information per serving with side dish (% based upon daily values) ¾ cup couscous prepared with water; 1 cup prepared asparagus:
Calories: 520; Total Fat: 14g, 21%; Saturated Fat: 3g, 12%; Cholesterol: 130mg, 43%; Sodium: 546mg, 22%; Total Carbohydrate: 38g, 11%; Dietary Fiber: 6g, 21%; Sugar: 2g; Protein: 62g

2 pounds boneless, skinless chicken breasts

3 tablespoons olive oil

½ – ¾ lemon, juice only (2 tablespoons juice)

¾ teaspoon dried oregano, or 2 teaspoons fresh

1 teaspoon minced garlic (about 2 cloves)

½ teaspoon kosher salt

Wrap the chicken breasts in plastic wrap and flatten them with a mallet to an even thickness. This allows them to cook more quickly and evenly. (Alternatively, cut them into 1-inch pieces.)

Put the chicken (without the plastic wrap, of course) in a flat dish large enough to hold it in one layer. Drizzle 2 tablespoons of the oil, the lemon juice, oregano, garlic, and salt over it. Flip the chicken several times to coat it. (Meanwhile, start the asparagus and the couscous.)

In a large heavy skillet over medium heat, add the remaining oil. When the pan is hot, cook the chicken on the first side for 4 to 5 minutes until it is just starting to brown. Flip the chicken and partially cover the pan. Reduce the heat to medium-low, and continue cooking the chicken for 4 to 5 more minutes until it is just cooked through. Transfer the chicken to a cutting board and cut it into strips to serve it.

Scramble Flavor Booster: Marinate the chicken for at least 15 minutes and up to 2 hours. Season the chicken with freshly ground black pepper at the table, and serve it with lemon wedges.

Tip: When substituting fresh herbs for dry herbs in a recipe, the ratio I use is generally 3:1, or about 3 times the amount of fresh herbs as dried.

Side Dish suggestion: Prepare couscous according to package directions, using water or broth for the liquid. For even more flavor, stir fresh herbs, toasted pine nuts or slivered almonds, or dried cranberries or currants into the hot couscous.

Side Dish suggestion: To make asparagus with pine nuts, trim 1 bunch (about 1 pound) of asparagus and cut it in thirds. In a medium skillet, heat 1 tablespoon olive oil over medium heat. Add 2 tablespoons pine nuts and toast them in the oil for 1 to 2 minutes, stirring frequently, until they are lightly browned. Add the asparagus and stir-fry it for 3 to 5 minutes until it is tender-crisp. Season it with salt and black pepper to taste.

I love the airiness of Japanese panko-style bread crumbs. Here's a great way to incorporate them into a delicious and kid-friendly dinner. Serve it with Roasted Baby Carrots and a loaf of whole grain bread.

crispy parmesan-panko crusted chicken cutlets

Prep + Cook = 20 minutes

6 servings

Nutritional Information per serving (% based upon daily values): Calories 350, Total Fat 13g, 20%, Saturated Fat 4g, 20%, Cholesterol 170mg, 57%, Sodium 260mg, 11%, Total Carbohydrate 18g, 6% Dietary Fiber 1g, 4%, Sugar 6g, Protein 39g

Nutritional Information per serving with side dish (% based upon daily values) 1 cup roasted carrots; 1 slice bread: Calories: 545; Total Fat: 20g, 31%; Saturated Fat: 7g, 32%; Cholesterol: 170mg, 57%; Sodium: 663mg, 28%; Total Carbohydrate: 48g, 16%; Dietary Fiber: 8g, 30%; Sugar: 13g; Protein: 44g

⅓ cup flour

¼–½ teaspoon dry mustard, to taste

¼ teaspoon salt

¼ teaspoon black pepper

2 eggs

1 cup panko (Japanese bread crumbs)

¼ cup grated Parmesan cheese

2 tablespoons butter

2 tablespoons olive oil

2 pounds chicken cutlets, or boneless, skinless chicken breasts, pounded flat

½ cup Dijon mustard

2 tablespoons honey

(Start the carrots first, if you are serving them.) Combine the flour, dry mustard, salt, and pepper in a shallow dish, beat the eggs in a separate shallow bowl, and combine the panko and Parmesan cheese in another shallow dish.

Heat half the butter and half the oil in a large nonstick skillet or heavy skillet coated with nonstick cooking spray over medium-high heat. When the butter is melted, coat each chicken cutlet in the flour, then the egg, allowing the excess to drip off, then coat it thoroughly with the panko-Parmesan mixture and put it in the hot pan. About 3 to 4 chicken cutlets should fit in the pan at a time. After about 2 minutes, rotate the chicken so it cooks evenly, but don't flip it. After about 2 more minutes, flip the chicken, and do the same on the second side, rotating it once so the chicken cooks evenly throughout. Cook the rest of the chicken, adding the rest of the butter and olive oil as needed. Remove the cooked chicken to a paper towel–lined plate.

While the chicken is cooking, combine the Dijon mustard and honey in a small serving bowl. Serve the chicken with the honey-mustard sauce for dipping.

Scramble Flavor Booster: Use ½ teaspoon dry mustard in the coating and make the dipping sauce with spicy or grainy mustard.

Side Dish suggestion: To make Roasted Baby Carrots, preheat the oven to 450 degrees. Toss 1 pound baby carrots (or use large carrots, sliced into 1-inch pieces) with 1 tablespoon olive oil, ¼ teaspoon kosher salt, ¼ teaspoon black pepper, and ⅛ teaspoon ground ginger (optional). Roast the carrots until they are lightly browned, 15 to 20 minutes, tossing once.

growing your own vegetables
start small and savor the rewards

When spring arrives many of us are drawn outdoors to dig in (literally) to the garden to prepare for the delectable edibles we can harvest in the summer and fall. Having your own garden truly feeds the body, mind, and spirit. What's more, growing our own food can save us money. And if we keep it small and manageable, it's not overly time-consuming, and in fact, it's rewarding to maintain our little corners of the earth.

I confess that I am not a seasoned gardener. Like most of us, my busy life juggling kids, work, friends, and community involvements leaves precious few hours for tilling the earth. So these tips on gardening come from the viewpoint of a Scrambling mom who wants a sustainable source of fresh food. Hopefully they will inspire you to try your hand at a garden this year, too:

Start small. While you may be enthusiastic about putting in a large garden in the spring, after a few months of fighting back weeds, bugs, and cute (but pesky!) little garden bunnies or roaming deer, your enthusiasm is likely to wane. Start with a small plot or even some containers and build up a little each year.

Location, location, location. Pick a spot that has a lot of sun. Without 4 to 6 hours of direct sunshine each day, you are unlikely to have a good harvest. Also try to have a spot that is easy to get to (maybe even close to the kitchen), if possible, so you are more likely to build the garden into your meal plans.

Prepare and plan. Prepare the soil with organic material and plan what you will plant and when. As we Scramblers know, planning takes about 80 percent of the stress out of any project.

Let your garden save you money. Plant those items that tend to cost you the most at the grocery store. Many herbs grow like weeds, yet at the store they cost $3 or more for a few sprigs! Also think of planting specialty "gourmet" or dwarf vegetables like Japanese eggplants and broccoli raab, grape tomatoes, and fancy leaf lettuces.

Make it a family affair. Include your kids, maybe even dedicating sections to each child. Purchase some child-size gardening gloves and tools so they have the ability and inspiration to help out. (I have a friend who includes these in her children's Easter baskets.)

Of course, I can't grow the majority of the produce my family eats in my little suburban backyard. Fortunately, there are several farmers markets nearby that will help us enjoy fresh and locally grown (and organic, whenever possible) produce throughout the growing season.

This is a terrific marinade to use for meat or fish. As with most marinades, the flavor intensifies the longer you marinate it, so overnight is ideal. Serve it with wild rice and one of my favorite spring side dishes, Wilted Spinach with Mushrooms.

bacon-wrapped chicken strips with orange-dijon sauce

Prep + Cook =
30 minutes + Marinate (1–24 hours)

6 servings

Nutritional Information per serving (% based upon daily values): Calories 230, Total Fat 9g, 14%, Saturated Fat 2g, 10%, Cholesterol 95mg, 32%, Sodium 990mg, 41%, Total Carbohydrate 3g, 1%, Dietary Fiber 0g, 0%, Sugar 2g, Protein 33g

Nutritional Information per serving with side dish (% based upon daily values) ¾ cup cooked rice; ⅙ of spinach and mushrooms: Calories: 411; Total Fat: 12g, 19%; Saturated Fat: 3g, 12%; Cholesterol: 95mg, 32%; Sodium: 1,089mg, 45%; Total Carbohydrate: 38g, 12%; Dietary Fiber: 5g, 21%; Sugar: 5g; Protein: 40g

1½–2 lbs. boneless, skinless chicken breasts

½ cup orange juice

2 tablespoons reduced-sodium soy sauce

1 teaspoon sesame oil

½ teaspoon garlic powder

1 tablespoon Dijon mustard

8 ounces turkey or pork bacon

Cut the chicken breasts lengthwise into several strips about 1 inch wide and lay them in a flat dish with sides.

In a large measuring cup or bowl, whisk together the remaining ingredients except the bacon. Pour the marinade over the chicken, stir the chicken to coat it, and marinate it, refrigerated, for at least 1 hour, and up to 24 hours.

(Start the wild rice first, if you are serving it.) When you are ready to cook, preheat the oven to 350 degrees. Remove the chicken from the marinade, reserve the marinade, and lay the chicken strips on a baking sheet. Wrap each chicken strip with a strip of bacon, wrapping it from one end to the other, trying to cover as much of the chicken as possible.

Bake the chicken for 15 minutes until the chicken is cooked through in the thickest part. (Meanwhile, make the spinach and mushrooms.) While the chicken is cooking, transfer the marinade to a small saucepan and bring it to a boil. Simmer it for 2 to 3 minutes to kill any bacteria from the raw chicken. Transfer the marinade to a small bowl to use as a sauce for the chicken and rice.

Scramble Flavor Booster: Add ¼ teaspoon black pepper to the marinade.

Tip: If the bacon isn't crispy after baking the chicken, you can put it under the broiler for 3 to 5 minutes to crisp it up.

Side Dish suggestion: Prepare 1½ to 2 cups wild rice, using water or chicken broth, according to the package directions. To make it even more interesting, stir 1 to 2 tablespoons each of dried cranberries and chopped pecans and 1 to 2 tablespoons vinaigrette dressing into the just-cooked rice.

Side Dish suggestion: To make Wilted Spinach with Mushrooms, in a large skillet, heat 1 to 2 tablespoons olive oil over medium to medium-low heat. Add 1 teaspoon minced garlic (1 to 2 cloves) and sauté it for about 30 seconds. Add 2 portobello mushrooms or 2 to 4 cups of other gourmet mushrooms, coarsely chopped. Sauté the mushrooms for about 5 minutes until they are dark and tender. Add 12 to 18 ounces baby spinach and 3 to 4 teaspoons balsamic vinegar. Mix everything together and cover the pan to wilt the spinach for about 3 to 4 minutes. Season it with salt and black pepper to taste, and ¼ teaspoon crushed red pepper flakes (optional) before serving.

This stir-fry from my friend Deb Ford tastes like the best Chinese take-out (Scramble recipe tester Margaret Mattocks said it was "better than take-out"), but it's quicker than waiting (and paying!) for a delivery. If you have chives growing in your garden, you can use those instead of the scallions. Serve it with steamed rice and Sesame-Soy Broccoli.

chinese chicken with peanuts

Prep + Cook =
20 minutes

6 servings

Nutritional
Information per
serving (% based
upon daily values):
Calories 220, Total
Fat 8g, 12%, Satu-
rated Fat 1.5g, 8%,
Cholesterol 65mg,
22%, Sodium 750mg,
31%, Total Carbohy-
drate 8g, 3%, Dietary
Fiber 1g, 4%, Protein
29g, Sugar 3g

Nutritional
Information per
serving (% based
upon daily values):
3/4 cup white rice;
1 cup broccoli:
Calories: 463; Total
Fat: 12g, 20%; Satu-
rated Fat: 2g, 11%;
Cholesterol: 65mg,
22%; Sodium: 951 mg,
39%; Total Carbohy-
drate: 52g, 18%;
Dietary Fiber: 6g,
22%; Sugar: 6g;
Protein: 37g

3½ tablespoons reduced-sodium soy sauce

1 tablespoon cornstarch

1½ pounds boneless, skinless chicken breasts or thighs, cut into 1-inch pieces

1 tablespoon sherry

1 teaspoon honey or sugar

1 teaspoon red wine vinegar

½ teaspoon ground ginger

1 tablespoon peanut oil

1 red bell pepper, cut into 1-inch pieces (or use snow peas or diced water chestnuts)

4 scallions, sliced (about ⅓ cup)

½ cup unsalted peanuts (or use cashews or walnuts)

(If you are serving rice and broccoli, start those first.) In a medium bowl, combine 1½ tablespoons of the soy sauce and the cornstarch. Stir in the cut chicken and set it aside. In a small bowl, combine the remaining soy sauce, sherry, honey or sugar, vinegar, and ginger.

In a large wok or nonstick skillet, heat the oil over medium-high heat. Add the chicken with its juices to the pan and stir-fry it for 2 minutes, until the chicken starts to brown. Add the bell peppers and scallions and cook, stirring, for 2 more minutes. Add the soy-sherry mixture and the peanuts and cook for 1 more minute. Serve it immediately over rice or refrigerate it for up to 2 days or freeze it for up to 3 months.

Scramble Flavor Booster: Add ¼ teaspoon crushed red pepper flakes or a pinch of cayenne pepper to the stir-fry with the bell peppers.

Tip: As with almost any stir-fry, the key is having all the ingredients ready and near the stove before you start to cook, so you can add them quickly when needed.

Side Dish suggestion: To make Sesame-Soy Broccoli, heat 1 tablespoon sesame oil in a wok or skillet over medium-high heat. Lightly brown 2 teaspoons minced garlic (3 to 4 cloves). Add 1 pound broccoli spears and ⅛ cup water. Cover, reduce the heat to medium, and steam the broccoli for 4 to 5 minutes, until it is tender-crisp. Add 1 tablespoon reduced-sodium soy sauce, and stir-fry it for 1 more minute before serving. Top it with 1 to 2 teaspoons toasted sesame seeds, if desired.

This dish flooded my mind with warm memories of my grandmother, who always ordered Chicken or Veal Marsala at her favorite Italian restaurants (along with a screwdriver and decaf!). The Marsala and lemon combination gives the chicken a sweet and tangy flavor and fills the house with a wonderful scent. Serve it with gnocchi (Italian potato dumplings) and a green salad with avocado, walnuts, and Parmesan cheese.

chicken marsala with mushrooms and garlic

Prep + Cook =
30 minutes

6 servings

Nutritional Information per serving (% based upon daily values): Calories 220, Total Fat 7g, 11%, Saturated Fat 2g, 10%, Cholesterol 70mg, 23%, Sodium 300mg, 13%, Total Carbohydrate 5g, 2%, Dietary Fiber 0g, 0%, Sugar 1g, Protein 28g

Nutritional Information per serving with side dish (% based upon daily values) ¾ cup prepared gnocchi; 1¾ cups salad: Calories: 596; Total Fat: 23g, 35%; Saturated Fat: 5g, 21%; Cholesterol: 74mg, 24%; Sodium: 926mg, 40%; Total Carbohydrate: 57g, 19%; Dietary Fiber: 7g, 28%; Sugar: 5g; Protein: 38g

3 tablespoons flour

¼ teaspoon salt plus additional to taste

¼ teaspoon black pepper

1½–2 pounds boneless, skinless chicken breasts, cut into 1-inch pieces

1 tablespoon plus 1 teaspoon olive oil

1 tablespoon butter or margarine

1 package (8 ounces) fresh sliced mushrooms

1½ teaspoons minced garlic (about 3 cloves)

½ cup Marsala wine

½ cup low-sodium chicken broth (freeze or refrigerate remaining broth for future use)

½ lemon, juice only (about 2 tablespoons)

1 tablespoon chopped fresh parsley (optional)

In a medium bowl, combine the flour, salt, and black pepper. Add the diced chicken and toss it gently to coat it thoroughly. Heat a large heavy skillet over medium heat. (Meanwhile, heat the water for the gnocchi, if you are making it.) Add 1 tablespoon oil and the butter and let the butter melt. Add the chicken and cook it for several minutes on each side until it is brown and cooked partially through. Remove the chicken from the pan and set it aside.

Add the remaining oil to the same pan without cleaning it. Sauté the mushrooms and garlic for 1 minute, and then add the wine, broth, and lemon juice. Bring the liquid to a low boil, scraping any bits of chicken from the bottom of the pan. Simmer the mixture for about 10 minutes until the mushrooms are tender and the liquid is reduced and slightly thickened. (Meanwhile, make the green salad if you are serving that.)

Add the chicken back into the pan, spoon the sauce over it, and cook it for 3 to 5 more minutes until the chicken is just cooked through. Season it with additional salt, if desired, and sprinkle the chicken with parsley before serving it (optional).

Scramble Flavor Booster: Use the fresh parsley and serve the chicken with additional lemon wedges.

Tip: If you have parsley growing in your garden, adding it to this dish at the end will really bring out its fresh flavor.

Side Dish suggestion: Cook 1 package of gnocchi according to the package directions. Drain and toss it with 1 to 2 tablespoons olive oil.

Side Dish suggestion: For the green salad, combine 6 to 8 cups lettuce, 1 diced avocado, ¼ cup walnuts, and ¼ cup grated Parmesan cheese. Top everything with 2 to 4 tablespoons light vinaigrette dressing, and toss gently.

seven steps to keeping
the six o'clock scramble on schedule

It seems as if for every year our kids get older the evening routine gets that much more complicated. Sure, on the weekends I often don't feel like making my weekly menu plan and going to the grocery store. But when dinnertime rolls around each weeknight (and I'm often just rolling in the driveway at 6:00 or later), I want to kiss myself for taking the time to get organized in advance. I breathe a deep sigh of relief, knowing I have everything I need to get a healthy, tasty meal on the table quickly.

If you've been with the Scramble for a while, you probably know that I think that the key to keeping our sanity around dinnertime is to plan a few meals in advance and try to grocery shop just once a week. However, I do have a few other suggestions for keeping dinners on track:

1. Schedule your meals for the week based on which ingredients are most perishable (i.e., meat, fish, and spinach), and which nights you will be shortest on time. You can put your recipes in that order or jot a note in your calendar to remember what you're making when.

2. Have a system for your kitchen. If you know where the vegetables are in your refrigerator (I keep one drawer for fruit and one for veggies), and can quickly lay your hands on the black beans and bowtie noodles, dinner prep will go a lot faster.

3. Get a head start during the day. While the kids are eating breakfast or doing homework, or while you are on a long call, wash and/or chop the vegetables you'll need, make your spice rubs, and pull out the pots and pans you'll need later.

4. Before you begin to cook, clear off the kitchen counters, empty the dishwasher, and pull out all of the ingredients. These steps make dinner preparation a lot less chaotic.

5. Before you start cooking, take a moment to think through the whole meal (and quickly read the whole recipe), including side dishes and table settings, so you know what you need to start preparing when. Enlist help from other family members if you can.

6. When you use up an ingredient that you consider a staple, write it on your grocery list right away so you'll be fully stocked after your next grocery trip. Teach your family to do this, too, and you'll all have your essentials on hand when you need them.

7. Put the ingredients away as you use them, so cleanup goes more quickly. When you are ready to do the dishes, stack all of the dirty dishes by the sink and load the dishwasher first (most dishes don't need to be pre-rinsed), so your dishwashing goes quickly and you use less water.

Sometimes having a system can sound daunting, but I have found that a little planning ahead saves so much time and effort that it makes cooking dinner for my family a pleasure most days, rather than a chore.

You can prepare this delicious Indian chicken in the morning or the night before you cook it, and then put it in the oven shortly before dinnertime. Scramble recipe tester Nancy Bolen said her children rated this dish a 10 out of 10. If your kids find it too flavorful, you can always wash the sauce off their cooked chicken before serving it to them. Serve it with basmati rice and Curried Carrots with Dill.

tandoori chicken

Prep (10 minutes) + Cook (25 minutes) + Marinate (1–24 hours)

4 servings

Nutritional Information per serving (with chicken breasts) (% based upon daily values): Calories 230, Total Fat 3g, 5%, Saturated Fat 1g, 5%, Cholesterol 100mg, 33%, Sodium 440mg, 18%, Total Carbohydrate 6g, 2%, Dietary Fiber <1g, 4%, Sugar 3g, Protein 42g

Nutritional Information per serving with side dish (% based upon daily values) ¾ cup rice with broth; ¼ of carrots: Calories: 450; Total Fat: 7g, 11%; Saturated Fat: 2g, 8%; Cholesterol: 105mg, 35%; Sodium: 575mg, 24%; Total Carbohydrate: 48g, 16%; Dietary Fiber: 4g, 16%; Sugar: 7g; Protein: 48g

¾ cup low-fat plain yogurt, preferably thick Greek yogurt

2 teaspoons minced fresh ginger, or ½ teaspoon ground ginger

2 teaspoons minced garlic (about 4 cloves)

1 teaspoon paprika

1 teaspoon ground cumin

1 teaspoon garam masala (an Indian spice blend)

½ teaspoon salt

1 lime, juice only (about 2 tablespoons juice)

1½–2 pounds boneless, skinless chicken thighs or breasts

¼ cup mango chutney for serving (optional)

In a large bowl, combine all the ingredients except the chutney (optional) and mix well to coat the chicken. Cover and refrigerate it for at least 1 and up to 24 hours; the longer the better.

Preheat the oven to 400 degrees (and start the rice, if you are serving it). Transfer the chicken to a glass or ceramic baking dish, allowing some sauce to cling to it. Bake the chicken, uncovered, for 20 to 25 minutes, until it is cooked through (the thighs will be tender but still dark in the middle when cooked through). (Meanwhile, prepare the carrots.) Serve it immediately, or refrigerate it for up to 24 hours.

Scramble Flavor Booster: Add ½ teaspoon cayenne pepper to the marinade.

Tip: If you can't find garam masala at your market, you can make your own blend with equal parts (or to your taste) of ground coriander, cumin, ginger, black pepper, cinnamon, cardamom, cloves, and nutmeg.

Side Dish suggestion: To make Curried Carrots with Dill, heat 2 teaspoons olive oil in a small saucepan over medium heat. Add 4 to 6 large carrots, sliced, ½ teaspoon curry powder, ½ teaspoon dried or fresh dill, to taste, and a pinch of salt. Sauté it for 2 minutes, stirring occasionally. Cover the pan, reduce the heat, and steam the carrots for about 8 minutes until just tender when pierced with a fork.

This recipe makes very juicy and flavorful chicken, and it's so nutritious. Serve it with boiled new or red potatoes.

baked chicken romano

Prep (20 minutes) +
Cook (30 minutes)

4 servings

Nutritional
Information per
serving (% based
upon daily values):
Calories 260, Total
Fat 7g, 11%, Saturated Fat 1g, 5%,
Cholesterol 100mg,
33%, Sodium 260mg,
11%, Total Carbohydrate 9g, 3%, Fiber
2g, 8%, Sugar 4g,
Protein 42g

Nutritional
Information per
serving with side dish
(% based upon daily
values) 3 small
potatoes:
Calories: 350; Total
Fat: 10g, 14%; Saturated Fat: 1g, 7%;
Cholesterol: 100mg,
33%; Sodium: 296mg,
13%; Total Carbohydrate: 30g, 10%;
Dietary Fiber: 6g,
21%; Sugar: 13g;
Protein: 44g

1 tablespoon olive oil

1 package (8 ounces) sliced fresh mushrooms

1 teaspoon minced garlic (about 2 cloves)

¼ large yellow onion, finely diced (about 1 cup)

3 plum tomatoes (also called Roma tomatoes), diced (or substitute 1 cup canned diced tomatoes)

¼ cup chopped fresh herbs, such as basil, oregano, and/or thyme

¼ teaspoon salt

¼ cup white wine (or use 1 lemon, juice only)

1½ pounds boneless, skinless chicken breasts, cut in half crosswise

Preheat the oven to 350 degrees. In a large skillet, heat the oil over medium heat. Sauté the mushrooms, garlic, and onions for 5 minutes until the onions soften and the mushrooms start to shrink. Stir in the tomatoes, herbs, salt, and white wine or lemon juice and cook for about 2 more minutes.

Put the chicken breasts in a flat baking dish with sides, just large enough to hold them in one layer. Pour the mushroom-tomato sauce on top, and bake the chicken for 25 to 30 minutes, until it is just cooked through. (Meanwhile, prepare the potatoes, if you are serving them.)

Scramble Flavor Booster: Add ¼ teaspoon crushed red pepper flakes with the garlic and onions and sprinkle the chicken with freshly ground black pepper to taste.

Tip: If the tomatoes in your market aren't too fresh or flavorful yet, use the canned tomatoes, which are picked and canned when they are perfectly ripe.

Side Dish suggestion: For boiled new or red potatoes, cover 1 to 2 pounds potatoes with water in a medium pot. Add about ½ teaspoon salt, and bring the water to a boil. Simmer the potatoes until they are fork-tender, 10 to 15 minutes, and drain them. Toss them immediately (cut them in half first, if desired) with 1 tablespoon of olive oil or butter, ⅛ teaspoon garlic powder, and ¼ teaspoon salt-free lemon-pepper seasoning (optional).

This delightful family friendly recipe from The Scramble's business advisor, Robin Thieme, gives us the perfect opportunity to get our grill ready for the season. It only takes a few minutes to make the marinade in the morning, then a few more minutes to grill it at dinnertime. But that's time enough to make you feel like you've been transported to a tropical paradise! Serve it with steamed brown or white rice and a Caribbean Sun Smoothie.

grilled island chicken

Prep (10 minutes) + Cook (10 minutes) + Marinate (30 minutes–24 hours)

4 servings

Nutritional Information per serving (% based upon daily values): Calories 270, Total Fat 4.5g, 7%, Saturated Fat 0.5g, 3%, Cholesterol 100mg, 33%, Sodium 310mg, 13%, Total Carbohydrate 15g, 5%, Dietary Fiber 1g, 4%, Sugar 13g, Protein 40g

Nutritional Information per serving with side dish (% based upon daily values) ³⁄₄ cup white rice; ¹⁄₄ of smoothie: Calories: 564; Total Fat: 5.5g, 10%; Saturated Fat: 1g, 3%; Cholesterol: 110mg, 33%; Sodium: 501 mg, 21%; Total Carbohydrate: 116g, 38%; Dietary Fiber: 6g, 22%; Sugar: 67g; Protein: 59g

3 tablespoons canola or vegetable oil

20 ounces pineapple slices or rings in 100 percent juice, juice reserved

3 tablespoons reduced-sodium soy sauce

1 teaspoon minced garlic (about 2 cloves)

¹⁄₄ teaspoon ground ginger

¹⁄₄ teaspoon black pepper

1¹⁄₂ –2 pounds boneless, skinless chicken breasts

In an 8-inch flat dish with sides, combine the oil, 3 tablespoons pineapple juice, soy sauce, garlic, ginger, and black pepper. Slice each chicken breast lengthwise into three long strips, and add them to the marinade. Set the pineapple rings aside (reserve the remaining juice for the smoothie). Cover and refrigerate the chicken for at least 30 minutes and up to 24 hours.

Preheat the grill or broiler to high heat (if you are using the broiler, set the rack 4 to 6 inches from the heat source). (Prepare the rice, if you are serving it.) Grill or broil the chicken strips (reserve the marinade for brushing on the chicken after you flip it). Grill the pineapple rings directly on the grates of the grill for 3 to 5 minutes per side, until they are browned and the chicken is just cooked through, or broil until browned. (Meanwhile, make the smoothies.) Flip the chicken once and brush it with the marinade, then discard the remaining marinade. Top the cooked chicken with the grilled pineapple rings to serve it.

Scramble Flavor Booster: Add a few dashes of hot pepper sauce, such as Tabasco, and up to 1 tablespoon minced fresh ginger to the marinade.

Tip: If you don't have or don't like to use an outdoor grill, you can use an indoor grill pan, or even a cast-iron skillet, right on your stove.

Side Dish suggestion: For the smoothies, in a blender combine the remaining pineapple juice (8–10 ounces), 1 cup of orange juice, 2 ripe bananas, 2 cups of nonfat plain or vanilla yogurt, and 1 cup of ice.

My friend Madhavi Naik, originally from Mumbai (Mumbai is the Indian name for what we used to call Bombay, India), gave me her appetizer recipe for Indian meatballs. The meatballs were so good that I thought they would make a unique, family-friendly dinner, too (no utensils except toothpicks required!). Serve the meatballs on colorful toothpicks with a few dipping sauces (even ketchup and mustard), with snow peas or sugar snap peas (a late spring favorite!) and Indian naan or pita bread.

mumbai meatballs with yogurt-chutney dipping sauce

Prep (10 minutes) + Cook (25 minutes)

4 servings

Nutritional Information per serving (% based upon daily values): Calories 260, Total Fat 10g, 15%, Saturated Fat 3g, 15%, Cholesterol 125mg, 42%, Sodium 530mg, 22%, Total Carbohydrate 16g, 5%, Dietary Fiber 1g, 4%, Sugar 3g, Protein 27g

Nutritional Information per serving with side dish (% based upon daily values) $\frac{1}{2}$ cup snow peas with 1 tsp. ranch; 1 whole wheat pita pocket: Calories: 467; Total Fat: 15g, 22%; Saturated Fat: 4g, 18%; Cholesterol: 127mg, 43%; Sodium: 912mg, 38%; Total Carbohydrate: 54g, 18%; Dietary Fiber: 7g, 26%; Sugar: 5g; Protein: 35g

1 pound ground turkey, chicken, or beef

1 slice wheat or white bread, moistened with water

$\frac{1}{4}$ cup minced yellow or white onion (about $\frac{1}{4}$ of a small onion)

1 egg, lightly beaten

1 teaspoon ground coriander (or use ground cumin or 1 teaspoon of each if you like more spice)

1 teaspoon garam masala (buy it or make your own—see Tip, page 27)

1 teaspoon curry powder

1 teaspoon minced garlic or fresh ginger or $\frac{1}{4}$ teaspoon ground garlic or fresh ginger (or both if you like more flavor)

$\frac{1}{2}$ teaspoon salt

$\frac{1}{2}$ cup plain nonfat yogurt

$\frac{1}{4}$–$\frac{1}{2}$ cup mango chutney or any variety (or use apricot jam if you can't find chutney), to taste

Preheat the oven to 350 degrees. Put the meat in a medium bowl and crumble in the moistened bread with your fingers. Add the onions, egg, coriander, garam masala, curry powder, garlic or ginger, and salt, and mix it thoroughly. (At this point you can refrigerate it for up to 24 hours or proceed with the recipe.) Using wet hands, form the mixture into 25 to 30 meatballs, about $1\frac{1}{2}$ inches wide.

Put the meatballs on a large baking sheet sprayed with nonstick cooking spray, and bake them for 20 to 25 minutes until they are cooked through (cut the largest meatball in half to see if it is brown and firm throughout).

While the meatballs bake, combine the yogurt and chutney in a small serving bowl, and put any other dipping sauces, such as ketchup and mustard, in small bowls, too.

Serve the meatballs with toothpicks, if desired.

Scramble Flavor Booster: Use a spicy curry powder and use both the garlic and ginger.

Tip: Chutney is an intensely fruity and often sour or spicy Indian condiment. Mango is one of the most common chutneys, which are usually sold in supermarkets with international ingredients.

Side Dish suggestion: Dip 8 ounces snow peas or sugar snap peas in ½ cup ranch or salad dressing of your choice.

Side Dish suggestion: Serve it with Indian naan or pita bread either warmed in the microwave for about 1 minute or wrapped in foil and warmed in the oven at 300 degrees for 8 to 10 minutes.

solomon's mother's day poem for peace

In 1872, social reformer and poet Julia Ward Howe founded the first American Mother's Day as a celebration of mothers and a dedication to peace. It is fitting, then, that my son, Solomon, at age eleven, was inspired to write this poem celebrating the sense of tranquility we mothers can bring to our young ones. The poem was actually his birthday gift to me, but Solomon agreed to let me share it with you for Mother's Day.

Happy Mother's Day to all you Scrambling moms, who not only do so much to protect your families' health by making nutritious home-cooked meals for them, but also do your utmost to protect your children from war, climate change, and other dangers to their health. I hope you will join me in praying for peace and health this Mother's Day for our families and for families throughout the world.

Mothers

Soft hands tuck me in tonight,
A shadowy figure turns off the light,
And as I drift to sleep, I think,
People say this world is on the brink,
Of chaos, corruption, maybe despair,
That too many pollutants are in the air,
And sisters fight sisters, and brothers fight brothers,
But not everything is wrong, because there are still mothers.

—Solomon Goldfarb

Empanadas are an Argentinean specialty, reminiscent of Italian calzones or Australian meat pies. Using a prepared pie crust, rather than making and rolling your own dough, makes them easy enough for a weeknight dinner. To save time in the evening, make the filling up to a day ahead, and fill the empanadas and bake them right before dinner. Serve them with homemade Baked Potato Chips and Lemony-Garlic Spinach.

beef or turkey empanadas (flaky meat pies)

Prep (25 minutes) +
Cook (20 minutes)

8 servings

Nutritional
Information per
serving (with beef)
(% based upon daily
values):
Calories 370, Fat 22g,
34%, Saturated Fat
7g, 35%, Cholesterol
40mg, 13%, Sodium
550mg, 23%, Total
Carbohydrate 30g,
10%, Fiber 1g, 4%,
Sugar 7g, Protein 14g

Nutritional
Information per
serving with side dish
(% based upon daily
values) ½ cup baked
potato chips; ¼ cup
of spinach:
Calories: 500; Total
Fat: 29g, 42%; Saturated Fat: 8g, 37%;
Cholesterol: 40mg,
13%; Sodium: 865mg,
36%; Total Carbohydrate: 44g, 14%;
Dietary Fiber: 9g,
36%; Sugar: 8g;
Protein: 18g

1 teaspoon canola oil

1 pound ground beef, turkey, or vegetarian ground "meat"

1 medium yellow onion, finely chopped

¾ teaspoon salt

¼ teaspoon garlic powder

¾ teaspoon ground cinnamon

¼ teaspoon ground cumin

⅛ teaspoon ground cloves

2 tablespoons balsamic vinegar

½ cup raisins or ¼ cup pine nuts

2 ready-made refrigerated pie crusts (the kind you unroll, such as
    Pillsbury Refrigerated Pie Crusts)

Preheat the oven to 375 degrees, and spray a baking sheet with nonstick cooking spray.

In a large heavy skillet, heat the oil over medium-high heat and brown the meat and onions. Once the meat is browned (about 5 minutes) add the salt, garlic powder, cinnamon, cumin, cloves, vinegar, and raisins or pine nuts and simmer it for about 10 minutes. Remove it from the heat. (Meanwhile, prepare the potato chips, if you are making them.)

Unroll and cut each of the pie crusts into 4 even quarters. Put each section of the crust on the baking sheet, fold it gently in half to find the middle seam, and put a small scoop of the meat mixture along the seam. Fold it over and seal the edges with the tines of a fork to make a pocket. Bake the empanadas for 20 minutes, or until golden brown. (Meanwhile, make the spinach, if you are serving it.) Allow the empanadas to cool for a few minutes before serving.

Scramble Flavor Booster: Double the garlic powder and cumin and use both raisins and pine nuts.

Tip: By using ground turkey instead of beef, you'll reduce the calories by about 50 and the fat by 5 grams.

Side Dish suggestion: To make Baked Potato Chips, preheat the oven to 400 degrees. Thinly slice 2 russet potatoes and toss the slices in a bowl with 1 tablespoon olive oil and ¼ to ½ teaspoon kosher salt (add ½ teaspoon dried rosemary, oregano, or other herbs, if desired). Lay the slices in a single layer on a baking sheet coated with nonstick cooking spray, and spray the tops of the potatoes with the spray, too. Bake them for about 20 minutes until they are lightly browned and crispy, flipping them once. Serve them with ketchup.

Side Dish suggestion: To make Lemony-Garlic Spinach, heat 1 tablespoon olive oil in a nonstick skillet over medium heat. Sauté 1 teaspoon minced garlic (about 2 cloves) for 30 seconds (don't let it burn!). Add 1 package (9 to 12 ounces) fresh baby spinach. Stir, cover, and steam it for 3 to 5 minutes, or until the spinach is limp, but not overcooked. Sprinkle it with 1 tablespoon fresh lemon juice (about ¼ lemon).

taking fresh veggies out for a dip

Fresh raw veggies make a quick, easy, and oh-so-healthy side dish or appetizer while you're waiting for dinner to cook. Sometimes we just eat them plain, but here are a few of our favorite ways to take them out for a dip.

Salad dressings such as light ranch, Annie's Naturals Goddess, or Caesar

Hummus

Baba gannoush (a roasted eggplant spread)

Black bean dip

Guacamole

Salsa

Peanut or other nut butter

Whipped or light cream cheese

Boursin cheese

Olive tapenade

Sprinkled with kosher salt

Drizzled with fresh lime juice and cayenne pepper or paprika

I love this sweet and smoky flavored meatloaf—it's ultra-moist and has much more pizzazz than the typical meatloaf. It's also a great use for that open bottle of barbecue sauce from your last grilling adventure. Serve it with lightly toasted whole grain English muffins for making sandwiches, and red or orange bell peppers with light ranch dressing or dip of your choice.

smokin' barbecue meatloaf

Prep (10 minutes) + Cook (60–70 minutes)

6 servings

Nutritional Information per serving (with ground chicken) (% based upon daily values): Calories 368, Total Fat 39g, 28%, Saturated Fat 4g, 20%, Cholesterol 162mg, 54%, Sodium 481 mg, 20%, Total Carbohydrate 17.5g, 5%, Dietary Fiber 1g, 4%, Sugar 4g, Protein 32g

Nutritional Information per serving with side dish (% based upon daily values) 1 whole grain English muffin; ½ pepper and 4 tsp. dressing: Calories: 564; Total Fat: 44g, 36%; Saturated Fat: 4g, 22%; Cholesterol: 166mg, 56%; Sodium: 939mg, 39%; Total Carbohydrate: 51g, 17%; Dietary Fiber: 6g, 22%; Sugar: 10g; Protein: 38g

2 pounds ground chicken, lean turkey, or lean beef

1 egg, lightly beaten

¾ cup oats or bread crumbs, or use a combination

1 cup barbecue sauce

½ teaspoon garlic powder

1 teaspoon chili powder or ½ teaspoon chipotle chili powder

½ teaspoon dry mustard

½ small yellow onion, minced (about ½ cup)

Preheat the oven to 375 degrees and spray a loaf pan with nonstick cooking spray. In a large bowl, thoroughly mix all the ingredients together. Put the mixture in the loaf pan and smooth it into a loaf shape. Bake the meatloaf for 1 hour (or up to 70 minutes), or until it is cooked through (a thermometer should read 165 degrees for chicken or turkey, or 160 degrees for beef). Let it sit for 10 minutes if time allows, then cut it into slices and serve. The meatloaf can also be refrigerated for up to 2 days and served warm or cold in sandwiches. Or, it can be frozen, thawed, and reheated in the oven or microwave.

Scramble Flavor Booster: Use chipotle chili powder rather than traditional chili powder and use spicy barbecue sauce.

Our kids devoured these simple pork chops, infused with my favorite flavor-boosting ingredient, lemon-pepper seasoning (thank you, Deb Ford, for introducing me to it!). Scramble recipe tester Debbie Firestone said, "This recipe was a home run!" Serve it with whatever condiments your family enjoys; Andrew and I like ours dipped in Dijon mustard while the kids prefer ketchup and barbecue sauce. Serve it with thin crispy Italian breadsticks and steamed broccoli tossed with olive oil and grated Parmesan cheese.

lemon-pepper pork chops

Prep + Cook = 20 minutes

6 servings

Nutritional Information per serving (% based upon daily values): Calories 270, Total Fat 15g, 23%, Saturated Fat 6g, 30%, Cholesterol 100mg, 33%, Sodium 190mg, 8%, Total Carbohydrate 0g, 0%, Dietary Fiber 0g, 0%, Sugar 0g, Protein 29g

Nutritional Information per serving with side dish (% based upon daily values) 5 breadsticks; 1 cup prepared broccoli: Calories: 483; Total Fat: 21g, 29%; Saturated Fat: 8g, 37%; Cholesterol: 104mg, 34%; Sodium: 527mg, 23%; Total Carbohydrate: 35g, 12%; Dietary Fiber: 7g, 28%; Sugar: 3g; Protein: 38g

1 tablespoon olive oil

1 tablespoon butter

2 pounds thin center-cut boneless pork chops

¼ teaspoon salt, or to taste

4 teaspoons salt-free lemon-pepper seasoning, or to taste

Preheat the oven to 400 degrees. (Meanwhile, start the broccoli, if you are serving it.) When the oven is hot, heat a large heavy ovenproof skillet, preferably cast iron, over medium-high heat. When it's hot, add the oil and the butter and swirl them around in the pan. Add the pork chops to the pan and season them with half the salt and half the lemon-pepper seasoning. Allow them to cook for about 3 minutes until they are lightly browned on the bottom, then flip them, season them with the remaining salt and lemon-pepper seasoning, and brown the second side for about 3 minutes.

Transfer the skillet to the oven and let the pork chops cook for about 4 to 5 more minutes until they are just cooked through (cut into the thickest one to make sure it is no longer pink in the center). For extra-thick chops you may need 8 to 10 minutes. Remove them from the oven and serve them immediately.

Scramble Flavor Booster: Serve them with Dijon mustard or spicy barbecue sauce.

Tip: To keep a cast-iron skillet going strong for decades, wash it with water only (no soap), always dry it immediately, and rub it occasionally with a lightly oiled paper towel.

Side Dish suggestion: To make the broccoli, steam 1 pound broccoli, cut into spears, until tender, 7 to 10 minutes. Drain the broccoli and toss it immediately with 1 tablespoon olive oil and 1 to 2 tablespoons grated Parmesan cheese.

This recipe has received rave reviews from Scramble subscribers. The ginger-soy marinade is fabulous on almost any meat or fish—you can try it with salmon or chicken if you prefer. Serve it with brown or white rice and steamed edamame.

ginger-soy flank steak

Prep + Cook = 25 minutes + optional Marinate (30 minutes–24 hours)

6 servings

Nutritional Information per serving (% based upon daily values): Calories 220, Total Fat 12g, 18%, Saturated Fat 4g, 20%, Cholesterol 55mg, 18%, Sodium 600mg, 25%, Total Carbohydrate 2g, 1%, Dietary Fiber 0g, 0%, Sugar 0g, Protein 24g

Nutritional Information per serving with side dish (% based upon daily values) ¾ cup brown rice; ½ cup edamame in their pods: Calories: 509; Total Fat: 19g, 29%; Saturated Fat: 6g, 27%; Cholesterol: 55mg, 18%; Sodium: 620mg, 27%; Total Carbohydrate: 46g, 11%; Dietary Fiber: 7g, 26%; Sugar: 1g; Protein: 39g

1½–2 pounds flank steak

1 tablespoon minced garlic (about 6 cloves)

1 tablespoon minced fresh ginger

3 scallions, white and green parts, finely sliced

2 tablespoons peanut oil

3 tablespoons reduced-sodium soy sauce

2 teaspoons rice vinegar

Put the steak in a flat dish with sides, just large enough to hold it in one layer.

In a small bowl, whisk together the remaining ingredients and pour them over the steak. Flip the steak a few times to coat it with the sauce. If time allows, refrigerate it for at least 30 minutes and up to 24 hours.

Preheat the grill to medium-high heat, or preheat the broiler. (Start the rice and edamame, if you are serving them.) Transfer the steak to the grill or a broiler pan, reserving any remaining sauce. Grill or broil the meat for 4 to 6 minutes per side until it is browned on the outside and only slightly pink in the center. In a small saucepan, bring any remaining marinade to a low boil for 2 minutes, and transfer it to a small serving bowl. Slice the meat on the diagonal (against the grain so it won't be tough to chew) and serve it with the sauce on the side.

Scramble Flavor Booster: Add ½ teaspoon chili garlic paste or ¼ teaspoon crushed red pepper flakes to the marinade.

Tip: You can reuse almost any liquid-based marinade as a sauce if you bring it to a low boil for 2 minutes before serving it, to kill any bacteria it may contain from the raw meat.

Side Dish suggestion: Prepare 1 pound edamame (or use frozen peas) according to the package directions. Sprinkle the cooked edamame with a little kosher salt. (If you are using frozen peas, no salt is needed.)

Corned beef, or cured brisket, is often part of meals celebrating this Irish holiday, which falls just a few days before the official start of spring. This recipe, from my mother-in-law Barbara Goldfarb, makes an irresistible family meal. It's easy to make, but cooks slowly, so it's best reserved for a non-Scrambling evening (unless you want to leave all the work to your slow-cooker!). By the way, this is higher in fat and sodium than the usual Scramble fare, so best to make it an annual indulgence. Serve it with spicy or grainy mustard, and boiled new or red potatoes (see page 28). Wash it down with green beer (or milk)!

st. patrick's day special:
sweet glazed corned beef and cabbage

Prep (10 minutes) + Cook (3½ hours!)

8 servings

Nutritional Information per serving (% based upon daily values): Calories 400, Total Fat 27g, 42%, Saturated Fat 9g, 45%, Cholesterol 95mg, 32%, Sodium 2240mg, 93%, Total Carbohydrate 12g, 4%, Dietary Fiber 1g, 4%, Sugar 12g, Protein 26g

Nutritional Information per serving with side dish (% based upon daily values) 3 small potatoes: Calories: 490; Total Fat: 30g, 45%; Saturated Fat: 9g, 47%; Cholesterol: 95mg, 32%; Sodium: 2,276mg, 95%; Total Carbohydrate: 33g, 11%; Dietary Fiber: 5g, 17%; Sugar: 21g; Protein: 28g

1 corned beef or brisket (3–4 pounds)

½ yellow or white onion, sliced thinly crosswise (use 3 of the slices)

1 bay leaf

1 celery stalk, sliced

4–6 cups shredded green cabbage (optional)

5 tablespoons ketchup

1 tablespoon Dijon mustard

3 tablespoons red wine vinegar

⅓ cup brown sugar

1 tablespoon butter or margarine

Put the beef into a Dutch oven or other large pot and cover it with cold water, with about 2 inches of water over the meat. Bring it to a boil over medium-high heat. Add the onions, bay leaf, and celery to the water, and simmer it gently, partially covered, for 2½ to 3 hours, until the beef is tender (it will pull apart easily). The meat will shrink. Check the water level periodically while it is cooking, and if you need to, add boiling water to keep the meat covered.

After about 2 hours and 15 minutes, add the cabbage to the pot with the meat (optional) and preheat the oven to 350 degrees. Combine the ketchup, mustard, vinegar, brown sugar, and butter or margarine in a small saucepan and bring it to a boil. Simmer it for 1 to 2 minutes, and then remove it from the heat. (Meanwhile, start the potatoes.)

Drain the meat and vegetables and return them to the pot. Discard the bay leaf. Spoon the ketchup mixture evenly over the meat and bake it for about 10 minutes, until the edges turn brown. Slice the meat across the grain into thin slices and serve it with the vegetables in the pot.

Scramble Flavor Booster: Serve it with creamy horseradish sauce or spicy mustard.

Slow Cooker directions: On the bottom of the slow cooker, place 8 small red potatoes (and a bag of baby carrots, if desired). Place the corned beef on top with the onion slices, celery, cabbage, and bay leaf. Cover it with water as above and cook on High for 6 hours or on Low for 10 to 12 hours. Remove the corned beef from the slow cooker and put it in a baking pan. Finish it as above.

grocery bags can do double (or triple) duty for a cleaner environment

In our house, grocery bags often live a long and prosperous life. After unloading my weekly groceries, I put most of the bags right back in my car so I can reuse them next time I shop. An enthusiastic environmentalist, I reuse and recycle whatever I can, including aluminum foil, self-sealing bags, even newspaper bags to clean up after our dogs. My husband, Andrew, calls me the recycling police, because I carefully eye what he throws away, ready to pounce if he accidentally tosses a takeout menu or coupon mailer in the trash, rather than the recycling bin.

I've often pondered the age-old environmental question—plastic or paper? My research suggests that it hardly matters. What matters most is that you recycle whichever type of bag you choose, preferably by using it as many times as possible.

And the most sustainable (and practical) solution is to just keep a stock of reusable canvas or nylon bags in your car at all times, bypassing the need for disposable bags altogether. As more stores and states offer financial incentives for bringing your own bags (every nickel counts!) you'll save money, too.

Our friend (and Scramble subscriber since way back when) Jolynn Dellinger sent me this delightfully easy yet sophisticated recipe for salmon. It goes beautifully with the bright green spinach that starts to appear in many farmers markets in late spring. Serve it with basmati rice and a spinach salad with mushrooms and cherry tomatoes.

indian spiced salmon

Prep + Cook =
20 minutes

4 servings

Nutritional Information per serving (% based upon daily values): Calories 320, Total Fat 17g, 26%, Saturated Fat 3g, 14%, Cholesterol 125mg, 41%, Sodium 380mg, 16%, Total Carbohydrate 1g, 0%, Dietary Fiber 0g, 0%, Sugar 1g, Protein 39g

Nutritional Information per serving with side dish (% based upon daily values) ¾ cup rice with broth; ¼ of salad:
Calories: 539; Total Fat: 22g, 32%; Saturated Fat: 4g, 18%; Cholesterol: 130mg, 43%; Sodium: 515mg, 22%; Total Carbohydrate: 40g, 12%; Dietary Fiber: 3g, 12%; Sugar: 4g; Protein: 46g

1½ **pounds salmon fillet**

1 **teaspoon olive oil**

2 **teaspoons brown sugar**

½ **teaspoon curry powder**

½ **teaspoon kosher salt**

Preheat the broiler. (If you are making the rice, start that first.) Line a baking pan with aluminum foil, and set the rack about 4 inches from the heating source.

Cut the salmon into 4 serving-size pieces. Pour the olive oil in a small bowl or dish and, using a pastry brush, brush it over the fish.

In a small bowl, combine the brown sugar, curry powder, and salt and rub it evenly over the fillets.

Broil the fish for about 12 to 14 minutes, without flipping it, until it is browned on top and cooked through, and flakes easily in the thickest part of a fillet. Watch it carefully so it doesn't burn, and lower the rack if it is browning too quickly before the inside is cooked through. (While the fish is cooking, prepare the spinach salad.)

Scramble Flavor Booster: Spice it up by doubling the curry powder and adding ½ teaspoon ground cumin and ¼ to ½ teaspoon cayenne pepper.

Tip: Kosher salt is a coarse-grained salt with a slightly milder flavor than table salt.

Side Dish suggestion: Cook 1½ cups of basmati rice according to the package directions, cooking it in chicken or vegetable broth for extra flavor, if desired. For an authentic Indian flavor, cook the rice using chicken or vegetable broth instead of water, and add a stick of cinnamon, 6 whole cloves, and 2 cloves of peeled garlic to the liquid with the rice. Remove the cinnamon, cloves, and garlic before serving.

Side Dish suggestion: To make the salad, combine 4 cups baby spinach, 1 cup sliced mushrooms, 1 cup cherry or grape tomatoes, halved, and toss with 2 to 4 tablespoons balsamic vinaigrette.

My family polished off this delectable salmon, suggested by Scramble subscriber and recipe tester Alice Clark of Seattle. It's a fabulous dish to serve to company with steamed rice and a green salad with diced red bell peppers, toasted slivered almonds, shredded carrots, chopped scallions, and ginger dressing.

grilled caramelized ginger salmon

Prep (10 minutes) +
Cook (20 minutes) +
Marinate (30 minutes–12 hours)

4 servings

Nutritional Information per serving (% based upon daily values): Calories 300, Total Fat 14g, 22%, Saturated Fat 2g, 10%, Cholesterol 95mg, 32%, Sodium 920mg, 38%, Total Carbohydrate 7g, 2%, Dietary Fiber 1g, 4%, Sugar 5g, Protein 35g

Nutritional Information per serving (% based upon daily values) ¾ cup steamed rice; 1½ cups salad : Calories: 490; Total Fat: 16g, 25%; Saturated Fat: 2g, 10%; Cholesterol: 95mg, 32%; Sodium: 990mg, 41%; Total Carbohydrate: 46g, 15%; Dietary Fiber: 3g, 12%; Sugar: 8g; Protein: 40g

¼ cup reduced-sodium soy sauce

1 tablespoon canola oil

1 tablespoon salt-free lemon-pepper seasoning

1 tablespoon grated or minced fresh ginger

4 scallions or 8 chives, chopped

2 tablespoons brown sugar

1½ pounds (or use up to 2 pounds for 6 servings) salmon fillet, preferably wild salmon

In a large measuring cup, stir together the soy sauce and the remaining ingredients except for the salmon. Pour the mixture in a large flat dish with sides, and add the salmon, flesh down. Marinate the salmon for at least 30 minutes and up to 12 hours.

Preheat the grill to medium heat; about 350 degrees on a gas grill (or, cook the salmon in the oven at 350 degrees for 20 to 25 minutes). (Meanwhile, prepare the rice.) Bend up the edges of a sheet of heavy-duty aluminum foil that is slightly larger than the fillet. Put the foil on the grill, and put the salmon flesh side up on top of the foil, spooning the extra marinade evenly over the top of the fish. Close the grill, and cook the salmon over indirect heat for 20 to 25 minutes (depending on the thickness of the fish and your grill's heat), until the fish is cooked through in the thickest part—do not flip it. (While the fish is cooking, prepare the salad.)

Scramble Flavor Booster: Season the fish with freshly ground black pepper.

Tip: Whenever possible, buy wild Alaskan salmon (also called chinook, coho, pink, or sockeye). These varieties are not as heavily overfished and don't contain the high levels of environmental contaminants that many types of farmed salmon do.

Side Dish suggestion: In a salad bowl, combine 6 to 8 cups romaine lettuce, ½ diced red bell pepper, 1 to 2 tablespoons toasted slivered almonds, 1 cup shredded carrots, ¼ cup chopped scallions, and 2 to 4 tablespoons (store-bought) ginger dressing.

eight essential pots and pans
for scrambling families

Although I count fifteen pots and pans in my bulging cabinet, nearly half of them are mostly just taking up space. Here are the pots and pans that I have found to be indispensable for making my family's meals (if you're just starting out, or in very cramped quarters, you could get by with just numbers 1, 3, 4, and 5 below):

1. **Large (10- to 12-inch) stainless steel skillet (also called a frying pan):** My All-Clad skillet, probably the best wedding gift we received back in 1994 (a million thanks to my brother, Lincoln!), is excellent for browning or searing meats, sautéing onions and other vegetables, and making sauces. It's my first choice for sautéing unless I need a nonstick skillet.

2. **Large (10- to 12-inch) nonstick skillet (also called a frying pan):** A good nonstick skillet is vital for cooking eggs, making stir-fries, browning breaded fish or chicken fillets, or cooking anything else that may stick to regular cooking surfaces. I recently switched from Teflon-coated pans that wear out after a couple of years to the more expensive but longer lasting and exceedingly more durable Scanpan cookware (made in Denmark), and I love it!

3. **Small or medium (8- to 10-inch) nonstick skillet:** Like the above, but this one is perfect for making omelets, scrambled eggs, and other smaller and potentially sticky meals.

4. **Stockpot (6- to 12-quart, also called a pasta pot):** This is essential for making pasta, big pots of soup, boiling lots of potatoes, and making homemade popcorn.

5. **Saucepan (3- to 4-quart stainless steel stockpot):** I use this beauty (my All-Clad was also a wedding gift from my brother!) for steaming vegetables or rice or making small quantities of noodles. It's smaller than the stockpot, so I can pull it out more easily for smaller jobs.

6. **Small saucepan:** Look for a stainless steel saucepan, which is perfect for making small amounts of sauce, single servings of soup, and for melting chocolate.

7. **Dutch oven:** This heavy-duty pot, often made of coated cast iron, goes easily from stovetop to oven to table, and can work well for making a roast, a stew, or a soup.

8. **Cast-iron skillet:** This isn't one of my daily pans, but it can't be beat for browning steaks and pork chops—I use it like an indoor grill. If properly seasoned (don't wash it with soap, dry it immediately, and rub it with a little oil on a paper towel occasionally), a cast-iron skillet can also be used as a nonstick skillet.

I have found that it's worth investing in good quality pots and pans that can really help us get great meals on the table and don't need to be replaced often, if ever. For help choosing great pots, I recommend a professional kitchen store such as Sur la Table or Williams-Sonoma, and/or using the product ratings and advice in *Cook's Illustrated* and *Consumer Reports*.

Six O'Clock Scramble subscriber Lizzy Smith shared her family's favorite fish recipe with me. You can use chicken tenderloins or thin chicken cutlets in the packets instead of the fish, and you can vary the vegetables, herbs, and seasonings to your tastes and your garden or market's bounty. Try shredded carrots or slivered onions or use dill or oregano instead of the suggested herbs. Serve it with quinoa (a light whole grain).

tilapia packets with fresh herbs and baby spinach

Prep + Cook = 30 minutes

4 servings

Nutritional Information per serving (% based upon daily values): Calories 290, Total Fat 16g, 25%, Saturated Fat 2.5g, 13%, Cholesterol 45mg, 15%, Sodium 330mg, 14%, Total Carbohydrate 19g, 6%, Dietary Fiber 2g, 8%, Sugar 4g, Protein 17g

Nutritional Information per serving with side dish (% based upon daily values) ¾ cup cooked quinoa: Calories: 481; Total Fat: 19g, 30%; Saturated Fat: 3g, 13%; Cholesterol: 45mg, 15%; Sodium: 345mg, 15%; Total Carbohydrate: 54g, 18%; Dietary Fiber: 5g, 20%; Sugar: 4g; Protein: 24g

1–1½ **pounds tilapia or other thin white fish fillets such as flounder or cod**

1 **tablespoon olive oil**

½ **lemon, juice only (about 2 tablespoons)**

2 **tablespoons white wine (or use chicken or vegetable broth or 1 additional tablespoon olive oil)**

1 **tablespoon chopped fresh herbs, such as sage, thyme, parsley, basil, or any combination (or substitute 1 teaspoon dried herbs)**

¼–½ **teaspoon salt, to taste**

⅛–¼ **teaspoon black pepper, to taste**

1 **yellow bell pepper, cut in thin strips (or use 1 cup slivered carrots or slivered onions)**

2 **cups baby spinach**

Preheat the oven to 400 degrees.

Put each fillet in the center of its own large square of heavy-duty aluminum foil. Drizzle the olive oil, lemon juice, and white wine evenly over the fish and season it with the herbs, salt, and black pepper.

Top the fillets with the bell peppers and spinach, divided evenly, and fold and seal the foil packets (Meanwhile, start the quinoa, if you are serving it.)

Place the packets directly on the oven rack and bake them for 15 to 20 minutes (check doneness after 15 minutes) until the fish flakes easily with a fork and is opaque throughout. Unwrap the packets carefully (to avoid getting burned by the steam) and serve.

Scramble Flavor Booster: Add ¼ teaspoon fresh lemon zest with the lemon juice, and use fresh herbs.

Tip: When possible, buy organic spinach, as conventional spinach tends to be high in pesticides, according to the Environmental Working Group (http://www.foodnews.org/fulllist.php). Asparagus, broccoli, and avocados, on the other hand, tend to be low in pesticides.

Side Dish suggestion: Prepare 1 to 2 cups quinoa (or use couscous) according to the package directions, making sure to rinse the quinoa with cold water before cooking it (I use a fine metal strainer to rinse it).

the safest seafood for kids

When I was a teenager, my dad used to take us sailing near our home in Southern California on *The Evely,* the sailboat he fixed up and named after my mom. Once we got some distance offshore, my dad would catch whatever grabbed his bait, and, to my horror, would clean it, slice it up, slather it with horseradish and cocktail sauce, and eat it raw (despite his encouragement, I refused to taste it).

Even though we don't have to catch it ourselves, seafood may be the trickiest of all foods I feed my family and recommend in The Scramble. While certain types of fish are among the healthiest foods we can eat, others are tainted with contaminants such as mercury and PCBs (a regrettable result of human pollution). Once I narrow the list of edible fish down to those that are safest for human consumption, environmentally friendly, and appeal to finicky eaters, I often feel like the options are limited.

Despite those challenges, I still love cooking fish. Fish is generally a low-fat protein that has a mild flavor and is quick and easy to cook. When it's fresh and prepared right, it tastes fabulous.

The Scramble has teamed up with SeaWeb and Environmental Defense to provide guidance on the very best seafood to serve kids—seafood that is nutritious, low in toxic pollutants, and ocean-friendly (some varieties of fish are being overfished to the brink of extinction). At the top of the list of best seafood for kids are tilapia, wild Alaskan salmon, and Northern U.S. and Canadian shrimp, which are three of my favorite types of seafood to cook.

For more information about Kidsafe Seafood, visit www.kidsafeseafood.org. For an even broader list of acceptable seafood for adults, visit www.oceansalive.org.

Scramble recipe tester Melinda Kelley of Potomac, Maryland, said her picky four-year-old gave this recipe "two thumbs up." Melinda also said it was so easy to make that she's going to let her eight-year-old prepare it next time. The fragrant fresh basil is optional but if it's bursting to life in your garden, I recommend using it. Serve it with baked breadsticks and green salad with celery, walnuts, and feta cheese.

basil-parmesan baked snapper

Prep + Cook = 20 minutes

4 servings

Nutritional Information per serving (% based upon daily values): Calories 170, Total Fat 10g, 15%, Saturated Fat 2.5g, 13%, Cholesterol 55mg, 18%, Sodium 120mg, 5%, Total Carbohydrate 1g, 0%, Dietary Fiber 0g, 0%, Sugar 0g, Protein 19g

Nutritional Information per serving with side dish (% based upon daily values) 1 baked breadstick; 1½ cups salad: Calories: 296; Total Fat: 15g, 22%; Saturated Fat: 4g, 20%; Cholesterol: 55mg, 20%; Sodium: 466mg, 51%; Total Carbohydrate: 20g, 6%; Dietary Fiber: 2g, 9%; Sugar: 4g; Protein: 24g

1–1½ **pounds red snapper, flounder, tilapia, or other white fish fillets**

½ **lemon (about 2 tablespoons juice)**

1½ **teaspoons dried basil**

3 **tablespoons grated Parmesan cheese**

¼–½ **teaspoon garlic powder, to taste**

¼ **teaspoon black pepper**

3 **fresh basil leaves, cut in strips (optional)**

Preheat the oven to 400 degrees. Lay the fillets in a large baking dish and pour the lemon juice over them. (Meanwhile, prepare the breadsticks, if you are serving them.)

In a small bowl, combine the dried basil, cheese, garlic powder, and black pepper. Sprinkle the mixture evenly over the fillets, and spray the top with nonstick cooking spray. Bake the fillets for 10 to 15 minutes, depending on the thickness of the fish, until it is opaque and flakes easily in the thickest part.

(Make the salad while the fish is baking.)

Sprinkle the fish with the fresh basil before serving it (optional).

Scramble Flavor Booster: Use the extra garlic powder to season the fish or substitute 1 teaspoon fresh minced garlic.

Tip: Planting a few fresh herbs in your garden or even on a windowsill will likely save you so much money on those expensive and highly perishable little herb packets at the grocery store.

Side Dish suggestion: To make the salad, combine 6 cups chopped iceberg or other lettuce, 2 celery stalks, sliced, 2 tablespoons walnuts, and 2 tablespoons crumbled feta cheese. To make maple-Dijon dressing, whisk together ¼ cup olive oil, ⅛ cup red wine vinegar, 1 tablespoon pure maple syrup, 1 teaspoon Dijon mustard, and ½ teaspoon herbes de Provence or dried thyme. Toss the salad with 2 to 4 tablespoons dressing or to taste.

This preparation has a fantastic flavor and texture that my family loves. It's a great family meal for all ages, as the fish is plain enough for picky eaters, and can be smothered with the savory salsa for those with more adventurous palates. Serve it with fresh or canned pineapple chunks or rings.

cornmeal-crusted fish with black bean and corn salsa

Prep + Cook = 30 minutes

4 servings

Nutritional Information per serving (% based upon daily values): Calories 350, Total Fat 14g, 22%, Saturated Fat 2.5g, 13%, Cholesterol 55mg, 18%, Sodium 830mg, 35%, Total Carbohydrate 33g, 11%, Dietary Fiber 7g, 28%, Sugar 4g, Protein 25g

Nutritional Information per serving with side dish (% based upon daily values) 1 cup pineapple: Calories: 420; Total Fat: 14g, 22%; Saturated Fat: 3g, 13%; Cholesterol: 55mg, 18%; Sodium: 832mg, 35%; Total Carbohydrate: 53g, 18%; Dietary Fiber: 9g, 37%; Sugar: 19g; Protein: 26g

1 can (15 ounces) black beans, drained and rinsed

1 cup chunky salsa

1 cup frozen corn kernels

2 teaspoons Old Bay seasoning

⅓ cup yellow cornmeal

1 pound catfish, white roughy, tilapia, or other boneless, skinless white fish fillets (or chicken cutlets)

1–2 tablespoons olive oil

In a small saucepan, combine the beans and salsa and bring them to a boil. Add the corn and simmer it for 10 to 15 minutes, stirring it occasionally, until the fish is ready.

Mix the Old Bay seasoning and cornmeal together thoroughly with a fork. Spread it on a shallow plate. Pat the fish dry with paper towels, if necessary, and dredge the fillets in the cornmeal mixture, patting on extra coating, if necessary, to completely cover the fish. Set the fillets aside.

Coat a large heavy skillet thoroughly with nonstick cooking spray. Heat it over medium-high heat, and add 1 tablespoon oil. When the pan is hot, cook the fillets for about 4 to 5 minutes per side, without moving them, until the bottoms are lightly browned. (Cook them in two batches or use two pans if they won't fit without overlapping.) If the fillets start to stick, add the additional oil after flipping them.

Serve the fish topped with the bean and corn salsa.

Scramble Flavor Booster: Use spicy salsa and add ¼ teaspoon cayenne pepper or ½ teaspoon chili powder or ground cumin to the coating along with the Old Bay seasoning.

Tip: To help you remember to reuse your grocery bags or your canvas/cloth bags, load them right back into your car after you unpack them. I keep a separate reusable shopping bag in the car for smaller errands, too.

Here's a fabulous recipe for a gourmet dinner in ten minutes from Scramble subscriber and recipe tester Alice Clark of Seattle. Serve it with steamed broccoli tossed with lemon-pepper seasoning.

spice-tossed shrimp with parmesan grits

Prep + Cook =
10 minutes

4 servings

Nutritional
Information per
serving (% based
upon daily values):
Calories 400, Total
Fat 15g, 23%, Saturated Fat 5g, 25%,
Cholesterol 190mg,
63%, Sodium 695mg,
41%, Total Carbohydrate 34g, 11%
Dietary Fiber 2g, 8%
Sugar 0g, Protein 30g

Nutritional
Information per
serving with side dish
(% based upon daily
values) 1 cup broccoli:
Calories: 455; Total
Fat: 16g, 24%; Saturated Fat: 5g, 26%;
Cholesterol: 190mg,
63%; Sodium: 759mg,
32%; Total Carbohydrate: 45g, 15%;
Dietary Fiber: 7g,
29%; Sugar: 2g;
Protein: 34g

4 cups water

1 cup quick-cooking (not instant) grits

$\frac{1}{4}$–$\frac{1}{2}$ teaspoon salt

1 tablespoon butter or margarine

$\frac{1}{2}$ cup grated Parmesan cheese, or use shredded Cheddar cheese

1 pound large shrimp, peeled and deveined (or use tempeh for a vegetarian alternative)

1 tablespoon dried oregano

$\frac{1}{2}$ teaspoon dried thyme

1 teaspoon salt-free lemon-pepper seasoning

$\frac{1}{2}$ teaspoon chili powder, or use $\frac{1}{4}$ teaspoon chipotle chili powder

$\frac{1}{2}$ teaspoon black pepper

2 tablespoons olive oil

(Start the broccoli first, if you are serving it.) In a medium saucepan, bring the water to a boil. Stir in the grits and $\frac{1}{4}$ teaspoon salt, reduce the heat, cover, and simmer it for 5 minutes, removing the cover to stir it occasionally. Remove the grits from the heat and stir in the butter or margarine and the cheese.

Meanwhile, wrap the shrimp in a clean kitchen towel to dry thoroughly.

In a medium bowl, combine the oregano, thyme, lemon-pepper seasoning, chili powder, $\frac{1}{4}$ teaspoon salt (optional), and black pepper. Toss the shrimp thoroughly with the spices to coat it.

In a large heavy skillet, heat the oil over medium-high heat. When it is very hot, add the shrimp and cook it for about 2 minutes per side (use tongs to flip it) until it is pink and firm. Serve the shrimp immediately, spooned over the grits.

Scramble Flavor Booster: Use the chipotle chili powder to season the shrimp. Season the grits with additional black pepper.

Tip: Grits, a traditional Southern grain made from ground corn, are low in calories and fat and have a decent amount of fiber per serving. They are also rich in iron, thiamin, and folic acid, so they're a healthy indulgence, especially if you don't stir in too much butter.

Side Dish suggestion: Steam 1 pound broccoli florets or spears until tender, 5 to 8 minutes. Drain and season them with lemon-pepper seasoning.

My family couldn't believe how delicious this humble salad was. Not only is it inexpensive to make and heart-healthy, but it is so versatile. You can serve it over greens, stuff it in a pita, or eat it on crackers. However you serve it, it's a super combination of tastes. This recipe is adapted from the HEARTy Salmon Salad recipe from City Harvest food rescue program. Serve it with celery sticks with Boursin cheese.

salmon salad with lemon and dill

Prep (no cook) = 15 minutes

4 servings

Nutritional Information per serving (without pita) (% based upon daily values):
Calories 220, Total Fat 10g, 16%, Saturated Fat 2g, 9.5%, Cholesterol 69mg, 23%, Sodium 568mg, 23.5%, Total Carbohydrate 13g, 4%, Dietary Fiber 4g, 15.5%, Sugar 4g, Protein 25g

Nutritional Information per serving with side dish (% based upon daily values) 1 cup celery and 2 tbsp. Boursin light cheese:
Calories: 281; Total Fat: 14g, 21%; Saturated Fat: 4g, 20%; Cholesterol: 83mg, 28%; Sodium: 805mg, 34%; Total Carbohydrate: 17g, 5%; Dietary Fiber: 6g, 22%; Sugar: 6g; Protein: 30g

1 can (15 ounces) wild salmon

4 tablespoons reduced-fat mayonnaise, or plain nonfat or low-fat yogurt

1 lemon, juice only (about ¼ cup)

1 small bunch fresh dill, finely chopped (¼ cup)

¼–½ yellow or white onion, finely diced (1 cup) or use celery

1 package (10 ounces) frozen peas, thawed

4 pita pockets for serving (optional)

Drain the salmon in a colander and discard any skin or bones (though they are edible and very healthy if you don't want to discard them.)

In a medium bowl, combine the salmon, mayonnaise or yogurt, lemon juice, dill, and onions and stir to combine. Gently mix in the peas. Serve it immediately stuffed inside the pita pockets (optional), or chill the salad until you are ready to serve it, up to 24 hours.

Scramble Flavor Booster: Add ½ to 1 teaspoon fresh lemon zest and ¼ teaspoon freshly ground black pepper to the salad.

Tip: For an elegant presentation, serve the salad in a hollowed out tomato or bell pepper.

Side Dish suggestion: Trim and cut celery stalks into thirds and dip in Boursin light herbed cheese. Or, fill the celery with the cheese before serving it.

This pasta salad is bursting with flavor. If you fear it may be too flavorful for your kids, make an extra package of tortellini to serve plain with extra pepperoni and olives on the side. This is a terrific dish for a picnic or a casual dinner, served with diced honeydew melon.

cool tortellini with artichokes and pepperoni

Prep + Cook = 20 minutes

6 servings

Nutritional Information per serving (% based upon daily values): Calories 290, Total Fat 13g, 20%, Saturated Fat 4g, 20%, Cholesterol 65mg, 22%, Sodium 910mg, 38%, Total Carbohydrate 28g, 9%, Dietary Fiber 4g, 16%, Protein 17g, Sugar 3g

Nutritional Information per serving with side dish (% based upon daily values) 1 cup melon: Calories: 351; Total Fat: 13g, 20%; Saturated Fat: 4g, 20%; Cholesterol: 65mg, 22%; Sodium: 941 mg, 39%; Total Carbohydrate: 44g, 14%; Dietary Fiber: 6g, 21%; Sugar: 17g; Protein: 18g

1–2 packages (9–18 ounces) cheese tortellini (use 9 ounces for the recipe plus an extra 9 ounces to serve to picky eaters)

6 ounces sliced turkey pepperoni (or use regular or vegetarian pepperoni), sliced in strips

1 jar or can (14 ounces) artichoke hearts, drained and coarsely chopped

½ cup sliced black olives

½ teaspoon minced garlic (about 1 clove)

¼ cup crumbled Gorgonzola cheese (or use diced mozzarella for a milder flavor), or more to taste

¼ cup chopped fresh basil

2 tablespoons olive oil

1½ tablespoons balsamic vinegar

Cook the tortellini according to the package directions and drain it.

Meanwhile, in a large bowl, combine the pepperoni, artichokes, olives, and garlic. Add the cooked and drained tortellini to the mixture and toss it slightly, then add the cheese, basil, oil, and vinegar and toss it gently. Serve warm or cold.

Scramble Flavor Booster: Add a little extra Gorgonzola cheese to the pasta and season it with freshly ground black pepper.

Tip: To save time, stack the pepperoni before slicing it into strips. Opt for turkey pepperoni, when possible, as it has about half the calories and one-fourth of the fat of regular pepperoni.

This dinner has a combination of sweet, spicy, and savory that I love. It may look like a large quantity of spinach at first, but it melts away to practically nothing once it's cooked, so the kids probably won't even mind it—ours don't. Serve it with a green salad with grapes, walnuts, and Gorgonzola cheese.

ravioli with spinach and sun-dried tomatoes

Prep + Cook = 25 minutes

6 servings

Nutritional Information per serving (% based upon daily values): Calories 390, Total Fat 13g, 20%, Saturated Fat 6g, 30%, Cholesterol 75mg, 25%, Sodium 730mg, 30%, Total Carbohydrate 48g, 16%, Dietary Fiber 8g, 32%, Sugar 7g, Protein 18g

Nutritional Information per serving with side dish (% based upon daily values) 1½ cups salad: Calories: 443; Total Fat: 16g, 25%; Saturated Fat: 7g, 35%; Cholesterol: 79mg, 26%; Sodium: 874mg, 36%; Total Carbohydrate: 53g, 17%; Dietary Fiber: 10g, 38%; Sugar: 10g; Protein: 20g

1 family-size package (20 ounces) cheese ravioli

1 package (6–9 ounces) baby spinach

1 tablespoon olive oil

½ yellow onion, finely diced

1 teaspoon minced garlic (1–2 cloves)

5 sun-dried tomatoes, marinated or dry, chopped

¼–½ teaspoon crushed red pepper flakes, to taste (optional)

1½ cups red pasta sauce

Cook the ravioli according to the package directions. When it is 1 minute from being done, add the spinach to the water with the ravioli, then drain the spinach and pasta.

Meanwhile, in a large heavy skillet, heat the oil over medium heat. Add the onions and sauté them for about 4 minutes until they are softened. (Meanwhile, make the salad, if you are serving it.) Add the garlic, sun-dried tomatoes, and crushed red pepper flakes (optional) and sauté them with the onions for about 1 minute. Add the pasta sauce and bring it to a low boil. Reduce the heat, if necessary, and simmer the sauce, stirring occasionally, until the ravioli and spinach are cooked and drained.

Combine the ravioli and spinach with the sauce, and serve it immediately or refrigerate it for up to 48 hours or freeze it for up to 3 months.

Scramble Flavor Booster: Serve it with extra crushed red pepper flakes.

Tip: If your young children like to help you in the kitchen, you can give them a plastic knife and a cutting board and ask them to cut the grapes in half for the salad (they can even re-wash all of the grapes that roll off the board!). Older children can help you make the sauce for the ravioli.

Side Dish suggestion: In a large bowl, combine 6 to 8 cups lettuce (1 small head), 1 cup purple seedless grapes, halved, ¼ cup chopped walnuts, 2 tablespoons crumbled Gorgonzola cheese, and 2 to 4 tablespoons vinaigrette dressing or other dressing of your choice.

Subscriber Susan Oliver shared her family's recipe for lo mein noodles, which she describes as "melt in your mouth," Especially if you make it with freshly picked asparagus. I ran into a longtime Scramble subscriber recently who said this is his family's favorite dish! The sauce is very mild and kid-friendly (Susan's three kids love it). Serve it with an Asian Cucumber Salad.

chinese lo mein noodles with asparagus

Prep + Cook = 30 minutes

8 servings

Nutritional Information per serving (with chicken) (% based upon daily values): Calories 320, Fat 8g, 12%, Saturated Fat 1.5g, 8%, Cholesterol 15mg, 5%, Sodium 340mg, 14%, Total Carbohydrate 47g, 16%, Fiber 7g, 28%, Sugar 2g, Protein 15g

Nutritional Information per serving with side dish (% based upon daily values) 1/6 of salad: Calories: 345; Total Fat: 9g, 14%; Saturated Fat: 2g, 8%; Cholesterol: 15mg, 5%; Sodium: 440mg, 18%; Total Carbohydrate: 50g, 17%; Dietary Fiber: 8g, 32%; Sugar: 4g; Protein: 16g

¼ cup reduced-sodium soy sauce, plus additional for serving

1 teaspoon superfine sugar (or use granulated sugar)

1½ teaspoons minced garlic (2–3 cloves)

½ pound boneless chicken, beef, or extra-firm tofu (if using the meat, cut it into thin strips, if using the tofu, dice into ½-inch pieces)

1 package (16 ounces) Chinese lo mein noodles (sold with Asian foods), or spaghetti

¼ cup peanut oil

1 yellow or white onion, quartered from top to bottom and cut crosswise into thin slices

1 pound asparagus, ends trimmed and cut into thirds

In a flat dish, combine the soy sauce, sugar, and ½ teaspoon of the garlic and add the chicken, beef, or tofu. Stir to coat it thoroughly and set it aside. (You can refrigerate the chicken or beef at this point for up to 24 hours, but not the tofu, as it will absorb all the marinade.)

Cook the noodles according to the package directions until they are al dente. Meanwhile, in a wok or large nonstick skillet, heat 1 teaspoon of the oil over medium to medium-high heat. Sauté the meat or tofu, with the marinade, until it is cooked through, about 5 minutes. (Meanwhile, prepare the salad, if you are serving it.) Remove the meat or tofu from the pan and set it aside (don't return the chicken or beef to the same bowl in which you marinated it).

In the same skillet, sauté the onions and remaining 1 teaspoon garlic for about 2 minutes over medium to medium-high heat, then add the asparagus and toss the mixture for another 3 to 4 minutes until the asparagus is tender-crisp.

Drain the noodles thoroughly, return them to the cooking pot, and toss them with the remaining oil. Add the noodles to the skillet with the vegetables, or if the pan is too small, combine them in the pasta pot. Add the cooked meat or tofu and toss thoroughly to combine. Add additional soy sauce to taste, and serve it immediately or refrigerate it for up to 2 days.

Scramble Flavor Booster: Add ¼ to ½ teaspoon chili garlic paste or crushed red pepper flakes to the marinade for the meat or tofu.

Tip: You can use leftover cooked chicken or steak in this recipe. You would still marinate it, but sauté it for only 1 or 2 minutes to heat it through.

Side Dish suggestion: To make an Asian Cucumber Salad, in a medium bowl with a lid, whisk together 1 tablespoon reduced-sodium soy sauce, 2 teaspoons rice vinegar, and 1 teaspoon sugar. Add 2 seeded and diced or thinly sliced cucumbers, and toss it thoroughly to coat the cucumbers with the dressing. Top it with 1 tablespoon sesame seeds. Serve immediately, or refrigerate for up to 24 hours.

ten best dishes for school potlucks or other gatherings

I get some of my best ideas for new recipes at school or neighborhood potlucks. I love the creativity and cooperative spirit that they elicit. My ideal potluck dishes are flavorful (so they'll stand out from the crowd), and easy to prepare (of course!), can easily be doled out in small portions, and can sit out for an hour or two without needing to be refrigerated (if your potluck is outdoors on a hot day, be careful not to bring a dish that contains meat, mayonnaise, eggs, or other ingredients that can cause dangerous bacteria to grow on the food). Here are a few of my favorite Scramble dishes to share at potlucks—you might as well bring extra copies of the recipe to hand out because people are going to ask for them!

Spinach Pie with Portobello Mushrooms (page 79)

Ginger-Soy Flank Steak (page 36)

Danish Egg Salad Sandwiches with Smoked Salmon (page 236)

Orzo Salad with Peas and Feta Cheese (page 52)

Mediterranean Quinoa Salad (page 81)

Curried Chicken Salad with Grapes (page 147)

Mango and Black Bean Salad (page 80)

Lemon-Basil Summer Pasta Salad (page 127)

Asian Shrimp Pilaf (page 118)

Indonesian Chicken Satay with Peanut Sauce (page 96)

I begged our friend Elizabeth Zehner for the recipe for this pasta salad after she brought it to our house for a potluck. It's great for a gathering or a light family meal, and also makes an excellent side dish with chicken, fish, or steak—you can even stir in additional goodies, such as halved cherry or grape tomatoes. If your kids are picky eaters, make some extra plain orzo and toss it with butter or olive oil and peas. Serve it with Zucchini Fritters.

orzo salad with peas and feta cheese

Prep + Cook =
20 minutes +
30 minutes–3 days
to chill

6 servings

Nutritional Information per serving (% based upon daily values):
Calories 260, Total Fat 10g, 15%, Saturated Fat 3.5g, 18%, Cholesterol 15mg, 5%, Sodium 490mg, 20%, Total Carbohydrate 33g, 11%, Dietary Fiber 3g, 12%, Sugar 4g, Protein 10g

Nutritional Information per serving with side dish (% based upon daily values) 1½ zucchini fritters:
Calories: 400; Total Fat: 16g, 24%; Saturated Fat: 4.5g, 23%; Cholesterol: 70mg, 23%; Sodium: 730mg, 30%; Total Carbohydrate: 49g, 16; Dietary Fiber: 4g, 16%; Sugar: 6g; Protein: 15g

2 cups orzo

1½–2 cups frozen peas (or use fresh peas, if they are available in your market)

¼ cup pine nuts (optional)

1 teaspoon minced garlic (about 2 cloves)

1 cup crumbled feta cheese

¼ cup chopped fresh parsley or dill (or 1 tablespoon dried parsley or dill)

1–2 tablespoons balsamic vinegar, to taste

2 tablespoons olive oil

½ teaspoon salt

¼ teaspoon black pepper

Cook the orzo according to the package directions, or for 7 to 8 minutes (for some reason many orzo packages don't list the cooking times!). For the final 30 seconds, throw the peas in the water with the orzo to thaw them, then drain the orzo and peas and rinse them with cold water.

Toast the pine nuts (optional) in a toaster oven on the lightest setting for about 2 minutes, until lightly browned. (Alternatively, toast the pine nuts and garlic in 1 teaspoon olive oil in a skillet over medium heat for 3 to 4 minutes until they are lightly browned.)

Combine all the ingredients in a large bowl, toss it thoroughly, and chill it for at least 30 minutes, if time allows, and up to 3 days. (Meanwhile, prepare the Zucchini Fritters.)

Scramble Flavor Booster: Use the fresh dill and 2 tablespoons balsamic vinegar. Serve with extra freshly ground black pepper.

Tip: Orzo is rice-shaped pasta, made from refined wheat. I used to confuse it with Italian risotto, which is actually made with Arborio rice.

Side Dish suggestion: To make Zucchini Fritters, in a medium bowl, thoroughly combine 1 grated zucchini (about 2 cups), 1 lightly beaten egg, ¾ cup bread crumbs or crushed crackers, ½ teaspoon Old Bay seasoning, and ½ teaspoon salt-free lemon-pepper seasoning. In a large nonstick skillet, heat 1 to 2 tablespoons butter or vegetable oil over medium to medium-high heat until the butter starts to bubble or the oil starts to smoke. Form the zucchini mixture into about 6 thin pancakes and sauté them in the butter or oil until they are browned, flipping them once, 3 to 4 minutes per side. If the outsides are getting too brown, reduce the heat.

my child is a vegetarian!
what the heck should i do now?

When Andrew and I had our first child, he was, like all newborns, as sweet as they come. It would crack us up to envision a future when Solomon would be a floppy-headed, surly teenager who would slam the door to his room and yell at his clueless and inhumane parents, "I'm a vegetarian!" Well, that baby, who is still pretty sweet at age twelve (though his hair is pretty floppy), remains an omnivore. However, his little sister Celia, now ten, recently decided to swear off meat.

That Celia should decide to become a vegetarian was pretty surprising to us. This is a girl whose very favorite dinner has always been steak. But one of Celia's closest friends is a vegetarian, and recently Celia, who has always loved animals, has become uncomfortable with the thought of eating them.

Our family is clearly not alone in having a family member who doesn't eat meat. We all know people who follow a vegetarian diet in some form. A recent Six O'Clock Scramble poll showed that nearly half of you have family members who don't eat some type of meat. Nationwide, somewhere between 4 and 10 percent of Americans consider themselves vegetarian.

Celia's vegetarianism might be a short-lived dietary experiment; however, Andrew and I want to support her as she tries to develop her own sense of herself and be true to her own values.

We only eat meat once or twice a week for dinner, so the transition has been pretty smooth. When I do serve meat, I make sure to also serve something healthy that she can eat, such as beans, carrots, and hummus, or yogurt, and we can all enjoy the same side dishes. We've talked to Celia about how to make sure she maintains a healthy and balanced diet, and she's agreed that she needs to be even more adventurous with foods so she gets enough protein, vitamins, and variety in her diet. One nice change I've noticed is that she is eating more fruits and vegetables than ever.

Another challenge for us has been packing lunch. Celia used to bring a turkey sandwich to school, along with fruit, yogurt, and cheese. She's never liked peanut butter. We're still exploring main course options, but so far we've muddled through by alternating pasta, black beans and tortilla chips, bagels and cream cheese, and hard-boiled eggs.

While this change in Celia's eating habits has taken a little more energy and thought on all of our parts, I'm proud of Celia for following her heart. I'd love to hear from other Scrambling families about how you manage varying diets in your homes. Please send me a note at aviva@thescramble.com or post your comment for others to read on the Scramblog (www.thescramble.com/healthymenuplanning).

My friend Bev Abrams, of Santa Barbara, California, sent me this delicious recipe, which is perfect for celebrating spring's harvest. Serve it with an Ambrosia Fruit Salad.

lemon-parmesan fusilli
with asparagus and spinach

Prep + Cook =
25 minutes

8 servings

Nutritional
Information per
serving (% based
upon daily values):
Calories 290, Total
Fat 7g, 11%, Saturated Fat 2.5g, 13%,
Cholesterol 10mg,
3%, Sodium 105mg,
4%, Total Carbohydrate 45g, 15%,
Dietary Fiber 4g,
16%, Sugar 2g,
Protein 11g

Nutritional
Information per
serving with side dish
(% based upon daily
values) 1 cup fruit
salad:
Calories: 390; Total
Fat: 9g, 14%; Saturated Fat: 3g, 13%;
Cholesterol: 10mg,
3%; Sodium: 120mg,
5%; Total Carbohydrate: 69g, 23%;
Dietary Fiber: 7g,
28%; Sugar: 20g;
Protein: 13g

1 package (16 ounces) fusilli pasta

1 pound asparagus spears

2 tablespoons olive oil

1 tablespoon butter

1 teaspoon minced garlic (about 2 cloves)

1 package (6 ounces) baby spinach

¼–½ lemon, juice only (1–2 tablespoons, to taste)

salt and black pepper, to taste

½ cup grated Parmesan cheese

Cook the pasta according to the package directions. Meanwhile, break off the tough ends of the asparagus and cut the spears into 1-inch pieces. (Prepare the fruit salad, if you are serving it.)

When the pasta goes into the boiling water, heat the olive oil and butter in a large heavy skillet over medium heat. When the butter is melted, stir in the garlic, then immediately add the asparagus, stirring to coat it. Sauté the asparagus, stirring occasionally, for about 4 minutes until it is tender-crisp. Stir in the spinach and lemon juice, cover, and steam it for about 2 minutes, then uncover it and cook it, stirring frequently, for about 2 more minutes until the spinach is completely wilted. Season the vegetables with salt and pepper to taste.

Drain the pasta, combine it with the asparagus and spinach mixture, and stir in the Parmesan cheese until it melts. Serve it immediately.

Scramble Flavor Booster: Add ½ teaspoon lemon zest and 2 to 4 tablespoons pesto sauce. Sauté 2 teaspoons capers with the asparagus, if desired.

Tip: A covered pot of water will boil faster and save energy.

Side Dish suggestion: To make an Ambrosia Fruit Salad, combine 2 tablespoons plain yogurt or sour cream, ⅛ lemon, juice only (about 1 teaspoon fresh lemon juice), and 1 tablespoon honey in a medium bowl. Add about 6 cups of cut fresh fruit, such as cantaloupe, blueberries, strawberries, bananas, and/or grapes and stir gently.

Kids and kids-at-heart can't resist this oh-so-simple yet ah-so-delicious spaghetti that our daughter, Celia, begs me to make for her (if by some miracle there are any leftovers, I pack them in her lunch. Given the chance, she'll even have it for breakfast.) Serve it with Baked Asparagus.

celia's simply irresistible spaghetti

Prep + Cook =
20 minutes

8 servings

Nutritional
Information per
serving (% based
upon daily values):
Calories 330, Total
Fat 13g, 20%, Satu-
rated Fat 2.5g, 23%,
Cholesterol 15mg,
5%, Sodium 190mg,
8%, Total Carbohy-
drate 43g, 14%,
Dietary Fiber 2g, 8%,
Sugar 1g, Protein 9g

Nutritional
Information per
serving with side
dish (% based upon
daily values) 1 cup
asparagus:
Calories: 390; Total
Fat: 16g, 34%; Satu-
rated Fat: 3g, 26%,
Cholesterol; 15mg,
5%; Sodium: 370mg,
15%; Total Carbohy-
drate: 50g, 16%;
Dietary Fiber: 6g,
22%; Sugar: 3g;
Protein: 13g

1 package (16 ounces) spaghetti

3 tablespoons butter or margarine

¼ cup olive oil

2–3 teaspoons minced garlic (about 4–6 cloves), to taste

½ teaspoon salt, or to taste

½ cup flat-leaf parsley, chopped

¼ cup grated Parmesan cheese, for serving

Cook the spaghetti according to the package directions until it is al dente. (Meanwhile, prepare the asparagus.)

After the spaghetti has cooked for about 5 minutes, heat the butter and olive oil in a small saucepan over medium heat. Once the butter has melted, stir in the garlic for 30 to 60 seconds, until it is fragrant. Keep it warm over low heat until the spaghetti is cooked and drained.

After draining the spaghetti, return it to the pot and stir in the butter mixture and the salt. Stir in the parsley, and serve it with the Parmesan cheese.

Scramble Flavor Booster: Serve the spaghetti with crushed red pepper flakes or freshly ground black pepper. To jazz it up, you can add toasted pine nuts, canned clams, or crumbled bacon.

Tip: To save energy, wait to run your dishwasher until it is completely full. For most dishwashers, you can just scrape the food into the trash can (or composter) and load the dishes without pre-washing them, saving water, too.

Side Dish suggestion: To make Baked Asparagus, toss 1 pound of trimmed asparagus spears with 1 tablespoon olive oil, ¼ teaspoon kosher salt, ⅛ teaspoon black pepper, and a squeeze of fresh lemon juice or salt-free lemon-pepper seasoning, if desired. Roast it flat in a baking dish in a single layer in the oven at 375 to 400 degrees (depending on what else you are baking) until they are slightly browned (about 20 minutes).

This light and colorful pasta is perfect for welcoming spring. Serve it with a spinach salad with strawberries (one of the most welcome signs of spring) and slivered almonds.

pasta primavera

Prep + Cook = 25 minutes

8 servings

Nutritional Information per serving (% based upon daily values): Calories 350, Total Fat 10g, 15%, Saturated Fat 6g, 30%, Cholesterol 30mg, 10%, Sodium 280mg, 12%, Total Carbohydrate 48g, 16%, Dietary Fiber 3g, 12%, Sugar 3g, Protein 15g

Nutritional Information per serving with side dish (% based upon daily values) 1½ cups salad: Calories: 423; Total Fat: 15g, 22%; Saturated Fat: 6g, 32%; Cholesterol: 30mg, 10%; Sodium: 310mg, 13%; Total Carbohydrate: 55g, 18%; Dietary Fiber: 5g, 21%; Sugar: 7g; Protein: 17g

1 package (16 ounces) campanelle pasta (which means bellflowers)

1 package (16 ounces) frozen or fresh broccoli florets

2 carrots, sliced (about 1 cup)

2 tablespoons butter or margarine

2 tablespoons milk, any variety

1 cup shredded Swiss cheese

½ cup grated Parmesan cheese

¾ teaspoon dried basil

½ teaspoon salt

¼ teaspoon black pepper

In a large pot, cook the pasta according to the package directions until it is al dente.

Meanwhile, in a separate pot, steam the broccoli and carrots in 1 inch of simmering water, covered, for about 5 minutes until they are tender but not mushy. (While the vegetables are cooking, prepare the salad.) Drain the vegetables, retaining ½ cup of their cooking water.

Drain the pasta and return it to the pot over medium-low heat. Add the butter, milk, cheeses, basil, salt, and black pepper and stir it thoroughly until the cheeses melt. If the sauce is too thick, stir in the reserved cooking water. Toss in the vegetables and serve it hot.

Scramble Flavor Booster: Stir ½ cup of chopped fresh basil or parsley into the sauce when you add the pasta. Serve it with crushed red pepper flakes.

Tip: Primavera means springtime in Italian and Spanish. This colorful dish will remind you of spring, my favorite season! If the broccoli in your grocery store isn't looking very fresh, use frozen broccoli florets, which are picked and frozen at the peak of freshness.

Side Dish suggestion: For the salad, in a large bowl, combine 1 package (6 to 9 ounces) baby spinach, 1 cup sliced strawberries, and ¼ cup slivered almonds. Toss it with 2 to 4 tablespoons vinaigrette dressing and serve it immediately.

Scramble subscriber Jennifer Brockett sent me her family's favorite pasta recipe, which can be served cold, warm, or in between. After finishing his fifth helping, our ten-year-old dinner guest, Matthew Warner, gave it the thumbs up. Serve it with baby carrots dipped in ginger dressing, or dip of your choice (see page 33 for dip suggestions).

honey sesame spaghetti

Prep + Cook =
25 minutes +
30 minutes–2 days to
chill (optional)

8 servings

Nutritional
Information per
serving (with
edamame) (% based
upon daily values):
Calories 510, Total
Fat 23g, 35%, Saturated Fat 2.5g, 13%,
Cholesterol 0mg, 0%,
Sodium 320mg, 13%,
Total Carbohydrate
62g, 21%, Dietary
Fiber 5g, 20%, Sugar
17g, Protein 17g

Nutritional
Information per
serving with side dish
(% based upon daily
values) ¾ cup
carrots:
Calories: 570; Total
Fat: 26g, 38%; Saturated Fat: 2.5g, 13%;
Cholesterol: 0mg,
0%; Sodium: 365mg,
15%; Total Carbohydrate: 72g, 24%;
Dietary Fiber: 7g,
28%; Sugar: 23g;
Protein: 18g

1 package (16 ounces) thin spaghetti

2 cups frozen shelled edamame or peas, or use precooked shrimp or slivered red bell pepper

¼ cup canola or vegetable oil

⅓ cup sesame oil

¼ – ½ teaspoon crushed red pepper flakes (optional)

5 tablespoons honey

4 tablespoons reduced-sodium soy sauce

¼ cup chopped fresh cilantro (optional)

2 scallions, green and a little of the white parts only, thinly sliced (¼ cup total)

3 tablespoons toasted sesame seeds

Cook the pasta according to the package directions. For the last 5 minutes of cooking (or 1 minute for the peas), add the edamame to the boiling water with the pasta, then drain. If using cooked shrimp or red bell pepper, add it to the just cooked and drained pasta.

In a large measuring cup or a bowl, heat the oils and red pepper flakes (optional) in the microwave oven until they are hot and fragrant, about 1 minute. (Alternatively, heat them in a saucepan on the stovetop over medium heat.) Stir in the honey and soy sauce. Pour the sauce over the cooked pasta, and toss. Mix in the cilantro (optional), scallions, and sesame seeds. Refrigerate the pasta for 30 minutes or up to 2 days, or serve immediately if it is already dinnertime!

Scramble Flavor Booster: For a bolder flavor, increase the amount of red pepper flakes, substitute hot chili oil for part of the sesame oil, and add extra cilantro.

Tip: Buy toasted sesame seeds where Asian foods are sold, or toast them on the lightest setting in the toaster oven or a 300-degree oven until they are lightly browned. I sometimes find less expensive sesame seeds sold with Asian foods rather than in the spice section of the supermarket.

Our son, Solomon, was eleven when he was the executive chef for this dish, though I stayed very close. He was so proud that he volunteered to serve the whole family! An added bonus—with the flavorful sauce, our kids didn't mind eating whole wheat pasta. Serve it with Quick-Steamed Artichokes with Lemon Butter.

solomon's mushroom-sausage penne pasta

Prep + Cook = 20 minutes

8 servings

Nutritional Information per serving (% based upon daily values): Calories 380, Total Fat 10g, 15%, Saturated Fat 2.5g, 13%, Cholesterol 45mg, 15%, Sodium 640mg, 27%, Total Carbohydrate 54g, 18%, Dietary Fiber 4g, 16%, Protein 20g, Sugar 8g

Nutritional Information per serving with side dish (% based upon daily values) ⅓ artichoke: Calories: 520; Total Fat: 23g, 35%; Saturated Fat: 9g, 43%; Cholesterol: 65mg, 22%; Sodium: 735mg, 31%; Total Carbohydrate: 59g, 20%; Dietary Fiber: 6g, 24%; Sugar: 8g; Protein: 22g

1 package (16 ounces) whole wheat or regular penne pasta

1 tablespoon olive oil

1 teaspoon minced garlic (about 1 clove)

8 ounces fresh sliced mushrooms

12–16 ounces precooked turkey or vegetarian sausage, halved lengthwise and sliced into semicircles

1 jar (26 ounces) tomato-basil pasta sauce

1 cup frozen peas, thawed slightly

¼ cup grated or shredded Parmesan cheese, or to taste

(Start the artichokes, if you are serving them.) In a large stockpot, cook the pasta according to package directions, and drain it.

Meanwhile, in a large heavy skillet, heat the oil over medium heat and add the garlic. When it starts to get fragrant and brown (less than 1 minute), add the mushrooms and sausage and cook, stirring occasionally, for about 10 minutes until the mushrooms have shrunken and the sausage is slightly browned.

Add the pasta sauce and peas and bring it to a boil. Reduce the heat and let it simmer for 1 to 2 minutes. In a large metal bowl or in the stockpot that you used to cook the pasta, combine the sauce with the drained pasta. Serve it immediately topped with Parmesan cheese, or store it in the refrigerator for up to 3 days.

Scramble Flavor Booster: Use spicy sausage and add ⅛ to ¼ teaspoon crushed red pepper flakes to the skillet with the mushrooms and sausage.

Tip: When possible, involve your children in making dinner. Kids are more likely to eat something they've helped create, and they learn valuable life skills by cooking with us.

Side Dish suggestion: To make Quick-Steamed Artichokes with Lemon Butter, cut off the stems of 2 artichokes so they can sit without falling over, and trim the pointy leaves with kitchen scissors, if desired. Fill a bowl with cold water and soak the artichokes for 3 to 5 minutes; rinse them thoroughly. Stand the artichokes in a microwave-safe dish with the leaves pointing up and pour 1 cup water and the juice of half a lemon over them. Cover tightly with plastic wrap and cook them in the microwave for 15 to 20 minutes on high (depending on your microwave oven), turning them halfway through, until they are tender. (You can check their tenderness by seeing if an inner leaf pulls easily from the stem.) While the artichokes are cooling, divide 4 tablespoons butter or margarine between 2 small bowls and melt it, covered, in the microwave (10 to 40 seconds) on high power. Into each bowl, stir in 1 tablespoon olive oil, 1 teaspoon grated Parmesan cheese, $\frac{1}{8}$ teaspoon garlic powder, $\frac{1}{8}$ teaspoon salt, and a squeeze of fresh lemon juice. Serve the artichokes with lemon-butter sauce for dipping.

It's hard to believe that this was my first attempt at using prosciutto (thinly sliced Italian cured ham) in a recipe. The flavorful results made me wonder what took me so long! Look for the least salty brand of prosciutto that you can find so you can enjoy more of its smoky sweetness. Serve it with Sugar Snap Peas (one of my favorite spring delights!) with Cashews.

penne with prosciutto and goat cheese

Prep + Cook = 30 minutes

8 servings

Nutritional Information per serving (% based upon daily values): Calories 370, Total Fat 15.5g, 24%, Saturated Fat 6.5g, 33%, Cholesterol 13.5mg, 4.5%, Sodium 411mg, 17%, Total Carbohydrate 45.5g, 15%, Dietary Fiber 2.5g, 10.5%, Sugar 2g, Protein 10.5g

Nutritional Information per serving with side dish (% based upon daily values) ¾ cup sugar snap peas: Calories: 460; Total Fat: 23g, 35%; Saturated Fat: 8g, 41%; Cholesterol: 14mg, 5%; Sodium: 411mg, 17%; Total Carbohydrate: 51g, 17%; Dietary Fiber: 4g, 15%; Sugar: 4g; Protein: 13g

1 package (16 ounces) penne paste

3 ounces prosciutto, cut into thin strips or diced

2 tomatoes, chopped (or use 1 can [15 ounces] tomatoes, with a little of their liquid)

¼ cup olive oil

1 cup pitted black olives, chopped (optional)

1 cup fresh basil and/or parsley, chopped

4 ounces goat cheese, crumbled or diced (about 1 cup)

Cook the pasta according to the package directions until it is al dente, drain it, and rinse it briefly in cool water. (If you are making the sugar snap peas, start them while the pasta is cooking.)

Toss the cooled pasta with the remaining ingredients, except the cheese (if the pasta is still warm, the cheese will melt). Gently stir in the cheese just before serving.

Scramble Flavor Booster: Season the finished dish with lots of freshly ground black pepper, and use kalamata or another flavorful black olive.

Tip: For a meatless version of this dish, you can omit the prosciutto and use a few extra olives.

Side Dish suggestion: In a small skillet, heat 1 tablespoon olive oil over medium heat. Add 8 ounces (about 2 cups) sugar snap peas and sauté them, stirring frequently, for 3 to 4 minutes. Add ¼ cup chopped cashews, sauté them for about 2 more minutes, and serve.

Spaghetti with bacon and eggs? Now that was something I had to try making, and the result was superb. Serve it with steamed broccoli with lemon-pepper seasoning (page 46).

spaghetti carbonara

Prep + Cook =
25 minutes

8 servings

Nutritional
Information per
serving (% based
upon daily values):
Calories 340, Total
Fat 12g, 18%, Satu-
rated Fat 3.5g, 18%,
Cholesterol 80mg,
27%, Sodium 540mg,
23%, Total Carbohy-
drate 43g, 14%,
Dietary Fiber 1g, 4%,
Sugar 1g, Protein 16g

Nutritional
Information per
serving with side dish
(% based upon daily
values) 1 cup broccoli:
Calories: 395; Total
Fat: 12.5g, 19%; Satu-
rated Fat: 3.5g, 19%;
Cholesterol: 80mg,
27%; Sodium: 604mg,
26%; Total Carbohy-
drate: 54g, 18%;
Dietary Fiber: 6g,
25%; Sugar: 3g;
Protein: 19.5g

1 package (16 ounces) spaghetti

1 tablespoon olive oil

8 ounces turkey bacon, preferably nitrite-free, sliced into thin strips
    (or use sliced mushrooms or vegetarian bacon)

1½ teaspoons minced garlic (about 3 cloves)

2 eggs

1 cup grated Parmesan cheese

¼ cup fresh minced parsley (optional)

Cook the spaghetti in salted water according to the package directions, until it is al dente. (Meanwhile, prepare the broccoli, if you are serving it.)

Heat the oil in a large heavy skillet over medium heat. Add the bacon and sauté it for about 8 to 10 minutes until it is crisp. Add the garlic and sauté it for 1 minute.

While the bacon cooks, in a medium bowl, beat the eggs and stir in the cheese. Heat the eggs and cheese in the microwave, loosely covered, for about 1 minute on high power, and then stir the mixture until the cheese melts into the eggs.

Drain the spaghetti and add it immediately to the pan with the bacon while it is still hot (alternatively, combine the spaghetti and bacon in a large metal bowl that will retain the heat.) Remove the pan from the heat and immediately stir in the egg and cheese mixture, tossing quickly, until the eggs thicken. It's very important that the spaghetti is still hot so the eggs cook quickly on contact. Try not to get distracted during this final stage! Serve immediately, sprinkled with the parsley (optional).

Scramble Flavor Booster: Add ¼ teaspoon crushed red pepper flakes to the spaghetti with the egg and cheese mixture. Use freshly grated aged Parmesan cheese.

Tip: If you shop at a store that carries nitrite-free turkey bacon (such as Applegate Farms brand), use that instead of cured bacon. I try to avoid serving meats that contain sodium nitrites to my family any more than necessary, as they are possible carcinogens.

I served this meal to vegetarians and Midwestern steak eaters (even an avowed tofu-hater from Texas) and all agreed it was delicious. You can use the same recipe for chicken tenderloins or breasts (or even steak!), if you are adamantly opposed to tofu. Serve it with sliced oranges, (which are grown in the U.S. from November through June).

crispy tofu triangles with fried rice

Prep + Cook = 30 minutes

6 servings

Nutritional Information per serving (% based upon daily values): Calories 340, Total Fat 13g, 20%, Saturated Fat 2g, 10%, Cholesterol 35mg, 12%, Sodium 620mg, 26%, Total Carbohydrate 42g, 14%, Dietary Fiber 3g, 12%, Sugar 2g, Protein 14g

Nutritional Information per serving with side dish (% based upon daily values) 1 orange: Calories: 371; Total Fat: 13g, 20%; Saturated Fat: 2g, 10%; Cholesterol: 35mg, 12%; Sodium: 620mg, 26%; Total Carbohydrate: 50g, 17%; Dietary Fiber: 5g, 18%; Sugar: 8g; Protein: 15g

1½ cups white or brown rice

1 pound extra-firm tofu packed in water, drained

6 tablespoons reduced-sodium soy sauce

2 tablespoons pure maple syrup or honey

1 tablespoon sesame oil

2 teaspoons rice vinegar

¼ teaspoon ground ginger

5 scallions, green parts only, thinly sliced

2 tablespoons peanut oil

1 egg

1 cup finely diced carrots or peas (optional)

¼–½ teaspoon black pepper

Cook the rice according to the package directions. Meanwhile, cut the tofu lengthwise from end to end (like cutting a deck of cards), making 3 even slices. Wrap those slices in a clean kitchen towel to absorb any excess water.

To prepare the tofu, combine 2 tablespoons soy sauce, the maple syrup or honey, sesame oil, vinegar, and ginger in the bottom of a flat baking dish that's large enough to hold the tofu in a single layer. Cut the tofu slices in half, then diagonally again into triangles. Add them to the dish with the marinade and flip them several times to coat them with the sauce. Heat a large nonstick skillet over medium heat. Transfer the tofu and marinade to the skillet. Cook it, flipping occasionally, until the tofu is nicely browned on both sides, 10 to 12 minutes. Transfer it to a serving plate and sprinkle it with 2 sliced scallions.

When the rice is 5 minutes from done, heat the peanut oil in a large skillet. Fry the egg in the oil, chopping it as it cooks, until it is well done. Add 3 sliced scallions, carrots or peas (optional) and stir-fry them with the egg for 1 minute. Add 3 cups cooked rice, 4 tablespoons soy sauce, and the pepper and toss it thoroughly. Serve the fried rice immediately with the tofu.

Tip: My rice and grains come out perfect every time when I use my All-Clad stainless saucepan. My brother gave it to us for our wedding fifteen years ago and it is certainly the gift I've used most. Its tight-fitting lid seals in the steam and its heavy weight conducts heat evenly so the grains never scorch.

Scramble Flavor Booster: Serve the tofu and rice with Asian chili garlic sauce or sweet chili sauce.

kids and calcium
how much is enough?

The American Academy of Pediatrics recommends three servings per day of calcium for 4- to 8-year-olds (and adults), and four servings for 9- to 18-year-olds. What counts as a serving? One cup (8 ounces) of milk or yogurt or 1½ ounces of cheese (about ¼ cup of shredded cheese).

The best way to make sure your kids get enough calcium is to make calcium-rich foods a daily habit. In our house, milk is the only drink option for the kids at dinner. The kids also get yogurt and cheese in their lunches, and they sometimes have cereal with milk for a snack.

For those families where kids don't like or can't tolerate milk, introduce calcium-fortified fruit juices or soy milk. Many doctors and dieticians also recommend adding chocolate or other flavoring to milk if kids won't drink plain milk, believing that the health benefits of drinking milk outweigh the downside from the extra sugar. If your kids don't like any of these options, tofu, broccoli, chickpeas, lentils, canned sardines, salmon, and other fish with bones are also good sources of calcium.

P.S. Don't neglect your own nutritional needs: If you aren't getting your 2 to 3 servings of calcium each day, consider taking a daily calcium supplement.

This delicious stew is flavored with fresh herbs and a touch of honey. Serve it over Israeli (large-grain) couscous.

earth day vegetable stew with feta cheese

Prep (20 minutes) + Cook (20 minutes)

6 servings

Nutritional Information per serving (% based upon daily values): Calories 147, Total Fat 6g, 9%, Saturated Fat 3g, 13%, Cholesterol 13mg, 4%, Sodium 627mg, 27%, Total Carbohydrate 19g, 7%, Dietary Fiber 4g, 16%, Sugar 9g, Protein 5g

Nutritional Information per serving with side dish (% based upon daily values) ¾ cup cooked couscous: Calories: 279; Total Fat: 6g, 9%; Saturated Fat: 3g, 13%; Cholesterol: 13mg, 4%; Sodium: 633mg, 27%; Total Carbohydrate: 46g, 16%; Dietary Fiber: 6g, 23%; Sugar: 9g; Protein: 10g

1 tablespoon olive oil

1 large yellow onion, chopped

1 large sweet potato, diced into ½-inch chunks

1 can (28 ounces) diced tomatoes with their liquid, or 1½–2 pounds fresh tomatoes

1 package (14–16 ounces) frozen cut green beans (or use fresh)

1 tablespoon fresh oregano leaves (or ½ teaspoon dried)

2 tablespoons fresh parsley, chopped (optional)

20 fresh basil leaves, chopped, or 2 teaspoons dried basil

½ teaspoon salt

1 tablespoon honey

4 ounces crumbled feta cheese for serving (about 1 cup)

In a large pot, heat the oil over medium heat. Add the onions and cook, stirring often, until softened, about 5 minutes. Add the sweet potatoes and tomatoes and bring it to a low boil.

Reduce the heat, partially cover, and simmer the mixture for 10 to 15 minutes, stirring occasionally, while you prepare the remaining ingredients, letting the potatoes soften.

Add the green beans and herbs and simmer it for 10 more minutes. (Meanwhile, prepare the couscous if you are making it.)

Stir in the salt and honey. Serve it immediately, topped with crumbled feta cheese (optional), or refrigerate it for 1 to 2 days, or freeze it and add the feta when you are ready to serve it.

Scramble Flavor Booster: Add ¼ teaspoon black pepper or crushed red pepper flakes to the stew with the salt and honey.

Tip: Before you throw them out, try to think of creative ways to reuse those muffin containers, spice jars, gift bags, and other household waste. We reuse large spice jars to organize the workbench, and muffin containers to deliver baked goods to friends.

When we were in Costa Rica last year, we stayed in a tent camp in the rainforest that was very rustic, except for the French-trained chef who prepared our meals. I was shocked when our kids not only devoured his asparagus soup, but asked me to get the recipe so I could make it at home. Although the chef shared his recipe with no measurements or instructions (just the ingredients written in Spanish!), I've finally managed to create a very close facsimile to his soothing tropical elixir. Serve it with the remaining baguette and a green salad with raisins, cashews, and sunflower seeds.

cream of asparagus soup with fresh croutons

Prep + Cook =
30 minutes

6 servings

Nutritional Information per serving (% based upon daily values): Calories 320, Total Fat 12.5g, 19%, Saturated Fat 4g, 20%, Cholesterol 10mg, 3.5%, Sodium 567mg, 23%, Total Carbohydrate 43g, 15%, Dietary Fiber 4.5g, 18.5%, Sugar 2.5g, Protein 10g

Nutritional Information per serving with side dish (% based upon daily values) ¼ of baguette; 1½ cups salad:
Calories: 596; Total Fat: 20g, 30%; Saturated Fat: 5g, 23%; Cholesterol: 16mg, 6%; Sodium: 1,119mg, 46%; Total Carbohydrate: 90g, 31%; Dietary Fiber: 8g, 30%; Sugar: 9g; Protein: 21g

1 tablespoon butter

3 tablespoons olive oil

1 teaspoon minced garlic (about 2 cloves)

2 russet (baking) potatoes, peeled and diced

1 pound asparagus, trimmed and cut into 1-inch pieces

1 box (32 ounces) reduced-sodium chicken or vegetable broth

1 teaspoon dried tarragon, or 1 tablespoon fresh

1 baguette (use ½ for croutons and reserve ½ for serving)

½ teaspoon salt

¼ teaspoon black pepper

¼ cup half-and-half or heavy cream

Preheat the oven to 400 degrees. In a large saucepan, heat the butter and 1 tablespoon of the oil over medium heat. When the butter starts to bubble, add the garlic and stir it for about 30 seconds until it becomes fragrant. Add the potatoes and asparagus, and cook for about 3 minutes, stirring often.

Add the broth and dried tarragon (if using fresh tarragon, add it with the salt and pepper) and bring it to a low boil. Cook, stirring often, for about 15 minutes until the potatoes are tender. (Prepare the salad, if you are serving it.)

Meanwhile, to make the croutons, cut half of the baguette into thin slices and lay them on a baking sheet. Brush the tops of the slices with olive oil and bake them for about 10 minutes until they are crisp and just starting to brown at the edges. Remove them from the oven and set them aside.

Add the salt and pepper to the soup and puree it. Stir in the half-and-half or cream, and serve it with the croutons.

Scramble Flavor Booster: Season the soup with freshly ground black pepper or lemon-pepper seasoning. For a meatier meal, stir some crisp crumbled bacon into the soup.

Side Dish suggestion: To make the salad, combine 6 to 8 cups chopped lettuce, ¼ cup raisins, ¼ cup unsalted cashews, 2 tablespoons shelled sunflower seeds, and toss with 2 to 4 tablespoons vinaigrette, or dressing of your choice.

During the Passover seder this filling soup signals the beginning of the meal and is always the kids' favorite part of the dinner. Our kids like it so much that I usually make it at least once more during the year. Traditionally matzo ball soup takes a couple of hours to make, and involves many pots, strained herbs and vegetables, and too many steps for a Scramble meal. This version takes only about 20 minutes of actual work. Serve it with Dr. Praeger's potato or broccoli pancakes (sold frozen) and with a green salad with diced red bell peppers, pine nuts, and Gorgonzola cheese.

speedy quick matzo ball soup

Prep (20 minutes) + Cook (30 minutes)

8 servings

Nutritional Information per serving:
Calories 237, Fat 14g, 21%, Saturated Fat 1g, 4%, Cholesterol 0mg, 0%, Sodium 1550mg, 65%, Total Carbohydrate 20g, 6%, Dietary Fiber 3g, 10%, Sugar 3g, Protein 4g

Nutritional Information per serving with side dish (% based upon daily values) 2 potato pancakes, 1½ cups salad:
Calories: 501; Total Fat: 34g, 51%; Saturated Fat: 5g, 22%; Cholesterol: 134mg, 45%; Sodium: 722mg, 31%; Total Carbohydrate: 37g, 12%; Dietary Fiber: 10g, 37%; Sugar: 6g; Protein: 13g

1 package (4.5 ounces) matzo ball mix (sold in supermarkets with kosher foods)

4 eggs

½ cup vegetable oil

2 teaspoons salt

2 boxes (32 ounces each) reduced-sodium chicken or vegetable broth

3 large carrots, sliced

3 celery stalks, sliced

1 tablespoon chopped fresh dill (or use 1 teaspoon dried)

Prepare the matzo ball mix according to the package directions. (For most packages, mix the matzo meal with 4 beaten eggs and ½ cup oil, stir, and refrigerate for 15 minutes.)

Set a large pot of water to boil. Once it boils, add the salt to the boiling water. Using wet hands, gently form the matzo ball mixture into 1-inch balls and carefully drop them into the water. Cover the pot and cook them for 30 minutes, reducing the heat, if necessary, to keep it at a low boil.

After adding the matzo balls to the boiling water, bring the broth to a boil in a separate large pot. Add the carrots and celery and simmer them for 15 minutes. (Meanwhile, prepare the potato or broccoli pancakes and salad.) When the matzo balls are cooked, using a slotted spoon, carefully remove them from the salted water and add them to the pot with the vegetables. (At this point you can serve the soup immediately or refrigerate it for up to 3 days). Add the dill and serve it hot, making sure to put a matzo ball and some vegetables into each bowl.

Scramble Flavor Booster: Use fresh dill, and sprinkle a little extra over each bowl.

Side Dish suggestion: Heat 1 package potato pancakes or other vegetable pancakes (Dr. Praeger's or other variety) according to the package directions (if you only have one oven, like I do, you can use a toaster oven to heat them). Serve them hot, topped with nonfat or low-fat sour cream and/or applesauce, if desired.

Side Dish suggestion: In a large bowl, combine 6 to 8 cups lettuce, ½ red bell pepper, diced, 1 tablespoon pine nuts, and 2 tablespoons Gorgonzola cheese. Toss it with 2 to 4 tablespoons dressing of your choice.

Scramble subscriber and recipe tester Alice Clark sent me her version of Sloppy Joes—the white wine, garlic, and sourdough bread give it a Northern California twist. Serve it with red bell peppers and carrots with dressing.

san francisco joes

Prep + Cook =
15 minutes

6 servings

Nutritional
Information per
serving (with 2 slices
of bread) (% based
upon daily values):
Calories 320, Total
Fat 8g, 12%, Satu-
rated Fat 2g, 10%,
Cholesterol 105mg,
35%, Sodium 660mg,
28%, Total Carbohy-
drate 32g, 11%,
Dietary Fiber 3g,
12%, Sugar 4g,
Protein 28g

Nutritional
Information per
serving with side dish
(% based upon daily
values) ¼ bell pep-
per, 1 carrot, 1 tbsp.
ranch dressing:
Calories: 426; Total
Fat: 16g, 24%; Satu-
rated Fat: 3g, 16%;
Cholesterol: 110mg,
37%; Sodium: 825mg,
35%; Total Carbohy-
drate: 41g, 14%;
Dietary Fiber: 6g,
21%; Sugar: 9g;
Protein: 29g

1 package (10 ounces) frozen chopped spinach (or use fresh spinach, and add it after meat is browned)

1 tablespoon olive oil

1 pound ground beef or turkey or vegetarian ground "meat"

1 small yellow onion, diced

8 ounces sliced mushrooms

2 tablespoons Worcestershire sauce

½ teaspoon garlic powder

2 eggs, beaten

¼ cup grated Parmesan cheese

¼ cup white wine

¼ teaspoon salt

⅛–¼ teaspoon black pepper, to taste

1 loaf sourdough bread

In a microwave-safe dish, thaw the spinach in the microwave and drain it thoroughly.

In a large skillet, heat the oil over medium heat. Brown the meat, onions, and mushrooms until the meat is just cooked through. Drain the excess liquid (I find that a turkey baster works well for this) and discard. Stir in the Worcestershire sauce, garlic powder, and spinach, distributing the spinach evenly.

Stir in the eggs, cheese, and wine until the eggs are fully cooked, and season with the salt and black pepper. Serve over warm bread, or make sandwiches.

Scramble Flavor Booster: Double the garlic powder, top the bread with pesto sauce, and/or serve it with hot pepper sauce, such as Tabasco.

Tip: If you don't cook with wine, you can use 1 tablespoon of white vinegar and 2 to 3 tablespoons of chicken or vegetable broth instead.

This recipe is inspired by a suggestion from Scramble subscriber Alyce Traverso. It's a healthy and filling vegetarian meal that your family members can each enjoy in their own way. Serve it with freshly popped popcorn.

chili potatoes with sweet peppers

Prep + Cook = 30 minutes

4 servings

Nutritional Information per serving (% based upon daily values): Calories 490, Total Fat 18g, 28%, Saturated Fat 9g, 45%, Cholesterol 40mg, 13%, Sodium 700mg, 29%, Total Carbohydrate 63g, 21%, Dietary Fiber 10g, 40%, Sugar 5g, Protein 21g

Nutritional Information per serving with side dish (% based upon daily values) 1½ cups popped corn: Calories: 660; Total Fat: 32g, 50%; Saturated Fat: 14g, 68%; Cholesterol: 55mg, 18%; Sodium: 720mg, 30%; Total Carbohydrate: 72g, 24%; Dietary Fiber: 12g, 48%; Sugar: 5g; Protein: 23g

4 russet (baking) potatoes

1 tablespoon olive oil

1 red or green bell pepper, diced

1 jalapeño pepper, seeds removed and finely diced

1 small yellow or white onion, diced

¾ teaspoon chili powder, or more to taste

¼ teaspoon ground cumin, or more to taste

½ teaspoon dried oregano or 1½ teaspoons fresh oregano leaves

¼ teaspoon salt

1 can (15 ounces) black beans, drained and rinsed (or use combination of beans and corn kernels)

½ cup shredded Cheddar cheese

½ cup shredded Monterey Jack or mozzarella cheese

½ cup salsa for serving (optional)

½ cup nonfat sour cream for serving (optional)

Scrub the potatoes, pat them dry, and pierce the skins in several places with a fork. Place the potatoes in a microwave-safe glass dish and cover it with wax paper. Cook the potatoes on high power for 15 to 20 minutes (depending on your microwave), turning them once, until they are tender.

Meanwhile, in a heavy skillet, heat the oil over medium heat. Add the bell peppers, jalapeños, onions, chili powder, cumin, oregano, and salt. After about 10 minutes, stir in the beans (or bean and corn combination). Cook the vegetables, stirring often, until they are very tender, 10 to 15 minutes. (Make the popcorn, if you are serving it.)

Cut the potatoes lengthwise and press them open. Top each potato with one-fourth of the vegetables, one-fourth of the cheese, and 1 to 2 tablespoons of salsa and sour cream, if desired.

Scramble Flavor Booster: Use extra dry spices or substitute chipotle chili powder for the chili powder, and serve the potatoes topped with lots of salsa. Top the potatoes with a thin layer of butter or margarine before adding the toppings.

Tip: For a lower-calorie dinner, half a potato with an eighth of the topping would still be a filling main dish (245 calories), served with 1 cup of popcorn (113 calories) and a big glass of water.

Side Dish suggestion: Popcorn for dinner? Why not? Put 3 tablespoons vegetable oil and ⅓ cup popcorn kernels into a heavy-bottom stockpot over medium heat (or use a popcorn popper, if you have one). Cover the pot, leaving the top slightly ajar, gently shaking the popcorn around occasionally. When popping slows to every few seconds, remove the pan from the heat. Season the popcorn with 2 to 4 tablespoons melted butter or margarine and ¼ teaspoon salt or 1 to 2 tablespoons grated Parmesan cheese, to taste. Some people also like to toss it with chili powder or Cajun spices.

This is a nearly instant meal for a bustling night. Or you can pack the tuna mixture, the lettuce, and the tortillas separately for a picnic or school lunches. For a low-carb version, serve the tuna salad over the lettuce without the wraps, or use whole pieces of lettuce as the wraps themselves! Serve them with a green salad with diced orange, walnuts, and shredded Parmesan cheese.

mandarin tuna roll-ups

Prep (no cook) = 10 minutes

4 servings

Nutritional Information per serving (% based upon daily values):
Calories 270, Total Fat 3.5g, 5%, Saturated Fat 1g, 5%, Cholesterol 45mg, 15%, Sodium 890mg, 37%, Total Carbohydrate 36g, 12%, Dietary Fiber 3g, 12%, Sugar 10g, Protein 24g

Nutritional Information per serving with side dish (% based upon daily values) 1½ cups salad:
Calories: 346; Total Fat: 9g, 12%; Saturated Fat: 2g, 9%; Cholesterol: 47mg, 16%; Sodium: 952mg, 40%; Total Carbohydrate: 43g, 14%; Dietary Fiber: 5g, 21%; Sugar: 15g; Protein: 26g

1 large can or 2 small cans (12 ounces total) chunk light tuna in water, drained

¼ cup fat-free or reduced-fat mayonnaise

1 teaspoon curry powder

1–2 stalks finely chopped celery or canned water chestnuts, drained thoroughly (½ cup)

1 cup (from 1 large can) mandarin orange segments, drained thoroughly (or use diced fresh orange or pineapple tidbits)

4 whole wheat tortillas or pita pockets

2 cups chopped romaine or other crunchy lettuce

In a medium bowl, combine the tuna, mayonnaise, curry powder, and celery or water chestnuts.

Gently stir in the oranges or pineapple. (Make the green salad, if you are serving it.)

Spread one-fourth of the tuna mixture in a tortilla or pita pocket, top it with one-fourth of the lettuce, and roll it up. Slice it in half crosswise (if using a tortilla), and serve.

Scramble Flavor Booster: Stir 1 tablespoon of Indian chutney or 1 teaspoon of jerk seasoning into the tuna mixture.

Tip: I always use chunk light tuna instead of white because it is much lower in mercury.

Side Dish suggestion: In a salad bowl, combine 6 to 8 cups washed, dried, and torn lettuce with 1 diced orange (pour juice in, too), 2 to 4 tablespoons coarsely chopped walnuts, and 2 tablespoons shredded Parmesan cheese. Toss it with 2 to 4 tablespoons vinaigrette or your favorite salad dressing and serve it immediately.

These burritos are a standby meal at our house because they are so easy, healthy, and versatile. You can get creative and sauté some bell peppers or other vegetables with the onions, or add some diced chiles. Serve it with Lemony Asparagus.

chipotle bean and corn burritos

Prep + Cook =
15 minutes

6 servings

Nutritional
Information per
serving (% based
upon daily values):
Calories 360, Total
Fat 9g, 14%, Satu-
rated Fat 3g, 15%,
Cholesterol 5mg, 2%,
Sodium 930mg, 39%,
Total Carbohydrate
55g, 18%, Dietary
Fiber 9g, 36%, Sugar
5g, Protein 17g

Nutritional
Information per
serving with side
dish (% based upon
daily values) ¼ of
asparagus:
Calories: 385; Total
Fat: 10g, 16%; Satu-
rated Fat: 3g, 15%;
Cholesterol: 5mg,
2%; Sodium: 930mg,
39%; Total Carbohy-
drate: 58g, 19%;
Dietary Fiber: 10g,
40%; Sugar: 6g;
Protein: 18g

1 tablespoon olive oil

½ yellow onion, chopped

2 cans (14 or 15 ounces each) pinto or black beans, drained and rinsed

10–14 ounces canned or frozen unsweetened corn kernels, drained if using canned

1 tablespoon balsamic vinegar

6 large (burrito-size) whole wheat or flour tortillas

1 cup shredded Cheddar cheese

1 cup chipotle salsa

Heat the oil in a large heavy skillet over medium heat. Add the onions and cook, stirring occasionally, until the onions are softened, about 5 minutes.

Add the beans, corn, and vinegar and stir until heated through, about 5 minutes. (Meanwhile, prepare the asparagus, if you are serving it.)

Heat the tortillas in the microwave. (To heat them in the oven, wrap them in foil and warm them at 350 degrees for 5 to 10 minutes).

Scoop a large spoonful of the bean mixture into the tortillas. Top them with cheese and salsa and wrap them burrito style.

Scramble Flavor Booster: Use spicy salsa and sharp Cheddar cheese. Sauté 1 diced jalapeño pepper with the onions, if desired.

Tip: Burrito means little burro (or donkey) in Spanish. No one knows for sure how burritos came to be named after donkeys (maybe because the rolled-up burrito looks a little like the packs that burros carry on their backs). If your family comes up with any other theories while eating them please send me a note!

Side Dish suggestion: To make Lemony Asparagus, trim 1 pound asparagus and cut it into thirds. In a heavy skillet over medium heat, sauté ½ teaspoon minced garlic (about 1 clove) in 1 teaspoon olive oil, add the asparagus, and sauté it for 4 to 5 minutes until it is tender-crisp. Sprinkle it with the juice of ¼ fresh lemon or with ½ to 1 teaspoon salt-free lemon-pepper seasoning, to taste.

A quick and healthy no-cook meal, these sandwiches are fun to eat on a busy night. We top them with sliced tomatoes and add a layer of tortilla chips for extra crunch! Serve them with celery sticks with Boursin cheese (see page 47).

salmon salad sandwiches

Prep (no cook) = 10 minutes

6 servings

Nutritional Information per serving (% based upon daily values): Calories 270, Total Fat 10g, 15%, Saturated Fat 2g, 10%, Cholesterol 30mg, 10%, Sodium 730mg, 30%, Total Carbohydrate 25g, 8%, Dietary Fiber 1g, 4%, Sugar 4g, Protein 19g

Nutritional Information per serving with side dish (% based upon daily values) 1 cup celery and 2 tbsp. Boursin light cheese: Calories: 331; Total Fat: 14g, 20%; Saturated Fat: 4g, 20%; Cholesterol: 44mg, 15%; Sodium: 967mg, 40%; Total Carbohydrate: 29g, 9%; Dietary Fiber: 3g, 10%; Sugar 6g; Protein: 24g

¼ cup reduced-fat mayonnaise

1 tablespoon Dijon mustard

1 teaspoon honey

½ lemon, juice only (2 tablespoons fresh lemon juice)

1 can (15 ounces) wild Alaskan pink salmon, drained

2 celery stalks, finely chopped (about 1 cup)

6 hamburger/sandwich buns, whole wheat or white

1 tomato, sliced (optional)

1 cup tortilla chips (optional)

In the measuring cup used to measure the mayonnaise, combine the mayonnaise, mustard, honey, and lemon juice. In a medium bowl, mix the salmon, celery, and mayonnaise mixture. (At this point you can refrigerate the salmon salad for up to 24 hours until you are ready to serve it.)

Put a scoop of the salmon salad in each bun, top it with sliced tomato and/or tortilla chips, if desired, and serve immediately.

Scramble Flavor Booster: Add ½ teaspoon lemon zest to the salad.

Tip: Canned salmon is a true power food—high in protein, calcium, and omega-3s, this is a great food to add to your family's diet.

My family loves these little pizzas. The variations are endless—try sliced olives, hot peppers, mushrooms, or whatever you like on your pizza—just don't pile too much on top, or the tortillas will sag from the weight. Serve them with Strawberry-Banana Smoothies.

tortilla pepperoni pizzas

Prep + Cook =
20 minutes

8 servings

Nutritional Information per serving (% based upon daily values): Calories 240, Total Fat 8g, 12%, Saturated Fat 1.5g, 8%, Cholesterol 5mg, 1%, Sodium 580mg, 24%, Total Carbohydrate 29g, 10%, Dietary Fiber 1g, 4%, Protein 15g, Sugar 1g

Nutritional Information per serving with side dish (% based upon daily values) ¼ of smoothie: Calories: 370; Total Fat: 9g, 14%; Saturated Fat: 2g, 11%; Cholesterol: 10mg, 3%; Sodium: 620mg, 26%; Total Carbohydrate: 57g, 19%; Dietary Fiber: 4g, 16%; Sugar: 21g; Protein: 19g

2 tablespoons olive oil

½ teaspoon garlic powder

8 small to medium (soft taco-size) wheat or flour tortillas

½ cup tomato-basil flavored pasta sauce

1½ cups reduced-fat shredded mozzarella cheese, or to taste

4 ounces sliced pepperoni (traditional, turkey, or veggie), or toppings of your choice

Preheat the oven to 400 degrees. In a small bowl, combine the oil and garlic powder. Using a pastry brush, coat each tortilla with a thin layer of the garlic oil. Spread a thin layer (about 1 tablespoon) of sauce on each tortilla, and sprinkle them with cheese. Top them with pepperoni (or a very thin layer of toppings of your choice).

For a crispy crust (our preferred method), carefully transfer the tortilla pizzas directly to the oven rack and cook them for 3 to 4 minutes. For a softer crust, cook them on a baking sheet coated with nonstick cooking spray for 4 to 6 minutes. (Meanwhile, make the smoothies.) Remove the pizzas from the oven when the tortillas start to brown on the edges—watch them carefully so they don't burn!

Scramble Flavor Booster: Sprinkle crushed red pepper flakes, dried oregano, and dried basil directly on top of the sauce before adding the cheese, and top the pizza with hot peppers.

Tip: Let your kids design their own pizzas—they can even make funny faces with the toppings. I have found that kids are more likely to eat something they have helped create.

Side Dish suggestion: To make a Strawberry-Banana Smoothie, in a blender, puree 2 cups fresh or frozen strawberries, 2 ripe bananas, 1 cup orange juice, and 1 cup nonfat vanilla or plain yogurt.

These versatile wraps can make a simple, cool dinner on a hot night, a gourmet lunch, or a fun finger food for a party if you slice them into smaller pieces. Serve the wraps with a White Bean and Red Onion Salad.

spinach, basil, and red pepper wraps

Prep (no cook) =
10 minutes

4 servings

Nutritional Information per serving (% based upon daily values): Calories 310, Total Fat 12g, 18%, Saturated Fat 6g, 30%, Cholesterol 30mg, 10%, Sodium 790mg, 33%, Total Carbohydrate 38g, 13%, Dietary Fiber 6g, 24%, Sugar 14g, Protein 12g

Nutritional Information per serving with side dish (% based upon daily values) ¼ of bean salad:
Calories: 460; Total Fat: 16g, 24%; Saturated Fat: 6.5g, 33%; Cholesterol: 30mg, 10%; Sodium: 1,300mg, 54%; Total Carbohydrate: 61g, 21%; Dietary Fiber: 12g, 48%; Sugar: 15g; Protein: 20g

4 large whole wheat or flour tortillas

8 teaspoons mango chutney or honey mustard

24 fresh basil leaves

8 slices Havarti or Cheddar cheese

1 red bell pepper, seeds and ribs removed, cut into long thin strips

4 cups baby spinach

(If you are serving the bean salad, make that first.) Heat the tortillas in the microwave (some people prefer to heat them over an open flame on the stovetop for a few seconds) until they are warm and soft. Spread 2 teaspoons mango chutney or honey mustard on one side of each tortilla. Top the spread on each wrap with 6 basil leaves spread from one end to the other. Top the basil with 2 slices of cheese, one-fourth of the bell pepper (lay the strips across the middle of the tortilla so you can roll it up), and 1 cup spinach. Roll the wrap as tightly as possible, and slice it in half before serving.

Scramble Flavor Booster: Use spicy chutney or Pepper Jack cheese and extra basil.

Tip: When slicing bell peppers, cut them in large pieces from top to bottom, remove the stem and seeds. Put the smooth skin down on the cutting board to slice or chop it, as it's easier for your knife to grip the rough inside of the pepper.

Side Dish suggestion: To make the White Bean and Red Onion Salad, drain and rinse 1 can (15 ounces) cannellini beans. In a medium bowl, combine the juice of ½ lemon and 1 tablespoon olive oil. Gently stir in the beans, one-fourth of a red onion, finely diced, and 1 to 2 teaspoons drained capers, to taste. Chill until you are ready to serve it, up to 24 hours.

You might not expect these ingredients to taste so great together—but you'll be surprised. (Beware: It doesn't get any extra points for looks.) If you are feeling ambitious or have leftover produce on hand, sauté some bell peppers and onions in the oil before you add the chips. For a meatier meal, serve it with chorizo or any type of flavorful sausage on the side. Serve it with bowls of nonfat vanilla yogurt topped with granola and raisins.

easy-cheesy
tex-mex scramble

Prep + Cook = 10 minutes

4 servings

Nutritional Information per serving (with 1 tablespoon oil and no pepper, onion, or sausage) (% based upon daily values): Calories 290, Total Fat 15g, 23%, Saturated Fat 3g, 15%, Cholesterol 215mg, 71%, Sodium 840mg, 35%, Total Carbohydrate 22g, 7%, Dietary Fiber 2g, 7%, Sugar 5g, Protein 16g

Nutritional Information per serving with side dish (% based upon daily values) 1 cup yogurt, 1 tablespoon granola, 1½ teaspoons raisins: Calories: 503; Total Fat: 15.5g, 23%; Saturated Fat: 3g, 15%; Cholesterol: 215mg, 71%; Sodium: 1004mg, 42%; Total Carbohydrate: 62.5g, 11%; Dietary Fiber: 2.5g, 9%; Sugar: 41.5g; Protein: 26.5g

1–2 tablespoons vegetable oil
½ green bell pepper, diced (optional)
¼ yellow onion, diced (optional)
2 cups tortilla chips, broken
1 cup chunky salsa
4 eggs, beaten
⅔ cup reduced-fat shredded Cheddar cheese

In a medium to large nonstick skillet, heat the oil over medium heat. Sauté the bell peppers and onions (optional) in the oil until they are softened and starting to brown. Add the chips and sauté them in the oil for 1 minute. Add the salsa and stir it until the chips soak up some of the liquid.

Top the mixture with the beaten eggs. Cook, stirring gently, until the eggs are set and the mixture is somewhat dry, 5 to 7 minutes. Top it with the cheese and serve it hot.

Scramble Flavor Booster: Use spicy salsa and sauté a jalapeño pepper in the oil with the bell peppers and onions.

Tip: Use cold water when running your garbage disposal. Cold water congeals grease better (though most grease should go in the trash, instead of down the drain) and keeps the disposal cooler, helping it run more efficiently.

Side Dish suggestion: In small serving bowls, top 1 cup of nonfat vanilla yogurt with 1 to 2 tablespoons granola and 1 to 2 teaspoons raisins, or use fresh berries.

At our children's school, one of the most popular dishes in the cafeteria is called Chips Olé. My son, Solomon, and I decided to re-create his favorite lunch dish at home—and make it a little healthier in the process. Now our kids like our version even better than the cafeteria stuff, which is too salty and greasy for their tastes. Serve it with a Caesar Salad.

chips olé

Prep + Cook =
15 minutes

8 servings

Nutritional
Information per
serving (% based
upon daily values):
Calories 340, Fat 15g,
23%, Saturated Fat
2.5g, 13%, Choles-
terol 70mg, 23%,
Sodium 250mg, 10%,
Total Carbohydrate
28g, 9%, Dietary
Fiber 4g, 16%, Sugar
6%, Protein 26%

Nutritional
Information per
serving with side dish
(% based upon daily
values) ¼ of the
salad:
Calories: 480; Total
Fat: 25g, 38%; Satu-
rated Fat: 5g, 23%;
Cholesterol: 75mg,
25%; Sodium: 500mg,
20%; Total Carbohy-
drate: 38g, 12%;
Dietary Fiber: 7g,
28%; Sugar: 8g;
Protein: 30g

2 pounds ground turkey, chicken, or beef
    (or use 32 ounces vegetarian ground "meat")

2 tablespoons chili powder or chipotle chili powder

1 teaspoon garlic powder

1–2 cans (28–30 ounces total) no-salt-added tomato sauce

4 cups whole grain tortilla chips (use the round kind for scooping,
    if you can find them)

Spray a large heavy skillet with nonstick cooking spray. Brown the meat over medium heat, breaking it up with a spatula as it cooks. If you are using ground beef, drain any oil, if necessary. (If you are using vegetarian ground "meat," add the tomato sauce and spices first, then the "meat") (Meanwhile, prepare the salad, if you are serving it.)

When the meat is about halfway cooked through, add the chili powder and garlic powder and continue cooking. When it is almost cooked through, with just a little pink remaining, stir in the tomato sauce and bring it to a low boil. Reduce the heat and continue to simmer it for about 5 minutes.

To serve, use the chips to scoop up the meat mixture (which our son calls the Olé!).

Scramble Flavor Booster: Replace some or all of the tomato sauce with salsa. Add a can of diced green chiles or a fresh jalapeño pepper with the chili and garlic powder.

Tip: You can adapt this recipe to your taste: Make it more vegetable laden by adding a package of frozen chopped spinach, or spicier by adding a can of diced green chiles or a fresh chopped jalapeño pepper.

Side Dish suggestion: To make a Caesar salad, in a large bowl combine 8 cups chopped romaine lettuce, ¼ cup (or to taste) shredded Parmesan cheese, and ¾ cup to 1 cup croutons, pita chips, or toasted baguette slices (optional). To make the dressing, whisk together 2 tablespoons reduced-fat mayonnaise, 2 tablespoons olive oil, ½ teaspoon minced garlic (about 1 clove), ½ lemon, juice only (about 2 table-spoons), 1 teaspoon Worcestershire sauce, and ½ teaspoon anchovy paste. Toss the salad with the dressing just before serving it.

This recipe for crustless spinach pie was suggested by event planner extraordinaire Claudia Ades. It is simple and delicious, and tastes great the next day, too. Serve it with Claudia's favorite baked sweet potatoes for an elegant, colorful spring meal.

spinach pie with portobello mushrooms

Prep (20 minutes) + Cook (30–35 minutes)

6 servings

Nutritional Information per serving (% based upon daily values): Calories 173, Fat 9g, 15%, Saturated Fat 5g, 25%, Cholesterol 160mg, 55%, Sodium 320mg, 13%, Total Carbohydrate 7g, 3%, Dietary Fiber 1g, 6%, Sugar 3g, Protein 17g

Nutritional Information per serving with side dish (% based upon daily values) 1 sweet potato with 2 tsp. butter, 1 tsp. maple syrup, and 1 tsp. pecans: Calories: 327; Total Fat: 13g, 21%; Saturated Fat: 8g, 37%; Cholesterol: 170mg, 58%; Sodium: 363mg, 15%; Total Carbohydrate: 35g, 12%; Dietary Fiber: 5g, 21%; Sugar: 17g; Protein: 20g

1 package (10 ounces) frozen chopped spinach

4 eggs

1 cup part-skim ricotta cheese

¾ cup grated Parmesan cheese

¾ cup portobello, cremini, or conventional mushrooms, chopped

4 scallions, finely chopped (½ cup total)

½ teaspoon dried oregano, or 1½ teaspoons fresh

½ teaspoon dried basil, or 1 tablespoon chopped fresh

¼ teaspoon salt, or to taste

⅛ teaspoon black pepper, or to taste

Preheat the oven to 375 degrees. (If you are baking the sweet potatoes, start them first.) Spray a 9-inch pie dish with nonstick cooking spray. Defrost the spinach in the microwave or on the stovetop, and drain it thoroughly, pressing it to squeeze out excess water.

In a large bowl, combine all the ingredients. Pour the mixture into the pie dish. Bake it for 30 to 35 minutes until it is lightly browned and set. Let the pie cool slightly before cutting and serving it, or refrigerate it for up to 2 days, or freeze it for up to 3 months.

Scramble Flavor Booster: Use an extra ¼ cup of scallions and stir ¼ teaspoon crushed red pepper flakes into the pie before baking it.

Tip: I recently learned that portobello mushrooms are actually giant cremini mushrooms. Select plump, firm mushrooms, and refrigerate them for up to 6 days.

Side Dish suggestion: To make baked sweet potatoes, preheat the oven to 375 to 400 degrees (depending on what else you are making.) Poke several holes in the potatoes and place them directly on the oven rack. Bake them for 50 to 60 minutes until they are soft. If you're in a hurry, you can microwave them for 10 to 15 minutes until they are soft, turning them every 5 minutes. Split the potatoes lengthwise and mash in desired toppings (I recommend a little butter, maple syrup, and chopped pecans).

I've re-created a delightful salad that our friend Tricia Nudelman enjoyed at the Genesis retreat in El Balam, Mexico. It's spa-healthy yet satisfying enough for hearty eaters. Serve it with sliced avocados sprinkled with fresh lime juice and lightly salted.

mango and black bean salad

Prep + Cook =
20 minutes + 10 minutes–24 hours to chill
(optional)

6 servings

Nutritional Information per serving (with 1 whole wheat tortilla) (% based upon daily values): Calories 300, Total Fat 4.5g, 7%, Saturated Fat 1.5g, 8%, Cholesterol 0mg, 0%, Sodium 760mg, 31%, Total Carbohydrate 57g, 19%, Dietary Fiber 7g, 28%, Sugar 6g, Protein 9g

Nutritional Information per serving with side dish (% based upon daily values) ½ avocado, dash salt, lime juice: Calories: 444; Total Fat: 18g, 28%; Saturated Fat: 4g, 17%; Cholesterol: 0mg, 0%; Sodium: 767mg, 31%; Total Carbohydrate: 65g, 21%; Dietary Fiber: 13g, 52%; Sugar: 7g; Protein: 11 g

¾–1 cup quick-cooking brown rice (2 cups prepared)

1 can (15 ounces) black beans, drained and rinsed

1–1½ cups fresh or frozen mango, cut in ½-inch chunks

¼ sweet yellow onion, such as Vidalia, finely diced (about 1 cup)

¼ cup scallions, green parts only, or chives, finely chopped

1 lime, juice only (2–3 tablespoons)

¼ cup fresh cilantro, chopped (optional)

¼ teaspoon salt, or more to taste

6 large Boston or butter lettuce leaves (optional)

6 whole wheat tortillas for serving (optional)

Cook the rice according to the package directions. Remove it from the heat immediately when it is done cooking. (If you want to serve the Mango and Black Bean Salad immediately rather than waiting for it to chill, put the rice in the freezer for 5 minutes to cool it.)

Meanwhile, in a large bowl, combine the beans, mango, onions, scallions, lime juice, and cilantro (optional). Combine the rice with the ingredients in the large bowl, season it with the salt, and toss it gently. Chill it for at least 10 minutes (an hour or more is ideal) and up to 24 hours. (Meanwhile, prepare the avocados.)

Serve the salad on its own or wrapped in large lettuce leaves or warm tortillas, or both, topped with the sliced avocado, if desired.

Scramble Flavor Booster: Stir in fresh cilantro and serve the salad with spicy salsa.

Tip: If you don't like raw onions, sauté the onions first until they are lightly browned. If you have picky eaters, put some of the beans and rice aside before combining all the ingredients and let them have simple black bean and rice burritos with mango on the side.

Side Dish suggestion: Peel and slice 2 to 4 avocados and sprinkle them with 1 to 4 teaspoons fresh lime juice (about 1 teaspoon per avocado) and ⅛ to ½ teaspoon salt (about ⅛ teaspoon per avocado) (or mash the avocados, lime juice, and salt to make guacamole).

You can turn that powerhouse of a healthy grain, quinoa, into a light lunch or dinner with some flavorful additions. Serve it alone or topped with plain yogurt, or over a bed of greens, accompanied by homemade pita chips.

mediterranean quinoa salad

Prep + Cook = 20 minutes + 30 minutes–2 days to chill

4 servings

Nutritional Information per serving (% based upon daily values): Calories 535, Total Fat 30, 46%, Saturated Fat 5.5g, 27%, Cholesterol 15mg, 5%, Sodium 958mg, 40%, Total Carbohydrate 53g, 19% Dietary Fiber 8.5g, 33%, Sugar 4.5g, Protein 16.5g

Nutritional Information per serving with side dish (% based upon daily values) with ⅙ of pita chips: Calories: 605; Total Fat: 32.5g, 60%; Saturated Fat: 5.5g, 27%; Cholesterol: 15mg, 5%; Sodium: 1,063mg, 44%; Total Carbohydrate: 64g, 23%; Dietary Fiber: 8.5g, 33%; Sugar: 4.5g; Protein: 18.5g

1 cup quinoa (sold with grains) or use orzo or rice
¼ cup olive oil
2 tablespoons balsamic vinegar
¼–½ lemon, juice only (1 tablespoon or more to taste)
¾ cup sun-dried tomatoes, packed in oil or dry, diced
⅓ cup pine nuts, lightly toasted
¾ cup crumbled feta cheese
½ cup flat-leaf parsley or fresh basil, finely chopped (or more to taste)
15 pitted black or kalamata olives, chopped
1 cup plain nonfat or low-fat yogurt for serving (optional)
4 cups mixed salad greens for serving (optional)

Cook 1 cup quinoa according to the package directions. Remove it from the heat and fluff it with a fork.

In a medium bowl, combine the quinoa with all the other ingredients. Refrigerate it for at least 30 minutes and up to 2 days before serving.

Scramble Flavor Booster: Add freshly ground black pepper and additional fresh herbs to the salad. Add ½ cup finely diced yellow or white onion and/or finely diced carrots.

Tip: Because parsley grows out from the center, harvest the outer leaves first, to keep it producing longer.

Side Dish suggestion: To make homemade pita chips, preheat the oven to 350 degrees. Cut 2 to 3 pita pockets in half, separating the tops from the bottoms, and cut each top and bottom into about 6 triangular wedges (like a pizza). In a medium bowl, toss the pita with 2 tablespoons olive oil and ½ teaspoon kosher salt (optional). Lay the pita wedges on a large baking sheet and bake them for 10 to 12 minutes until they start to brown. Serve them with hummus or baba gannoush, if desired.

summer

five weekly summer menus

To help you celebrate all the vibrant flavors of summer, here are five weekly menus. (You can also make shopping a breeze by grabbing the accompanying organized grocery list for each of these menus at www.thescramble.com/SOS.)

week 1

Grilled Chipotle Chicken with Mango Salsa
Tortuguero Tilapia with Cilantro-Lime Sauce
Farfalle with Pine Nuts and Fresh Herbs
Vegetarian Enchiladas
Turkey Club Panini

week 2

Three-Pepper Flank Steak with Red Onions
Curried Chicken Salad with Grapes
Grilled Balsamic-glazed Salmon
Ravioli with Walnut and Parsley Pesto
Moo Shu Vegetable Wraps

week 3

Pork Cutlets with Mushroom-Sherry Sauce
Lemony Fish Bake with Vegetable Confetti
Grilled Quicki Souvlaki Sandwich
Southwestern Cobb Salad with Avocado Ranch Dressing
Divine Eggplant and Chickpeas with Mint

week 4

Chicken Tricolore
Yummi Yummi Mahi Mahi
Ultimate Juicy Turkey Burgers
Lemon-Basil Summer Pasta Salad
Costa Rican Black Beans and Rice

week 5

Chicken Parmesan with Garden Herbs
Asian Shrimp Pilaf
Italian Caprese Sandwiches
Classic Spinach Salad with Turkey Bacon
Golden Tofu (or Chicken) with Ginger and Peppers

poultry, pork, and beef

fish

pastas, grains, soups, and stews

Key: (V) = Vegetarian or vegetarian optional;
       * = Scramble Express: 30 minutes or less total;
    (M) = Make-ahead, freeze, or slow-cooker option

sandwiches, wraps, salads, and other lighter fare

Key: (V) = Vegetarian or vegetarian optional;
          * = Scramble Express: 30 minutes or less total;
        (M) = Make-ahead, freeze, or slow-cooker option

Key: (V) = Vegetarian or vegetarian optional;
        * = Scramble Express: 30 minutes or less total;
      (M) = Make-ahead, freeze, or slow-cooker option

summertime, and the dining is easy

WHEN OUR KIDS were toddlers, my neighbor Chrissie McHenry, who has three older kids, told me that she breathes a huge sigh of relief when summer arrives because the obligations of the school year come to an end.

At the time, I must admit, I couldn't relate. Our kids were still at the ages where the days seemed long and time moved slowly. They only went to preschool for a few hours, and didn't participate in sports or many other activities. We'd fill a whole afternoon rolling shapes out of Play-Doh or searching for buried treasure (i.e. pennies) in the sandbox. Summer was just another season, albeit too hot and buggy to stay outside for long.

Now that Celia and Solomon are ten and twelve, I'm overjoyed that summer is here! No homework to supervise, no after-school activities to rush to, no soccer carpools to remember. With all this extra time in the afternoons, you might think I'd like to cook some more complex dinners—but I don't! I'd prefer to take things light and easy with no-cook meals, dinner sandwiches, and salads, grilling, and simple dishes for potlucks and picnics.

But my favorite thing about summer is the bounty of fresh and delicious produce from local farms. I salivate over the plump and juicy tomatoes, corn, eggplants, peaches, and strawberries and find ways to incorporate the fresh local produce into our summer meals.

So relax and savor summer the Scramble way—with meals that are light on effort, loaded with flavor, and feature the many luscious fresh fruits and vegetables of the season.

happy summer!

My family devoured this fabulous chicken, suggested by Scramble subscriber Elizabeth Fenimore. It's a great dish to serve to company because it looks as good as it tastes, with the colors of the Italian flag, and can be prepared in advance, then baked before dinner. I like to make it in the summer using fresh tomatoes and freshly cut herbs. Serve it with sweet summer corn on the cob.

chicken tricolore

Prep (20 minutes) +
Cook (50 minutes)

6 servings

Nutritional
Information per
serving (% based
upon daily values):
Calories 450, Total
Fat 30g, 46%, Satu-
rated Fat 7g, 35%,
Cholesterol 145mg,
48%, Sodium 710mg,
30%, Total Carbohy-
drate 3g, 1%, Dietary
Fiber <1g, 4%, Sugar
1g, Protein 39g

Nutritional
Information per
serving with side dish
(% based upon daily
values) 1 ear corn, $\frac{1}{2}$
tsp. butter, sprinkle
of salt:
Calories: 526; Total
Fat: 33g, 50%; Satu-
rated Fat: 9g, 41%;
Cholesterol: 150mg,
50%; Sodium: 879mg,
37%; Total Carbohy-
drate: 17g, 6%;
Dietary Fiber: 3g,
11%; Sugar: 4g;
Protein: 41g

1 whole chicken, cut up (you can purchase a cut-up chicken), or
   8 to 10 bone-in pieces of your choice

¾ cup pitted green olives, halved

1 pint grape or cherry tomatoes, halved

2 teaspoons chopped garlic (about 4 cloves)

½ cup chopped fresh parsley

1 teaspoon lemon zest or 1 tablespoon fresh lemon juice (¼–½ lemon)

½ teaspoon kosher salt

¼ teaspoon black pepper

2 tablespoons olive oil

Preheat the oven to 400 degrees. (Alternatively, you can prepare the chicken up to a day in advance and bake it when needed.)

Place the chicken in a baking dish large enough to fit the pieces in a single layer, skin side up. In a medium bowl, combine the olives, tomatoes, garlic, parsley, lemon zest or juice, salt, black pepper, and olive oil. Spoon the mixture evenly over the chicken.

Bake the chicken, uncovered and without flipping it, for 45 minutes, or until the breasts are cooked through. Then put it under the broiler for an additional 5 minutes until the skins are browned. If the breasts (white meat) are done before the thighs and legs (dark meat), you can remove the white meat from the pan and continue to cook the dark meat for about 10 more minutes. (While the chicken is cooking, prepare the corn.)

Scramble Flavor Booster: Serve the chicken with hot pepper sauce, such as Tabasco.

Side Dish suggestion: Steam 4 to 6 ears of corn in the microwave or over boiling water for 3 to 5 minutes (sprinkle them with water, partially cover the bowl, and cook on high power) and then toss them in the still-warm bowl with 1 to 2 teaspoons of butter or margarine and a little salt before serving. (Some people like to cook corn longer, but we prefer it crisp and juicy.) For a flavor boost, add a few shakes of chili powder and/or a squeeze of lime juice just before serving the corn.

My friend and colleague Jeanne Rossomme picked up this fabulous recipe during her years living in Mexico. The salsa is so colorful and flavorful, you can also use it as a dip with chips, or just to liven up any Mexican meal. Serve it with quesadillas, which are also delicious stuffed with the barbecue sauce and salsa.

grilled chipotle chicken with mango salsa

Prep + Cook =
30 minutes + optional Marinate (up to 12 hours)

4 servings

Nutritional Information per serving (% based upon daily values): Calories 330, Total Fat 3.5g, 5%, Saturated Fat 1g, 5%, Cholesterol 130mg, 43%, Sodium 600mg, 25%, Total Carbohydrate 22g, 7%, Dietary Fiber 3g, 12%, Sugar 17g, Protein 54g

Nutritional Information per serving with side dish (% based upon daily values) 1 quesadilla: Calories: 590; Total Fat: 15g, 23%; Saturated Fat: 7g, 35%; Cholesterol: 160mg, 53%; Sodium: 1160mg, 48%; Total Carbohydrate: 48g, 16%; Dietary Fiber: 5g, 20%; Sugar: 20g; Protein: 65g

1 cup canned crushed tomatoes (or 2 fresh ripe tomatoes)

1 large mango, peeled and cubed, or 1½ cups frozen mango chunks

2 tablespoons white wine vinegar

1 tablespoon honey or sugar

2 teaspoons canned chopped chipotles in adobo sauce (sold with Latino foods), or ½ teaspoon chipotle chili powder, or 1 teaspoon chili powder

½ teaspoon salt

2 pounds boneless, skinless chicken breasts (about 6 chicken breast halves)

1 large tomato, seeded and diced (about 1 cup)

½ small yellow or white onion, finely chopped (about ½ cup)

2 tablespoons chopped fresh cilantro or flat-leaf parsley

1 lime, juice only (about 2 tablespoons)

First make the barbecue sauce: In a blender, combine the tomatoes, ½ cup of the mango, the vinegar, honey or sugar, chipotle peppers or chili powder, and salt and puree it. (You can make the sauce up to 24 hours in advance.) Pour ½ cup of the barbecue sauce over the chicken breasts, flip them a couple of times to coat, and set them aside. If time allows, marinate the chicken for up to 12 hours in the refrigerator. Reserve half of the remaining barbecue sauce for serving.

Preheat the grill to medium-high heat (if you plan to cook the chicken immediately), and make the salsa: In a medium bowl, combine the remaining mango, the fresh tomato, onions, cilantro or parsley, and lime juice. Set it aside, or refrigerate it for up to 24 hours.

Grill the chicken for about 4 to 5 minutes per side until it is just cooked through, brushing the tops of the breasts with the barbecue sauce before and after flipping them. (Meanwhile, make the quesadillas.) Serve the chicken topped with the reserved barbecue sauce and salsa.

Scramble Flavor Booster: For a spicier flavor, add more chipotle peppers, but be careful—they're very hot! To spice up the salsa, add 1 seeded and minced jalapeño pepper.

Tip: For the freshest flavor, always store tomatoes at room temperature, rather than in the refrigerator.

Side Dish suggestion: To make quesadillas, spray a large skillet with nonstick cooking spray. Spread about ¼ cup of Cheddar cheese in each wheat or flour tortilla, fold them in half, and allow them to cook on each side for 3 to 4 minutes over medium heat, flipping once, until lightly browned.

My Scramble colleague Betsy Goldstein says that this is one of her kids' favorite dinners. She sometimes uses a spoonful of pesto instead of or in addition to the fresh herbs. Serve it with whipped potatoes.

chicken parmesan with garden herbs

Prep + Cook = 30 minutes

6 servings

Nutritional Information per serving (% based upon daily values): Calories 260, Total Fat 5g, 8%, Saturated Fat 2g, 10%, Cholesterol 110mg, 37%, Sodium 380mg, 16%, Total Carbohydrate 19g, 6%, Dietary Fiber 1g, 4%, Sugar 2g, Protein 33g

Nutritional Information per serving with side dish (% based upon daily values) ⅙ of potatoes: Calories: 417; Total Fat: 7g, 12%; Saturated Fat: 3g, 12%; Cholesterol: 111mg, 37%; Sodium: 593mg, 25%; Total Carbohydrate: 51g, 17%; Dietary Fiber: 3g, 13%; Sugar: 6g; Protein: 37g

¾ **cup flour**

¼ **teaspoon salt**

1–2 **eggs**

¾ **cup bread crumbs or panko**

1½ **pounds chicken cutlets (or cut chicken breasts in half and pound them to an even thickness)**

⅓ **cup shredded part-skim mozzarella cheese**

¼ **cup grated Parmesan cheese**

½ –¾ **cup red pasta sauce**

2 **tablespoons fresh minced basil and sage leaves**

Preheat the oven to 425 degrees. (Start the potatoes, if you are making them.) Spray a baking sheet with nonstick cooking spray.

Combine the flour and salt in a shallow dish, and put the egg(s) and the bread crumbs or panko in 2 separate shallow dishes. Coat each chicken cutlet lightly with the flour, then the egg, then the bread crumbs, and lay them on the baking sheet. Bake them for 6 to 8 minutes. Meanwhile, combine the cheeses.

Remove the chicken from the oven, flip each cutlet over, and top each one with 1 tablespoon of the sauce, spreading it to the edges, and a sprinkling of the fresh herbs and the cheese (make sure to use up all of the herbs and cheese).

Return the chicken to the oven for 6 to 8 more minutes until it is cooked through and the cheese is melted. Serve it immediately.

Scramble Flavor Booster: Use aged Parmesan such as Parmigiano-Reggiano and add a little black or cayenne pepper to the bread crumb mixture.

Tip: You can also serve the chicken over angel hair noodles or on whole wheat hamburger rolls topped with extra marinara sauce.

Side Dish suggestion: To make the potatoes, bring a medium pot of water to a boil. Peel and cut 2 pounds of Yukon gold (or your favorite potatoes) into 1-inch pieces. Add the potatoes, 1 peeled clove of garlic, and about 1 teaspoon salt to the water and simmer the potatoes for 10 to 15 minutes, until they are fork tender. Drain the potatoes and garlic and return them to the pot over medium heat, shaking them until any remaining water dries. Transfer the potatoes to a large mixing bowl, add 2 tablespoons butter or margarine, ½ cup nonfat or low-fat milk, ½ teaspoon fresh or ¼ teaspoon dried thyme, and ¼ teaspoon salt, and beat them on medium speed until they are smooth. Serve them immediately or transfer them to an oven-safe serving bowl and keep them warm in a 300-degree oven until you are ready to serve them.

Subscriber Consie Mote asked me if I could create a Scramble version of the delicious grilled chicken sold at so many Peruvian grilled chicken outlets around the country. After a little experimenting, I think if I sold this version from my kitchen there would be lines out the door! It's super juicy and delicious. If time allows, marinate the chicken for 24 hours for enhanced flavor. Serve it with steamed broccoli with lemon-pepper seasoning (page 46), and with corn or wheat tortillas.

pollo a la brasa
(peruvian grilled chicken)

Prep (15 minutes) + Cook (35 minutes) + Marinate (8–24 hours)

6 servings

Nutritional Information per serving (% based upon daily values): Calories 400, Total Fat 24g, 37%, Saturated Fat 6g, 30%, Cholesterol 145mg, 48%, Sodium 135mg, 6%, Total Carbohydrate 4g, 1%, Dietary Fiber 0g, 0%, Sugar 3g, Protein 39g

Nutritional Information per serving with side dish (% based upon daily values) 1 cup broccoli; 1 corn tortilla: Calories: 507; Total Fat: 25g, 39%; Saturated Fat: 6g, 32%; Cholesterol: 145mg, 48%; Sodium: 210mg, 9%; Total Carbohydrate: 26g, 9%; Dietary Fiber: 7g, 27%; Sugar: 5g; Protein: 44g

1 tablespoon brown sugar

2 teaspoons ground cumin

1 teaspoon paprika

½ teaspoon black pepper

1 teaspoon dried oregano

2 tablespoons Worcestershire sauce

1 lime, juice only (about 2 tablespoons juice)

1 tablespoon olive oil

2 teaspoons minced garlic (3–4 cloves)

1 whole chicken, quartered

In a small bowl, whisk together all the ingredients except the chicken. Put the chicken in a large flat container with a tight-fitting lid and pour the marinade evenly over it. Flip and shake the chicken to coat it in the marinade. Marinate the chicken for at least 8 hours and up to 24 hours (the longer the better), shaking or flipping it a couple of times. By the time the chicken is finished marinating, most of the marinade will have been absorbed.

Preheat the grill to high heat. (Alternatively, you can roast the chicken at 450 degrees, covered for 15 minutes and then uncovered for 20 to 25 minutes.)

If using a gas grill, turn the back burner to its lowest setting and put the chicken, skin side down, over the back burner, so it is over indirect heat. Grill the chicken for 15 to 20 minutes, then flip it and grill it for 15 to 20 minutes more, until the skin is nicely browned and the chicken is cooked through (cut into the thickest part of the breast with a sharp knife to make sure there is no pink remaining). (Meanwhile, prepare the broccoli). Slice the chicken into smaller pieces to serve it, if desired.

Scramble Flavor Booster: Marinate the chicken for 24 hours and add ½ teaspoon lime zest, in addition to the fresh lime juice.

Side Dish suggestion: Serve it with 6 corn or wheat tortillas, warmed in the microwave for 30 seconds to 1 minute, or over an open flame on a gas stove for a few seconds per side, using tongs.

Chicken satay is a kid-pleaser! Even if your kids don't like the peanut sauce, which many do, the flavorful chicken is great for all ages. If you have extra time (does that ever happen?) you can thread the chicken onto wooden skewers before or after cooking it (if you do it before cooking it, soak the skewers in water first so they don't burn). These also make a fabulous appetizer. Serve it with steamed rice and a colorful platter of baby carrots, red bell pepper slices, and snow peas, which are also good dipped in the peanut sauce.

indonesian chicken satay with peanut sauce

Prep (10 minutes) + Cook (10 minutes) + Marinate (30 minutes–24 hours)

8 servings

Nutritional Information per serving (% based upon daily values): Calories 260, Total Fat 9g, 14%, Saturated Fat 1.5g, 8%, Cholesterol 65mg, 22%, Sodium 310mg, 13%, Total Carbohydrate 10g, 3%, Dietary Fiber 1g, 4%, Sugar 4g, Protein 31g

Nutritional Information per serving with side dish (% based upon daily values) 1 cup mixed veggies; ¾ cup cooked rice: Calories: 460; Total Fat: 11g, 17%; Saturated Fat: 2g, 10%; Cholesterol: 65mg, 22%; Sodium: 340mg, 14%; Total Carbohydrate: 52g, 17%; Dietary Fiber: 6g, 24%; Sugar: 9g; Protein: 36g

4 tablespoons plus 1 teaspoon reduced-sodium soy sauce or tamari

2 tablespoons plus 1 teaspoon honey

2 tablespoons vegetable oil

2 teaspoons minced garlic (about 4 cloves)

2 teaspoons minced fresh ginger

¼ teaspoon crushed red pepper flakes, or more to taste

2 pounds chicken tenderloins or boneless, skinless chicken breasts cut into 1-inch-wide strips

½ cup hot water

½ cup creamy or chunky natural peanut butter

1 lime, juice only (about 2 tablespoons juice)

First, make the marinade: In a small bowl, mix together 4 tablespoons soy sauce, 2 tablespoons honey, the oil, garlic, 1 teaspoon minced ginger, and the crushed red pepper flakes. Put the chicken in a large flat dish with sides, pour the marinade over it, and turn the chicken several times to coat it. Cover it and refrigerate it for at least 30 minutes and up to 24 hours.

When you are ready to cook it, preheat the grill or the broiler (with the rack 3 to 4 inches from the heat source), and coat a grilling tray or baking sheet with nonstick cooking spray or line it with foil. (Start the rice and prepare the vegetables if you are serving them.) Drain the chicken from the marinade and transfer it to the tray or pan, discarding the marinade. Grill or broil the chicken for 4 to 5 minutes per side, flipping once, until it is cooked through and the edges are browned.

While the chicken is cooking, make the peanut sauce. In a medium bowl, whisk together the hot water, peanut butter, lime juice, 1 teaspoon soy sauce, 1 teaspoon honey, and 1 teaspoon ginger until it is smooth.

Add a few crushed red pepper flakes for a spicy sauce, if desired. Serve the chicken over rice with the sauce on the side for dipping.

Scramble Flavor Booster: Double the crushed red pepper flakes and add a little fresh lime zest to the peanut sauce.

Tip: To prevent the peanut butter and honey from sticking, spray the spoon and cup you use to measure them with nonstick cooking spray before using them.

Side Dish suggestion: Make a colorful veggie platter with 1 cup of baby or sliced carrots, 1 red bell pepper, sliced, and 8 ounces snow peas.

Subscriber Molly Thompson of Bozeman, Montana, asked me if I could update the recipe for the wonderful stuffed peppers that her dad used to make. The result is an extremely healthy and elegant comfort food that you can make for a family dinner or company, especially if you use a variety of beautifully colored peppers. Serve it with garlic bread and a salad of mixed greens with fresh or dried blueberries and crumbled feta cheese.

mediterranean stuffed green peppers

Prep (30 minutes) + Cook (30 minutes)

6 servings

Nutritional Information per serving (% based upon daily values): Calories 240, Total Fat 4g, 6%, Saturated Fat 1g, 5%, Cholesterol 30mg, 10%, Sodium 240mg, 10%, Total Carbohydrate 32g, 11%, Dietary Fiber 5g, 20%, Sugar 11g, Protein 23g

Nutritional Information per serving with side dish (% based upon daily values) 1/8 of garlic broad; 1 1/2 cups salad: Calories: 456; Total Fat: 15g, 22%; Saturated Fat: 4g, 20%; Cholesterol: 41 mg, 12%; Sodium: 663mg, 28%; Total Carbohydrate: 56g, 19%; Dietary Fiber: 8g, 32%; Sugar: 15g; Protein: 30g

6 medium green bell peppers, or use a variety of colored bell peppers

1 tablespoon olive oil

1/2 large yellow onion, diced (about 1 cup)

1 pound ground chicken, turkey, beef, or vegetarian ground "meat"

1/4 cup pine nuts (optional)

1 can (28 ounces) crushed tomatoes

2 teaspoons dried Italian seasoning or 1 teaspoon dried basil and 1 teaspoon dried oregano

2 tablespoons brown sugar

1/2 cup couscous

1/2 cup water

1 tablespoon Worcestershire sauce

1/2 teaspoon salt (optional)

Preheat the oven to 400 degrees. Slice the tops off of the peppers and scoop out the seeds and ribs. In a large pot, steam the peppers in an inch of water for 3 to 5 minutes, or microwave them on high heat for 5 to 7 minutes until they are slightly tender.

Meanwhile, in a large heavy skillet, heat the oil over medium heat and sauté the onions, meat (if you are using vegetarian "meat," add it after the tomatoes) and pine nuts (optional) for 8 to 10 minutes, until the meat is no longer pink. Add the tomatoes, Italian seasoning, sugar, couscous, water, and Worcestershire sauce to the skillet and simmer for about 5 minutes until the couscous is tender. Stir in the salt (optional).

Stand the peppers in a flat baking dish just large enough to hold them. Using a ladle or large spoon, fill the peppers with the meat sauce. If there is any extra filling, the peppers can overflow, or you can pour it around the bottoms of the peppers. (At this point you can proceed with the recipe or refrigerate the peppers for up to 2 days before cooking.) Bake the peppers in the preheated oven for abut 30 minutes until they are tender and starting to wrinkle or brown at the tops. (Meanwhile, make the garlic bread and salad.) Remove the peppers from the oven and allow them to cool for about 10 minutes before serving. (Alternatively, cover them tightly and freeze them for up to 3 months.)

Scramble Flavor Booster: Serve the stuffed peppers with hot pepper sauce, such as Tabasco.

Tip: Enjoy a little summer all year long: If you pick or buy extra berries while they are in season, consider freezing some. Gently rinse and dry them (remove stems from strawberries), lay them on a cookie sheet in the freezer, and then transfer them to a freezer bag or other container once they are frozen.

Side Dish suggestion: To make garlic bread, cut a loaf of French or Italian bread in half lengthwise and cut ½-inch-deep slits in the top about 1 inch apart. Mash together 3 tablespoons margarine or softened butter, 1 tablespoon olive oil, and 1 to 2 teaspoons minced garlic and spread it evenly over the cut sides of the bread. Put it on a baking sheet, buttered side up, and sprinkle ¼ cup grated Parmesan cheese on top, if desired. Bake it along with the peppers for 6 to 8 minutes until the edges are lightly browned.

Side Dish suggestion: In a large bowl, combine 6 to 8 cups mixed greens with ½ cup of fresh or ¼ cup of dried blueberries, ¼ cup of crumbled feta cheese, and 2 to 4 tablespoons vinaigrette dressing, to taste.

CSAs
a way to connect with your local farm community

CSA (or Community Supported Agriculture) groups are created to help local smaller farmers have a steady, predictable income by selling "shares" of their seasonal produce to community members. Subscribing members may pay by the week, for the entire season, or even donate or barter their time in harvesting and planting. This communal relationship is getting quite "trendy," with CSAs growing from about 50 in 1990 to over 2,200 in 2008 (according to localharvest.org).

There are many valuable benefits to participating in CSAs:

- They connect local farmers with consumers.

- Communities develop a local food supply.

- A larger sense of community is formed connecting rural and urban areas.

- The practice encourages land stewardship so small farmers are not "forced" into selling their land to suburban developers.

- The knowledge and experience of traditional farming (and many organic, sustainable practices) are preserved.

- There is greater biodiversity through the rotation of a wide variety of crops throughout the growing season.

Through membership in a CSA you can get fresh, often organic, produce at a reasonable price. The only drawback is that Mother Nature determines what you get in your CSA basket each week. Some families get frustrated with too much of one vegetable or produce they are unfamiliar with (like Swiss chard or garlic scapes). To help you get the most out of your CSA, here are some practical tips:

- Use the most perishable produce first when planning your weekly meals.

- If you feel you have too much for your family, consider splitting a share with a neighbor.

- Think of your farm basket as a weekly "surprise" or an opportunity for a culinary adventure as you create new salads and soups with these fresh vegetables.

- Search the index in this cookbook (or by subscribing online at www.thescramble.com) by vegetable to find ways to use your weekly produce in your meals.

- Think of freezing portions for use in those dreary months when much produce is expensive and bland (there are many great guides to freezing fresh vegetables available online.)

If a full seasonal membership in a CSA still seems a bit intimidating, at least take advantage of your local farmers market each week, where you can select your own "basket" of produce and take weeks off when you are traveling or need time to catch up, and also have the benefit of supporting local farms and farmers by enjoying their freshly picked, locally grown fruits and vegetables.

These grilled chops have a nice and light Greek flavor that we really enjoy. Scramble recipe tester Bobbi Woods said, "It was a thumbs-up all around the table! My fourteen-year-old son and my five-year-old daughter both ate everything on their plate and even loved the yogurt sauce!" Serve it with Baked Potato Chips (page 33) and steamed green beans.

rosemary-lemon pork chops with yogurt-feta sauce

Prep + Cook =
30 minutes

4 servings

Nutritional
Information per
serving (% based
upon daily values):
Calories 410, Total
Fat 24g, 37%, Satu-
rated Fat 8g, 40%,
Cholesterol 120mg,
40%, Sodium 340mg,
14%, Total Carbohy-
drate 9g, 3%, Dietary
Fiber 2g, 8%, Sugar
5g, Protein 38g

Nutritional
Information per
serving with side dish
(% based upon daily
values) ½ cup baked
potato chips; 1 cup
green beans:
Calories: 534; Total
Fat: 28g, 42%; Satu-
rated Fat: 8g, 40%;
Cholesterol: 120mg,
40%; Sodium: 587mg,
24%; Total Carbohy-
drate: 30g, 10%;
Dietary Fiber: 8g,
31%; Sugar: 8g;
Protein: 42g

- 1½ **pounds, boneless pork chops**
- 1¼ **lemons (juice only)**
- 2 **tablespoons olive oil**
- 1 **teaspoon fresh or dried rosemary**
- 1 **teaspoon minced garlic (about 2 cloves)**
- ½ **teaspoon kosher salt**
- 1 **cup plain nonfat Greek yogurt**
- ½ **cup crumbled feta cheese**
- 1–2 **teaspoons fresh oregano or ¾ teaspoon dried**
- ¼ **teaspoon black pepper**

Put the pork chops in a large flat dish with sides. Whisk together the juice of 1 lemon, the olive oil, rosemary, garlic, and kosher salt. Pour the mixture evenly over the meat, and turn it to coat both sides. (Start the potato chips now, if you are serving them.)

Meanwhile, heat the grill to medium-high heat. In a medium serving bowl, combine the yogurt, feta cheese, 1 tablespoon lemon juice, the oregano, and the black pepper. Set it aside. (Meanwhile, start the green beans.)

When the grill is hot, cook the pork for 2 to 4 minutes per side, depending on the thickness, until it is just cooked through. Remove it to a serving plate, and serve it immediately with the yogurt sauce.

Scramble Flavor Booster: Add the zest of 1 lemon to the marinade.

Side Dish suggestion: Trim and steam 1 pound of green beans for 8 to 10 minutes to desired tenderness. Drain and serve them plain or seasoned with salt and pepper or drizzled with fresh lemon juice.

This simple, elegant meal will make your family feel like they are eating in a fine French restaurant! Serve it with Zucchini Fritters (page 52).

pork cutlets with mushroom-sherry sauce

Prep + Cook = 15 minutes

4 servings

Nutritional Information per serving (% based upon daily values) (4.5 oz pork per serving): Calories 310, Total Fat 14g, 22%, Saturated Fat 5g, 25%, Cholesterol 115mg, 38%, Sodium 420mg, 18%, Total Carbohydrate 3g, 1%, Dietary Fiber 0g, 0%, Sugar 1g, Protein 41g

Nutritional Information per serving with side dish (% based upon daily values) 1½ fritters: Calories: 450; Total Fat: 20g, 31%; Saturated Fat: 6g, 30%; Cholesterol: 170mg, 56%; Sodium: 660mg, 28%; Total Carbohydrate: 19g, 6%; Dietary Fiber: 1g, 4%; Sugar: 3g; Protein: 46g

1 tablespoon butter or margarine

4 thin pork cutlets (or use turkey cutlets or thin steaks), cut crosswise into 2 pieces

½ teaspoon salt

¼ teaspoon black pepper

2 shallots, finely chopped

8 ounces sliced mushrooms

¼ cup sherry

1 teaspoon Dijon mustard

(If you are making the Zucchini Fritters, start them first.) In a large heavy skillet, preferably cast-iron, melt half the butter or margarine over medium-high heat. Season the pork with salt and pepper to taste, and add it to the skillet. Cook it for 2 to 3 minutes per side until it is lightly browned. Remove the pork to a plate and set it aside.

Melt the remaining butter in the skillet, and add the shallots. Let them brown for 1 minute until they are fragrant, and then add the mushrooms. Cook them for about 3 minutes until they start to brown and shrink, season them with salt and pepper, then add the sherry and mustard. Continue cooking for 2 to 3 more minutes, and then add the meat and its juices back to the pan. Serve it immediately.

Scramble Flavor Booster: Use spicy or grainy Dijon mustard in the sauce, and season the cutlets with extra black pepper.

Tip: A shallot is a small onion-like bulb, whose flavor is like a blend of onion and garlic.

My family made this magical Japanese-style dish disappear almost instantly! It's particularly wonderful if you use farm-fresh carrots and scallions. If you prefer, use chicken or tofu instead of the beef. Scramble recipe tester Debbie Firestone said this dish got "rave reviews" from her whole family, and her nine-year-old-daughter asked if they could have it again soon. Serve it with steamed brown or white rice.

beef and broccoli teriyaki

Prep + Cook = 20 minutes

4 servings

Nutritional Information per serving (% based upon daily values): Calories 430, Total Fat 9g, 14%, Saturated Fat 2.5g, 13%, Cholesterol 70mg, 23%, Sodium 150mg, 6%, Total Carbohydrate 55g, 18%, Dietary Fiber 5g, 20%, Protein 32g, Sugar 4g

Nutritional Information per serving with side dish (% based upon daily values) $3/4$ cup brown rice: Calories: 592; Total Fat: 10g, 16%; Saturated Fat: 4g, 17%; Cholesterol: 70mg, 23%; Sodium: 157mg, 7%; Total Carbohydrate: 89g, 25%; Dietary Fiber: 8g, 31%; Sugar: 5g; Protein: 36g

1 tablespoon sesame oil

1 pound boneless beef steak, such as top round or top sirloin, sliced against the grain into thin strips

1 pound broccoli, trimmed and cut into spears

2 large carrots, sliced (about 1 cup)

$3/4$ cup reduced-sodium teriyaki sauce (store-bought or make your own—see Tip below)

4 scallions, sliced (about $1/4$ cup)

(Prepare the rice according to the package directions.) In a large nonstick skillet, heat the oil over medium-high heat. Sear (cook without moving) the sliced steak for about 1 minute on each side. Add the broccoli, carrots, and teriyaki sauce to the skillet and toss to coat the meat and vegetables. Reduce the heat slightly and cover the pan to steam the vegetables for 3 to 5 minutes, until they are tender-crisp. Remove the cover and stir in the scallions until warmed through.

Serve the beef and vegetables over the rice, spooning the sauce over everything.

Scramble Flavor Booster: Add up to 1 teaspoon chili garlic sauce or $1/2$ teaspoon crushed red pepper flakes with the teriyaki sauce, if desired.

Tip: To make your own teriyaki sauce, combine 4 tablespoons reduced-sodium soy sauce, 4 tablespoons rice vinegar, 4 tablespoons rice wine, $1/2$ teaspoon each of ground ginger and garlic powder, and 1 tablespoon plus $3/4$ teaspoon brown sugar. Whisk it well until the sugar dissolves. Add a tablespoon of orange juice if you like it a little sweeter.

These ranch-style steaks don't require a mesquite barbeque to taste smoky and flavorful, and if it's a balmy night, maybe you can even serve your little wranglers dinner by the campfire. Serve it with Garlic Toast and Pan-browned Yellow Squash (or Zucchini).

three-pepper flank steak with red onions

Prep + Cook =
20 minutes +
Marinate (30
minutes–24 hours)

6 servings

Nutritional
Information per
serving (% based
upon daily values):
Calories 290, Total
Fat 16g, 25% Satu-
rated Fat 5g, 25%,
Cholesterol 75mg,
25%, Sodium 310mg,
13%, Total Carbohy-
drate 4g, 1%, Dietary
Fiber 1g, 4%, Sugar
3g, Protein 31g

Nutritional
Information per
serving with side dish
(% based upon daily
values) ⅛ of garlic
bread; ¼ of squash:
Calories: 520; Total
Fat: 31g, 48%; Satu-
rated Fat: 10g, 48%;
Cholesterol: 90mg,
28%; Sodium: 610mg,
26%; Total Carbohy-
drate: 25g, 8%;
Dietary Fiber: 4g,
16%; Sugar: 3g;
Protein: 36g

2 pounds flank steak

1 red onion, finely diced (about 2 cups)

½ cup balsamic vinegar

1 tablespoon chili powder

1 tablespoon brown sugar

⅛–¼ teaspoon chipotle chili powder or cayenne pepper, to taste

1 teaspoon paprika

1 teaspoon sage or rosemary

½ teaspoon salt

2 tablespoons olive oil

Lay the steak flat in a large dish with sides. Prick the meat in several places with the tines of a fork. Spread the onions on top of the steak. In a large measuring cup, combine the remaining ingredients and stir them thoroughly with a fork or whisk. Pour the mixture over the steak, and flip the meat several times to coat it thoroughly. Marinate the steak and onions, refrigerated, for at least 30 minutes and up to 24 hours.

Preheat the broiler and set the rack about 4 inches from the heat source. (Mean-while, prepare the Garlic Toast, if you are serving it.) Remove the steak from the marinade and set it on a broiling pan, letting the sauce and onions fall back in to the marinating dish. Reserve the marinade and onions.

Broil the steak on the first side for about 4 minutes for medium rare or 5 to 6 min-utes for medium. (Meanwhile, prepare the squash.) Remove the meat from the oven, flip it, and top it with the remaining marinade and onions, spreading the onions evenly over the meat. Return it to the broiler for 5 to 6 more minutes until the onions are browned and the steak is cooked to desired doneness.

Transfer the steak to a cutting board and slice it against the grain. Serve it topped with any remaining sauce and the onions.

Scramble Flavor Booster: Marinate the steak for 12 to 24 hours and use the higher range of chipotle chili powder or cayenne pepper.

Side Dish suggestion: To make Garlic Toast, preheat the oven to 400 degrees. (If you don't have two ovens, use a toaster oven or just use the oil mixture as a dip for bread.) In a small bowl, combine 3 tablespoons olive oil, 1 teaspoon minced garlic, ¼ teaspoon kosher salt, ¼ teaspoon rosemary, and ¼ teaspoon crushed red pepper flakes (optional). Cut the bread (such as sourdough, French, or challah) into ½-inch-thick slices (you only need about 6 slices). Brush the olive oil mixture evenly over the bread. Bake it for 7 to 10 minutes until it starts to brown.

Side Dish suggestion: To make Pan-browned Yellow Squash (or Zucchini), cut 2 to 3 yellow squash into medium-thin slices. In one or two large skillets (depending on how large your skillets and squash are), heat 1 tablespoon olive oil and 1 tablespoon butter over medium to medium-high heat. Sauté the squash slices until they are well browned (but not burned!), about 5 minutes per side. After flipping the slices, season them with salt and chili powder or black pepper. Serve them hot.

The key to searing the salmon, which gives it those nice grill marks, is using very high heat and not moving the salmon for a couple of minutes, so it doesn't stick to the grates. Scramble recipe tester Nancy Bolen reports, "The salmon was a hit! The best endorsement came from six-year-old Anna-Grace, who usually will not eat any kind of fish, who said 'I love it!' and cleaned her plate! My son, Scot, who is not a big fish eater either, rated it 1,000 on a 10-point scale." Serve the salmon with grilled broccoli and couscous with toasted pine nuts and currants or raisins.

grilled balsamic-glazed salmon

Prep + Cook = 25 minutes

6 servings

Nutritional Information per serving (% based upon daily values): Calories 230, Total Fat 15g, 23%, Saturated Fat 3g, 15%, Cholesterol 65mg, 22%, Sodium 410mg, 17%, Total Carbohydrate 1g, 0%, Dietary Fiber 0g, 0%, Sugar 0g, Protein 23g

Nutritional Information per serving with side dish (% based upon daily values) 1/4 of broccoli; 3/4 cup prepared couscous made with water: Calories: 486; Total Fat: 21g, 31%; Saturated Fat: 3g, 16%; Cholesterol: 65mg, 22%; Sodium: 463mg, 19%; Total Carbohydrate: 45g, 14%; Dietary Fiber: 5g, 21%; Sugar: 3g; Protein: 33g

1 tablespoon olive oil

1 teaspoon minced garlic (about 2 cloves)

1 tablespoon balsamic vinegar

1 teaspoon Dijon mustard

1–2 teaspoons minced fresh chives, basil, or parsley

1 1/2 –2 pounds salmon fillet

1 teaspoon kosher salt

1/4 teaspoon black pepper, or to taste

Preheat the grill to high heat. (Alternatively, you can use the oven's broiler for this recipe, with the rack about 5 inches from the heat source.)

Meanwhile, in a small bowl, whisk together the oil, garlic, vinegar, mustard, and chives. Season the flesh side of the salmon with the salt and black pepper, and coat both sides of the salmon thoroughly with nonstick cooking spray.

When the grill is very hot (about 500 degrees), grill the salmon flesh side down for 2 to 3 minutes with the lid closed. Carefully flip the salmon and spoon the balsamic mixture over the flesh side of the fish, spreading it evenly with the back of the spoon. (Start the broccoli now, too, if you are making it.) Reduce the grill heat to low (or move the salmon off the direct heat) and cover the grill. Grill the salmon for about 10 more minutes until it is cooked through in the thickest part and flakes easily. (Meanwhile, prepare the couscous, if you are serving it.) Remove the salmon to a clean plate and serve it immediately.

Scramble Flavor Booster: Serve it with freshly ground black pepper.

Side Dish suggestion: For grilled broccoli, cut 1 to 2 heads broccoli into long spears. Grill the spears directly on the grill or on a vegetable tray or aluminum foil, until they are lightly browned (about 10 minutes). Toss the grilled broccoli with 1 tablespoon olive oil and 1 tablespoon grated Parmesan cheese.

Side Dish suggestion: Prepare 1 package couscous according to the package directions, using broth or water as the liquid. Stir 2 tablespoons toasted pine nuts and 2 tablespoons currants or raisins into the hot prepared couscous and cover it until ready to serve.

smart shopping for organic produce

We know that organic produce is better for your body and the earth. But most of us have grocery budgets and need to balance the realities of cost versus benefit. Consumer Reports cites organic products as 50 percent to 100 percent more expensive than conventional brands. So if we have to choose, what organic foods should we spend that extra money on?

Luckily, the Environmental Working Group (one of my favorite environmental nonprofits) has created a list of the fruits and vegetables that are higher in pesticides, and therefore, are worth the extra expense of buying organic to avoid ingesting those potentially harmful chemicals. (You can get printable pocket guides to carry to the grocery store from www.ewg.org.)

Best Choice Organic Fruits: Peaches, apples, nectarines, strawberries, cherries, grapes, pears, raspberries, plums.

Best Choice Organic Vegetables: Bell peppers, celery, kale, lettuce, carrots, collard greens, spinach, potatoes, green beans, summer squash, cucumbers.

But some fruits and vegetables, either because of growing conditions, their own cellular makeup, or tougher skins, are less susceptible to the effects of pesticides or pests. If you need to, you can save money by buying the following produce from conventional, non-organic sources (but keep in mind that buying organic produce is almost always better for the earth).

Save Money on These Fruits: Pineapples, mangoes, kiwis, papayas, watermelon, grapefruit, honeydew, cranberries, cantaloupe, and bananas.

Save Money on These Vegetables: Onions, avocados, sweet corn, asparagus, sweet peas, cabbage, eggplant, broccoli, tomatoes, and sweet potatoes.

You can also introduce more organic foods economically by trying the following:

- Shop with a list so you only buy what is needed. The savings on less waste can then be used to purchase those higher-quality organic items.

- Buy fruits and vegetables in season from local organic farmers (or grow your own—see page 19). Prices will be lower and the taste at its best.

- Organic goes on sale, too. Look for specials and coupons, especially for canned and frozen organic items that you can save and use anytime.

- Consider generic brands. Many supermarket chains have their own generic brand of organic products. Here you can save money by taking advantage of their bulk purchases.

- Consider joining a CSA. Community Supported Agriculture groups (see box, page 100) provide an economic way to get a steady supply of fresh, often organic, produce during the growing season.

This brightly flavored tilapia was first prepared for us by Chef Valentín Corral at the remote Tortuguero Lodge in Costa Rica, and he was kind enough to share his recipe. Serve it with quinoa (page 43) and baby greens with sliced peaches and pecans.

tortuguero tilapia with cilantro-lime sauce

Prep + Cook = 15 minutes

4 servings

Nutritional Information per serving (% based upon daily values): Calories 200, Total Fat 8g, 12%, Saturated Fat 1.5g, 8%, Cholesterol 80mg, 27%, Sodium 135mg, 6%, Total Carbohydrate 2g, 1%, Dietary Fiber 1g, 4%, Sugar 0g, Protein 29g

Nutritional Information per serving with side dish (% based upon daily values) ¾ cup cooked quinoa; 1½ cups salad: Calories: 457; Total Fat: 15g, 22%; Saturated Fat: 2g, 9%; Cholesterol: 80mg, 27%; Sodium: 167mg, 8%; Total Carbohydrate: 46g, 16%; Dietary Fiber: 7g, 27%; Sugar: 5g; Protein: 37g

2 tablespoons olive oil

1–1½ pounds tilapia fillets

¼ teaspoon salt, or to taste

⅛ teaspoon black pepper, or to taste

⅓ cup fresh cilantro leaves

3 whole cloves garlic

1 lime (use the juice of half and serve the other half cut into wedges)

(If you are making the quinoa, start it first.) In a large nonstick skillet, heat 1 tablespoon oil over medium-high heat. Place the tilapia fillets in the pan and press them down with a spatula to ensure each fillet is completely touching the pan. Cook the fillets on each side until they are lightly browned, 3 to 4 minutes per side. After flipping the fish, season it with salt and pepper.

While the fish is cooking, make the sauce one of two ways: Either puree the cilantro, garlic, 1 tablespoon olive oil, and the juice of half the lime, or, by hand, finely chop the cilantro and garlic, put them in a small serving bowl, and stir in 1 tablespoon olive oil and the juice of half a lime. Season it with salt and pepper to taste.

When the fish is done, put it on a serving plate and top it with the sauce (or serve the sauce on the side.) Cut the remaining half lime into wedges for serving.

Scramble Flavor Booster: Add some fresh lime zest to the cilantro-lime mixture.

Side Dish suggestion: Serve it with a salad of baby greens tossed with 1 sliced peach, 4 teaspoons coarsely chopped pecans, lightly toasted, if desired, and 2 to 4 tablespoons vinaigrette dressing.

This is a really simple preparation for delicate sole. It's also a great use for any little tomatoes you have clinging to your vines or sitting on your counter begging to be used. Serve it with whole grain rolls and a cucumber salad with honey and feta cheese.

lime-butter sole
with grape tomatoes

Prep + Cook =
20 minutes

4 servings

Nutritional
Information per
serving (% based
upon daily values):
Calories 150, Fat 6g,
9%, Saturated Fat
2.5g, 13%, Choles-
terol 60mg, 20%,
Sodium 95mg, 4%,
Total Carbohydrate
5g, 2%, Dietary Fiber
1g, 4%, Sugar 3g,
Protein 20g

Nutritional
Information per
serving with side dish
(% based upon daily
values) 1 roll; ¼ of
salad:
Calories: 290; Total
Fat: 10g, 15%; Satu-
rated Fat: 4g, 21%;
Cholesterol: 70mg,
23%; Sodium: 370mg,
15%; Total Carbohy-
drate: 27g, 10%;
Dietary Fiber: 5g,
20%; Sugar: 9g;
Protein: 26g

1 tablespoons butter

1 teaspoon olive oil

1–1½ pounds sole fillets (or use flounder, tilapia, or other thin white fish)

1 lime or lemon, juice only (about 2 tablespoons)

1 tablespoon white wine (or use 1 additional tablespoon lime or lemon juice)

¼ teaspoon salt, or to taste

⅛ teaspoon black pepper, or to taste

1 pint grape or cherry tomatoes, halved

handful of fresh parsley, chopped (optional)

Preheat the oven to 425 degrees. Put the butter and olive oil in the bottom of a 9 × 13-inch baking dish and put it in the oven until the butter melts. Remove the pan from the oven (don't forget to use mitts!), and lay the fillets flat in the baking dish. Top them with the lime juice, wine, salt, pepper, and tomatoes.

Bake it in the preheated oven for 10 minutes until the fish is opaque and flakes easily, and the tomatoes are softened. (Meanwhile, make the salad, if you are serving it, and warm the rolls.) Top it with the parsley, if desired.

Scramble Flavor Booster: Top the fish with about ½ teaspoon lime or lemon zest or lemon-pepper seasoning before baking it and sprinkle the tomatoes with some crushed red pepper flakes.

Tip: Grape tomatoes are smaller, firmer, and sweeter than cherry tomatoes, and are a great choice for eating raw, adding to salads, or for quick cooking. A hybrid tomato, they originated in Asia, and have soared in popularity in the U.S., where many farms now grow this healthy gem.

Side Dish suggestion: To make the salad, toss 2 peeled, chopped, and seeded cucumbers with ¼ cup crumbled feta cheese, 10 chopped fresh mint leaves, and 1 teaspoon honey. Serve immediately or chill for up to 1 hour until ready to serve.

A scrumptious sauce like this one enhances the flavor of mild white fish like halibut. Serve it with brown or white rice, and a green salad with avocado, walnuts, and Parmesan cheese (page 25).

halibut with caramelized red pepper sauce

Prep + Cook = 30 minutes

4 servings

Nutritional Information per serving (% based upon daily values): Calories 270, Total Fat 13g, 20%, Saturated Fat 2g, 10%, Cholesterol 45mg, 15%, Sodium 80mg, 3%, Total Carbohydrate 7g, 2%, Dietary Fiber 1g, 4%, Sugar 4g, Protein 30g

Nutritional Information per serving with side dish (% based upon daily values) $^3/_4$ cup brown rice; $1^3/_4$ cups salad: Calories: 598; Total Fat: 28g, 42%; Saturated Fat: 5g 24%; Cholesterol: 49mg, 16%; Sodium: 270mg, 12%; Total Carbohydrate: 49g, 11%; Dietary Fiber: 9g, 35%; Sugar: 7g; Protein: 40g

3 tablespoons olive oil

1 large yellow onion (preferably sweet Vidalia or Walla Walla onion), halved and sliced

1 large red bell pepper, sliced or diced

$1^1/_4$–$1^1/_2$ pounds halibut fillet (or other thick fish fillets, such as flounder or salmon)

$^1/_2$ lemon (1 tablespoon plus 2 teaspoons lemon juice)

$^1/_4$ teaspoon salt, or to taste

$^1/_8$ teaspoon black pepper, or to taste

1–2 teaspoons honey, to taste

Preheat the oven to 400 degrees.

In a heavy skillet, heat 1 tablespoon of the oil over medium heat. Caramelize the onions and peppers by sautéing them, stirring occasionally, until they are well browned (but not blackened), 15 to 20 minutes.

Meanwhile, put the fish in the bottom of a flat ovenproof dish with sides. In a small bowl, combine 2 tablespoons oil and 1 tablespoon lemon juice and pour it over the fish. Flip the fish in the juice a couple of times to coat it, and season the fillet with salt and black pepper. Bake the fish for about 20 minutes, until it is opaque and flakes easily. (Meanwhile, prepare the salad and rice, if you are making them.)

Once the onions and peppers are nicely browned, remove them from the heat. Puree them in a blender or food processor, adding 2 teaspoons lemon juice and the honey. Remove the sauce from the blender and put it in individual-size serving bowls or one larger bowl. Serve the fish immediately, smothered with the sauce.

Scramble Flavor Booster: Add additional lemon juice to the fish and sauce, and top the fish with the zest of 1 lemon after baking it.

Tip: You can substitute yellow or orange bell peppers for the red, but don't use green bell peppers, as they don't have the same sweet flavor.

This was my effort to use up all our vegetables before going away on vacation, and the result was remarkably delicious! Scramble recipe tester Margaret Mattocks said this dish has "a bright, fresh, and satisfying flavor." Serve it with a Chopped Cucumber and Avocado Salad and sourdough bread.

yummi yummi mahi mahi

Prep + Cook = 25 minutes

4 servings

Nutritional Information per serving (% based upon daily values): Calories 150, Total Fat 4.5g, 7% Saturated Fat 0.5g, 3%, Cholesterol 85mg, 28%, Sodium 250mg, 10%, Total Carbohydrate 6g, 2%, Dietary Fiber 1g, 4%, Sugar 3g, Protein 22g

Nutritional Information per serving with side dish (% based upon daily values) 1 cup salad; 1 slice bread: Calories: 410; Total Fat: 8g, 11%; Saturated Fat: 1g, 3%; Cholesterol: 85mg, 28%; Sodium: 650mg, 26%; Total Carbohydrate: 56g, 18%; Dietary Fiber: 3g, 12%; Sugar: 3g; Protein: 32g

1 tablespoon olive oil

¼ yellow onion, chopped (about ½ cup)

1 teaspoon minced garlic (about 2 cloves)

1 pound skinless mahi mahi fillets, or other firm white fish (or use boneless chicken breasts)

¼ teaspoon salt, or to taste

⅛ teaspoon black pepper, or to taste

2 tomatoes, chopped

½ cup chopped fresh flat-leaf parsley

½ lemon, juice only (about 2 tablespoons) (reserve remaining lemon for side dish)

2 teaspoons capers (optional)

In a large heavy skillet, heat the oil over medium heat. Add the onions and garlic and sauté them for about 5 minutes until the onions are translucent.

Push the onions and garlic to the sides of the pan and add the fish to the center of the pan. Season the fish with salt and black pepper to taste, and top it with the tomatoes, parsley, lemon juice, and capers (optional). Cook the fish for about 4 minutes per side, flipping it once, until it is cooked through. (Meanwhile, prepare the salad and warm the bread, if you are serving them.)

Serve the mahi mahi topped with the pan sauce.

Scramble Flavor Booster: Double the garlic and be sure to use the optional capers.

Tip: Don't judge an organic tomato (or apple, peach, or zucchini) by its peel: Sometimes the organic and/or locally grown fruit at the markets doesn't look perfect, but that doesn't mean that it doesn't taste great. Judge fresh produce, especially when it's locally grown, by its shape, smell, weight, or even how well you know and trust the farmer, rather than searching for the most perfect-looking produce. Farmers often sell their blemished fruits and vegetables at the farm markets because the big supermarkets won't buy them, but a little discoloration or imperfection usually won't affect the flavor one bit, and buying them supports the farmers and reduces wasted food.

Side Dish suggestion: To make a Chopped Cucumber and Avocado Salad, in a medium bowl, combine 1 small chopped cucumber, 2 chopped avocados, and 1 tablespoon blue cheese or Gorgonzola. Top everything with 1 teaspoon lemon juice and ½ teaspoon (or more to taste) balsamic vinegar. Toss gently and serve it immediately.

Side Dish suggestion: Serve it with a loaf of sourdough bread, warmed in a 300-degree oven for about 5 minutes.

let kids get their hands dirty in the kitchen

Kids love getting their hands dirty so let them help you with kitchen tasks that do just that—like forming meatballs, working with pastry dough, and hand-mixing pasta salads (just make sure they scrub their grubby mitts first!). Here are a few other ideas for getting kids involved with your meal preparations:

- Let them use their creativity by "painting" sauce on your next pizza or sandwich creation.
- Let them be "smoothie" king or queen and invent their own versions with healthy yogurt, fruit juices, and fresh or frozen fruit chunks.
- If your child loves to build, let them help construct the next lasagna or any other layered dish.
- Encourage them to exercise their developing muscles by squeezing lemons and limes, peeling carrots, and grating zucchini or potatoes.

Before long they'll actually be making your job easier by being a real help in the kitchen, and hopefully you will also be helping them develop a love of cooking healthy homemade meals.

This is a flavorful fish with a beautiful presentation. If you have fresh herbs on hand, they would also be wonderful stirred into the vegetables before you layer them over the fish. Serve it with Israeli couscous and a French Beet Salad.

lemony fish bake with vegetable confetti

Prep (20 minutes) + Cook (25 minutes)

4 servings

Nutritional Information per serving (% based upon daily values): Calories 160, Total Fat 8g, 12%, Saturated Fat 1g, 5%, Cholesterol 25mg, 8%, Sodium 80mg, 3%, Total Carbohydrate 6g, 2%, Dietary Fiber 1g, 4%, Sugar 2g, Protein 18g

Nutritional Information per serving with side dish (% based upon daily values) ³⁄₄ cup prepared couscous; ¹⁄₄ of salad: Calories: 328; Total Fat: 8g, 12%; Saturated Fat: 1g, 5%; Cholesterol: 25mg, 8%; Sodium: 169mg, 7%; Total Carbohydrate: 41g, 14%; Dietary Fiber: 5g, 17%; Sugar: 8g; Protein: 24g

2 tablespoons olive oil

½ red onion, diced

1 teaspoon minced garlic (about 2 cloves)

1 zucchini, diced

1 red bell pepper, diced

1 teaspoon herbes de Provence (or use dried thyme or basil or fresh herbs)

¼ teaspoon salt, or to taste

⅛ teaspoon black pepper, or to taste

1–1½ pounds white roughy, cod, tilapia, or other white fish fillets

1 lemon, juice only (about ¼ cup)

¼ cup shredded Parmesan cheese, or to taste (optional)

(If you are making the beets, start them first.) Preheat the oven to 350 degrees. In a heavy skillet, heat the oil over medium heat. Sauté the onions and garlic for about 2 minutes, while you chop the other vegetables. Add the zucchini, bell peppers, and herbes de Provence to the pan and continue to sauté them until the vegetables are soft, about 10 minutes. Season them with salt and black pepper to taste.

Lay the fish in a single layer in a large baking dish. Spoon the vegetables evenly over the fillets, and pour the lemon juice over everything.

Bake it for 20 to 25 minutes, until the fish is cooked through and the vegetables are softened. (Meanwhile, prepare the couscous if you are making it.) Top the fish with Parmesan cheese, if desired.

Scramble Flavor Booster: Double the garlic and herbes de Provence (add up to 2 teaspoons), and sprinkle the fish and vegetables with fresh parsley, basil, or thyme.

Tip: We sometimes use a Vidalia Chop Wizard to quickly and easily dice and julienne softer vegetables like peppers, zucchini, mushrooms, and onions (I almost sprained my shoulder trying to use it to chop carrots, though). While I usually prefer my trusty knife, my kids love using it and I don't have to worry about them cutting their fingers.

Side Dish suggestion: To make a French Beet Salad, scrub 3 medium to large beets. Cut off the greens, leaving about 1 inch of stems, and steam them in about 1 inch of gently boiling water, covered, for 45 minutes, until they are fork tender. (You can cook and peel the beets up to 24 hours in advance.) Drain the beets, rinse them in cold water, and remove the skins, using your fingers or a vegetable peeler. Dice the beets and place them in a medium bowl. Combine 2 teaspoons grainy Dijon mustard and 2 teaspoons white wine vinegar and pour over the beets, tossing thoroughly. Refrigerate the salad for at least 20 minutes and up to 48 hours.

the perfect salad
(or at least a really great one!)

While I am pretty sure there is not a gene for salad-making, my sister and I both inherited the ability to make great salads from my mom. Sometimes our salads are a meal—a hearty lunchtime or dinner salad with chicken, hard-boiled egg, or beans, for example—though usually they're just a great side dish for a healthy and delicious dinner. Whether passed down by nature or nurture, here's our basic technique:

- **The key is to start with the freshest looking lettuce**—I lean toward romaine, Boston or Bibb lettuces, or baby spinach. I wash it very well (few things are as icky as gritty salad), tear it into bite-size pieces, and use a salad spinner to dry it completely.

- **Our favorite trick is to include lots of goodies in the salad.** My preferred combinations usually involve fresh or dried fruit, nuts, beans, or chopped hard-boiled egg, and cheese. (I often follow this guideline: A fruit, a nut, and a cheese.) Sometimes I also include diced or small vegetables, such as bell peppers, tomatoes, corn kernels, or peas. In the warmer months, a handful of fresh herbs is a wonderful addition.

- **For fruits, I lean toward oranges, apples, pears, dried cranberries, strawberries, halved grapes, and avocado**—I've even been known to use blueberries. For nuts, I prefer walnuts (glazed or plain), pecans, pistachios, or pine nuts. For cheese, I like Parmesan, feta, Gorgonzola, blue, or goat cheese. It's cheaper to crumble the cheese myself, but if I know that time will be tight I buy cheeses already crumbled at the supermarket. For softer additions, such as avocado and goat cheese, I add them after tossing the salad so they don't get squished at the bottom of the bowl.

- **Finally, we use just a little bit of high-quality dressing**, store-bought or homemade (a simple combination of olive oil, balsamic vinegar, and Dijon or honey-Dijon mustard works well), and toss the salad thoroughly just before serving it. You don't need much dressing, because the array of ingredients gives the salad lots of flavor.

This terrific recipe is from my friend and food writer April Fulton. I just love making trout because it tastes wonderful, never too fishy, and is so versatile. What makes it even better is that trout is on the "eco-best" list of the Environmental Defense Fund's Oceans Alive project. Serve it with gnocchi (Italian potato dumplings) and Swiss Chard with Garlic.

grilled trout stuffed with fresh herbs and lemon slices

Prep + Cook = 20 minutes

4 servings

Nutritional Information per serving (% based upon daily values): Calories 250, Total Fat 12g, 18%, Saturated Fat 3g, 15%, Cholesterol 90mg, 30%, Sodium 300mg, 13%, Total Carbohydrate 0g, 0%, Dietary Fiber 0g, 0%, Sugar 0g, Protein 33g

Nutritional Information per serving with side dish (% based upon daily values) ¾ cup prepared gnocchi; ¼ Swiss chard: Calories: 531; Total Fat: 20g, 30%; Saturated Fat: 6g, 24%; Cholesterol: 96mg, 32%; Sodium: 1,065mg, 48%; Total Carbohydrate: 47g, 16%; Dietary Fiber: 3g, 12%; Sugar: 3g; Protein: 41g

2 tablespoons fresh mint leaves, finely chopped

2 tablespoons fresh rosemary, finely chopped

2 lemons

4 whole trout, cleaned, gutted, heads removed (the fishmonger can do this for you)

1–2 tablespoons olive oil

½ teaspoon kosher salt

¼ teaspoon black pepper

Preheat the grill to medium heat and oil the grates to prevent the fish from sticking. (Alternatively, bake the trout at 400 degrees for about 25 minutes.) (Start the gnocchi, if you are making it.) In a small bowl, combine the chopped herbs, the zest of 1½ lemons, and the juice of 1 lemon. Cut the other lemon into thin slices. (Start the Swiss chard now, if you are making it.)

Open each trout and lay them on a cutting board skin side up. Brush the skin of each trout with olive oil to coat it. Flip the fish and rub the lemon-herb mixture over the flesh of the trout, season it with the salt and black pepper, and lay the lemon slices on top of one half of the flesh of each trout. Close the trout around the herbs and lemon slices, and transfer the fish to the grill. Grill the fish with the lid closed and without flipping the trout for 8 minutes, until the flesh is opaque and flaky. Using a thin spatula, carefully transfer the trout to a serving plate. Serve garnished with a few fresh mint leaves and sprigs of rosemary, if desired.

Scramble Flavor Booster: Season the fish with freshly ground black pepper or lemon-pepper seasoning at the table.

Tip: Swiss chard is such an easy green to grow—my friend Tricia Nudelman grows it in her yard next to her front walk and it looks beautiful! When you're ready to use it, just trim the outer leaves and let the center keep growing.

Side Dish suggestion: To make Swiss Chard with Garlic, wash 1 head of Swiss chard thoroughly and trim the stalks. Chop the leaves and stems. Heat 1 tablespoon olive oil over medium heat in a large nonstick skillet and add 1 teaspoon minced garlic (about 2 cloves). When the garlic starts to brown, add the Swiss chard and ¼ cup water, reduce the heat, cover, and cook for about 10 minutes. Remove the cover, raise heat to medium-low, and let the Swiss chard cook, stirring occasionally, until it is very tender, about 10 more minutes. Top it with a little salt and shredded Parmesan cheese.

This light dish can be served warm or cold, so it can be made in advance for an especially hectic night, or chilled and toted to a picnic. Serve it with diced cantaloupe and Sugar Snap Peas with Cashews (page 60).

asian shrimp pilaf

Prep + Cook =
30 minutes

6 servings

Nutritional Information per serving (% based upon daily values): Calories 250, Total Fat 6g, 9%, Saturated Fat 1g, 5%, Cholesterol 115mg, 38%, Sodium 700mg, 29%, Total Carbohydrate 29g, 10%, Dietary Fiber 2g, 8%, Sugar 4g, Protein 20g

Nutritional Information per serving with side dish (% based upon daily values) 1 cup cantaloupe; ¾ cup sugar snap peas: Calories: 394; Total Fat 13g, 20%; Saturated Fat: 3g, 13%; Cholesterol: 115mg, 38%; Sodium: 726mg, 30%; Total Carbohydrate: 47g, 16%; Dietary Fiber: 4g, 18%; Sugar: 19g; Protein: 23g

1 package (6 ounces) rice pilaf, such as Near East Original Style (or use 1½ cups white rice)

1 tablespoon reduced-sodium soy sauce

2 teaspoons sesame oil

1 tablespoon honey

½ teaspoon minced garlic (about 1 clove)

1 large carrot, diced or shredded (½ cup)

½ red bell pepper, diced (½ cup)

2–3 scallions, sliced (¼ cup)

¼ cup unsalted peanuts, coarsely chopped

1 pound large shrimp, peeled and deveined (alternatively, use drained, diced, and sautéed extra-firm tofu or cooked and diced chicken breast)

Prepare the rice pilaf mix according to package directions, omitting the butter or oil.

Bring a separate large pot of water to a boil for the shrimp. (If you are making sugar snap peas, prepare that now, too.)

In a small bowl, combine the soy sauce, sesame oil, honey, and garlic (if you don't like the taste of raw garlic, sauté the garlic first in a tiny bit of olive oil until it is lightly browned).

Put the carrots, bell peppers, scallions, and peanuts in a medium bowl. When the rice is cooked, stir it into the vegetables and stir in the soy-sauce mixture.

Drop the shrimp in the boiling water for 2 to 3 minutes and cook it until it is pink and opaque. Drain it well and add it to the rice mixture. Serve the pilaf warm or cold.

Scramble Flavor Booster: Top the pilaf at the table with Asian chili sauce or hot pepper sauce, such as Tabasco.

Tip: Bell peppers have a tangy taste and crunchy texture. They are a great source of vitamins A and C, two powerful antioxidants. Peppers are also a good source of dietary fiber, niacin, magnesium, and copper.

This dish hits the spot for simple summer pasta that's great for the whole family. Scramble recipe tester, Maria Mullen, said, "I love the flavors in this dish and it was so easy. I usually have all the ingredients on hand so it's a great meal to make on a crazy night." Serve it with steamed green beans with goat or feta cheese.

light and garlicky penne with plum tomatoes

Prep + Cook = 20 minutes

8 servings

Nutritional Information per serving (% based upon daily values): Calories 290, Total Fat 8g, 12%, Saturated Fat 1g, 5%, Cholesterol 0mg, 0%, Sodium 80mg, 3%, Total Carbohydrate 46g, 15%, Dietary Fiber 2g, 8%, Sugar 3g, Protein 8g

Nutritional Information per serving with side dish (% based upon daily values) 1 cup green beans, 1 tsp. goat cheese: Calories: 351; Total Fat: 10g, 15%; Saturated Fat: 2g, 10%; Cholesterol: 4mg, 1%; Sodium: 260mg, 10%; Total Carbohydrate: 56g, 18%; Dietary Fiber: 6g, 24%; Sugar: 5g; Protein: 11g

1 package (16 ounces) penne pasta

¼ cup olive oil

½ red onion, finely diced (about 1 cup)

1 tablespoon minced garlic (about 6 cloves)

4 plum tomatoes, diced

¼ teaspoon salt

½ cup grated Parmesan cheese (optional)

Cook the penne according to the package directions until it is al dente.

Meanwhile, in a large heavy skillet, heat the oil over medium heat. Add the onions and sauté them for about 3 minutes until they start to soften. (Meanwhile, make the green beans if you are serving them.) Add the garlic and sauté it for about 2 more minutes.

Add the tomatoes to the skillet and cook them until they soften but don't completely lose their shape, about 5 minutes, stirring often. Lower the heat to medium-low if they are sticking to the pan.

Drain the penne and add it to the skillet with the tomatoes. Season with the salt and top it, at the table, with the cheese, if desired.

Scramble Flavor Booster: Use freshly grated aged Parmesan cheese and stir a handful of chopped fresh basil or parsley into the finished pasta.

Tip: Prepared trail mix (the type without chocolate chips or M&Ms, of course) makes a speedy mix-in for green salads.

Side Dish suggestion: Trim and halve 1 pound green beans and steam in 1 to 2 inches of boiling water for 5 to 8 minutes to desired tenderness. Drain and toss immediately with 1 to 2 tablespoons goat or feta cheese, 1 tablespoon fresh lemon juice (about ¼ lemon), and salt and black pepper to taste.

This sophisticated pasta was a big hit with the adults I served it to and several of the more adventurous kids. If your kids are picky, remove some of the pasta before you toss it with the Gorgonzola, or use a milder cheese such as goat cheese or ricotta. Serve it with sweet summer cherries.

rotini with arugula or spinach and pine nuts

Prep + Cook = 25 minutes

8 servings

Nutritional Information per serving (% based upon daily values): Calories 340, Total Fat 12g, 18%, Saturated Fat 4g, 20%, Cholesterol 15mg, 5%, Sodium 320mg, 13%, Total Carbohydrate 45g, 15%, Dietary Fiber 2g, 8%, Sugar 2g, Protein 11g

Nutritional Information per serving with side dish (% based upon daily values) 1 cup cherries: Calories: 414; Total Fat: 12g, 18%; Saturated Fat: 4g, 20%; Cholesterol: 15mg, 5%; Sodium: 320mg, 13%; Total Carbohydrate: 64g, 21%; Dietary Fiber: 5g, 18%; Sugar: 17g; Protein: 12g

1 package (16 ounces) rotini pasta

4 tablespoons olive oil

½ cup pine nuts

½ teaspoon kosher salt

¼ teaspoon black pepper

2 large tomatoes, diced

4–6 ounces arugula or baby spinach leaves, roughly chopped (baby spinach leaves don't need to be chopped)

½ cup crumbled Gorgonzola cheese (or use goat cheese or ricotta)

¼ lemon, juice only (about 1 tablespoon)

In a large pot, cook the pasta according to package directions until it is al dente.

Once you add the rotini to the boiling water, make the sauce. Heat the olive oil in a large heavy skillet over medium heat. Add the pine nuts, salt, and pepper and cook for about 2 minutes, until the pine nuts are lightly browned. Add the tomatoes and arugula or spinach to the skillet and cook for 2 more minutes.

Drain the cooked pasta, allowing some water to cling to the pasta, and add it to the skillet with the pine nut mixture. Add the cheese and lemon juice and toss until the cheese is melted. Remove it from the heat and serve it immediately.

Scramble Flavor Booster: Use the arugula, which is more peppery than spinach, and add a little extra lemon juice and freshly ground black pepper.

Tip: To keep nuts tasting fresh for a long time, keep them tightly sealed in the freezer. Because of their high oil content, they don't actually freeze, and they stay fresh for many months.

This is a wonderful dish to highlight those sweet and juicy summer tomatoes, suggested by our friend Nachama Wilker. Serve it with steamed green beans (page 101).

penne with fresh tomatoes and basil

Prep + Cook = 20 minutes

6 servings

Nutritional Information per serving (% based upon daily values): Calories 410, Total Fat 13g, 20%, Saturated Fat 2g, 10%, Cholesterol 0mg, 0%, Sodium 210mg, 9%, Total Carbohydrate 63g, 21%, Dietary Fiber 4g, 16%, Sugar 5g, Protein 11g

Nutritional Information per serving with side dish (% based upon daily values) 1 cup green beans: Calories: 444; Total Fat: 13g, 20%; Saturated Fat: 2g, 10%; Cholesterol: 0mg, 0%; Sodium: 217mg, 9%; Total Carbohydrate: 71g, 24%; Dietary Fiber: 8g, 31%; Sugar: 7g; Protein: 13g

1 package (16 ounces) penne or other cut pasta

2 pounds fresh tomatoes, chopped (about 8 tomatoes)

⅓–½ cup olive oil, to taste

1 teaspoon minced garlic (about 2 cloves)

½–¾ teaspoon salt, to taste

20 leaves fresh basil, chopped (or a combination of fresh basil, parsley, and oregano)

¼ cup shredded Parmesan cheese to taste (optional)

Cook the penne according to the package directions.

Meanwhile, in a large bowl, mix the tomatoes, oil, garlic, salt, and basil. Smash the tomatoes in the oil with a fork or potato masher and let the mixture stand. (Prepare the green beans, if you are serving them.)

When the pasta is cooked, drain it well and toss it with the tomato mixture. Top it with Parmesan cheese, if desired.

Scramble Flavor Booster: Double the garlic and season the pasta with freshly ground black pepper.

Tip: The quality of the tomatoes makes a big difference in this dish. If possible, use fresh, locally grown tomatoes. If your tomatoes aren't too flavorful, add a teaspoon of sugar to the tomato mixture to add flavor.

Scramble subscriber Vanessa Jones of Dumfries, Virginia, sent me this recipe after she misread a Scramble recipe and had to build a meal on a busy night around a pound of sausage she had in her freezer. Vanessa's Scramble meal was a surprising hit in her family, and mine loved it, too. Serve it with a green salad with shredded carrots, diced avocado, and crumbled goat or feta cheese.

rotini pasta with sweet sausage and peppers

Prep + Cook = 30 minutes

10 servings

Nutritional Information per serving (% based upon daily values): Calories 410, Total Fat 6g, 9%, Saturated Fat 1.5g, 8%, Cholesterol 25mg, 8%, Sodium 2,080mg, 87%, Total Carbohydrate 76g, 25%, Dietary Fiber 13g, 52%, Sugar 28g, Protein 20g

Nutritional Information per serving with side dish (% based upon daily values) 1½ cups salad: Calories: 517; Total Fat: 13g, 20%; Saturated Fat: 3g, 16%; Cholesterol: 31mg, 10%; Sodium: 2,296mg, 96%; Total Carbohydrate: 86g, 28%; Dietary Fiber: 17g, 70%; Sugar: 31g; Protein: 55g

1 package (16 ounces) whole wheat or regular rotini pasta (or any short shape)

1 tablespoon olive oil

1 pound sweet Italian sausage (uncooked or cooked), turkey sausage, or vegetarian sausage, diced if using pre-cooked sausage

1 medium yellow onion, diced

1 medium green bell pepper (or any color), diced

½ teaspoon dried basil or 1 tablespoon chopped fresh

½ teaspoon dried oregano or 1–2 teaspoons fresh

½ teaspoon dried thyme or 1–2 teaspoons fresh

1–2 cans (28–30 ounces total) diced tomatoes

1 can (15 ounces) tomato sauce

¼ cup grated Parmesan cheese for serving

Cook the pasta according to the package directions until they are al dente, and drain it.

Meanwhile, in a large skillet, heat the oil over medium heat, and brown the sausage. While it's cooking, add the onions, bell peppers, and dried herbs (if using fresh herbs, stir them in toward the end of cooking) and continue to sauté it until the sausage is browned and the vegetables are softened, 8 to 10 minutes.

Add the diced tomatoes and tomato sauce and simmer it, uncovered, for about 15 minutes until the liquid has thickened slightly and the pasta is cooked. (While the sauce is cooking, prepare the salad, if you are making it.)

Combine the rotini and the sauce, and serve it hot, topped with Parmesan cheese to taste.

Scramble Flavor Booster: Serve the dish with crushed red pepper flakes or hot pepper sauce, such as Tabasco.

Tip: Watch the pasta so it doesn't overcook, which can make it mushy or sticky. The pasta should still have some firmness when you bite through a piece to test it. I find it's best not to rinse pasta in cold water after cooking, unless the directions on your package specifically say to do so, or you are making a cold pasta dish.

Side Dish suggestion: To make the salad, gently toss 6 to 8 cups lettuce, 1 shredded or finely chopped carrot, $\frac{1}{2}$ to 1 peeled and diced avocado, and 2 to 4 tablespoons crumbled goat or feta cheese with salad dressing to taste.

putting extra fresh herbs to great use

If your backyard in July is anything like ours, your fresh potted herbs are starting to look a little like the multiplying pods from that old movie, *Invasion of the Body Snatchers,* with tentacles (or in this case, fragrant offshoots) threatening to invade the house while you sleep! Normally, I hate to see anything go to waste. But since they are growing so rapidly, there's little hope of actually using all the herbs right away (except maybe the basil, which I use frequently in pesto and other sauces).

Since they taste so wonderful and are abundant here for only half the year, I try to find loads of uses for these flavorful leaves. Here are some of my favorites, including a few creative suggestions from Scramble subscribers—these ideas also work well for using up leftover herbs from the supermarket:

- Mix a handful of fresh oregano, mint, dill, or basil leaves into green salads or make a tomato, basil, and mozzarella salad.

- Make pesto out of basil, parsley, or mint, and use it as a topping for pasta, pizza, fish, chicken, sandwiches, or crackers. Pesto also freezes well, so you can enjoy some now and some later.

- Top pizza with fresh basil or oregano, or stuff the leaves in sandwiches.

- Add herbs to almost any pasta, especially pasta salads.

- Before roasting vegetables or potatoes, toss them with rosemary, thyme, or oregano.

- Rub meat or fish with a paste of fresh herbs before baking or grilling it.

- Make lemonade or ice tea with sprigs of fresh mint.

- Use herbs as a garnish on a platter, or put bunches in small vases for table decorations.

If you live in a hot climate, don't forget to water your herbs nearly every day—that's an ideal chore for kids of all ages to help with.

This is a light and lovely pasta to enjoy in the warm weather. Our daughter, Celia, said it was the best thing I've ever made! You can certainly get creative with this recipe, using walnuts instead of the pine nuts, for example, and goat cheese or pecorino romano instead of the Parmesan. Serve it with a spinach salad with sliced strawberries and crumbled Gorgonzola cheese.

farfalle with pine nuts and fresh herbs

Prep + Cook = 25 minutes

6 servings

Nutritional Information per serving (% based upon daily values): Calories 390, Total Fat 12g, 18%, Saturated Fat 4.5g, 22%, Cholesterol 15mg, 5%, Sodium 150mg, 6%, Total Carbohydrate 58g, 9%, Dietary Fiber 2g, 8%, Sugar 2g, Protein 12g

Nutritional Information per serving with side dish (% based upon daily values) 1½ cups salad: Calories: 512; Total Fat: 19g, 29%; Saturated Fat: 7g, 34%; Cholesterol: 25mg, 8%; Sodium: 372mg, 16%; Total Carbohydrate: 71g, 13%; Dietary Fiber: 6g, 25%; Sugar: 6g; Protein: 17g

1 package (16 ounces) farfalle or other pasta

2 tablespoons butter

2 tablespoons olive oil

1 teaspoon minced garlic (about 2 cloves)

2 tablespoons pine nuts

1 cup fresh basil (or try a mixture of mostly basil and some sage), chopped

¼ teaspoon salt

¼–½ cup grated Parmesan cheese, to taste

Cook the pasta according to package directions until it is al dente. (Meanwhile, prepare the salad if you are serving it.)

Five minutes before the pasta is done, melt the butter in a large heavy skillet over medium heat. Add the oil, garlic, and pine nuts and cook for about 2 minutes, stirring occasionally. (If you don't cook with nuts, the dish is still delicious without them.)

Before draining the pasta, use a ladle to scoop out ¼ to ½ cup of the pasta's cooking water.

To the skillet with the butter and garlic, add the drained pasta, the reserved cooking liquid, the basil, salt, and Parmesan cheese and toss over low heat for 1 to 2 minutes until it is warmed through and the cheese is melted. Serve it hot.

Scramble Flavor Booster: Season the pasta with lots of freshly ground black pepper and use freshly grated Parmesan cheese.

Tip: Be careful not to overcook the pasta or it will get too gummy when you toss it with the sauce.

Side Dish suggestion: Serve it with a spinach salad made with 6 ounces baby spinach, 1 to 2 cups sliced strawberries, and ¼ cup crumbled Gorgonzola cheese, and tossed with 2 to 4 tablespoons raspberry vinaigrette dressing, to taste.

Subscriber Linda Willard sent me this kid-friendly stir-fry recipe that can be enjoyed hot or cold. Recipe tester Debbie Firestone said that her nine-year-old daughter declared it her "absolute favorite recipe!" This is a meal in itself for a busy night, or serve it with sliced watermelon.

teriyaki noodle stir-fry

Prep + Cook =
30 minutes

6 servings (4 servings without chicken)

Nutritional Information per serving (with chicken and store-bought sauce):
Calories 260, Total Fat 3.5g, 5%, Saturated Fat 0.5g, 3%, Cholesterol 45mg, 15%, Sodium 820mg, 34%, Total Carbohydrate 35g, 12%, Dietary Fiber 3g, 12%, Protein 24g, Sugar 3g

Nutritional Information per serving with side dish (% based upon daily values) 2 slices watermelon:
Calories: 346; Total Fat: 4g, 6%; Saturated Fat: 1g, 3%; Cholesterol: 45mg, 15%; Sodium: 823mg, 34%; Total Carbohydrate: 57g, 19%; Dietary Fiber: 4g, 17%; Sugar: 21g; Protein: 26g

1 package (8 ounces) Japanese soba noodles (or use whole wheat linguine)

1 tablespoon sesame oil

1 pound boneless, skinless chicken breasts, cut into ½-inch strips or 1 pound extra-firm tofu, diced

2–4 tablespoons vegetable or canola oil

1 red, orange, or yellow bell pepper, cut into 1-inch strips

1½ cups sliced carrots (about 3 large carrots)

½ large red onion (or 1 small red onion), thinly sliced

3 scallions, sliced

¼ teaspoon crushed red pepper flakes (optional)

2 tablespoons reduced-sodium soy sauce

4 tablespoons teriyaki or stir-fry sauce (Soy Vey makes a great-tasting teriyaki sauce), or more to taste

Cook noodles according to the package directions until they are al dente. Drain and toss them immediately in a large bowl with the sesame oil. (If you are making your own teriyaki sauce, make that now, too—see Tip below.)

While the noodles are cooking, heat 2 tablespoons vegetable or canola oil over medium-high heat in a wok or large skillet (use a nonstick skillet for tofu) and add the cut chicken (or tofu). Cook, tossing often, until the chicken is no longer pink, about 3 minutes (or the tofu is lightly browned, about 5 minutes). Add the chicken (or tofu) to the bowl with the noodles.

Add the remaining 2 tablespoons vegetable or canola oil to a skillet over medium-high heat and add the peppers, carrots, onions, scallions, and red pepper flakes (optional). Cook, stirring frequently, until the vegetables are tender-crisp, about 3 minutes. Add the noodles, chicken or tofu, soy sauce, and teriyaki or stir-fry sauce to the pan and toss it all together for 1 minute.

Serve hot or chill for up to 24 hours and serve it cold.

Scramble Flavor Booster: Use the optional crushed red pepper flakes.

Tip: If you prefer to make your own teriyaki sauce, combine 1½ tablespoons reduced-sodium soy sauce, 1½ tablespoons rice vinegar, 1½ tablespoons rice wine, ¼ teaspoon each of ground ginger and garlic powder, and 1½ teaspoons brown sugar.

This pasta tastes light and delicious, and is so simple to prepare. It's the kind of dish I could eat over and over—the traditional Greek flavors blend together beautifully. Serve it with Sautéed Sweet Corn, Onions, and Zucchini.

farfalle with feta cheese and plum tomatoes

Prep + Cook = 25 minutes

8 servings

Nutritional Information per serving (% based upon daily values): Calories 350, Total Fat 14g, 22%, Saturated Fat 4g, 20%, Cholesterol 15mg, 5%, Sodium 360mg, 15%, Total Carbohydrate 46g, 15%, Dietary Fiber 2g, 8%, Sugar 3g, Protein 11g

Nutritional Information per serving with side dish (% based upon daily values) 1 cup corn mixture: Calories: 480; Total Fat: 21g, 33%; Saturated Fat: 7g, 32%; Cholesterol: 25mg, 8%; Sodium: 440mg, 18%; Total Carbohydrate: 63g, 21%; Dietary Fiber: 4g, 16%; Sugar: 7g; Protein: 14g

1 package (16 ounces) farfalle (butterfly-shaped) pasta
¼ cup olive oil
3 tablespoons pine nuts
1 tablespoon minced garlic (about 6 cloves)
½ teaspoon dried oregano or 1½ teaspoons fresh
½ teaspoon salt
¼ teaspoon black pepper
4 plum tomatoes or 2 conventional tomatoes, diced
½ cup pitted kalamata olives, coarsely chopped (optional)
¾ cup crumbled feta cheese

Cook the pasta according to the package directions. (Meanwhile, start the vegetables, if you are serving them.) When you add the pasta to the water, heat the oil in a medium skillet over medium heat. Add the pine nuts and garlic and cook them, stirring, until the pine nuts are lightly browned, 3 to 5 minutes. Add the spices and stir well (if you are using fresh oregano, add it at the end with the pasta). Add the tomatoes and olives (optional) and cook them for 3 to 5 minutes, until everything is heated through and the tomatoes are slightly softened.

Drain the pasta and transfer it to a large metal bowl. Toss it with the sauce and top it with the cheese. Cover the bowl with plastic wrap and let it stand for about 5 minutes to let the flavors meld.

Scramble Flavor Booster: Use additional fresh or dried oregano and black pepper.

Side Dish suggestion: To make Sautéed Sweet Corn, Onions, and Zucchini, heat 1 tablespoon olive oil and 1 tablespoon butter or margarine in a heavy skillet over medium heat. Sauté ½ diced yellow onion for 2 minutes. Add 1 diced zucchini and sauté it for 2 to 3 minutes. Cut the kernels off 4 ears of corn (or use 2 cups frozen corn kernels) and add them to the skillet. Sauté everything for 3 to 5 more minutes. Reduce the heat if it's browning too much. Season it with salt and pepper to taste, or for a flavor boost, add ½ to 1 teaspoon curry powder or chili powder.

This light pasta salad, suggested by subscriber Koren Bowie, tastes like a summer day in Italy—the key is to use fresh mozzarella and the freshest and most flavorful tomatoes you can find. Serve it with whole grain bread.

lemon-basil
summer pasta salad

Prep + Cook =
25 minutes + optional
Marinate (up to 24
hours)

8 servings

Nutritional
Information per
serving (% based
upon daily values):
Calories 336, Total
Fat 12.5g, 19%, Satu-
rated Fat 3.5g, 17%,
Cholesterol 15mg,
5%, Sodium 319mg,
13%, Total Carbohy-
drate 45.5g, 15%,
Dietary Fiber 3g,
11.5%, Sugar 3g,
Protein 8g

Nutritional
Information per
serving with side dish
(% based upon daily
values) 1 slice bread:
Calories: 446; Total
Fat: 15g, 22%; Satu-
rated Fat: 4g, 17%;
Cholesterol: 15mg,
5%; Sodium: 499mg,
21%; Total Carbohy-
drate: 66g, 22%;
Dietary Fiber: 6g,
24%; Sugar 6g;
Protein: 12g

1 package (16 ounces) farfalle pasta

6 plum (or Roma) tomatoes, seeded and diced (or use 4 large tomatoes)

20 basil leaves, cut into thin strips

1 lemon, juice only (about ¼ cup)

¼ cup olive oil

1 teaspoon mashed garlic cloves (1–2 cloves)

¾–1 teaspoon salt, to taste

8 ounces fresh mozzarella, diced (about 1½ cups)

In a large pot of salted water, cook the pasta according to package directions until it is al dente. Drain and rinse pasta with cold water to cool.

Meanwhile, in a large serving bowl, combine the remaining ingredients. Add the cooled pasta, toss, and chill it for up to 24 hours, or serve it immediately.

Scramble Flavor Booster: Add extra lemon juice and a little lemon zest for a tangier flavor. Add freshly ground black pepper and/or some crushed red pepper flakes for a spicy kick.

Tip: To get more juice out of your lemons, roll them on the counter while pressing firmly with your palm before juicing them.

I was skeptical when subscriber Robyn Muncy suggested I make her pesto recipe using more parsley than basil, and walnuts instead of pine nuts. But, suspecting that she has excellent taste, I plunged ahead and the results were wonderful. Serve this ravioli with a Tomato, Mozzarella, and Artichoke Salad.

ravioli with walnut and parsley pesto

Prep + Cook = 25 minutes

6 servings

Nutritional Information per serving (1% based upon daily values): Calories 254, Total Fat 11g, 16%, Saturated Fat 4.5g, 24%, Cholesterol 47mg, 16%, Sodium 325mg, 13.5%, Total Carbohydrate 28g, 9.5%, Dietary Fiber 1.5g, 5.5%, Sugar 2.5g, Protein 13.5g

Nutritional Information per serving with side dish (% based upon daily values) ⅙ of salad with no olives: Calories: 374; Total Fat: 19g, 28%; Saturated Fat: 8g, 42%; Cholesterol: 62mg, 21%; Sodium: 505mg, 21.5%; Total Carbohydrate: 32g, 10.5%; Dietary Fiber: 2.5g, 9.5%; Sugar: 3.5g; Protein: 21.5g

1 family-size package (20 ounces) reduced-fat cheese ravioli

1¾ cups tightly packed flat-leaf parsley

¼ cup tightly packed basil plus a handful of sliced basil for serving

½ cup walnuts

¾ cup grated Parmesan cheese

1 teaspoon minced garlic (about 2 cloves)

¼ teaspoon salt

¼ teaspoon black pepper

⅔ cup olive oil

2 tomatoes, chopped

Cook the ravioli according to package directions and drain it. (While the water is heating, prepare the salad, if you are serving it.)

Meanwhile, in a food processor or blender, coarsely chop the parsley, ¼ cup basil, walnuts, Parmesan cheese, garlic, salt, and black pepper. Then, slowly add the oil and continue to process the pesto until it is well combined.

Gently toss the warm ravioli with 1 cup of the pesto, reserving any remaining pesto for future use. Top the ravioli with the tomatoes and a handful of fresh basil before serving.

Scramble Flavor Booster: Add ¼ teaspoon crushed red pepper flakes to the blender with the pesto ingredients.

Tip: This recipe makes about 2 cups of pesto sauce, which is twice the amount that you will need for the ravioli. Freeze the extra for a future meal, or serve it as a spread for crackers, layer it over goat cheese for a tantalizing dip, spread it on a sandwich, or toss a couple of tablespoons of the sauce with green beans for an excellent side dish.

Side Dish suggestion: To make a Tomato, Mozzarella, and Artichoke Salad, combine 1 pint of cherry tomatoes, halved, 6 to 8 ounces fresh mozzarella cheese, diced, 1 jar (6 ounces) marinated artichokes, drained and coarsely chopped, ½ teaspoon dried basil or 1½ teaspoons chopped fresh, ½ teaspoon dried oregano or 1½ teaspoons fresh, 1 tablespoon olive oil, and 1 teaspoon balsamic vinegar. (Optional: Add ½ cup pitted Greek olives instead of, or in addition to, the cheese.)

nine secrets to easy composting for scrambling families

Composting is one of Mother Nature's miracles—it turns organic waste (like grass clippings, raked leaves, veggie peelings, fruit rinds, and other produce leftovers) into rich soil. And it is one of the easiest things the average family can do to reduce their footprint and help the environment naturally. Just think, by turning everyday waste into compost, you can not only reduce the amount of garbage picked up curbside, hauled by fossil fuel–operated trucks and dumped into landfills, but you will also gain free, 100 percent natural, organic fertilizer for your garden, flowerbeds, and lawn. In fact, you will be harvesting what nature already does with organic waste.

While many of us have heard about the benefits of composting, we have hesitated starting this project. Why? Because we are afraid it is complicated, messy, and yet another household chore that is unlikely to get done.

But in reality, there are easy ways to get started, and the benefits are vast. Here are some tips for composting simply without the mess and fuss.

1. **Start small.** One of the most common mistakes of any gardening project is to get overambitious, and then stare at a half complete project for months, drenched in guilt. You can simply start with a plastic bin or a designated corner where you dump organic refuse. As you enjoy the results you can expand to a larger area.

2. **Pick a convenient location.** If your compost pile is far from your kitchen or your garden, you will be unlikely to visit it when the weather is cold or rainy. You can creatively "beautify" your compost pile by using dark green or black colors to camouflage or having your kids paint the container bright colors. You don't really even need a "bin." You can simply make a pile of leaves in the corner of the yard and add material to it. Keep a plastic bin (with a tight-fitting lid, of course) under your sink for compostable kitchen waste and add it to your bin (or pile) when it's full.

3. **Stay with "brown" and "green" materials.** Brown materials, as the name implies, are dried pine needles, leaves, and dead plants. Green materials are "wet" fresh grass clippings and kitchen waste, such as vegetable peels, orange peels, watermelon rinds, egg shells (without egg contents), and coffee grounds (with filter paper). You can even add shredded newspaper and brown paper if you're

(continued)

feeling adventurous. Many experts recommend an ideal mix of two parts brown to one green, but in reality such suggestions just accelerate the process. Any combination will work so don't sweat it.

4. **Avoid adding meats, oils, and fruits.** While Mother Nature eventually breaks down anything, these materials are also likely to attract rodents and slow down the overall composting process.

5. **Keep things moist.** Water is needed to attract worms, bacteria, and fungi. If you live in a dry area or have dry seasons you can water with a hose and then place plastic covers on top to conserve the water and heat.

6. **Mixing is optional.** Contrary to many guides, turning your compost pile is not necessary—it merely speeds things up. When you are in the mood to marvel at the magic of earth's re-creation, take out a shovel and dig in.

7. **Compost season.** While you can and should compost year-round, compost will develop more quickly during the warm growing season when your garden and lawn is at its peak. So, don't worry if you seem to be adding material every day or two during the spring and summer because nature will also have the composting process on overdrive.

8. **Compost indoors with a worm bin.** While this may seem strange and even a bit gross, worm bins take little space and are very convenient, especially if you live in an apartment. And you will get lots of "cool parent" points!

9. **Finally (after 6 to 12 months) you can enjoy the "fruits" of your labor!** Sprinkle your compost on your lawn and garden, once it turns into dark and sweet-smelling dirt, and enjoy the beautiful flowers, vegetables, and fruits that your own rich soil will inspire.

This is a fabulous one-pot dish that has everything you need for a nutritious weeknight meal, especially flavor! Anne Berube, a self-described "Scramble devotee," learned this recipe from a roommate and invited me to share it with other Scramble fans. The shrimp can also be left out for a vegetarian version, or replaced with 1 can of garbanzo beans or 1½ cups of cashews. Serve it with Honey-Glazed Carrots.

tortellini with shrimp and broccoli pesto

Prep + Cook = 25 minutes

8 servings

Nutritional Information per serving (% based upon daily values): Calories 230, Total Fat 5g, 8%, Saturated Fat 2g, 10%, Cholesterol 110mg, 37%, Sodium 400mg, 17%, Total Carbohydrate 26g, 9%, Dietary Fiber 3g, 12%, Sugar 3g, Protein 19g

Nutritional Information per serving with side dish (% based upon daily values) ¼ of carrots: Calories: 296; Total Fat: 7g, 10%; Saturated Fat: 3g, 14%; Cholesterol: 113mg, 38%; Sodium: 479mg, 20%; Total Carbohydrate: 40g, 14%; Dietary Fiber: 6g, 24%; Sugar: 11g; Protein: 20g

1 package (12 ounces) mushroom or cheese tortellini

1 pound fresh or frozen broccoli spears or florets

1 pound medium cooked or uncooked shrimp, peeled, deveined, tails removed

1 pint grape tomatoes, halved

6 ounces refrigerated pesto sauce (Cibo brand is a great choice) (or make your own—see page 128)

¼ teaspoon salt, or to taste

⅛ teaspoon black pepper, or to taste

In a large pot, cook the tortellini according to the package directions. (Meanwhile, start the carrots, if you are serving them.) Add the broccoli to the water with the tortellini 2 to 3 minutes before the tortellini is done. Then add the shrimp if it is uncooked (if it is already cooked, add the shrimp 1 minute later). Return the water to a boil and cook it for 2 to 3 more minutes, then drain the tortellini, broccoli, and shrimp.

While the tortellini is cooking, put the halved tomatoes in the bottom of a large pasta bowl, preferably a metal one to retain the heat. Add the drained tortellini, broccoli, and shrimp and toss with the pesto sauce. Season with salt and black pepper to taste before serving.

Scramble Flavor Booster: Stir ¼ teaspoon crushed red pepper flakes into the pasta with the pesto sauce.

Side Dish suggestion: To make Honey-Glazed Carrots, heat 1 tablespoon butter in a large heavy skillet over medium heat. Add 1 pound sliced carrots and 1 to 2 teaspoons honey, and stir to coat the carrots with the butter and honey. Sauté the carrots, stirring occasionally, for 8 to 10 minutes until they are tender and slightly browned. If the carrots are getting too brown, reduce the heat. Season the carrots with up to ⅛ teaspoon salt before serving, if desired.

While most tuna casserole recipes might make you think of colder weather, this one, from Scramble subscriber and recipe tester Debbie Firestone, is just right for summer when you can take advantage of fresh zucchini and tomatoes. This casserole can also be cooked in the microwave oven to save time (directions below). For a meatless version, leave out the tuna or replace it with sliced mushrooms. Serve it with warm bread sticks (Pillsbury has a good low-fat version) and diced honeydew melon or cantaloupe.

light tuna casserole
with zucchini and tomatoes

Prep (25 minutes) + Cook (10–30 minutes)

6 servings

Nutritional Information per serving (% based upon daily values): Calories 300, Total Fat 11g, 17%, Saturated Fat 5g, 25%, Cholesterol 75mg, 25%, Sodium 520mg, 22%, Total Carbohydrate 32g, 11%, Dietary Fiber 2g, 8%, Sugar 4g, Protein 18g

Nutritional Information per serving with side dish (% based upon daily values) 1 baked breadstick; 1 cup melon: Calories: 424; Total Fat: 13g, 19%; Saturated Fat: 6g, 29%; Cholesterol: 75mg, 25%; Sodium: 731 mg, 31%; Total Carbohydrate: 58g, 19%; Dietary Fiber: 4g, 15%; Sugar: 18g; Protein: 21g

1 package (8 ounces) wide egg noodles

⅓ cup nonfat sour cream

2 tablespoons reduced-fat mayonnaise

½ teaspoon salt

½ teaspoon dried dill or 1½ teaspoons minced fresh

1 can (6 ounces) chunk light tuna, drained and flaked (or use 1 cup sliced mushrooms)

½ cup finely chopped celery (about 2 stalks)

1 medium zucchini, quartered lengthwise and thinly sliced

1 cup shredded Cheddar cheese

1 large tomato, diced

Cook the noodles according to package directions until al dente, and drain them. Spray a 2-quart casserole with nonstick cooking spray. Preheat the oven to 350 degrees (unless you plan to cook it in the microwave oven).

In a small bowl, combine the sour cream, mayonnaise, salt, and dill. In a larger bowl, combine the noodles, tuna, celery, and zucchini. Add the sour cream sauce and stir it well. Transfer it to the baking dish.

Bake it for 25 minutes, uncovered, then remove the casserole from the oven, top it with the cheese and tomato, and bake it for 5 minutes more. (For a crispier top, broil it, rather than bake it, for the final 5 minutes.) (Meanwhile, prepare the bread sticks and melon, if you are serving them.)

Microwave directions: Top the casserole dish with a paper towel and cook it on high heat for 6 to 8 minutes until it is heated through. Top it with the cheese and tomato and cook it, loosely covered, for about 3 more minutes until the cheese is melted.

Scramble Flavor Booster: Use fresh dill—it's delicious!

Side Dish suggestion: Serve it with 1 honeydew melon or cantaloupe, peeled and diced. If the melon needs extra flavor, sprinkle it with 1 to 2 teaspoons superfine sugar and the juice of ¼ lemon or lime.

If you love vegetables as much as I do, this recipe is for you. The sauce gets even better with age, so you can make it on the weekend and serve it during the week, or freeze it and defrost it for a busy night. Turn on some good music and enjoy a glass of red wine (you can even splash half a glass into the simmering sauce) while you dice the vegetables. Serve it with a French baguette.

rotini with italian vegetables

Prep (15 minutes) +
Cook (30 minutes)

8 servings

Nutritional Information per serving (% based upon daily values): Calories 350, Total Fat 10g, 15%, Saturated Fat 2g, 10%, Cholesterol 5mg, 2%, Sodium 420mg, 18%, Total Carbohydrate 57g, 19%, Dietary Fiber 6g, 24%, Sugar 10g, Protein 12g

Nutritional Information per serving with side dish (% based upon daily values) ⅛ baguette: Calories: 500; Total Fat: 11.5g, 17%; Saturated Fat: 2g, 10%; Cholesterol: 10mg, 4%; Sodium: 750mg, 32%; Total Carbohydrate: 87g, 29%; Dietary Fiber: 7g, 28%; Sugar: 11g; Protein 18g

¼ cup olive oil

1 red or yellow onion, diced

1½ teaspoons minced garlic (about 3 cloves)

1 red bell pepper, diced

1 zucchini, quartered lengthwise and sliced

1 small to medium eggplant, cut into ½-inch pieces

¼–½ teaspoon kosher salt, to taste

¼ teaspoon black pepper, or to taste

1½ teaspoons dried basil or 1 tablespoon fresh

1½ teaspoons dried oregano or 1 tablespoon fresh

1 can (28 ounces) crushed tomatoes

1 tablespoon brown sugar

1 package (16 ounces) tri-color rotini (spiral) pasta

½ cup shredded Parmesan cheese for serving, or to taste

In a large Dutch oven or stockpot, heat the oil over medium heat. Add the onions and garlic, and cook them for about 3 minutes until the onions start to soften. As you chop them, add the bell pepper and zucchini, stirring gently with each addition. Chop and add the eggplant, stirring gently, but try to keep the eggplant from touching the bottom of the pot, so it doesn't scorch.

Add the salt, pepper, basil, oregano, tomatoes, and sugar and stir gently. Bring the liquid to a boil, cover the pot, reduce the heat to a simmer, and continue cooking the sauce, stirring occasionally, for about 30 minutes, until the eggplant is very tender and dark.

Meanwhile, cook the pasta according to the package directions (unless you plan to refrigerate or freeze the sauce for later). When the pasta is cooked and drained, combine it with the sauce. Serve it hot, topped with the cheese.

Scramble Flavor Booster: Serve it at the table with hot pepper sauce, such as Tabasco.

Tip: Red bell peppers are actually mature green peppers (they become red and sweet as they ripen). They cost more because they take longer to mature.

Slow Cooker directions: In a skillet, cook the onions and garlic in the oil as directed above. Add the contents of the skillet along with the rest of the vegetables and spices to the slow cooker. Cook on High for 2 to 3 hours or on Low for 4 to 6 hours. Serve over pasta, topped with the cheese.

Who wants to cook risotto the traditional way on a busy night? It's just too time-consuming! Baking it instead makes it easy to enjoy risotto any night of the week. In this version the squash melts into the risotto so your kids won't even know it's there. Our son, Solomon, gobbled it up. Serve it with whole grain bread and a Chopped Cucumber and Avocado Salad (page 113).

creamy baked risotto with secret squash

Prep (15 minutes) + Cook (20 minutes)

4 servings

Nutritional Information per serving (% based upon daily values): Calories 320, Total Fat 13g, 20%, Saturated Fat 4g, 20%, Cholesterol 15mg, 5%, Sodium 300mg, 14%, Total Carbohydrate 43g, 14%, Dietary Fiber 2g, 8%, Sugar 2g, Protein 11g

Nutritional Information per serving with side dish (% based upon daily values) 1 slice bread; 1 cup salad: Calories: 560; Total Fat: 17g, 25%; Saturated Fat: 4g, 20%; Cholesterol: 15mg, 5%; Sodium: 650mg, 30%; Total Carbohydrate: 88g, 29%; Dietary Fiber: 6g, 24%; Sugar: 5g; Protein: 20g

2 tablespoons olive oil

1 small yellow onion, finely diced

1 cup Arborio rice

½ yellow squash, grated (1 cup total) (the kind that looks like yellow zucchini, no need to peel it)

1 can (15 ounces) reduced-sodium chicken or vegetable broth

¾ cup grated Parmesan cheese

Preheat the oven to 400 degrees. Spray a medium ovenproof heavy pot or a small Dutch oven with nonstick cooking spray, then add the oil and heat it over medium heat. Add the onions and sauté them for 3 to 4 minutes until they are translucent. Add the rice, stirring to coat with the oil, then add the squash, and cook it for about 1 minute. Add the broth and bring it to a simmer, raising the heat, if necessary. Stir in half the cheese, and sprinkle the remaining cheese on top.

Cover the pot and put it in the center of the oven. Bake it for 20 to 25 minutes until the rice is tender to the bite and the liquid is absorbed. (Meanwhile, prepare the salad.) Serve it immediately.

Scramble Flavor Booster: Use freshly grated aged Parmesan cheese and season it with freshly ground black pepper.

Tip: Grating vegetables like squash is a great job for children to help with. My twelve-year-old son, Solomon, still loves it when I find excuses for him to use the grater, and he still has all ten fingers.

how to keep fruits and veggies fresh and flavorful

Scramble recipes feature seasonal fruits and vegetables whenever possible. But how can you make sure that this precious produce does not spoil before you can enjoy it?

First, make sure you choose where to store your produce to give it the longest life possible:

- Fruits and vegetables that keep best in the refrigerator: Apples (if keeping for more than one week), berries, cherries, grapes, most vegetables (with the exception of those listed below that should be stored at room temperature), and any cut fruits or vegetables.

- Fruits that can be ripened on the counter first and then stored in the refrigerator: Avocados, bananas, kiwis, nectarines, peaches, pears, plums.

- Fruits and vegetables that are best stored at room temperature (out of direct sunlight): Apples (for less than a week), grapefruits, lemons, limes, oranges, mangoes, pineapple, pomegranates, and watermelon. Basil (with stems or roots in water), cucumbers, onions, garlic, peppers, potatoes (regular and sweet), winter squash, and tomatoes.

Next, use these tips on how best to store your fruits and vegetables:

- To prolong their shelf life, wait to wash fruits and vegetables until just before you plan to use them.

- Ripe fruits and vegetables should be kept in a dark, aerated place, such as a perforated (not sealed) plastic bag or a wide or vented bowl.

- Store potatoes away from light to avoid sprouting.

- Store fruits and vegetables separately. Fruits release ethylene, which speeds the ripening process of vegetables. Also, fruits easily pick up the flavors of nearby veggies so it is best to use separate drawers in your refrigerator for fruits and vegetables.

- Separate any bruised or rotten fruit from the others immediately to avoid spoiling nearby produce.

Finally, decide on *when* you will use each item:

- Depending on where you live and shop, some fresh items only last a few days after purchase, especially if they have traveled long distances to get to your supermarket. So save locally grown items for later in the week.

- When deciding which of your weekly Scramble meals to make first, it may be best to start with recipes that use ingredients which spoil the quickest, such as mushrooms, green leafy vegetables, and fresh corn.

I love polenta, an Italian comfort food made from cornmeal, because it tastes so rich and decadent yet it is low in fat. Usually I sauté or bake prepared polenta (sold in tubes), but this time I tried pan-frying and then broiling it, which gave it an irresistible texture, firm on the outside and creamy on the inside. Serve it with Wilted Spinach with Mushrooms (page 21) and whole grain bread.

pan-fried polenta with summer vegetables

Prep + Cook = 25 minutes

8 servings

Nutritional Information per serving (% based upon daily values): Calories 231, Total Fat 12g, 18%, Saturated Fat 3g, 14.5%, Cholesterol 7.5mg, 2.5%, Sodium 535mg, 22%, Total Carbohydrate 25.5g, 8%, Dietary Fiber 2.5g, 10.5%, Sugar 4.5g, Protein 7g

Nutritional Information per serving with side dish (% based upon daily values) $\frac{1}{6}$ of spinach and mushrooms; 1 slice bread: Calories: 398; Total Fat: 17g, 25%; Saturated Fat: 4g, 16%; Cholesterol: 8mg, 3%; Sodium: 810mg, 34%; Total Carbohydrate: 55g, 18%; Dietary Fiber: 9g, 35%; Sugar: 10g; Protein: 13g

$\frac{1}{4}$ cup plus 1 tablespoon olive oil

$1\frac{1}{2}$ tubes (36 ounces total) prepared polenta, sliced into $\frac{1}{2}$-inch-thick circular slices

1 yellow onion, diced

1 zucchini, diced

6 sun-dried tomatoes, dry or marinated, sliced

1 cup tomato sauce

$\frac{1}{4}$ cup fresh oregano and/or parsley, chopped

1 cup shredded mozzarella or crumbled Gorgonzola cheese

Preheat the broiler and set the broiling rack about 5 inches from the heat source. (If you are making the spinach and mushrooms, start them now.) In a large nonstick skillet or an electric frying pan, heat $\frac{1}{4}$ cup oil over medium to medium-high heat. Add the polenta slices and let them get crispy and lightly browned, then flip and repeat on the other side (about 5 minutes per side).

Meanwhile, in a heavy skillet, heat 1 tablespoon oil over medium heat and sauté the onions and zucchini until they are tender, about 5 minutes. Add the sun-dried tomatoes, tomato sauce, and herbs and continue to cook it, stirring occasionally, for about 5 more minutes.

Spray a 9 × 13-inch rectangular baking pan, preferably metal, with nonstick cooking spray. When the polenta is done, transfer the slices to the pan and top them evenly with the vegetable and tomato sauce mixture. Top everything with the cheese, and broil it for 3 to 4 minutes until the cheese is melted and browned in spots. Allow it to cool for a few minutes before serving.

Scramble Flavor Booster: Add up to ½ teaspoon crushed red pepper flakes to the sauce when you add the tomatoes, and use the Gorgonzola cheese.

Tip: Store mushrooms in a paper bag in the refrigerator until you are ready to use them.

This summery Middle-Eastern dish was suggested by longtime Scramble subscriber Diana Molavi of Maryland, who needed to find more ways to use the mint that threatened to take over her garden. We like to serve it over whole wheat couscous.

divine eggplant and chickpeas with mint

Prep + Cook = 30 minutes

6 servings

Nutritional Information per serving (% based upon daily values): Calories 410, Total Fat 16g, 25%, Saturated Fat 5g, 26%, Cholesterol 20mg, 7%, Sodium 620mg, 26%, Total Carbohydrate 64g, 21%, Dietary Fiber 13g, 52%, Sugar 11g, Protein 16g

Nutritional Information per serving with side dish (% based upon daily values) ½ cup whole wheat couscous: Calories: 580; Total Fat: 21g, 33%; Saturated Fat: 6g, 29%; Cholesterol: 20mg, 7%; Sodium: 620mg, 26%; Total Carbohydrate: 101g, 33%; Dietary Fiber: 19g, 76%; Sugar: 12g; Protein: 23g

2 tablespoons olive oil

1 medium eggplant, peeled and diced

½ teaspoon ground cumin

½ teaspoon paprika

¼ teaspoon salt

1 can (15 ounces) chickpeas (garbanzo beans), drained and rinsed

1 can (28 ounces) diced tomatoes with their liquid

⅓ cup fresh mint and/or parsley, chopped

1 cup crumbled feta cheese for serving (optional)

In a large skillet or medium stockpot, heat the oil over medium-high heat. Add the eggplant, cumin, paprika, and salt, and sauté it until the eggplant starts to get tender, stirring occasionally, about 5 minutes.

Add the chickpeas and tomatoes and simmer it for about 10 more minutes, stirring occasionally, until the eggplant is very tender. (Meanwhile, make the couscous, if you are serving it.) Stir in the herbs. Serve immediately, over couscous, topped with the cheese (optional). Or refrigerate it for up to 3 days, or freeze it for up to 3 months.

Scramble Flavor Booster: Double the cumin and paprika and use the optional feta cheese.

Tip: To peel an eggplant with ease, slice off the ends of the eggplant first so your peeler doesn't slip.

Costa Ricans eat a version of this dish, called Gallo Pinto (which translates as painted rooster), with nearly every meal, but it's especially typical to eat it for breakfast! The curry and lime give it a Caribbean flare (Costa Rica borders the Caribbean Sea), and the fresh cilantro gives it a bright summery flavor. For even more Caribbean flavor, cook the rice in half water and half coconut milk. Serve it with warm whole wheat tortillas, and with steamed corn sprinkled with fresh lime juice and chili powder.

costa rican black beans and rice

Prep + Cook =
25 minutes

6 servings

Nutritional
Information per
serving (% based
upon daily values):
Calories 228, Total
Fat 5g, 8%, Saturated
Fat 0.5g, 3.5%, Cho-
lesterol 0mg, 0%,
Sodium 296mg, 12%,
Total Carbohydrate
38g, 12.5%, Dietary
Fiber 4g, 16%, Sugar
1g, Protein 6g

Nutritional
Information per
serving with side dish
(% based upon daily
values) 1 whole
wheat tortilla; 1 ear
corn, 1/2 tsp. butter,
sprinkle of salt:
Calories: 444; Total
Fat: 10g, 15%; Satu-
rated Fat: 3g, 15%;
Cholesterol: 5mg,
2%; Sodium: 845mg,
35%; Total Carbohy-
drate: 78g, 27%;
Dietary Fiber: 8g,
31%; Sugar: 7g;
Protein: 12g

1 cup white rice

2 tablespoons olive oil

1 green bell pepper, finely diced

1 small yellow or white onion, finely diced

1½ teaspoons minced garlic (about 3 cloves)

1 teaspoon ground cumin

½ teaspoon curry powder

1 can (15 ounces) black beans with their liquid

2 tablespoons Worcestershire sauce (or use Salsa Lizano if you have it)

2 tablespoons salsa (optional)

½ cup fresh cilantro leaves (optional)

1 lime, cut into wedges for serving (optional)

Cook the rice with 2 cups of water according to the package directions. (The rice can be made up to a day in advance.)

In a large skillet, heat the oil over medium heat, and sauté the bell peppers, onions, and garlic for about 5 minutes until they are fragrant and slightly tender. While they are cooking, stir in the cumin and curry powder. Add the beans and their liquid, the Worcestershire sauce, and salsa (optional) and bring to a boil. (Meanwhile, prepare the corn, if you are serving it.) Let the beans simmer for about 5 more minutes. Stir in the cooked rice and continue to cook it, stirring frequently, for about 3 more minutes until it is heated through. Stir in the cilantro leaves, if desired, and serve it with the lime wedges (optional).

Scramble Flavor Booster: Double the curry powder, use spicy salsa, and add 1 diced jalapeño pepper with the bell pepper.

This humble soup was originally made by Italian peasants who would usually have all these ingredients on hand. It's quick and healthy comfort food, and can be spiced up to your heart's content. Serve it with a loaf of whole grain bread, and with a Sliced Tomato, Basil, and Mozzarella Salad.

italian peasant soup (minestrone)

Prep (15 minutes) + Cook (25 minutes)

6 servings

Nutritional Information per serving (% based upon daily values): Calories 160, Total Fat 3g, 5%, Saturated Fat .5g, 3%, Cholesterol 0mg, 0%, Sodium 390mg, 16%, Total Carbohydrate 24g, 8%, Dietary Fiber 5g, 20%, Sugar 4g, Protein 8g

Nutritional Information per serving with side dish (% based upon daily values) 1 slice bread; $\frac{1}{4}$ of salad: Calories: 360; Total Fat: 11 g, 17%; Saturated Fat: 4g, 21%; Cholesterol: 20mg, 7%; Sodium: 750mg, 32%; Total Carbohydrate: 46g, 16%; Dietary Fiber: 8g, 32%; Sugar: 8g; Protein: 18g

1 tablespoon olive oil

1 small yellow onion, diced

2 celery stalks, sliced

2 large carrots, sliced

$\frac{1}{2}$ teaspoon minced garlic (about 1 clove)

$\frac{1}{2}$ teaspoon dried basil, or 1 tablespoon fresh chopped basil

$\frac{1}{2}$ teaspoon dried thyme or oregano, or $1\frac{1}{2}$ teaspoons fresh thyme or oregano

1 can (15 ounces) reduced-sodium chicken or vegetable broth

$2\frac{1}{4}$ cups water

1 can (15 ounces) canned cannellini or pinto beans, drained and rinsed

1 can (14 ounces) canned diced tomatoes with their liquid

$\frac{1}{8}$ teaspoon black pepper, or to taste

1 cup mezzi tubetti pasta (little tubes) or elbow macaroni (be sure to use a small pasta for this soup, as a large pasta will absorb all the liquid)

$\frac{1}{2}$ cup shredded Parmesan cheese, or to taste (optional)

In a Dutch oven or stockpot, heat the oil over medium heat. Add the onions, celery, and carrots and cook them, stirring occasionally, until the onions are tender, 5 to 7 minutes. (Cut some extra carrots and celery to serve with dinner, if desired.) Add the garlic, basil, and thyme or oregano (if you are using fresh herbs, stir them in a couple of minutes before the soup is finished cooking) and stir it for a minute until it is fragrant.

Add the broth, water, beans, tomatoes, and black pepper, and bring to a boil. Simmer it for 10 minutes, and then add the pasta. Continue to simmer it for 8 to 10 minutes, or until the pasta is tender, stirring occasionally.

Serve the soup in bowls, topped with the cheese, if desired, or refrigerate the soup for up to 1 day, or freeze it for up to 3 months.

Scramble Flavor Booster: Stir slivered fresh basil into the soup before serving, and serve it with hot pepper sauce, such as Tabasco, at the table.

Tip: For an even healthier and more colorful version, stir fresh baby spinach into the soup before serving.

Side Dish suggestion: To make the Sliced Tomato, Basil, and Mozzarella Salad, layer 2 sliced tomatoes with 8 ounces fresh sliced mozzarella and about 10 whole basil leaves and drizzle it with balsamic vinegar (about 1 teaspoon total). (For a lower-fat version, skip the mozzarella and sprinkle crumbled feta cheese or blue cheese on top of the sliced tomatoes instead.)

light and healthy lunches
to stay energized in the afternoons

Whether we spend our days at home or in an office, few of us like to be weighed down by a heavy lunch. In many countries, lunch is the biggest meal of the day, but often in those same regions, everything shuts down in the afternoon for a few hours so everybody can sleep off their feasts!

Just as at dinnertime, I like my lunches quick and healthy. Unlike dinners, I'm happy to eat the same lunch nearly every day—I generally favor vanilla yogurt with fresh or dried berries with whole grain cereal or granola on top, or a small portion of leftovers from the previous night's meal. Since I'm short on lunch ideas, I asked some of my friends and family to share their favorite lunches that are nutritious yet quick to prepare and portable.

Meals on a Roll

- Top fresh bread with vine-ripened tomato slices, mozzarella cheese, and fresh basil, or, top tomato slices with Cheddar or Swiss cheese and put it under the broiler.
- Mash half an avocado on wheat bread, and drizzle it with fresh lemon juice, salt, and pepper. Top with red pepper strips or cucumbers, if desired.
- Top half a bagel with hummus, sliced tomato, fresh basil, salt, and pepper.
- Layer sliced Cheddar cheese, turkey, and pesto sauce on whole grain bread.
- Fill a wheat tortilla with beans, cheese, and salsa and heat it in the microwave. Add baby spinach or other greens, if desired.
- Make a quesadilla with Cheddar cheese, sliced avocado, baby spinach, and salsa.

(continued)

- Layer spreadable herbed cheese, turkey or salami, field greens, and sliced tomato on wheat bread.
- Make a sandwich with natural peanut or other nut butter and sliced bananas or apples.
- Wrap grilled tofu and mango in fresh lettuce leaves.
- Fill a wheat pita pocket with hummus and cucumbers.
- Mix tuna with a light olive oil and lemon juice in lieu of mayo. Spoon it onto a whole wheat English muffin.
- Pile grilled chicken breast, Cheddar cheese, and pico de gallo in a whole wheat wrap.
- Melt Brie cheese on half of a French roll. Top with sliced peaches, apples, or fig jam.
- Layer spinach leaves, sliced red pepper, onion, and tomato in a whole wheat pita. Drizzle with lime juice for added flavor.
- Slice a Kaiser roll in half and spread with mustard. Top with ham and a pineapple ring.
- Wrap peanut butter, sliced banana, apples, and raisins in a tortilla.
- Fill a roll with sliced hard-boiled eggs, lettuce, tomato, and mustard.

Meals in a Bowl

- Mix a can of tuna with chopped raw vegetables and drizzle it with olive oil and vinegar.
- Eat chicken, tuna, or egg salad with endive leaves, celery, or pita chips as the "spoon."
- Top a green salad with pistachios, halved grapes or dried cranberries, crumbled Gorgonzola cheese, and balsamic vinaigrette dressing.
- Drizzle raisins, cashews, roasted chicken, and sliced avocado with olive oil and vinegar.
- Top Greek yogurt with fresh or frozen fruit, a teaspoon of your favorite nuts, and a tablespoon of granola or muesli (European cereal with oats and dried fruit).
- Top whole grain cereal with skim milk and fresh berries or sliced bananas.
- Top warm quinoa or oatmeal with skim milk, blueberries, and peaches.
- Mix cooked couscous or quinoa with chopped tomatoes, black beans, scallions, and feta cheese. Splash with lemon juice. Serve chilled.
- Mix whole grain pasta with sun-dried tomatoes and pine nuts. Drizzle with pesto sauce or goat cheese.
- Mix cooked wild rice with chopped green apple, raisins, and pecans. Add fresh lemon juice.
- Top rice with steamed broccoli, cashews or peanuts, and teriyaki sauce.
- Make a quick omelet or scrambled eggs with leftover veggies and a little cheese or meat such as prosciutto.
- Sauté a few shrimp with a little olive oil and garlic (or try preseasoned grilled shrimp from Gorton's Seafood).

The key ingredient in these crisp and cool wraps, sweet chili sauce, is a popular Thai seasoning sauce, which is getting easier to find in North American grocery stores as those flavors gain in popularity. If you can't find it, you can make your own by combining ¼ cup orange marmalade, 1 tablespoon rice vinegar, and ⅛ to ¼ teaspoon crushed red pepper flakes. Serve it with steamed brown or white rice and sliced mangoes.

thai sweet-and-sour chicken wraps

Prep + Cook =
20 minutes

4 servings

Nutritional Information per serving (% based upon daily values): Calories 146, Total Fat 1.5g, 2%, Saturated Fat 0.5g, 1.5%, Cholesterol 49.5mg, 16.5%, Sodium 202mg, 8.5%, Total Carbohydrate 11g, 3.5%, Dietary Fiber 1.5g, 5%, Sugar 9g, Protein 22.5g

Nutritional Information per serving with side dish (% based upon daily values) ¾ cup brown rice; ½ mango: Calories: 375; Total Fat: 3g, 4%; Saturated Fat: 2g, 7%; Cholesterol: 50mg, 17%; Sodium: 211mg, 10%; Total Carbohydrate: 63g, 17%; Dietary Fiber: 7g, 23%; Sugar: 26g; Protein: 27g

1 pound boneless, skinless chicken breasts

¼ cup Asian sweet chili sauce (also called mae ploy) or make your own (see headnote)

2 limes (2 tablespoons juice, plus 4 lime wedges)

¼–½ cup fresh cilantro or mint, coarsely chopped (optional)

1 red bell pepper, seeded and thinly sliced

2 scallions, thinly sliced

1 head Boston or other wide-leaf lettuce, leaves separated

(Start the rice first, if you are making it.) Put the chicken in a microwave-safe dish with a lid. Partially cover it and microwave it on high until the chicken is just cooked through, 6 to 8 minutes, turning it once or twice. Drain the chicken. (Alternatively, to cook the chicken on the stove, cut the chicken breasts in half crosswise and sauté them in a skillet over medium heat in 1 tablespoon olive oil until they are cooked through, 8 to 10 minutes total.)

Cut the chicken crosswise, and using two forks, shred the chicken into bite-size pieces. Toss it with the chili sauce and lime juice, and the cilantro or mint (optional).

Put the chicken, bell peppers, scallions, and lettuce in serving bowls, and have each family member wrap the chicken and vegetables in the lettuce. Squeeze additional lime juice over the fillings before wrapping, if desired. Use 2 lettuce leaves for each wrap to prevent the sauce from dripping through torn lettuce.

Scramble Flavor Booster: Serve it with Vietnamese chili-garlic sauce or other hot sauce.

Tip: To make slicing scallions easy, snip the scallions with a clean, sharp pair of kitchen scissors.

Honestly, this satisfying sandwich is only a distant cousin of a true Greek souvlaki, but I couldn't think of a more descriptive name. Whatever you call it, our son, Solomon, called it delicious and polished it off. Serve it with a Greek Salad.

grilled quicki souvlaki sandwich

Prep + Cook =
30 minutes

4 servings

Nutritional Information per serving (with 2 tbsp. feta cheese) (% based upon daily values): Calories 450, Total Fat 23g, 35%, Saturated Fat 6g, 30%, Cholesterol 50mg, 17%, Sodium 1,310mg, 55%, Total Carbohydrate 42g, 14%, Dietary Fiber 6g, 24%, Sugar 3g, Protein 23g

Nutritional Information per serving with side dish (% based upon daily values) 2 tbsp. feta cheese; 1½ cups Greek salad: Calories: 530; Total Fat: 28g, 43%; Saturated Fat: 8g, 40%; Cholesterol: 60mg, 20%; Sodium: 1,450mg, 61%; Total Carbohydrate: 49g, 16%; Dietary Fiber: 7g, 28%; Sugar: 7g; Protein: 26g

3 tablespoons olive oil

1 yellow onion, halved and thinly sliced

1 green, red, or orange bell pepper, thinly sliced

½ teaspoon minced garlic (about 1 clove)

¼ teaspoon kosher salt

12 ounces sweet Italian-style precooked turkey or chicken sausage or vegetarian sausage, cut most of the way through, lengthwise

4 soft whole wheat or white pita pockets (get the softest and freshest type you can find)

½ cup crumbled feta cheese for serving (optional)

Preheat the grill to medium-high heat. Meanwhile, in a large heavy skillet, heat 1 tablespoon oil over medium heat and sauté the onions and bell peppers until they are soft and well browned, about 15 minutes total, stirring occasionally. (Meanwhile, prepare the salad, if you are serving it.) If they are getting too browned, reduce the heat. Remove them from the heat once they are soft and browned.

In a small bowl, combine 2 tablespoons olive oil, the garlic, and the salt and set aside.

Grill the sausages for 8 to 10 minutes until they are light to medium brown, flipping them once. Meanwhile, brush the olive oil mixture onto both outer sides of the pita pockets (don't cut them), stacking them as you go so they can share their oil. Next, lay the pita pockets on the grill for about 3 minutes per side, flipping once, until they start to puff up (if they are fresh enough) and are lightly browned in spots. Watch them carefully so they don't burn.

Fold one pita pocket around each sausage, and top the sausage with the onions and bell peppers, and feta cheese (optional).

Scramble Flavor Booster: Add 1 teaspoon fresh oregano to the peppers and onions while they are cooking. Serve the sandwiches with spicy mustard.

Side Dish suggestion: To make a Greek Salad, combine 2 large tomatoes, chopped, 2 cucumbers, peeled and diced, and ½ to 1 cup feta cheese (use real Greek feta in brine, if possible). Add ¼ to ½ cup sliced red onion, if desired. Toss it with 1 tablespoon olive oil and 1 teaspoon red wine vinegar. Add 2 tablespoons chopped fresh oregano or 1 to 2 teaspoons dried oregano, and black pepper to taste.

This fresh chicken salad has just the right combination of creaminess, sweetness, and crunch. Another great option is to double the sauce and stir in one pound of cooked radiatore or ziti pasta for a more filling meal. Try it on toasted wheat bread with a Sliced Tomato Salad.

curried chicken salad with grapes

Prep + Cook = 25 minutes + up to 48 hours to chill (optional)

6 servings

Nutritional Information per serving (% based upon daily values): Calories 180, Total Fat 4g, 6%, Saturated Fat 0.5g, 3%, Cholesterol 45mg, 15%, Sodium 105mg, 4%, Total Carbohydrate 15g, 5%, Dietary Fiber 1g, 4%, Sugar 11g, Protein 20g

Nutritional Information per serving with side dish (% based upon daily values) $\frac{1}{2}$ tomato, 1 tsp. onion, 1 tsp. feta cheese, $\frac{1}{2}$ tsp. dressing: Calories: 438; Total Fat: 12g, 17%; Saturated Fat: 3g, 12%; Cholesterol: 48mg, 16%; Sodium: 732mg, 30%; Total Carbohydrate: 61g, 20%; Dietary Fiber: 8g, 31%; Sugar: 16g; Protein: 29g

1–1$\frac{1}{2}$ pounds boneless, skinless chicken breasts

$\frac{1}{2}$ cup plain nonfat yogurt

$\frac{1}{4}$ cup reduced-fat mayonnaise

$\frac{1}{2}$ lemon, juice only (about 2 tablespoons)

2 tablespoons mango chutney or apricot jam

2 to 3 teaspoons curry powder, to taste

2 large celery stalks, finely diced

1 cup seedless red grapes, halved, or use chopped apple, mango, or pineapple

$\frac{1}{4}$ cup shelled and unsalted pistachio nuts, slivered almonds, or coarsely chopped pecans

Trim any excess fat from the chicken. Place the chicken in a large skillet and add just enough water to cover it. Bring the water to a boil over high heat, reduce the heat to a simmer, cover, and poach the chicken (steaming it lightly in the boiling water) for 7 to 10 minutes, until it is just cooked through; check by cutting into the thickest piece of chicken to make sure it is no longer pink. (Meanwhile, make the tomato salad.) Rinse the chicken under cold water to cool it. Shred it using 2 forks or chop it into $\frac{1}{2}$-inch pieces.

In a large bowl, combine the yogurt, mayonnaise, lemon juice, chutney or jam, and curry powder. Stir in the shredded chicken, celery, grapes, and nuts. Serve it immediately, or chill it for up to 48 hours.

Side Dish suggestion: To make a Sliced Tomato Salad, place 2 to 3 sliced tomatoes on a serving plate, and top them with $\frac{1}{8}$ to $\frac{1}{4}$ of a yellow onion, minced ($\frac{1}{4}$ to $\frac{1}{2}$ cup), and 1 to 2 tablespoons crumbled feta cheese, and drizzle everything with 1 to 3 teaspoons vinaigrette dressing, or to taste. (You can also add chopped fresh basil to the salad).

This is a summery meal with cooling cucumbers and creamy yogurt. For a vegetarian alternative, use chickpeas in the sandwiches instead of the chicken. Serve it with Greek-Style Green Beans. (You can also peel, slice, and serve the half cucumber that wasn't used in the recipe).

greek chicken sandwiches with yogurt-cucumber sauce

Prep + Cook = 30 minutes

4 servings

Nutritional Information per serving (% based upon daily values): Calories 370, Fat 6g, 9%, Saturated Fat 1g, 5%, Cholesterol 65mg, 22%, Sodium 450mg, 19%, Total Carbohydrate 42g, 14%, Dietary Fiber 2g, 8%, Sugar 8g, Protein 36g

Nutritional Information per serving with side dish (% based upon daily values) 1 cup prepared green beans: Calories: 452; Total Fat 10g, 16%; Saturated Fat: 2g, 9%; Cholesterol: 68mg, 23%; Sodium: 630mg, 26%; Total Carbohydrate: 52g, 17%; Dietary Fiber: 6g, 24%; Sugar: 10g; Protein: 39g

1 pound boneless, skinless chicken breasts
    (or use 1 can [15 ounces] garbanzo beans, drained)

1 tablespoon olive oil

¼ teaspoon salt, or to taste

⅛ teaspoon black pepper, or to taste

1 cup nonfat plain yogurt

1 teaspoon minced garlic (about 2 cloves)

2 teaspoons fresh mint, oregano, or dill, chopped

½ teaspoon honey

½ cucumber, peeled and finely diced or shredded (1 cup total)

4 whole wheat or white pita pockets

1 tomato, diced

(If you are making the green beans, start them first.) Cut the chicken into ½-inch-wide strips and toss it with the oil, salt, and pepper. (If using garbanzo beans, warm them in the microwave or on the stovetop with the oil, and omit the salt.)

Heat a large heavy skillet over medium heat. Cook the chicken until it is browned on the outside and no longer pink in the middle, turning occasionally, 5 to 7 minutes.

Meanwhile, in a medium serving bowl, combine the yogurt, garlic, mint, oregano or dill, honey, and cucumber.

Warm the pita in the microwave or conventional oven (10 to 15 minutes at 300 degrees, wrapped in foil) to soften it.

Assemble the sandwiches at the table by stuffing or wrapping the chicken (or garbanzo beans) in the pita pockets and topping it with the yogurt sauce and tomato. Serve the sandwiches warm.

Scramble Flavor Booster: Use lots of fresh herbs in the yogurt sauce, and season the chicken with freshly ground black pepper after cooking it.

Tip: If your market carries a range of yogurts, look for Greek yogurt, such as Fage, which has a much richer and smoother taste and texture than American yogurts.

Side Dish suggestion: To make Greek-Style Green Beans, steam 1 pound trimmed green beans for 7 to 10 minutes to desired tenderness. Drain and toss the cooked beans with 1 tablespoon olive oil, 1 teaspoon red wine vinegar, ¼ teaspoon salt, ⅛ teaspoon black pepper, and 1 teaspoon dried or 1 tablespoon fresh oregano or dill. Top it with 1 to 2 tablespoons crumbled feta cheese.

Who doesn't love sizzling fajitas? Part of their appeal is that each family member can design their own, so everyone leaves the table happy. The marinated meat makes these fajitas especially flavorful. Serve the fajitas with guacamole and carrots.

chicken or steak fajitas

Prep + Cook =
30 minutes

8 servings

Nutritional Information per serving (with 1 tbsp. sour cream, 2 tsp. salsa, 1 tbsp. Cheddar, and whole wheat tortilla) (% based upon daily values): Calories 380, Total Fat 12g, 18%, Saturated Fat 3g, 15%, Cholesterol 75mg, 25%, Sodium 670mg, 28%, Total Carbohydrate 34g, 11%, Dietary Fiber 4g, 16%, Sugar 5g, Protein 33g

Nutritional Information per serving with side dish (% based upon daily values) ¼ cup guacamole; ½ cup carrots: Calories: 440; Total Fat: 10g, 15%; Saturated Fat 1.5g, 8%; Cholesterol: 65mg, 22%; Sodium: 567mg, 24%; Total Carbohydrate: 50g, 17%; Dietary Fiber: 6g, 23%; Sugar: 11g; Protein: 37.5g

1 to 2 limes, juice only (about ¼ cup)

5 tablespoons olive oil

¼–½ teaspoon salt, to taste

½ teaspoon ground cumin

½ teaspoon chili powder

¼ teaspoon garlic powder

2 pounds boneless, skinless chicken breasts or boneless steak, sliced into thin strips (or use black beans)

1 large yellow onion, halved and thinly sliced

2 green or red bell peppers, cored and thinly sliced

8 medium (soft taco-size) whole wheat or flour tortillas

1–2 avocados, halved, pitted and sliced for serving (or use guacamole) (optional)

1 cup nonfat sour cream for serving (optional)

1 cup salsa for serving (optional)

1 cup shredded Cheddar cheese for serving (optional)

In a small bowl or measuring cup, combine the lime juice, 2 tablespoons oil, salt, cumin, chili powder, and garlic powder. In a resealable plastic bag or flat dish with sides, combine the meat with the marinade, and set it aside. (You can prepare the meat for this recipe up to 24 hours in advance and refrigerate it until you are ready to cook, so it has more time to absorb the marinade's flavor.)

While the meat is marinating, heat 2 tablespoons oil in a large heavy skillet over medium-high heat. Sauté the onions and bell peppers until they are softened and lightly browned, stirring occasionally, about 15 minutes. Transfer them to a serving bowl.

When the vegetables have been cooking about 5 minutes, heat the remaining oil in a large nonstick skillet over medium heat. (The meat can also be grilled.) Drain and transfer the meat to the skillet, and discard the marinade. Cook the meat, turning occasionally, until it is cooked through, about 10 minutes. (Meanwhile, make the guacamole, if you are serving it.)

Warm the tortillas in the microwave. Assemble the fajitas at the table, wrapping the meat or beans, onions and peppers, and optional fillings in the tortillas.

Scramble Flavor Booster: Serve the fajitas with fresh chopped jalapeño or Serrano chilies and/or fresh cilantro.

Tip: If you prefer a meatless version, you can combine 2 cans of drained and rinsed black beans with the marinade ingredients (omitting the salt), heat them on the stovetop over medium heat until heated through, and assemble the fajitas using the beans instead of the meat.

Side Dish suggestion: To make fresh guacamole, mash the flesh of 2 to 3 avocados with about 1 tablespoon fresh lime (or lemon) juice and ¼ to ½ lime or lemon. Add ¼ teaspoon salt and ¼ teaspoon garlic powder, or to taste. To jazz up your guacamole, try adding 1 tablespoon minced onions and/or cilantro and/or 1 teaspoon minced hot peppers. To keep the guacamole from turning brown, put the avocado pit in the center of it until you are ready to serve it. Serve it with baby carrots or carrot sticks.

At last, turkey burgers that are sweet and juicy (rather than dry and bland), and so quick to make. This recipe can easily be doubled for bigger families or appetites, and the burgers can also be cooked on the grill. Serve them topped with iceberg lettuce, sliced tomato, ketchup, and mustard, and with sweet potato fries and watermelon wedges.

ultimate juicy turkey burgers

Prep + Cook =
25 minutes

4 servings

Nutritional
Information per
serving (burgers only)
(% based upon daily
values):
Calories 230, Total
Fat 12g, 18% Saturated Fat 2.5g, 18%,
Cholesterol 70mg,
23%, Sodium 120mg,
5%, Total Carbohydrate 10g, 3%,
Dietary Fiber <1g,
4%, Sugar 9g,
Protein 24g

Nutritional
Information per
serving with side dish
(% based upon daily
values) ¾ cup sweet
potato fries; 2 slices
watermelon:
Calories: 357; Total
Fat: 14g, 22%; Saturated Fat: 3g, 20%;
Cholesterol: 70mg,
23%; Sodium: 206mg,
8%; Total Carbohydrate: 38g, 12%;
Dietary Fiber: 3g,
13%; Sugar: 29g;
Protein: 27g

1 pound ground turkey (not ground turkey breast)

2 tablespoons Worcestershire sauce or hoisin sauce

2 tablespoons apricot preserves or jam

1 tablespoon canola or vegetable oil

4 whole grain buns (optional)

4 lettuce leaves (optional)

1 tomato, sliced (optional)

(If you are making the fries, start them first.) In a large bowl, thoroughly combine the turkey, Worcestershire sauce, and apricot preserves or jam.

Heat a large, heavy-duty skillet over medium-high heat for 1 to 2 minutes, then add the oil and swirl it around to coat the bottom of the pan. Meanwhile, gently form the turkey mixture into 4 patties, about 1 inch thick, and add them to the skillet. Brown the patties without moving them for about 4 minutes on the first side. Then flip the patties and cook them for about 4 minutes on the second side. After they are browned on the second side, reduce the heat to medium-low, partially cover the skillet, and cook them for 8 to 10 more minutes (until no longer pink), flipping once. (Alternatively, cook the burgers on a grill over medium heat for 5 to 7 minutes per side.)

While the burgers are cooking, lightly toast the buns (optional). Transfer the burgers to a plate and serve immediately with lettuce and tomato, if desired.

Scramble Flavor Booster: Top the burgers with hot pepper slices and/or spicy mustard.

Side Dish suggestion: To make sweet potato fries, slice 2 medium sweet potatoes into thin, long strips. Toss them with 2 tablespoons vegetable or peanut oil, ¼ teaspoon salt, and ¼ teaspoon chili powder or cinnamon and roast them on a cookie sheet in the oven at 425 degrees, turning the potatoes every 10 minutes, until they are lightly browned (20 to 25 minutes total). Serve them with ketchup, if desired.

A hot pressed sandwich can be a fun family meal. Of course, if you happen to own a panini maker then by all means use it, but otherwise a grill pan or cast-iron skillet works well. You can make these sandwiches with endless combinations of fillings. Try adding fresh basil leaves, pesto, or baby spinach, or using mozzarella or provolone cheese rather than Cheddar. Serve it with fresh and juicy summer cherries.

turkey club panini

Prep + Cook =
30 minutes

4 servings

Nutritional Information per serving (% based upon daily values): Calories 330, Total Fat 18g, 28%, Saturated Fat 5g, 25%, Cholesterol 35mg, 12%, Sodium 880mg, 37%, Total Carbohydrate 30g, 10%, Dietary Fiber 2g, 8%, Sugar 3g, Protein 12g

Nutritional Information per serving with side dish (% based upon daily values) 1 cup cherries: Calories: 404; Total Fat: 18g, 28%; Saturated Fat: 5g, 25%; Cholesterol: 35mg, 12%; Sodium: 880mg, 37%; Total Carbohydrate: 49g, 16%; Dietary Fiber: 5g, 18%; Sugar: 18g; Protein: 13g

8 slices turkey bacon or vegetarian bacon

2 tablespoons fat-free or reduced-fat mayonnaise

1 tablespoon yellow or Dijon mustard

1 teaspoon honey

2 tablespoons olive oil

8 thin slices sourdough bread

½ pound reduced-salt sliced turkey breast or meatless deli slices

2 ounces Cheddar cheese, thinly sliced

1 large tomato, thinly sliced (or 2 cups baby spinach)

Cook the bacon according to the package directions until it is brown and crisp. In a small bowl, combine the mayonnaise, mustard, and honey. Put 1 tablespoon of olive oil in another small bowl. Spread the mayonnaise mixture on top of 4 slices of the bread. Top each bread slice with ¼ of the turkey, 2 slices of the bacon, and thin slices of Cheddar and tomato (or a handful of baby spinach). Top everything with the remaining bread slices. Using a pastry brush, brush the tops of the sandwiches with the olive oil in the bowl.

In a grill pan or large nonstick skillet over medium heat, heat the remaining oil. (You may need 2 skillets to cook all the sandwiches at once, or keep the first batch warm in a 250-degree oven). Add the sandwiches to the pan, with the side you brushed with olive oil facing up, and cover them with another heavy skillet, a foil-wrapped brick, or a heavy grill press. Cook the sandwiches for about 3 minutes per side until they are golden brown, pressing firmly with the top weight to flatten the sandwiches while they cook. Slice the panini in half before serving.

Scramble Flavor Booster: Be adventurous with condiments like wasabi mayonnaise or garlic mustard.

Tip: I prefer freshly sliced turkey from the deli counter or brands that are lower in salt and free of nitrites, such as Applegate Farms.

This is my take on a popular Chilean dish, Palta Reina, suggested by our friend Pamela Navarro-Watson. The avocados make a beautiful presentation for a hot summer night, and the best part is that no cooking is required! The avocados can also be stuffed with chicken, shrimp, or crab salad instead of the tuna. Serve them with hard-boiled eggs and a Black Bean and Corn Salad.

avocados stuffed with tuna salad

Prep (no cook) = 15 minutes

6 servings

Nutritional Information per serving (% based upon daily values): Calories 248, Total Fat 18g, 27%, Saturated Fat 2g, 12%, Cholesterol 29mg, 10%, Sodium 325mg, 14%, Total Carbohydrate 9g, 3%, Dietary Fiber 6g, 24%, Sugar 1g, Protein 17g

Nutritional Information per serving with side dish (% based upon daily values) 1 hard-boiled egg; 1 cup salad: Calories: 466; Total Fat: 25g, 37%; Saturated Fat: 4g, 22%; Cholesterol: 241 mg, 81%; Sodium: 857mg, 37%; Total Carbohydrate: 37g, 12%; Dietary Fiber: 12g, 48%; Sugar: 5g; Protein: 29g

2 cans (6 ounces each) chunk light tuna in water, drained

¼ cup reduced-fat mayonnaise

¼ red bell pepper, finely diced (about ¼ cup) (or substitute celery)

3 avocados

½ lemon

¼ teaspoon salt, or to taste

(If you are making hard-boiled eggs and the salad, start them first.) In a medium bowl, combine the tuna, mayonnaise, and bell pepper or celery.

Cut the avocados in half lengthwise, remove the pits, and sprinkle them with lemon juice and salt. Fill the avocados with the tuna salad, mounding the tuna. You can eat the salad and avocado flesh right out of the avocado skin bowl.

Scramble Flavor Booster: Add the zest of 1 lemon to the tuna or sprinkle it with lemon-pepper seasoning.

Tip: Chunk light tuna is much lower in mercury than albacore tuna, and is high in omega-3s and protein.

Side Dish suggestion: To make hard-boiled eggs, cover the eggs in cold water and bring the water to a boil. When the water boils, turn off the heat, cover the pot, and let the eggs sit in the hot water for 15 minutes (no peeking). Then rinse the eggs under cold running water, and peel them, starting by cracking the skinny pointed end and peeling down from there.

Side Dish suggestion: To make a Black Bean and Corn Salad, combine 1 can (15 ounces) black beans, drained and rinsed, 1 can (14 ounces) corn kernels, drained, ½ red bell pepper or ¼ to ½ cup red onion, finely diced, 1 teaspoon fresh lime juice (about ¼ lime), and ¼ to ½ cup fresh chopped cilantro (optional). Mix all the ingredients together in a medium bowl. Refrigerate until ready to serve.

If you close your eyes, you can almost imagine you are in Capri (the origin of the famous Caprese salad upon which these sandwiches are based) when you bite into one. Serve them with a spinach salad with strawberries and slivered almonds (page 56).

italian caprese sandwiches

Prep (no cook) =
10 minutes

4 servings

Nutritional
Information per
serving (% based
upon daily values):
Calories 430, Total
Fat 16g, 25%, Saturated Fat 9g, 45%,
Cholesterol 55mg,
18%, Sodium 920mg,
38%, Total Carbohydrate 44g, 15%,
Dietary Fiber 3g,
12%, Sugar 5g,
Protein 27g

Nutritional
Information per
serving with side dish
(% based open daily
values) 1½ cups
salad:
Calories 503; Total
Fat: 21g, 32%; Saturated Fat: 9g, 47%;
Cholesterol: 55mg,
18%; Sodium: 950mg,
39%; Total Carbohydrate: 51g, 17%;
Dietary Fiber: 5g,
21%; Sugar 9g;
Protein: 29g

1 ciabatta or other wide flat loaf of bread

12 ounces fresh mozzarella cheese, sliced

2–3 tomatoes, thinly sliced

20 fresh basil leaves

2 tablespoons balsamic vinaigrette dressing
(or whisk together 2 tablespoons olive oil and
1 tablespoon balsamic vinegar)

½ yellow or white onion, halved and thinly sliced (optional)

(Make the salad first, if you are serving it.) Slice the bread in half, separating the top from the bottom. On the bottom half of the bread, place a layer of the cheese, followed by the tomatoes and basil. Top the fillings with the vinaigrette dressing, and add the onions, if desired. Slice the loaf into 4 small sandwiches to serve it.

Tip: Turn the sandwich into a warm panini by brushing the outsides of the bread with olive oil or butter and cooking it in a cast-iron (or other heavy) skillet, under a heavy metal grill press or a brick wrapped in aluminum foil, until it is thin and the cheese is melted, about 2 minutes per side.

Scramble Flavor Booster: Add a thin layer of pesto to the sandwiches and use the optional onions.

This is a great no-cook meal for one of those busy evenings when you want to avoid eating fast food or cereal for dinner. You can make this dish in less time than it takes to heat a frozen pizza! Serve it with Fruity Swirl Smoothies.

middle eastern stuffed pitas

Prep (no cook) = 15 minutes

6 servings

Nutritional Information per serving (% based upon daily values): Calories 300, Total Fat 9g, 13.5%, Saturated Fat 2g, 10%, Cholesterol 11mg, 3.5%, Sodium 745mg, 31%, Total Carbohydrate 46g, 15.5%, Dietary Fiber 3g, 12.5%, Sugar 3.5g, Protein 9.5g

Nutritional Information per serving with side dish (% based upon daily values) ¼ of smoothie: Calories: 460: Total Fat: 10g, 15%; Saturated Fat: 2g, 10%; Cholesterol: 11mg, 4%; Sodium: 795mg 33%; Total Carbohydrate: 82g, 28%; Dietary Fiber: 6g, 25%; Sugar: 33g; Protein: 15g

10 ounces hummus, any variety

1 cucumber, peeled and sliced

2 tomatoes, diced

½ yellow or red onion, thinly sliced

½ cup fresh mint leaves

½ cup feta cheese, crumbled

6 pita pockets (get the softest and freshest you can find)

Put all the ingredients in separate bowls so each family member can design their own sandwich. Warm the pitas in the microwave oven for about 1 minute until they are very warm and soft. Cut them in half crosswise (so you have 2 semicircles), then cut the pockets open so you can fill them. (Make the smoothies now, unless you are serving them for dessert.)

Spread a layer of hummus in each pita half and top it with the fillings of your choice.

Tip: When possible, use real feta cheese made from sheep's milk and soaked in brine (available at Trader Joe's and other stores that sell gourmet cheeses). It has a more complex and less salty flavor than mass-produced feta cheese.

Scramble Flavor Booster: Use extra-garlicky hummus and/or extra onion.

Side Dish suggestion: To make a Fruity Swirl Smoothie (created by Celia Goldfarb and Rebecca Schrader), in a blender combine 1¼ cups orange juice, 1 cup nonfat vanilla yogurt, 2 cups fresh or frozen mango chunks, ½ cup fresh or frozen blueberries, and 1 ripe banana. Blend until smooth.

A colorful dish to celebrate the bounty of the season, these wraps are full of healthy vitamins, fiber, and lean protein and are sweet enough for the kids to enjoy. Serve them with sliced fresh peaches or nectarines.

warm garden wraps with corn and sweet potatoes

Prep + Cook = 30 minutes

8 servings

Nutritional Information per serving (% based upon daily values): Calories 360, Total Fat 9g, 14% Saturated Fat 3.5g, 18%, Cholesterol 10mg, 3%, Sodium 800mg, 33%, Total Carbohydrate 31g, 20%, Dietary Fiber 7g, 28%, Sugar 3g, Protein 11g

Nutritional Information per serving with side dish (% based upon daily values) 1 peach: Calories: 421; Total Fat: 10g, 15%; Saturated Fat: 4g, 18%; Cholesterol: 10mg, 3%; Sodium: 800mg, 33%; Total Carbohydrate: 46g, 25%; Dietary Fiber: 10g, 37%; Sugar: 16g; Protein: 13g

2 tablespoons butter or olive oil

1 medium sweet potato, diced into ¼-inch pieces (about 2 cups total)

1 small yellow onion (preferably a sweet Vidalia onion), diced into ¼-inch pieces (about 1 cup total)

1 red bell pepper, diced into ¼-inch pieces (about 1 cup total)

4 ears corn, kernels cut off (1½–2 cups total) or 1 can (15 ounces) unsweetened corn kernels

1 teaspoon ground cumin

½ teaspoon chili powder

½ cup chicken or vegetable broth or water (optional)

1 can (15 ounces) black or pinto beans, partially drained

¼ teaspoon salt (optional)

8 spinach wraps or whole wheat tortillas

1 cup salsa for serving (optional)

1 cup nonfat or low-fat sour cream for serving (optional)

In a large heavy skillet, melt the butter or heat the oil over medium heat. Add the sweet potatoes and onions and brown them, stirring occasionally, for 8 to 10 minutes. Add the bell pepper, corn, cumin, and chili powder and continue to cook it for about 5 minutes. If the mixture starts to dry out or stick, add the broth or water. Add the beans and salt (optional) and cook, stirring gently, until heated through. (Meanwhile, cut the fruit, if you are serving it.) (At this point you can refrigerate the filling for up to 24 hours, or serve it immediately.)

Put a scoop of the vegetable mixture onto the center of a wrap, and top it with salsa and sour cream, if desired. Fold one side of the wrap up about an inch to catch drips, and then roll it up burrito style.

Scramble Flavor Booster: Use chipotle chili powder rather than traditional chili powder and serve it with spicy salsa on the side.

Tip: To cut the kernels off an ear of corn, cut off the stem of the corn and stand the cob on its flat end in a shallow bowl. Using a serrated or paring knife, slice the kernels off from the top to bottom.

Far East goes South of the Border with these sweet hoisin-marinated vegetables, wrapped in whole wheat tortillas. If you prefer a meatier meal, you can add cooked chicken to the wraps with the rice and vegetables. Serve it with Asian dumplings or egg rolls and Asian Cucumber Salad (page 51).

moo shu vegetable wraps

Prep + Cook = 25 minutes

6 servings

Nutritional Information per serving (without chicken) (% based upon daily values): Calories 280, Total Fat 8g, 12%, Saturated Fat 1g, 5%, Cholesterol 0mg, 0%, Sodium 480mg, 20%, Total Carbohydrate 47g, 16%, Dietary Fiber 5g, 20%, Sugar 5g, Protein 7g

Nutritional Information per serving with side dish (% based upon daily values) 2 dumplings; $\frac{1}{6}$ of salad: Calories: 385; Total Fat 12g, 18%; Saturated Fat: 2g, 9%; Cholesterol: 9mg, 3%; Sodium: 737mg, 31%; Total Carbohydrate: 60g, 20%; Dietary Fiber: 7g, 27%; Sugar: 9g; Protein: 13g

1–1½ cups white or quick-cooking brown rice

2 tablespoons canola or vegetable oil

½ yellow or white onion, sliced into thin strips

1 zucchini, cut lengthwise into quarters and thinly sliced

½ red bell pepper, thinly sliced

8–12 ounces sliced mushrooms

2 scallions, thinly sliced

4 tablespoons hoisin sauce (a Chinese marinade and dipping sauce)

6 whole wheat or white tortillas

1½ cups cooked sliced chicken (optional)

1 teaspoon–1 tablespoon Asian chili sauce, Tabasco, or other hot pepper sauce for serving (optional)

Cook the rice according to package directions (and prepare the dumplings or egg rolls and salad, if you are serving them.)

Meanwhile, in a large heavy skillet over medium-high heat, heat the oil. Add the onions and zucchini and cook, stirring frequently, while you chop and add the other vegetables. Stir in 2 tablespoons hoisin sauce. Continue to sauté the vegetables for a few more minutes, stirring often, until they are tender but not mushy, 8 to 10 minutes total from when you first added the onions and zucchini. Remove the vegetables from the heat.

Put the tortillas on a microwave-safe plate, cover them with a damp paper towel, and heat them on high power for 1 to 2 minutes until they are very warm and soft.

At the table, lay a tortilla on each plate and brush a little hoisin sauce (about 1 teaspoon) in the middle of it with the back of a spoon. Add a scoop each of the rice, vegetables, chicken (optional), and a few drops of hot pepper or chili sauce (optional). Wrap the tortillas burrito-style.

Scramble Flavor Booster: Spice it up by adding the Asian chili sauce or Tabasco sauce to the wraps.

Tip: I find that if I let our kids fill their own wraps, they make healthy choices and are more likely to eat what they have created.

Side Dish suggestion: Prepare the dumplings (or egg rolls) according to the package directions. For the dumplings, make a dipping sauce, if desired, with ¼ cup reduced-sodium soy sauce, 1 tablespoon rice vinegar, and 1 teaspoon superfine sugar. Add 1 tablespoon finely chopped scallions or chives (optional). If you are using egg rolls, serve them with duck sauce and Chinese mustard.

This salad is flavorful, filling, and healthy as can be. If your kids are picky eaters, leave some of the bean mixture plain before adding the dressing, but Scramble recipe tester Alice Clark said she was amazed that her kids ate it. "My daughter is picky and she called it 'yummy' and even ate leftovers the next day!" You can also turn the salad into delicious wraps with whole wheat tortillas. Serve it with carrot and celery sticks with ranch dressing.

summer bean salad with turkey sausage

Prep + Cook =
20 minutes

10 servings

Nutritional Information per serving (% based upon daily values): Calories 460, Total Fat 14g, 22%, Saturated Fat 3g, 15%, Cholesterol 25mg, 8%, Sodium 1030mg, 43%, Total Carbohydrate 63g, 21%, Dietary Fiber 8g, 32%, Sugar 3g, Protein 20g

Nutritional Information per serving with side dish (% based upon daily values) 1 cup celery and carrots and 1 tbsp. light ranch dressing: Calories: 543; Total Fat: 17g, 26%; Saturated Fat: 5g, 23%; Cholesterol: 28mg, 9%; Sodium: 1,254mg, 53%; Total Carbohydrate: 77g, 26%; Dietary Fiber: 12g, 47%; Sugar: 9g; Protein: 22g

1 can (14 ounces) corn kernels, drained and rinsed, or
    1½ cups fresh sweet corn kernels from 2–3 ears of corn

1 can (15 ounces) black beans, drained and rinsed

1 can (15 ounces) kidney beans, drained and rinsed

1 orange bell pepper, finely diced

3 scallions, finely sliced

3 tablespoons olive oil

2 tablespoons balsamic vinegar

½ lemon, juice only (about 2 tablespoons)

1 tablespoon Dijon mustard

12–16 ounces precooked turkey sausage, quartered lengthwise and
    cut in ¼-inch slices (optional)

Combine the corn, both types of beans, bell peppers, and scallions in a serving bowl. In a small bowl, whisk together 2 tablespoons olive oil, vinegar, lemon juice, and mustard and add to the bean and corn mixture.

In a large skillet, heat the remaining 1 tablespoon olive oil over medium heat and brown the sausage (optional) for 3 to 5 minutes. Add it to the bean mixture and toss well.

Serve it immediately or refrigerate it for up to 3 days.

Scramble Flavor Booster: Use spicy sausage and serve the salad with hot pepper sauce, such as Tabasco.

light and delicious summer treats

While summer would not be summer for us without a liberal dose of ice cream and popsicles, I have devised a few frosty desserts and beverages that are just as satisfying, without filling us up with too many empty calories:

- **Fruit smoothies:** Blend ripe bananas, berries, and/or frozen fruit with nonfat vanilla yogurt or any kind of sorbet. One of our favorite concoctions is fresh strawberries, frozen blueberries, and bananas with vanilla yogurt, and a splash of orange juice.

- **Healthy popsicles:** In popsicle molds, freeze smoothies, fruit juice, or chocolate milk, for healthier popsicles.

- **Frozen fruit:** Many fruits taste candy-sweet when eaten frozen. Try freezing peeled and sliced bananas, grapes, blueberries, pineapple, mango, and strawberries. (Don't forget to wash and dry the berries and grapes before freezing.)

- **Ice cream sandwiches:** Top low-fat cookies (such as graham crackers or chocolate wafers) with softened frozen yogurt or low-fat ice cream to make your own ice cream sandwiches. Press a second cookie on top, then even edges with a dull knife. Eat immediately, or wrap in plastic wrap and freeze until ready to serve.

- **Parfaits:** For a light and delicious dessert, make a yogurt parfait in a tall sundae glass: For each parfait, layer 1 cup nonfat vanilla yogurt (or plain yogurt sweetened with a little honey and vanilla) with 1 cup fresh or frozen strawberries and/or blueberries (thawed, if frozen), and sprinkle 1 tablespoon granola on top.

- **Chocolate-covered strawberries (or other fruit):** Wash and dry strawberries and place in a flat dish. Melt semisweet chocolate in the microwave at half power for 1 minute and then at 30-second intervals, stirring until melted. Dip the strawberries in the chocolate or drizzle over the fruit and harden in the refrigerator.

- **Strawberries with sour cream and brown sugar:** Serve fresh strawberries with bowls of nonfat sour cream and brown sugar—first dip in the sour cream, then in the brown sugar.

- **Iced mochaccino (makes 2 servings):** In a standing blender, liquefy 2 heaping cups of ice cubes, 3 teaspoons regular or decaf instant coffee, 3/4 cup nonfat or low-fat milk, 2 tablespoons chocolate syrup, or more to taste, 1 teaspoon unsweetened cocoa powder, and 1 packet of Splenda or Equal or 1 teaspoon sugar.

- **Iced chococcino:** Follow directions above but skip the coffee and sweetener and double the chocolate syrup.

- **Earning our ice cream:** We have found that ice cream cones taste even better when we ride our bikes to our favorite scoop shop.

This casserole is a great one to make with your kids, though you should brown the tortillas yourself to prevent burns. It goes beautifully with sliced mangoes, which are at their peak from April through August.

mexican lasagna
with avocado salsa

Prep + Cook =
30 minutes

8 servings

Nutritional
Information per
serving (% based
upon daily values):
Calories 410, Total
Fat 19g, 29%, Satu-
rated Fat 8g, 40%,
Cholesterol 30mg,
10%, Sodium 1140mg,
48%, Total Carbohy-
drate 55g, 18%,
Dietary Fiber 10g,
40%, Sugar 3g,
Protein 17g

Nutritional
Information per
serving with side dish
(% based upon daily
values) $\frac{1}{2}$ mango:
Calories: 477; Total
Fat: 20g, 29%; Satu-
rated Fat: 9g, 41%;
Cholesterol: 30mg,
10%; Sodium:
1,142mg, 48%; Total
Carbohydrate: 73g,
24%; Dietary Fiber:
12g, 47%; Sugar: 19g;
Protein: 18g

1 can (15 ounces) black beans, drained and rinsed

1 can (15 ounces) vegetarian refried beans

1 can (15 ounces) corn kernels, naturally sweetened, drained

1 cup mild salsa

4 scallions, sliced

2 cups shredded Cheddar cheese

4 teaspoons vegetable oil

6 soft taco-size (8-inch) flour or wheat tortillas

1 avocado, peeled and diced

2 tomatoes, diced

$\frac{1}{2}$ lime, juice only (1 tablespoon juice)

$\frac{1}{4}$ teaspoon salt

Heat the oven to 400 degrees. Spray a 9 × 13-inch baking dish with nonstick cooking spray.

In a large bowl, stir together both types of beans, corn, salsa, scallions, and cheese.

Put the oil in a small bowl. Heat a large skillet over medium to medium-high heat. Brush both sides of each tortilla with a thin layer of oil and fry it in the skillet, turning once, until it is puffed and golden in spots, about 1 minute total. Stack the cooked tortillas on a plate.

To make the lasagna, put 2 tortillas in the bottom of the baking dish, top them with half the bean filling, then top that with 2 more tortillas, and the second half of the bean filling. Top with the final 2 tortillas. Press down with a spatula on the top tor-tillas to seal the layers.

Bake the lasagna, uncovered, for 10 to 12 minutes until it is heated through. Cut it into squares with a pizza cutter or serrated knife to serve it.

In a medium bowl, gently toss the diced avocado and tomatoes with the lime juice and salt. Top the lasagna squares with the avocado salsa at the table.

Scramble Flavor Booster: Use spicy salsa and add 1 minced hot chili pepper or some red onion to the salsa.

Tip: To dice an avocado, cut it in half lengthwise and separate the halves. Remove the pit and scoop out the flesh with a large spoon. Put the halves flat side down on a cutting board to dice them.

Side Dish suggestion: Serve the lasagna with 2 mangoes, peeled and sliced. To slice a mango, stand it on its end and slice each of the halves off as close to the oblong pit as possible. Score the flesh into strips or squares, turn the skin inside out, and cut the flesh off of the peel.

I first made this dish the night after we had a heavy, salty meal at a Chinese restaurant and decided Chinese "take-in" is much more satisfying. If you can catch the fresh snow peas when they're in season in early summer they are such a treat! Serve it with steamed rice and Orange-Ginger Glazed Carrots.

golden tofu (or chicken) with ginger and peppers

Prep + Cook =
25 minutes +

4 servings

Nutritional Information per serving (% based upon daily values): Calories 210, Total Fat 13g, 20%, Saturated Fat 1g, 5%, Cholesterol 0mg, 0%, Sodium 310mg, 13%, Total Carbohydrate 12g, 4%, Dietary Fiber 3g, 12%, Sugar 6g, Protein 13g

Nutritional Information per serving with side dish (% based upon daily values) ¾ cup white rice; ¾ cup carrots: Calories: 424; Total Fat: 16g, 25%; Saturated Fat: 1g, 5%; Cholesterol: 0mg, 0%; Sodium: 356mg, 15%; Total Carbohydrate: 55g, 18%; Dietary Fiber: 6g, 22%; Sugar: 12g; Protein: 17g

1 pound extra-firm tofu packed in water (or use boneless chicken breast or peeled and deveined large shrimp)

2 tablespoons vegetable oil

2 tablespoons reduced-sodium soy sauce or tamari

1 tablespoon rice wine or mirin

1 teaspoon sugar

½ small yellow onion, cut into matchsticks or thin strips (quarter the onion top to bottom first)

1 cup snow peas, cut lengthwise into matchsticks

1 red or yellow bell pepper, cut into matchsticks

2 teaspoons chopped fresh ginger

1 teaspoon chopped garlic (about 2 cloves)

Cut the tofu in half crosswise and wrap both halves in a clean absorbent kitchen towel for at least 10 minutes, and up to 12 hours. (Start the rice, if you are serving it.) When you are ready to cook, cut the tofu into ½-inch cubes.

Heat 1 tablespoon oil in a large nonstick skillet over medium heat. Cook the tofu, turning it every few minutes, until it is completely golden, about 15 minutes. (Meanwhile, prepare the carrots, if you are serving them.) Remove the tofu from the pan and set it aside.

Combine the soy sauce, rice wine, and sugar to make the sauce and set it aside.

Add the remaining oil to the skillet, and stir-fry the onions for about 2 minutes until they just start to brown. Add the snow peas, bell peppers, ginger, and garlic and stir-fry for about 2 more minutes until the vegetables are tender-crisp. Pour the sauce over the vegetables and stir-fry for 1 minute, then mix in the tofu. Serve immediately.

Scramble Flavor Booster: Add ¼ teaspoon Asian chili-garlic paste or crushed red pepper flakes to the sauce.

Tip: For great golden tofu, drain the tofu and wrap it in the dish towel as early in the day as possible to draw out a lot of the moisture.

Side Dish suggestion: To make Orange-Ginger Glazed Carrots, in a large skillet, heat 1 tablespoon olive oil over medium heat. Add 1 pound peeled and sliced large carrots or crinkle-cut carrots, and sauté them until they are coated, about 4 minutes. Meanwhile, combine ¼ cup orange juice, 1 teaspoon fresh lemon juice (about ⅛ lemon), 2 teaspoons honey, and ¼ teaspoon ground ginger in a measuring cup or bowl. Pour the mixture over the carrots, bring it to a boil, and allow it to simmer for about 3 minutes. Cover the carrots, reduce the heat to keep the liquid at a simmer, and steam them for about 5 minutes until they are tender. Sprinkle them liberally with about 1 teaspoon fresh or dried dill (optional) before serving.

This is a fantastic recipe from my friend Nachama Wilker, especially for those of us who are always looking for ways to use up summer's abundant zucchini harvest. Scramble recipe tester Debbie Firestone reports, "My husband balked at first, but by the end of the dinner he was asking to take the leftovers to work for lunch!! My nine-year-old exclaimed that they were 'yummy,' my two-year-old finished off every last bite, and my teenager asked me to save the recipe." Serve them with fresh guacamole and carrots (page 151).

vegetarian enchiladas

Prep (30 minutes) + Cook (25 minutes)

6 servings

Nutritional Information per serving (% based upon daily values): Calories 290, Total Fat 14g, 22%, Saturated Fat 8g, 40%, Cholesterol 35mg, 12%, Sodium 750mg, 31%, Total Carbohydrate 28g, 9%, Fiber 3g, 12%, Sugar 2g, Protein 12g

Nutritional Information per serving with side dish (% based upon daily values) ¼ cup guacamole; ½ cup carrots: Calories: 300; Total Fat: 18g, 28%; Saturated Fat: 8.5g, 43%; Cholesterol: 35mg, 12%; Sodium: 867mg, 36%; Total Carbohydrate: 36g, 12%; Dietary Fiber: 7g, 27%; Sugar: 5g; Protein: 13.5g

1 can (15 ounces) enchilada sauce, mild or spicy

2 tablespoons olive oil

1 teaspoon minced garlic (about 2 cloves)

½ red or yellow onion, diced

2 zucchini, cut lengthwise into 4 strips, and diced

¾ teaspoon ground cumin

¾ teaspoon chili powder

½ teaspoon salt (optional)

10–12 corn tortillas

2 cups shredded Mexican-blend cheese (or use Cheddar or Monterey Jack)

1 cup nonfat or low-fat sour cream for serving (optional)

Preheat the oven to 375 degrees, and spray the bottom of a 9 × 13-inch baking dish with nonstick cooking spray. Spread about one-fourth of the can of enchilada sauce on the bottom of the pan.

In a heavy skillet, heat the olive oil over medium heat. Cook the garlic for about 30 seconds, and then add the onions and zucchini. Season them with the cumin, chili powder, and salt (optional). Sauté the mixture, stirring it occasionally, for about 10 minutes until the vegetables are very soft.

Wrap the tortillas in a moist paper towel and heat them in the microwave oven for about 1 minute until they are soft. (Alternatively, warm each tortilla over medium heat in a nonstick skillet for 20 seconds per side, or until soft.)

On a plate, fill each tortilla with about 2 tablespoons of the vegetable mixture, and about 1 tablespoon of cheese. Roll it and place it in the pan. Repeat with the remaining tortillas until all the filling is used. Pour the remaining enchilada sauce evenly on top of the tortillas, and top them with any remaining cheese. Bake the enchiladas, uncovered, for 20 to 25 minutes until the sauce is bubbly. (Meanwhile, make the guacamole, if you are serving it.)

Serve the enchiladas hot, topped with the sour cream, if desired. (Alternatively, let them cool, cover tightly, and freeze them for up to 3 months.)

Scramble Flavor Booster: Use hot enchilada sauce and increase the amount of cumin and chili powder you use to 1 teaspoon each.

I've updated this classic American salad by using lower-fat turkey bacon and adding a few extra veggies to make it healthier. You can get creative and modify it to your own tastes, of course—glazed walnuts or sliced avocado would be great additions. For non-salad eaters in the family, serve the bacon, spinach, extra hard-boiled eggs, and tomatoes separately. Serve the salad with a loaf of whole grain bread.

classic spinach salad with turkey bacon

Prep + Cook = 20 minutes

4 servings

Nutritional Information per serving (% based upon daily values): Calories 220, Total Fat 16g, 25%, Saturated Fat 4.5g, 23%, Cholesterol 155mg, 52%, Sodium 1170mg, 49%, Total Carbohydrate 4g, 1%, Dietary Fiber 5g, 20%, Sugar 2g, Protein 16g

Nutritional Information per serving with side dish (% based upon daily values) 1 slice bread: Calories: 330; Total Fat: 18g, 8%; Saturated Fat: 5g, 23%; Cholesterol: 155mg, 52%; Sodium: 1,350mg, 57%; Total Carbohydrate: 24g, 8%; Dietary Fiber: 8g, 32%; Sugar: 5g; Protein: 20g

2 eggs, hard-boiled and sliced

8 ounces turkey, pork, or vegetarian bacon, preferably nitrite-free

1 bag (6–9 ounces) baby spinach

¼–⅓ cup crumbled blue cheese or Gorgonzola to taste

1 cup sliced mushrooms, coarsely chopped

¼ red or yellow onion, halved and thinly sliced

1 cup cherry tomatoes (about ½ pint), halved

¼ cup balsamic vinaigrette, (or to taste) store-bought or homemade (we like Annie's Naturals Balsamic Vinaigrette)

Hard-boil the eggs, if necessary (see directions, page 154), and soak them in cold water to cool them. Peel and slice them. Chop the turkey bacon into thin strips and cook it in a large nonstick skillet over medium heat, stirring occasionally, until it is browned and crispy, 8 to 10 minutes.

In a large bowl, top the spinach with the eggs, cheese, mushrooms, onions, and tomatoes. When the bacon is crisp, add it to the salad, top it with the dressing, and toss thoroughly. Serve it immediately.

Balsamic Vinaigrette Salad Dressing: You can make your own easy and delicious salad dressing by whisking together ¼ cup balsamic vinegar, ⅓ cup olive oil, 1 teaspoon superfine sugar (optional), and 1 teaspoon minced herbs such as basil and mint. Add 1 tablespoon Dijon mustard, if desired.

Scramble Flavor Booster: Use extra sliced onion in the salad, use aged blue cheese, and throw in a handful of fresh oregano or mint.

Tip: If you need to make the salad a few hours in advance, wait to dress it until the last minute so it doesn't get soggy.

My husband, Andrew, and I teamed up to make our own version of Italian Bread Salad. It was sublime, especially with fresh ingredients from the farmers market and our garden. Our daughter, Celia, liked the salad mixed together, but if you don't think your kids will eat it that way, serve the components of the salad separately for them. Serve it with corn on the cob and pineapple chunks (or serve pineapple dipped in melted chocolate or chocolate sauce for dessert!).

panzanella
(italian bread salad with salami)

Prep (no cook) = 15 minutes

4 servings

Nutritional Information per serving (% based upon daily values): Calories 270, Total Fat 14g, 22%, Saturated Fat 4g, 20%, Cholesterol 20mg, 7%, Sodium 660mg, 28%, Total Carbohydrate 28g, 9%, Dietary Fiber 2g, 8%, Sugar 7g, Protein 8g

Nutritional Information per serving with side dish (% based upon daily values) 1 ear corn, ½ tsp. butter, sprinkle of salt; 1 cup pineapple: Calories: 416; Total Fat: 17g; Saturated Fat: 6g, 26%; Cholesterol: 25mg, 9%; Sodium: 831mg, 35%; Total Carbohydrate: 62g, 21%; Dietary Fiber: 6g, 24%; Sugar: 25g; Protein: 11g

2 large tomatoes, diced into ¾-inch chunks (about 2 cups)

1 large cucumber, peeled and diced into ½ -inch chunks (about 1½ cups)

½ yellow or red onion, thinly sliced

1 cup (about 4 ounces) diced salami (or substitute diced fresh mozzarella or provolone cheese)

2 tablespoons slivered fresh basil (10–15 leaves)

¼ teaspoon kosher salt

½ teaspoon sugar

2 tablespoons balsamic vinegar

2 tablespoons olive oil

4 cups cubed (1-inch pieces) one-day-old hearty bread, such as a country white or wheat boule (a round loaf)

In a large serving bowl, combine all the ingredients except the bread and let them sit for a few minutes while you cut the bread (and prepare the corn, if you are making it). Add the bread a few minutes before serving the salad and toss it well to combine.

Tip: To make your own chocolate sauce for dipping fruit, melt semisweet chocolate bits in a microwave-safe bowl (make sure the bowl is completely dry). Stir the chocolate after 30 seconds, and then every 10 seconds until it is melted and smooth.

This is a versatile and zesty summer meal. If your kids don't eat salad, make a separate platter for them with all the healthy and delicious ingredients, such as the corn, beans, chicken, hard-boiled eggs (make a few extra), and cheese. To make this salad even easier, you can use store-bought ranch or vinaigrette dressing (or a combination). Serve it with homemade tortilla chips and salsa.

southwestern cobb salad
with avocado ranch dressing

Prep + Cook = 20 minutes

4 servings

Nutritional Information per serving (% based upon daily values): Calories 380, Total Fat 19g, 29%, Saturated Fat 5g, 25%, Cholesterol 95mg, 32%, Sodium 290mg, 12%, Total Carbohydrate 33g, 11%, Dietary Fiber 11g, 44%, Sugar 6g, Protein 24g

Nutritional Information per serving with side dish (% based upon daily values) ¼ of chips and ¼ cup salsa: Calories: 547; Total Fat: 24g, 36%; Saturated Fat: 6g, 28%; Cholesterol: 95mg, 32%; Sodium: 879mg, 36%; Total Carbohydrate: 61g, 20%; Dietary Fiber: 15g, 60%; Sugar: 8g; Protein: 28g

1 small head romaine lettuce, chopped (6 cups total)

1 cup canned black beans, drained and rinsed

1 cup cooked chicken breast or black beans

¼ red onion or red bell pepper, finely diced (½ cup onion or bell pepper)

1½ avocados, peeled and diced

1 cup corn kernels, fresh, frozen, or canned

½ cup diced or shredded Monterey Jack or Cheddar cheese

1 egg, hard-boiled, sliced

3 tablespoons nonfat sour cream

1–2 limes, juice only (about ¼ cup juice)

¼ teaspoon salt

1 teaspoon honey

1 teaspoon olive oil

hot pepper sauce (such as Tabasco), to taste (optional)

(Start the tortilla chips, if you are making them.) Hard-boil the egg, if necessary (see page 154), and cool and slice it. Put the lettuce in the bottom of a large serving bowl. Top it with the remaining salad ingredients (thaw the frozen corn, if you are using it), including 1 diced avocado.

In a blender, make the dressing by blending together the sour cream, half an avocado, the lime juice, salt, honey, olive oil, and hot pepper sauce (optional).

Just before you are ready to serve it, toss the salad with about half the dressing, then add more to taste.

Scramble Flavor Booster: Use the red onion and the optional hot sauce in the dressing.

Tip: Hard avocados? You can speed up the ripening process by putting them in a paper bag at room temperature for a few hours or up to a day, as necessary. Once they ripen, you can store them in the refrigerator for 5 to 7 days, but try to avoid bruising them.

Side Dish suggestion: To make your own tortilla chips, preheat the oven to 375 degrees. Put 1 tablespoon vegetable oil in a small bowl, and, using a pastry brush, lightly brush the top and bottom of 1 corn tortilla with the oil. Put the tortilla on a cutting board, and brush the top of the next tortilla with oil, putting the non-oiled side on top of the first tortilla so they share any extra oil. Continue with the remaining tortillas, brushing only the top side and stacking them (use 8 to 10 tortillas in total). Cut the tortillas into eighths, cutting across the middle so they are triangle-shaped, and scatter them on one or two large baking sheets in a single layer. Sprinkle them evenly with ½ teaspoon kosher salt, or to taste. Bake them for about 15 minutes until they are lightly browned and crisp, but remove them before they get dark brown. (Thanks to Scramble subscriber Kathy Stohr for the great recipe!). Serve them with salsa, if desired.

fall

five weekly fall menus

To help you embrace all the bountiful fall flavors, here are five weekly menus. (You can also make shopping a breeze by grabbing the accompanying organized grocery list for each week at www.thescramble.com/SOS.)

week 1

Sweet Harvest Baked Chicken
Seared Salmon with Orange-Rosemary Sauce
Warm Pasta Salad with Arugula or Spinach
Portobello Mushroom, Caramelized Onion, and Goat Cheese Pizza
Creamy Potato-Leek Soup

week 2

Rosemary-Garlic Pork Roast with Whipped Sweet Potatoes
Brazilian Halibut with Coconut-Lime Sauce
Philadelphia Cheese Steaks
Baked Risotto with Spinach and Cremini Mushrooms
Delectable Sweet-and-Sour Tofu

week 3

Flawless Roast Chicken with Sweet Onions
Broiled White Fish with Lemon, Tomatoes, and Olives
Sausage and Cabbage Sauté with Tart Apples
Tortellini Soup with Spinach and Tomatoes
Baked Green Chile Chimichangas

week 4

Hearty Beef Stew
Santa Barbara Salad with Apples, Dates, and Goat Cheese
Chili-rubbed Salmon with Garlic Roasted Fingerling Potatoes
Linguini with Basil and Clams
Three-Cheese Eggplant Melt

week 5

Chicken Thighs with Roasted Peppers and Black Olives
Pasta Shells with Zucchini, Leeks, and Melted Cheese
Greek Rice Bowl with Spinach, Feta, and Pine Nuts
Danish Egg Salad Sandwiches with Smoked Salmon
Mexican Confetti Casserole

poultry, pork, and beef

fish

pastas, grains, soups, and stews

Key: (V) = Vegetarian or vegetarian optional;
          * = Scramble Express: 30 minutes or less total;
       (M) = Make-ahead, freeze, or slow-cooker option

sandwiches, wraps, and other fare

Key: (V) = Vegetarian or vegetarian optional;
         * = Scramble Express: 30 minutes or less total;
        (M) = Make-ahead, freeze, or slow-cooker option

bringing our families together for nourishing fall dinners

THE FALL MORNING CRISPNESS is a sensory reminder that time is shifting once more away from long, sweltering summer days to the shorter days of a new season. With the change in the air come other changes in the pace of our days and even the flavors of our foods.

Fall weather brings transformations to the produce at the farmers' markets, which, in my area, shut down for the season at the end of October. The Scramble menus reflect the shift away from summer corn, tomatoes, fresh basil, and cooling salads and into fall favorites like sweet potatoes, apples, squash, and warming soups and casseroles.

As the new season begins, this is an excellent time for us Scramblers to renew our commitment to bringing our families together for healthy, homemade dinners whenever possible. As many of us have discovered, if we plan ahead for a few meals and shop once a week, we can easily prepare a healthy and delicious meal for our families in less time than it takes to heat up a frozen pizza or visit a drive-thru. I actually think it's easier to cook a simple meal than to drag the family out to dinner (though that's a treat once in a while, too).

Even in the bustling fall season we can continue to plan for and prepare nourishing meals, and include our families in the process—whether by letting them help us decide on the menu, cook with us, set the table, or clean up. And the resulting benefits are immense, both to our family's health and happiness, and to our own peace of mind.

happy fall!

This is the most delectable chicken, perfect for a family dinner or for company. It's a favorite in the home of our friends Elizabeth Cullen and Stephen Chertkof, who shared the recipe with me. Serve it with steamed broccoli with olive oil and grated Parmesan cheese (page 35) and wild rice.

sweet harvest baked chicken

Prep (15 minutes) + Cook (75 minutes)

6 servings

Nutritional Information per serving (% based upon daily values): Calories 430, Total Fat 18g, 28%, Saturated Fat 3.5g, 18%, Cholesterol 115mg, 38%, Sodium 170mg, 7%, Total Carbohydrate 40g, 13%, Dietary Fiber 2g, 8%, Sugar 34g, Protein 30g

Nutritional Information per serving with side dish (% based upon daily values) 1 cup prepared broccoli; ¾ cup cooked rice: Calories: 647; Total Fat: 22g, 35%; Saturated Fat: 5g, 25%; Cholesterol: 119mg, 39%; Sodium: 301mg, 13%; Total Carbohydrate: 77g, 25%; Dietary Fiber: 9g, 38%; Sugar: 37g; Protein: 40g

1 whole chicken, cut up, or 8–12 chicken pieces (about 4 pounds total)

2 carrots, thinly sliced

½ yellow onion, sliced

⅓ cup pitted prunes

½ cup dried apricots

¼ cup canola or vegetable oil

½ cup honey

½ cup reduced-sodium chicken broth

¼ cup white wine (or use additional broth)

2 teaspoons dried tarragon

Preheat the oven to 400 degrees. Put the chicken, carrots, onions, prunes, and apricots in a large roasting or baking pan.

In a large measuring cup or bowl, combine the oil, honey, broth, and wine. Pour the sauce over the chicken, and top it with the tarragon.

Bake the chicken for 30 minutes, then reduce the heat to 350 degrees and bake it for 45 more minutes, or until the chicken thighs are fully cooked. (Meanwhile, prepare the broccoli and rice, if you are serving them.) For browner chicken, put the pan under the broiler, about 5 inches from the heat source, for the final 5 minutes of cooking. Serve it immediately, or refrigerate it for up to 2 days or freeze it for up to 3 months.

Tip: If you have leftover chicken, you can slice it over greens for an easy lunch or dinner salad the next day. Add crumbled cheese, diced orange, and walnuts for a satisfying meal.

Hoisin is a sweet and salty Chinese cooking sauce and marinade that is so versatile; it's sometimes referred to as the ketchup of Asia. This is a good meal to make ahead during the day, or even a day or two in advance of when you plan to serve it. Serve it with Sesame-Stir-Fried Green Beans with Garlic and steamed brown or white rice.

hoisin baked chicken

Prep (5 minutes) + Cook (45 minutes) + Marinate 2 hours– 24 hours

6 servings

Nutritional Information per serving (% based upon daily values): Calories 190, Total Fat 5g, 8%, Saturated Fat 1g, 5%, Cholesterol 100mg, 33%, Sodium 560 mg., 23%, Total Carbohydrate 560mg, 23%, Dietary Fiber 0g, Sugar 6g, Protein 27g

Nutritional Information per serving with side dish (% based upon daily values) ³⁄₄ cup green beans; ³⁄₄ cup brown rice: Calories: 387; Total Fat: 8g, 12%; Saturated Fat: 2g, 9%; Cholesterol: 100mg, 33%; Sodium: 747mg, 32%; Total Carbohydrate: 45g, 11%; Dietary Fiber: 5g, 19%; Sugar: 8g; Protein: 32g

½ cup hoisin sauce (an Asian condiment or marinade)

2 tablespoons rice vinegar

1 tablespoon reduced-sodium soy sauce

3–4 pounds chicken drumsticks and thighs

In a large measuring cup, whisk together the hoisin sauce, vinegar, and soy sauce. In a resealable bag or plastic container with a lid, marinate the chicken in the hoisin mixture for at least 2 hours and up to 24 hours, flipping occasionally (if you use a plastic bag, make sure to put a plate under the bag in case of a leak).

Preheat the oven to 450 degrees. Line a roasting pan with aluminum foil. Using tongs, remove the chicken from the marinade and put it in the baking pan skin side down, reserving the marinade.

Bake the chicken for 20 minutes, then flip it and pour or brush some of the reserved marinade over the chicken pieces. (Preheat the broiler at this point, if your broiler is separate from your oven.) Continue baking the chicken for 20 more minutes (meanwhile, start the green beans and rice, if you are serving them), and then put the chicken under the preheated broiler for about 5 minutes, flipping once to brown the skin evenly.

Scramble Flavor Booster: Add ½ teaspoon Asian five-spice powder and 1 teaspoon chili garlic sauce to the marinade. You can also sprinkle toasted sesame seeds on the chicken and green beans.

Tip: If you prefer to use boneless chicken breasts instead of drumsticks and thighs, reduce the cooking time by about half (check for doneness) so the meat doesn't get too dry.

Side Dish suggestion: To make Sesame-Stir-Fried Green Beans with Garlic, heat 2 teaspoons sesame oil in a wok or medium skillet over medium heat. Lightly brown 1 to 2 teaspoons minced garlic (2 to 4 cloves). Add 1 pound green beans and ⅛ cup water. Cover and steam it for 3 to 4 minutes, or to desired tenderness. Remove the cover, add 1 tablespoon reduced-sodium soy sauce, and stir-fry everything for 1 minute before serving.

I adapted this recipe from one I picked up at an organic market called Home Farm Store in the quaint country town of Middleburg, Virginia. The chicken turns out so juicy and delectable, and the sauce is wonderful spooned over orzo. Scramble recipe tester Christina Ramus said the chicken was so tender that her family didn't need knives to cut it. Serve it with roasted acorn squash and orzo or Israeli couscous.

chicken thighs with roasted red peppers and black olives

Prep (15 minutes) + Cook (25 minutes)

5 servings

Nutritional Information per serving (% based upon daily values): Calories 220, Total Fat 9g, 14%, Saturated Fat 1.5g, 8%, Cholesterol 85mg, 28%, Sodium 330mg, 14%, Total Carbohydrate 12g, 4%, Dietary Fiber 2g, 8%, Sugar 4g, Protein 22g

Nutritional Information per serving with side dish (% based upon daily values) ¼ squash; ¾ cup cooked orzo with ½ tsp. butter: Calories: 478; Total Fat: 15g, 22%; Saturated Fat: 5g, 25%; Cholesterol: 98mg, 32%; Sodium: 335mg, 14%; Total Carbohydrate: 58g, 19%; Dietary Fiber: 9g, 33%; Sugar: 6g; Protein: 29g

3–4 leeks, coarsely chopped (use white part and a little of the light green part)

1 tablespoon olive oil

¾ cup jarred roasted red peppers, sliced (about 2 roasted peppers)

2 pounds boneless, skinless chicken thighs

1 cup reduced-sodium chicken broth

1 teaspoon dried thyme

½ teaspoon dried oregano

½ teaspoon paprika

¼ teaspoon salt

½ cup pitted kalamata olives, chopped

½ lemon (about 2 tablespoons juice)

(If you are making the squash, start it first.) Soak the chopped leeks in water for a few minutes to clean them thoroughly. Drain and rinse them well.

In a large heavy skillet, heat the oil over medium heat. Add the leeks and sauté them until they are tender, about 5 minutes. Arrange the pepper strips over the leeks, and arrange the chicken over the vegetables. Pour the broth over everything and sprinkle the chicken with the thyme, oregano, paprika, and salt.

Bring the liquid to a boil, reduce the heat, and simmer it, covered, for 10 minutes. (Meanwhile, start the orzo, if you are making it.) Flip the chicken and continue to simmer it, covered, for 10 more minutes. Add the olives and lemon juice and simmer, uncovered, for about 5 minutes or until the chicken is cooked through and cuts easily with a sharp knife. Serve it immediately, spooning the sauce over the orzo or couscous.

Scramble Flavor Booster: Double the paprika or use cayenne pepper instead of paprika.

Tip: When introducing a new vegetable, such as acorn squash, to your children, encourage them to take one or two bites before deciding how they like it, and give them a lot of praise for being adventurous. If our kids don't like a new food, we usually tell them that their taste buds mature as they get older so they may like it next time.

Side Dish suggestion: To make roasted acorn squash, cut 1 to 2 acorn squash in half and brush the yellow flesh of each squash with 1 tablespoon melted butter or margarine. Roast the squash halves, flesh side down, on a baking sheet at 400 degrees for 30 minutes. Then, turn them over and bake or broil the halves for 10 to 15 minutes more until they are soft and lightly browned. Remove them from the oven and sprinkle each half with ½ teaspoon brown sugar. Scoop out the flesh or cut the halves into wedges to serve.

Side Dish suggestion: Prepare 12 to 16 ounces orzo (or use Israeli couscous) according to the package directions. When it is finished cooking, stir in 1 tablespoon butter or margarine.

My family loves my healthy homemade chicken nuggets (which bolsters the theory that we're never too old to enjoy kid-food). For vegetarian family members, you can serve this with some meatless nuggets (we think Morningstar Farms Chik'n Nuggets are the tastiest and most reminiscent of the real thing). Serve it with baked potatoes and fruit kabobs.

buttermilk-bathed chicken nuggets

Prep (20 minutes) + Cook (20 minutes)

6 servings

Nutritional Information per serving (% based upon daily values): Calories 220, Total Fat 3.5g, 5%, Saturated Fat 1.5g, 8%, Cholesterol 70mg, 23%, Sodium 370mg, 15%, Total Carbohydrate 14g, 5%, Dietary Fiber 1g, 4%, Sugar 2g, Protein 31g

Nutritional Information per serving with side dish (% based upon daily values) ½ potato, ½ tsp. butter, 1 tbsp. sour cream, ½ tbsp. salsa, 1 tsp. scallions, 1 tsp. cheese; 1 cup mixed fruit: Calories: 399; Total Fat: 6g, 8%; Saturated Fat: 2g, 10%; Cholesterol: 71mg, 23%; Sodium: 478mg, 19%; Total Carbohydrate: 53g, 18%; Dietary Fiber: 6g, 21%; Sugar: 17g; Protein: 34g

½ **cup reduced-fat buttermilk**

¼ **teaspoon garlic powder**

1 **cup bread crumbs**

¼ **cup grated Parmesan cheese**

¼ **teaspoon salt**

⅛ **teaspoon black pepper**

1½ **pounds boneless, skinless chicken breasts**

½ **cup barbecue sauce and/or ketchup for dipping, or to taste**

Preheat the oven to 400 degrees, and spray a large baking sheet with nonstick cooking spray. (Start the potatoes first, if you are making them.)

In a shallow bowl, whisk together the buttermilk and garlic powder. In another shallow bowl, combine the bread crumbs, cheese, salt, and pepper.

Cut the chicken into nugget-size pieces, dip each piece into the buttermilk mixture, and then coat it well in the bread crumb mixture. Put the pieces on the baking sheet.

Bake the nuggets for 15 to 20 minutes, until they are just cooked through and lightly browned, flipping once after about 10 minutes. (Meanwhile, make the fruit kabobs.) Serve the nuggets immediately with the dipping sauce(s), or refrigerate them for up to 3 days, or freeze them for up to 3 months.

Scramble Flavor Booster: Use seasoned bread crumbs and add a pinch of cayenne pepper to the buttermilk mixture.

Tip: To easily flip small items like chicken nuggets, I like to use a pair of kitchen tongs.

Side Dish suggestion: Pierce 3–6 russet potatoes in several places. To microwave: Cook the potatoes on high for about 10 minutes, flipping them once, until they are tender when pierced with a knife. If they are not done after 10 minutes, keep checking every 2 minutes. To bake: Preheat the oven to 400 degrees. For more flavorful skin, rub the potatoes with olive oil and sprinkle them with salt before baking. Place the potatoes directly on the oven rack and bake them for 50 to 60 minutes, or until tender when pierced with a fork, turning them once. While the potatoes are cooking, make a sauce with 1 cup nonfat sour cream, ¼ cup salsa, and ¼ cup thinly sliced scallions or chives (optional). Slice the potatoes in half, and serve them topped with a thin layer of butter or margarine and with the sour cream sauce.

Side Dish suggestion: Thread 6–8 cups mixed fruit, such as strawberries, bananas, grapes, pineapple, and/or melon onto toothpicks or small skewers (kids can have fun doing this). Serve with small bowls of nonfat vanilla yogurt for dipping (optional).

This chicken, from Six O'Clock Scramble subscriber Sandra Swirski, is the perfect solution for those crazy fall days when you're running around until dinnertime. You can prepare the chicken anytime during the day and roast it a couple of hours before dinner is served. Serve it with Caramelized Brussels Sprouts and egg noodles.

flawless roast chicken with sweet onions

Prep (10 minutes) + Cook (90 minutes)

6 servings

Nutritional Information per serving (% based upon daily values): Calories 300, Total Fat 16g, 25%, Saturated Fat 3.5g, 18%, Cholesterol 125mg, 42%, Sodium 450mg, 19%, Total Carbohydrate 2g, 1%, Dietary Fiber 0g, 0%, Sugar 1g, Protein 36g

Nutritional Information per serving with side dish (% based upon daily values) ⅙ of Brussels sprouts; ½ cup egg noodles: Calories: 490; Total Fat: 23g, 35%; Saturated Fat: 5g, 23%; Cholesterol: 148mg, 50%; Sodium: 474mg, 20%; Total Carbohydrate: 30g, 11%; Dietary Fiber: 4g, 19%; Sugar: 5g; Protein: 43g

1 large yellow onion, halved and cut into half rings

2 tablespoons olive oil

1 teaspoon kosher salt

1 teaspoon black pepper

1 whole roasting chicken, 5 to 6 pounds

2 lemons, quartered

Preheat the oven to 425 degrees. Lay the onions in the bottom of a roasting pan, stir in 1 tablespoon olive oil, and sprinkle them with some of the kosher salt and black pepper (about ¼ teaspoon of each).

Remove the giblets, drain the cavity if necessary, and season the cavity with ½ teaspoon kosher salt and ½ teaspoon black pepper. Stuff the quartered lemons in the cavity, squeezing them a little as you put them in to soften them. Put the chicken on top of the onions. Rub the remaining olive oil on the skin of the chicken, and season it with about ¼ teaspoon each of the salt and black pepper.

Bake the chicken for a total of 90 minutes, removing it from the oven and basting it after 1 hour, then returning it to the oven for 30 minutes. (Meanwhile, prepare the side dishes.) Let it cool for 10 to 15 minutes before carving it, if time allows.

Scramble Flavor Booster: Sprinkle about ¾ teaspoon dried herbs such as rosemary and thyme over the chicken. My family likes to use Chinese hot mustard and duck sauce as condiments for roast chicken.

Slow Cooker directions: Follow the directions above, but instead of baking the chicken and onions, put them in the slow cooker on the High setting for 4 hours or the Low setting for 8 hours.

Side Dish suggestion: To make Caramelized Brussels Sprouts, heat 2 tablespoons olive oil in a heavy skillet over medium heat. Add ½ yellow onion, finely chopped, 1 pound chopped Brussels sprouts, and ½ teaspoon minced garlic (about 1 clove), and sauté it for about 10 minutes, stirring occasionally, until the Brussels sprouts are lightly browned and very tender. Add 2 teaspoons balsamic vinegar and salt and black pepper to taste, and continue cooking it for about 5 more minutes, stirring occasionally, and reducing the heat if it is getting too deeply browned.

Side Dish suggestion: Prepare 1 package (12–16 ounces) egg noodles according to the package directions. Toss with 1 teaspoon olive oil, butter, or margarine, to prevent sticking, and season it with salt to taste.

twenty creative ideas for healthy school lunches

While some kids are perfectly content and maybe even comforted by eating the same lunch day after day, other children prefer more variety. Here's a list of some of our favorite healthy homemade school lunch ideas:

1. Turkey, ham or salami, Swiss cheese, and lettuce on whole wheat bread.
2. Turkey or ham, red bell pepper strips, and Cheddar cheese wrapped in a whole wheat tortilla, with mayonnaise, spicy mustard, or salsa.
3. Tuna, chicken, or egg salad with whole grain crackers or on a bagel with cucumbers or lettuce.
4. Cheddar or Muenster cheese and sliced tomato sandwich (put the tomato between the slices of cheese so the bread doesn't get soggy) with a little mayonnaise or mustard.
5. Peanut or other nut butter with jelly, sliced bananas, honey, raisins, or apples.
6. Leftovers like pasta, tortellini with tomato sauce, pizza, chicken, turkey sausage, or steak (kids don't seem to mind eating them cold). Save little condiment packages from takeout food to use as dips.
7. Black beans and rice or other rice salad (try the Mango and Black Bean Salad [page 80] and Orzo Salad with Peas and Feta Cheese [page 52]).
8. Healthy soup or chili in a thermos.
9. Whole grain bagel or rice cakes with natural peanut butter or cream cheese.
10. Trail mix made with raisins, peanuts, and chocolate chips (or your kids' favorite healthy items).
11. Healthy dried cereals (milk is optional).
12. Baby carrots, celery, sliced cucumbers, red bell peppers, and pita chips with hummus or other dip.
13. All varieties of fresh fruit (cut apples, mango, oranges, and other hard-to-eat fruit, if needed).
14. Popcorn (a kid-friendly whole grain), alone or mixed with raisins and nuts.
15. Whole grain tortilla chips and salsa (look for a brand without added sugar) or black bean dip.
16. Low-fat yogurt or cottage cheese with fresh fruit and granola or other cereal (keep them separate and let your child combine them at lunch).
17. Drinkable, spoonable, or squeezable yogurt or kefir.
18. Cheese and whole grain crackers, or cheese and apple slices.
19. Proteins like cheese sticks or cubes, hard-boiled eggs, nuts, chickpeas, or other beans.
20. Diced tofu drizzled with teriyaki sauce.

To reduce environmental waste, pack everything in reusable containers and wash all the used plastic utensils in the dishwasher. We also love to use Lunch Skins, the reusable sandwich and snack wrappers from www.3greenmoms.com, and the Japanese-style bento boxes for kids from www.laptoplunches.com.

I finally found a great way to incorporate beautiful purple cabbage into a Scramble dinner. Its flavor melds wonderfully with zesty sausage and tart apples, and how often do you get to feed your family a purple dinner? Scramble recipe tester Jennifer Doig agrees, "It's a fantastic fall recipe." Serve it with Garlic Cheese Bread.

sausage and cabbage sauté with tart apples

Prep + Cook = 25 minutes

4 servings

Nutritional Information per serving (% based upon daily values): Calories 200, Total Fat 10g, 15%, Saturated Fat 2.5g, 13%, Cholesterol 55mg, 18%, Sodium 920mg, 38%, Total Carbohydrate 14g, 5%, Dietary Fiber 4g, 16%, Sugar 11g, Protein 16g

Nutritional Information per serving with side dish (% based upon daily values) with 1 slice garlic cheese bread (½ pita): Calories: 349; Total Fat: 16g, 25%; Saturated Fat: 5g, 22%; Cholesterol: 63mg, 21%; Sodium: 1,161mg, 48%; Total Carbohydrate: 31g, 11%; Dietary Fiber: 5g, 19%; Sugar: 11g; Protein: 22g

1 to 2 tablespoons olive oil

12 ounces precooked turkey kielbasa sausage, diced

½ head red or purple cabbage, chopped

½ yellow or white onion, quartered and sliced

1 Granny Smith apple, cored and chopped

½ cup water

1 tablespoon cider vinegar

¼ teaspoon salt, or to taste

⅛ teaspoon black pepper, or to taste

(If you are making the Garlic Cheese Bread, preheat the oven first.) In a large pot with a tight-fitting lid, heat the oil over medium heat. Add the sausage and sauté it for about 5 minutes until it starts to brown. Add the cabbage, onions, apples, water, and vinegar, and stir to mix. Cover the pot and steam the mixture for 15 minutes, stirring once or twice, until the cabbage is tender. (Meanwhile, prepare the bread.) Season the dish with the salt and pepper and serve it immediately, or refrigerate it for up to 48 hours.

Scramble Flavor Booster: Add up to ¼ teaspoon cayenne pepper instead of the black pepper, or use spicy sausage such as chorizo instead of kielbasa. Add 2 tablespoons raisins with the apples for a sweeter dish.

Tip: Slice extra purple cabbage into a green salad, use it to make coleslaw, or eat it raw with natural peanut butter, which is how my dad used to enjoy it every evening.

Side Dish suggestion: To make Garlic Cheese Bread, preheat the broiler or toaster oven. Split a large sub roll or 3 whole wheat pita pockets in half lengthwise. Spread the tops with a light coating of butter or margarine, sprinkle them with garlic powder, and top them with a small handful of shredded part-skim mozzarella cheese. Put the bread under the broiler, or in the toaster oven, until the cheese melts and the edges of the bread turn golden. (Thanks to subscriber Karen Singer for the great side dish suggestion!)

My friend Kim Tilley, who is a phenomenal cook, serves this flavorful pork roast to her family. She and I both love its quick preparation. The sweet potatoes, at their best in the fall, are the perfect complement to the savory pork. Serve it with a green salad with red cabbage, blue cheese, and walnuts.

rosemary-garlic pork roast with whipped sweet potatoes

Prep (20 minutes) + Cook (30-40 minutes)

6 servings

Nutritional Information per serving (% based upon daily values): Calories 360, Total Fat 10g, 15%, Saturated Fat 2.5g, 13%, Cholesterol 75mg, 25%, Sodium 270mg, 11%, Total Carbohydrate 38g, 13%, Dietary Fiber 6g, 24%, Sugar 10g, Protein 28g

Nutritional Information per serving with side dish (% based upon daily values) 1½ cups salad: Calories: 412; Total Fat: 14g, 19%; Saturated Fat: 3g, 17%; Cholesterol: 77mg, 26%; Sodium: 405mg, 17%; Total Carbohydrate: 43g, 14%; Dietary Fiber: 8g, 31%; Sugar: 12g; Protein: 30g

1½–2 pounds boneless pork loin roast or pork tenderloin

2 tablespoons olive oil

2½ teaspoons minced garlic (about 5 cloves)

1 tablespoon fresh or dried rosemary

½ teaspoon kosher salt

¾ teaspoon black pepper

2½ pounds sweet potatoes (about 5 potatoes), peeled and chopped into 1-inch pieces

1–2 tablespoons butter or margarine, to taste

1–2 tablespoons maple syrup or brown sugar, to taste

½ cup nonfat milk

Preheat the oven to 400 degrees. Put the meat in a large roasting pan. In a small bowl, combine the oil, garlic, rosemary, salt, and black pepper. Rub the mixture all over the top and sides of the meat. (If using pork tenderloin, fold the skinny piece under so you have a piece with somewhat uniform thickness.) Cook the meat for 30 to 40 minutes (check it after 25 minutes for pork tenderloin) until it is cooked through, or has an internal temperature of 160 degrees. Cut it into slices to serve it.

While the meat is cooking, cover the peeled and chopped sweet potatoes with water in a saucepan and bring it to a boil over high heat. Simmer the potatoes until they are fork-tender, 10 to 15 minutes. (Meanwhile, prepare the salad.) Drain them thoroughly, and whip them in a mixing bowl with the butter or margarine, syrup or sugar, and milk until they are smooth. [Optional: Transfer the whipped potatoes to a small casserole and put them in the oven with the pork roast until the tops of the potatoes start to brown.] Serve them hot.

Scramble Flavor Booster: Season the pork with extra freshly ground black pepper and serve it with spicy mustard.

Tip: Pork can dry out quickly, so rely on your meat thermometer rather than appearance to judge when it is done.

Side Dish suggestion: To make the salad, in a large bowl, combine 6 to 8 cups lettuce, 1 cup shredded red cabbage, 3 tablespoons crumbled blue cheese, 3 tablespoons walnuts, and 2 to 4 tablespoons balsamic vinaigrette or salad dressing of your choice.

My friend Ruth Robbins gave me a bottle of Cuban Mojo sauce, and I liked the complex flavors so much that I was inspired to make my own version. This sauce is great for marinating any meat or fish, but this pork version is most authentically Cuban, and we found it irresistible. Recipe tester Debbie Firestone gave this recipe 10 out of 10, and described it as "out-of-this-world delicious!" Serve it with Cuban Black Beans and grilled zucchini or yellow squash.

grilled pork tenderloin with cuban mojo sauce

Prep (10 minutes) + Cook (25 minutes) + Marinate (30 minutes– 12 hours)

4 servings

Nutritional Information per serving (% based upon daily values): Calories 280, Total Fat 13g, 20%, Saturated Fat 3g, 15%, Cholesterol 110mg, 37%, Sodium 570mg, 24%, Total Carbohydrate 4g, 1%, Dietary Fiber 0g, 0%, Sugar 2g, Protein 36g

Nutritional Information per serving with side dish (% based upon daily values) ¼ of beans; ¾ cup cooked squash or zucchini: Calories: 440; Total Fat: 20g, 31%; Saturated Fat: 4g, 18%; Cholesterol: 110mg, 37%; Sodium: 988mg, 41%; Total Carbohydrate: 24g, 8%; Dietary Fiber: 6g, 24%; Sugar: 5g; Protein: 43g

1½ pounds pork tenderloin, or 1 whole chicken cut into parts

2 limes, juice only (about ¼ cup juice)

¼ cup orange juice

1 teaspoon dried oregano or 1 tablespoon fresh

1 teaspoon kosher salt

½ teaspoon ground cumin

½ teaspoon black pepper

2 teaspoons minced garlic (3–4 cloves)

2 tablespoons olive oil

Put the pork (or chicken) in a flat dish large enough to hold it in one layer. In a measuring cup, mix together all the remaining ingredients and pour them over the meat, flipping it a couple of times to coat it. Marinate the meat, covered and refrigerated, for at least 30 minutes and up to 12 hours, flipping it once or twice.

Preheat the grill to medium heat (about 400 degrees, if you are using a gas grill). (Alternatively, you can bake it with the marinade at 400 degrees for 25 to 30 minutes.) (Meanwhile, prepare the squash, if you are serving it.) Remove the meat from the marinade, reserving the marinade, and grill it for 20 to 25 minutes (or 5 to 10 minutes longer for bone-in chicken), flipping it once, until it is no longer pink in the center. (Meanwhile, prepare the beans.) When the meat is almost done cooking, pour the marinade into a small pot, bring it to a boil, and simmer it for 2 minutes to kill any bacteria and intensify the flavor. Cut the tenderloin into thin slices to serve it, pouring the cooked marinade over it, if desired.

Scramble Flavor Booster: Double the cumin and the black pepper and add a few splashes of hot pepper sauce (such as Tabasco) or jerk seasoning to the marinade and the Cuban Black Beans.

Side Dish suggestion: To make Cuban Black Beans, sauté 1 teaspoon minced or chopped garlic (about 2 cloves) in 1 tablespoon olive oil over medium heat. Add ½ cup finely diced bell pepper or onion and sauté it for several minutes until it is tender. Add 1 can (15 ounces) black beans with their liquid, ½ teaspoon ground cumin, 1 teaspoon sugar or balsamic vinegar, and ¼ teaspoon black pepper, and simmer it, covered, for 5 to 7 minutes, stirring occasionally.

Side Dish suggestion: To make grilled zucchini or yellow squash, cut 2 to 3 zucchini or yellow squash lengthwise into quarters, and then cut the strips crosswise into several shorter strips. Toss them with about 1 tablespoon olive oil and a dash of salt and black pepper, to taste. Place the squash on a vegetable tray or sturdy piece of aluminum foil, and grill it for 10 to 20 minutes, flipping it once, until it reaches the desired tenderness. (Alternatively, sauté the zucchini or yellow squash in the oil over medium heat for about 10 minutes until it is lightly browned and tender.)

eight parent-tested tips to get kids to embrace new foods

I'm sure we all know kids with some very particular food rules: "I only eat plain noodles," "I hate green beans!," "I don't like water or milk." No wonder worn out parents get into a rut of serving the same five foods over and over.

Unfortunately the dinner table can turn into a battleground between the emerging wills of young kids and the desire of parents to nourish with healthy, balanced, and varied foods. We worry that our family will never be able to sit down and eat the same thing for dinner. I've been there and I know how frustrating this can be!

Having spoken to hundreds of parents and experts on this issue, and brought up two children who have been very picky at different times in their lives (but are now great eaters), I want to share my nearly foolproof suggestions for encouraging children to try new foods:

1. **Cut down on (or eliminate) snacks and juice between meals.** If kids are not hungry at mealtime, they are unlikely to eat much. If they do need snacks between meals, make sure they're healthy ones, or even part of the dinner you have planned. Leaving fresh fruit or cut-up veggies out makes for a great "grab snack."

2. **Don't push too hard.** Kids won't starve themselves, but they can be amazingly strident and you will likely lose the power struggle. However, I do believe in a one-bite rule. Kids often need repeated exposure to new tastes before they will begin to accept them. (And don't forget to shower them with praise if they try more than one bite.)

3. **Don't get into a food rut.** Vary the foods that you serve, and don't shy away from something just because your children didn't like it last time.

4. **Try to eat meals together at least a few nights (or mornings) each week, even if it seems inconvenient.** Your children will be more likely to eat what the rest of the family is eating when you sit together.

5. **Talk up the health benefits of new foods.** My husband, Andrew, has convinced many kids to eat green beans by telling them how strong they make their fingers and toes. After they eat 10 to 20 string beans, he lets them demonstrate their new finger power by pushing him over or taking him on in a spirited game of "Mercy"!

6. **Enjoy meals with friends.** Kids will often try something new if other kids, especially older kids, at the table are eating it.

7. **Cook with your kids.** We've found that our kids are more likely to eat food they've helped create, and they learn a priceless life skill in the process.

8. **Adapt your dinners.** Many cooked foods, including meat and pasta, can be rinsed to tone down sauces or flavors that the kids find to be too intense. I sometimes set a portion of a dish aside before adding a stronger spice or sauce—that way I can prepare just one meal, and still accommodate the more sensitive palates in the family.

This is a super-easy and delicious way to prepare salmon, suggested by my friend, Lisa Newman. You can adapt the seasoning to your taste, making it spicier or more or less salty. Serve it with Garlic Roasted Fingerling Potatoes.

chili-rubbed salmon with garlic roasted fingerling potatoes

Prep + Cook = 30 minutes

4 servings

Nutritional Information per serving (% based upon daily values): Calories 270, Total Fat 14g, 22%, Saturated Fat 2g, 10%, Cholesterol 95mg, 32%, Sodium 200mg, 8%, Total Carbohydrate <1g, 0%, Dietary Fiber 0g, 0%, Sugar 0g, Protein 34g

Nutritional Information per serving with side dish (% based upon daily values) ¼ of the potatoes: Calories: 320; Total Fat: 19g, 29%; Saturated Fat: 3g, 15%; Cholesterol: 95mg, 32%; Sodium: 290mg, 12%; Total Carbohydrate: 25g, 8%; Dietary Fiber: 3g, 12%; Sugar: 1g; Protein: 37g

1½ **pounds salmon fillet (preferably wild Alaskan salmon)**

1 **teaspoon chili powder, or more to taste**

¾ **teaspoon dried oregano**

¼ **teaspoon kosher salt, or more to taste**

⅛ **teaspoon black pepper**

1 **tablespoon olive oil**

Preheat the oven to 450 degrees. (If you are making the potatoes, start them first.) Lay a sheet of aluminum foil on a baking sheet for easy cleanup, and lay the salmon on the foil, skin side down. In a small bowl, combine the chili powder, oregano, salt, and black pepper. Sprinkle and rub the spices evenly over the salmon. Drizzle the olive oil in swirls over the salmon and spices.

Bake the fish for 10 to 15 minutes, depending on the fish's thickness, until it is nearly cooked through and flakes easily in the thickest part. Optional: Put the salmon under the broiler for the final 2 to 4 minutes of cooking for a crispier finish. Cut it into 4 pieces to serve.

Scramble Flavor Booster: Double the chili powder and black pepper and add ¼ teaspoon of white pepper or cayenne pepper.

Tip: If you have picky eaters in your family, consider leaving a portion of the salmon plain rather than rubbing it with the spices.

Side Dish suggestion: To make Garlic Roasted Fingerling Potatoes, in a baking or broiling pan, toss 1 to 1½ pounds fingerling potatoes (little potatoes that almost look like fingers—you can also use new potatoes, halved or quartered) with 1 tablespoon olive oil, ¼ teaspoon garlic powder, ¼ teaspoon kosher salt, and ¼ to ½ teaspoon dried or fresh rosemary leaves. Bake them at 450 degrees for about 30 minutes, until they are slightly browned, tossing every 10 minutes. Broil for the final few minutes with the salmon, if desired.

This was a popular recipe at our house, especially with our eleven-year-old guest, Ben Martel, who would have eaten all the salmon by himself if we hadn't begged some off of him. Serve it with roasted parsnips or carrots and Bulgur Wheat Pilaf with Grapes and Pecans.

seared salmon with orange-rosemary sauce

Prep + Cook =
30 minutes

4 servings

Nutritional Information per serving (% based upon daily values): Calories 330, Total Fat 18g, 28% Saturated Fat 2.5g, 13%, Cholesterol 95mg, 32%, Sodium 90mg, 4%, Total Carbohydrate 6g, 2%, Dietary Fiber 0g, 0%, Sugar 1g, Protein 34g

Nutritional Information per serving with side dish (% based upon daily values) ⅙ of parsnips; ¾ cup cooked bulgur pilaf: Calories: 548; Total Fat: 25g, 38%; Saturated Fat: 4g, 17%; Cholesterol: 95mg, 32%; Sodium: 158mg, 12%; Total Carbohydrate: 43g, 14%; Dietary Fiber: 10g, 38%; Sugar: 5g; Protein: 41g

2 tablespoons olive oil

1½ pounds salmon fillet

⅛–¼ teaspoon salt, to taste

⅛ teaspoon black pepper, or to taste

⅛–¼ lemon, juice only (about 1 teaspoon)

1–2 juicing oranges (use ¾ cup juice and 1 teaspoon orange zest)

1 tablespoon balsamic vinegar

⅛ yellow or white onion, minced (about 2 tablespoons)

1 tablespoon chopped fresh rosemary

Preheat the oven to 450 degrees. (Start the parsnips, if you are serving them.) In a large heavy, ovenproof skillet, heat 1 tablespoon olive oil over medium-high heat. Put the salmon in the skillet (skin side down unless it is skinless), season it with salt and black pepper, and sear the fish (cooking without moving it) for about 3 minutes. (Meanwhile, start the bulgur pilaf.)

Transfer the skillet to the oven, and cook the salmon for about 15 minutes until it is cooked through (use a sharp knife to peek in the thickest part of the salmon). Remove it from the oven and sprinkle it with the lemon juice.

Meanwhile, in a small saucepan, combine the orange zest, orange juice, remaining oil, vinegar, and onions and bring them to a boil. Reduce the heat and simmer the sauce for about 10 minutes until the fish is ready. After the sauce has been cooking for 5 minutes, add the rosemary and continue to simmer it. Serve the salmon with the orange-rosemary sauce spooned over it.

Scramble Flavor Booster: Serve the fish with lemon wedges.

Tip: To zest an orange, wash and thoroughly dry it, and use a zester, peeler, or sharp paring knife to slice the outer orange part of the peel from the orange, and dice the zest if necessary. Try to avoid the bitter white pith underneath the orange peel. I find my Microplane zester/grater to be a very handy kitchen tool.

Side Dish suggestion: To make roasted parsnips or carrots, cut 1 pound of parsnips or carrots lengthwise into quarters and cut those strips into 1-inch pieces. In a roasting pan, toss the pieces with 1 to 2 tablespoons olive oil, ½ teaspoon kosher salt, and ¼ teaspoon black pepper. Roast them in the oven at 450 degrees until they are slightly browned, 15 to 20 minutes, tossing once. The longer you cook them, the sweeter they will become.

Side Dish suggestion: To make the bulgur pilaf, bring 16 ounces reduced-sodium chicken or vegetable broth or water (or a mixture of broth and water) and 1 cup bulgur to a boil. Cover and simmer it for 15 minutes. Remove it from the heat and stir in ¼ cup halved grapes or whole raisins and ¼ cup lightly toasted, coarsely chopped pecans.

dinners can be a whole lot healthier with whole grains

As chief recipe developer for the Scramble, I scour the supermarket aisles looking for interesting new foods to try. Sure, I strike out sometimes—nobody but me liked the chili-salsa grits, and even I couldn't eat the frozen plantains. But I also learned that I enjoy quinoa (pronounced "keen-wah"), a light whole grain from South America, and barley. (My husband, Andrew, thinks "Quinoa & Barley" sounds like a great name for a folk-music duo.) While they may not make beautiful music, whole grains can help you maintain a healthy weight and prevent heart attacks, strokes, and Type II diabetes, and they can be a great part of delicious family dinners.

Lately, I have been trying to incorporate more whole grains into our meals. I try to follow the USDA's suggestion to "make half your grains whole," which gives us a realistic goal. (Some examples of whole grains are brown rice, wild rice, whole wheat, oats, quinoa, barley, bulgur, corn, and other foods with the words "whole grain" on the label.) According to the American Dietetic Association, "Whole grain foods give nutritional benefits of the entire grain—vitamins, minerals, dietary fiber, and other natural plant compounds called phytochemicals." In contrast, refined grains such as white rice and all-purpose flour contain only the center of the grains. Eating whole wheat bread and whole grain cereals also gives you the health advantages of whole grains.

Some whole grains take longer to cook, although others like quinoa, bulgur, and quick-cooking brown rice don't take any longer than refined grains. You can often reduce cooking time for the denser grains by soaking them overnight. I find that when I use them in stews, the grains take on the texture and flavor of the other ingredients and are more palatable to those unaccustomed to eating whole grains.

I still cook with refined grains, especially on busy weeknights, but I am always looking for opportunities to incorporate healthier and delicious whole grains into my family's diet and Scramble recipes.

Hint: If your kids (or spouse!) aren't taking well to brown rice, try mixing half white and half brown rice, or experiment with a few different brands.

This Island-inspired fish stew is adapted from an Atkins diet recipe, and it's really different from any fish I've tried—I think your family will love it. Serve it with couscous and steamed broccoli.

brazilian halibut with coconut-lime sauce

Prep + Cook =
20 minutes

4 servings

Nutritional Information per serving (% based upon daily values): Calories 299, Total Fat 13g, 20%, Saturated Fat 3g, 16%, Cholesterol 55mg, 18%, Sodium 536mg, 22%, Total Carbohydrate 9g, 3%, Dietary Fiber 1g, 4%, Sugar 4g, Protein 42g

Nutritional Information per serving with side dish (% based upon daily values) ¾ cup couscous prepared with water; 1 cup steamed broccoli: Calories: 486; Total Fat: 14g, 21%; Saturated Fat: 4g, 17%; Cholesterol: 55mg, 18%; Sodium: 606mg, 25%; Total Carbohydrate: 49g, 16%; Dietary Fiber: 8g, 32%; Sugar: 6g; Protein: 50g

2 tablespoons olive oil

1 lime, juice only (about 2 tablespoons)

1½ pounds halibut fillet, skin removed and cut into 1-inch chunks (have the market do this, if possible), or use other thick white fish fillets or boneless, skinless chicken breasts

1 small yellow onion, chopped

1 yellow bell pepper, diced

1½ teaspoons minced garlic (about 3 cloves)

½ cup unsweetened light coconut milk (sold with Asian foods)

1 tomato, diced

¾ teaspoon salt

In a flat dish with sides, combine 1 tablespoon of the oil and the lime juice. Marinate the fish flesh side down in the mixture while the other ingredients are cooking (or marinate it in the refrigerator for up to 2 hours).

In a large heavy skillet, heat the remaining oil over medium heat, and sauté the onions, bell peppers, and garlic for 5 to 7 minutes, until the vegetables are just tender. (Meanwhile, start the broccoli, if you are serving it.)

Add the fish to the skillet, flesh side up, and pour the marinade and coconut milk over it. Add the tomatoes to the pan and sprinkle the salt over everything. Simmer the fish for 8 to 10 minutes until it is cooked through and flakes easily, flipping it halfway through. (Meanwhile, prepare the couscous.) Serve it hot.

Scramble Flavor Booster: Add the zest of 1 lime to the marinade.

Tip: I don't usually cook with fresh tomatoes when it's not summer (their growing season), but in this recipe I've made an exception because the tomato gets cooked with other ingredients so it doesn't need to be particularly flavorful. If you prefer, you can use 1¼ cups of canned diced tomatoes instead of a fresh one.

Side Dish suggestion: Trim 1 to 2 heads broccoli and cut it into spears (or use frozen broccoli). Steam the broccoli in 1 inch of simmering water for 8 to 10 minutes, to the desired tenderness. Drain and season to taste with salt and black pepper and/or lemon-pepper seasoning.

This was my father-in-law Mark Goldfarb's fantastic preparation for fish. You won't believe how flavorful and elegant it is for such little effort. Serve it with whole grain bread and steamed green beans (page 101).

broiled white fish
with lemon, tomatoes, and olives

Prep + Cook =
20 minutes

4 servings

Nutritional
Information per
serving (% based
upon daily values):
Calories 220, Total
Fat 12.5g, 19%, Satu-
rated Fat 0.5g, 3%,
Cholesterol 80mg,
27%, Sodium 740mg,
31%, Total Carbohy-
drate 6g, 2%, Dietary
Fiber 3g, 12%, Sugar
1g, Protein 20g

Nutritional
Information per
serving with side dish
(% based upon daily
values) 1 slice bread;
1 cup green beans:
Calories: 364; Total
Fat: 15g, 22%; Satu-
rated Fat: 1g, 3%;
Cholesterol: 80mg,
27%; Sodium: 927mg,
39%; Total Carbohy-
drate: 34g, 12%;
Dietary Fiber: 10g,
39%; Sugar: 6g;
Protein: 26g

1 pound walleye, bluefish, catfish, or other thick white fish fillets

1 tablespoon olive oil

1½ teaspoons minced garlic (2–3 cloves)

¼ teaspoon salt, or to taste

⅛ teaspoon black pepper, or to taste

1 lemon, thinly sliced

1 cup cherry tomatoes, halved or quartered (or any fresh or canned tomatoes)

½ cup pitted kalamata olives

Preheat the broiler and put the rack about 5 or 6 inches from the heat source. Lay the fish, skin side down, in a medium baking dish or on an aluminum foil–lined baking sheet. Brush the oil and garlic evenly over the top of the fish, season it with salt and black pepper, and lay the lemon slices evenly on top of the fish. Scatter the tomatoes and olives on top of and around the fish.

Broil the fish for 10 to 12 minutes until it is cooked through and flakes easily. (Meanwhile, prepare the green beans.) Serve it immediately.

Scramble Flavor Booster: Top the cooked fish with 2 tablespoons chopped fresh parsley, and/or use extra kalamata olives and freshly ground black pepper.

Tip: Walleye is a freshwater fish, usually found in the Northern U.S. and in Canada.

I am honored that Scramble subscriber Alice Nolen of Mobile, Alabama, was willing to share her family's secret recipe for Southern-style broiled trout. Alice and I lightened up the original recipe a bit for healthier palates, but it still has just the right amount of flavor for a wonderful family dinner. Serve it with Parmesan grits and a Carrot and Apple Salad.

creole trout with lemon butter and tarragon

Prep + Cook = 20 minutes

4 servings

Nutritional Information per serving (% based upon daily values): Calories 210, Total Fat 13g, 20%, Saturated Fat 5g, 25%, Cholesterol 110mg, 37%, Sodium 220mg, 9%, Total Carbohydrate 1g, 0%, Dietary Fiber 0g, 0%, Sugar 0g, Protein 36g

Nutritional Information per serving with side dish (% based upon daily values) ¼ of grits; ½ cup salad: Calories: 450; Total Fat: 19g, 29%; Saturated Fat: 9g, 43%; Cholesterol: 125mg, 42%; Sodium: 550mg, 23%; Total Carbohydrate: 43g, 14%; Dietary Fiber: 4g, 16%; Sugar: 6g; Protein: 44g

1½ pounds whole boned trout or trout fillets, or use catfish, Arctic char, or other boneless fillets

1 lemon, halved

1 teaspoon Creole seasoning, seasoning salt (such as Lawry's), or Old Bay seasoning

1 teaspoon dried tarragon

4 teaspoons butter

Preheat the broiler and spray the bottom of a 9 × 13-inch baking dish or a baking sheet with nonstick cooking spray. (Heat the water for the grits, if you are serving them, but don't add the grits until the fish is in the oven.)

Put the fish (skin side down, if using a whole trout) in the dish, and squeeze the juice of ½ lemon over the fillets. Top them evenly with the seasoning salt and tarragon. Cut the pats of butter in half and put them in the center of each fillet.

Place the fish under the broiler for 7 to 10 minutes until it flakes easily with a fork and is lightly browned on the edges. (Meanwhile, make the salad and add the grits to the boiling water.)

Serve it immediately, with additional lemon wedges, if desired.

Scramble Flavor Booster: Use extra seasoning salt and sprinkle a little bit of cayenne pepper or black pepper on top.

Tip: Apples and apple juice, particularly apple cider, have been found to contain disease-fighting antioxidants and phytochemicals. Nonetheless, parents should still limit their children's juice consumption to one cup per day, according to pediatricians.

Side Dish suggestion: In a medium saucepan, bring 4 cups of water to a boil. Stir in 1 cup quick-cooking (not instant) grits and ¼ teaspoon salt, reduce the heat, cover, and simmer it for 5 minutes, removing the cover to stir it occasionally. Remove the grits from the heat and stir in 1 tablespoon butter or margarine and ½ cup grated Parmesan cheese. Serve it immediately.

Side Dish suggestion: To make a Carrot and Apple Salad, toss 1½ cups each of shredded carrots (about 3 large carrots) and shredded apples (about 2 apples) with 1 tablespoon each of orange juice and fresh lemon juice (about ¼ lemon). Chill the salad for at least 10 minutes before serving, if time allows.

I've always had mixed feelings about tabouli until I tried this version, suggested by Scramble subscriber Sara Rose Corcoran. With its big chunks of cucumber, tomato, shrimp, and feta cheese, I couldn't stop eating it. For a vegetarian version, use chickpeas instead of the shrimp. Serve it with homemade pita chips and hummus (page 81).

chopped tabouli salad with shrimp

Prep + Cook = 30 minutes + 30 minutes–2 days to chill

6 servings

Nutritional Information per serving (% based upon daily values): Calories 250, Total Fat 9g, 14%, Saturated Fat 2.5g, 13%, Cholesterol 120mg, 40%, Sodium 440mg, 18%, Total Carbohydrate 23g, 8%, Dietary Fiber 5g, 20%, Sugar 2g, Protein 21g

Nutritional Information per serving with side dish (% based upon daily values) $1/2$ piece pita and $1/4$ cup hummus: Calories: 437; Total Fat: 16g, 24%; Saturated Fat: 4g, 17%; Cholesterol: 120mg, 40%; Sodium: 838mg, 35%; Total Carbohydrate: 49g, 17%; Dietary Fiber: 10g, 38%; Sugar: 3g; Protein: 29g

1 cup bulgur wheat

1 pound shrimp, peeled and deveined (or use 1 can [15 ounces] chickpeas, drained and rinsed)

1 English cucumber, peeled and chopped

2 tomatoes, seeded and chopped

$1/4$ cup chopped flat-leaf Italian parsley

$1/4$ cup chopped fresh mint leaves

$1/2$–1 lemon, juice only (2–4 tablespoons), to taste

2 tablespoons olive oil

$1/2$ teaspoon salt

$1/4$ teaspoon black pepper

$1/2$ cup crumbled feta cheese

Bring $1\frac{1}{4}$ cups water to a boil, pour it over the bulgur wheat, cover, and let it sit for 20 to 25 minutes.

Steam the shrimp over a little bit of boiling water until they are pink and opaque, about 3 to 4 minutes. (Meanwhile, start the pita chips, if you are making them.) Run the shrimp under cold water to cool them, remove the tails, and cut each shrimp into 2 or 3 bite-sized pieces. Transfer them to a large serving bowl, and add the remaining ingredients, except the cheese.

When the bulgur wheat is done, fluff it with a fork and add it to the bowl, stirring with each addition. Add the cheese, toss gently, and refrigerate until ready to serve, at least 30 minutes and up to 2 days.

Scramble Flavor Booster: You can double the parsley, and for extra lemony flavor, add $1/4$–$1/2$ teaspoon lemon zest and extra lemon juice to the salad.

Tip: English cucumbers usually have small edible seeds, so you don't need to remove them before chopping them.

snack attack
fifty ideas for healthy snacks

Afternoon hunger strikes like a cobra! Before it attacks, it's best to be armed with some nourishing and delicious snacks for our kids (and ourselves). I've compiled a list from Scrambling parents for healthy and creative snack ideas.

1. Plain or flavored yogurt or cottage cheese with sliced fruit and granola.
2. Whole grain cereals or oatmeal, dry or with milk, yogurt, or raisins.
3. Cheese sticks, cubes, or shredded cheese.
4. Nuts and raisin mix, trail mix, or just nuts or raisins or dried cranberries and almonds.
5. Peanut butter sandwich on whole wheat bread with sliced apples or bananas.
6. Banana Dog (fill a whole wheat hot dog roll with peanut butter and a banana).
7. Peanut butter sandwich with raspberry jam and cashews.
8. Cinnamon toast (toasted whole grain bread spread lightly with butter and sprinkled with cinnamon and sugar).
9. Cinnamon graham crackers with nonfat cottage cheese.
10. Chocolate graham crackers with peanut butter.
11. Quesadillas (melted cheese on whole wheat tortillas).
12. Grilled cheese on whole grain bread.
13. Pancakes or waffles.
14. Rice cakes, plain or topped with peanut butter or cheese.
15. Popcorn, homemade or store-bought (look for a brand that is low in sodium and fat).
16. Pita chips, pretzels, or other healthy and flavorful chips.
17. Tortilla chips and salsa.
18. Tortilla chips with guacamole.
19. Tortilla chips topped with shredded cheese and put under the broiler.
20. Crackers with goat cheese or other spreadable cheese.
21. Healthy granola bars and fruit bars (look for high fiber and no trans fats).
22. Muffins or breads, such as banana, pumpkin, corn, or zucchini (you can make a batch and freeze it).
23. Mini bagels with cream cheese and sliced cucumbers.
24. Pizza bagels (bagel topped with sauce, cheese, and herbs)
25. Whole grain bagel chips with cream cheese or Cheddar spread. (continued)

26. Hummus dip with pita, crackers, or veggies.

27. Sliced avocados with wheat crackers.

28. Tapenade or other Mediterranean dip with whole grain crackers.

29. Hard-boiled eggs, whole or chopped over wheat bread.

30. Turkey slices served plain, rolled in a tortilla, or in a sandwich.

31. Celery filled with cream cheese, Boursin cheese, or peanut butter (plain or topped with raisins).

32. Sliced bell peppers, celery, baby carrots, or sugar snap peas with ranch dip or other dressing (see page 33 for suggested dips).

33. Edamame in the shell, sprinkled lightly with sea salt.

34. Chickpeas or other beans, eaten with fingers or toothpicks.

35. Scrambled egg and salsa wrapped in a whole wheat tortilla.

36. Olives, pickles, canned artichokes or hearts of palm.

37. Warm black beans topped with Cheddar cheese and salsa.

38. Frozen peas (not thawed!).

39. Apple slices with peanut butter, peanut butter and chocolate chips, or honey.

40. Apple or pear slices with Cheddar cheese or Gouda.

41. Fresh cut fruit, canned fruit (in water or fruit juice), or frozen fruit.

42. Fruit kabobs (cut fruit on a stick, dipped in vanilla yogurt).

43. Smoothies: combine fresh and/or frozen fruit, fruit juice, and yogurt or soy milk.

44. Pure fruit popsicles.

45. Dried fruit such as mango, apricots, raisins, or plums.

46. Banana Royale (slice a banana lengthwise and fill it with peanut butter and a couple of marshmallows or chocolate chips, then heat in microwave and eat with a spoon.

47. Ice cream cone or waffle bowl filled with yogurt and chopped fruit.

48. Bananas and/or strawberries with semisweet chocolate chips or chocolate syrup.

49. Naturally sweetened applesauce.

50. Leftovers from your healthy dinner!

This is a fresh-tasting dish for a weeknight dinner, and is great served hot or cold. Arugula has a light peppery taste that adventurous children may like, but you might want to leave some pasta plain just in case. If you can't find arugula, you can use baby spinach or other tender greens. Serve it with Italian Cauliflower, and Strawberry-Banana Smoothies for dessert (page 75).

warm pasta salad with arugula or spinach

Prep + Cook = 25 minutes

8 servings

Nutritional Information per serving (% based upon daily values): Calories 300, Total Fat 9g, 14%, Saturated Fat 3g, 15%, Cholesterol 10mg, 3%, Sodium 370mg, 15%, Total Carbohydrate 45g, 15%, Dietary Fiber 2g, 8%, Sugar 3g, Protein 10g

Nutritional Information per serving with side dish (% based upon daily values) 1 cup cauliflower; ¼ of smoothie: Calories: 497; Total Fat: 15g, 23%; Saturated Fat: 7g, 31%; Cholesterol: 26mg, 8%; Sodium: 445mg, 19%; Total Carbohydrate: 78g, 26%; Dietary Fiber: 8g, 33%; Sugar: 25g; Protein: 17g

1 package (16 ounces) penne pasta

1 bunch arugula, stemmed and roughly chopped (about 4 ounces), or baby spinach

4 plum (or Roma) tomatoes, chopped

4 ounces feta or goat cheese, crumbled (about 1 cup)

½ cup pitted kalamata or other strong olives, chopped

10 fresh basil or mint leaves, chopped

1 teaspoon balsamic vinegar, or more to taste

2 tablespoons olive oil

¼ teaspoon salt, or to taste

Cook the pasta according to package directions until it is al dente, then drain it. (Prepare the cauliflower now, if you are serving it.)

Meanwhile, soak the arugula in a bowl of cold water for a few minutes to thoroughly clean it, then dry it well.

In a large serving bowl, combine the arugula, tomatoes, feta or goat cheese, olives, basil or mint, vinegar, and oil. Set it aside.

Toss the pasta with the other ingredients in the large bowl. Season it with salt, if desired, and serve it immediately or refrigerate it for up to 24 hours.

Scramble Flavor Booster: Add ¼ teaspoon crushed red pepper flakes with the tomatoes and other ingredients. You can add a can or pouch of tuna for extra protein and flavor.

Tip: One more reason to love this recipe: Feta cheese has less fat and calories than most other cheeses.

Side Dish suggestion: To make Italian Cauliflower, cut 1 head cauliflower into florets and steam the florets until they are very soft (15 to 20 minutes). Toss them with 1 to 2 tablespoons butter or margarine, 1 tablespoon grated Parmesan cheese, 2 tablespoons bread crumbs, and 1 tablespoon chopped fresh parsley or 1 teaspoon dried (optional).

I could practically feel my muscles growing stronger after eating this tasty dish stacked with power foods like greens, onions, beans, and tomatoes, and my smile grew, too, when everyone in our family happily ate it. Serve it with a baguette.

farfalle with swiss chard and sun-dried tomatoes

Prep + Cook =
25 minutes

8 servings

Nutritional Information per serving (% based upon daily values): Calories 330, Total Fat 6g, 9%, Saturated Fat 1.5g, 8%, Cholesterol <5mg, 2%, Sodium 430mg, 18%, Total Carbohydrate 56g, 19%, Dietary Fiber 5g, 20%, Sugar 4g, Protein 13g

Nutritional Information per serving with side dish (% based upon daily values) ¼ of baguette: Calories: 517; Total Fat: 8g, 12%; Saturated Fat: 2g, 8%; Cholesterol: 11mg, 4%; Sodium: 841 mg, 35%; Total Carbohydrate: 94g, 31%; Dietary Fiber: 6g, 25%; Sugar: 5g; Protein: 21g

1 package (16 ounces) bow-tie or farfalle pasta

2 tablespoons olive oil

1 yellow onion, diced

2 teaspoons chopped garlic (about 4 cloves)

⅓ cup chopped sun-dried tomatoes (sold in a bag, not packed in oil)

1 head Swiss chard (about 1 pound), cleaned thoroughly, ends trimmed, and chopped

1 teaspoon chopped fresh rosemary or ½ teaspoon dried

1 tablespoon balsamic vinegar

¼ teaspoon salt, or to taste

1 can (15 ounces) cannellini beans (also called white kidney beans), drained and rinsed

½ cup shredded or grated Parmesan cheese

Cook the pasta according to the package directions until it is al dente. When it is nearly done cooking, scoop out about ¼ cup of the cooking water and set it aside.

Meanwhile, in a heavy skillet, heat the oil over medium heat. Add the onions and garlic and cook them for several minutes, stirring frequently, while you chop the chard. Stir in the tomatoes and chard, cover the skillet, reduce the heat (so the chard steams but doesn't burn) and steam the chard for about 5 minutes. Stir in the rosemary, vinegar, salt, and beans. Continue cooking it until the pasta is done.

Drain the pasta, allowing a little water to cling to it, and combine the chard mixture and the pasta. Stir in the cheese. If the pasta is too dry, stir in some, or all, of the reserved cooking water. Serve immediately.

Scramble Flavor Booster: Season the dish with freshly ground black pepper and use freshly grated aged Parmesan cheese.

Tip: If your market doesn't carry chard (many farm markets have it), use kale or spinach, but preferably not baby spinach because it's too delicate for this dish.

Great for a hearty family dinner or a casual gathering, this is a crowd-pleaser from Scramble subscriber Sarah Burke. Serve it with Roasted Brussels Sprouts and whole grain bread.

italian sausage linguine with grated carrots

Prep + Cook = 30 minutes

8 servings

Nutritional Information per serving (% based upon daily values): Calories 320, Total Fat 7g, 11%, Saturated Fat 1g, 5%, Cholesterol 15mg, 5%, Sodium 240mg, 10%, Total Carbohydrate 51g, 17%, Dietary Fiber 3g, 12%, Sugar 7g, Protein 12

Nutritional Information per serving with side dish (% based upon daily values) 1 cup Brussels sprouts; 1 slice whole grain bread: Calories: 470; Total Fat: 11.5g, 18%; Saturated Fat: 1g, 5%; Cholesterol: 15mg, 5%; Sodium: 610mg, 26%; Total Carbohydrate: 78g, 26%; Dietary Fiber: 9g, 36%; Sugar: 12g; Protein: 19

2 tablespoons olive oil

½ yellow onion, diced

8–12 ounces sweet or hot Italian-style chicken sausages, diced into ½-inch pieces (or use vegetarian sausage or mushrooms for a meatless version)

1 package (16 ounces) linguine

2 large carrots, grated (or 1½ cups pre-shredded carrots)

1 teaspoon dried oregano

1 can (28 ounces) whole tomatoes with their liquid

1 tablespoon sugar (optional)

¼ cup grated Parmesan cheese for serving (optional)

(If you are serving the Brussels sprouts, start them first.) In a large skillet, heat the oil over medium heat and sauté the onions and sausage for 3 to 5 minutes, until the onions are translucent and the sausage is starting to brown. Meanwhile, cook the pasta according to the package directions.

Add the carrots and oregano to the skillet, and cook them for 3 to 4 more minutes until the carrots are tender. Add the tomatoes and sugar (optional), breaking up the tomatoes into bite-size pieces with a spatula as they cook. Simmer the sauce for about 10 minutes while the linguine cooks.

Combine the linguini and sauce in a large bowl. Top it at the table with Parmesan cheese, if desired.

Scramble Flavor Booster: To spice this recipe up, use spicy Italian sausages, double the oregano, and add ¼ to ½ teaspoon crushed red pepper flakes to the skillet with the oregano.

Tip: To protect your local sources of water, use phosphate-free dishwashing liquid in your dishwasher (and use phosphate-free laundry detergent, whenever possible.)

Side Dish suggestion: Toss 1 pound Brussels sprouts with 1 to 2 tablespoons olive oil and ¼ to ½ teaspoon kosher salt and roast them in the oven for 25 to 30 minutes at 400 degrees, tossing them occasionally, until they are browned and tender.

This gem of a recipe is adapted from *Cooking for the Cure,* a wonderful cookbook created by some families in Bethesda, Maryland, to raise money for cancer research. Serve it with a green salad with sliced pears, pecans, and Gorgonzola cheese.

pasta shells with zucchini, leeks, and melted cheese

Prep + Cook = 30 minutes

8 servings

Nutritional Information per serving (% based upon daily values): Calories 330, Total Fat 8g, 12%, Saturated Fat 3g, 15%, Cholesterol 10mg, 3%, Sodium 350mg, 15%, Total Carbohydrate 54g, 18%, Dietary Fiber 4g, 16%, Sugar 6g, Protein 12g

Nutritional Information per serving with side dish (% based upon daily values) 1½ cups salad: Calories: 397; Total Fat: 13g, 20%; Saturated Fat: 4g, 19%; Cholesterol: 13mg, 4%; Sodium: 459mg, 19%; Total Carbohydrate: 59g, 20%; Dietary Fiber: 6g, 24%; Sugar: 13g; Protein: 32g

3 leeks, white and most of the green parts, thinly sliced

1 package (16 ounces) small pasta shells (conchiglie) or cavatelli

2 tablespoons olive oil

2 zucchini, halved lengthwise and thinly sliced

3 tablespoons fresh herbs, such as basil, oregano, or sage, chopped, or 1 teaspoon dried basil and 1 teaspoon dried oregano

¼ teaspoon crushed red pepper flakes (optional)

1 cup crumbled goat, feta, or shredded part-skim mozzarella cheese

¼ teaspoon salt, or to taste

⅛ teaspoon black pepper, or to taste

½ cup thinly sliced roasted red peppers, marinated sun-dried tomatoes, drained, or sliced pancetta (optional)

Soak the sliced leeks in cold water for a few minutes to remove any remaining dirt that may be clinging to the leaves. Drain them well.

Meanwhile, cook the pasta according to the package directions until it is al dente.

In a large heavy skillet, heat the oil over medium heat. Add the leeks and zucchini and stir them well. Cover the pan, reduce the heat to medium-low, and cook them, stirring occasionally, for about 10 minutes until they are very soft. (Meanwhile prepare the salad, if you are serving it.)

Add the herbs, red pepper flakes (optional), and cheese to the leeks and zucchini and toss it thoroughly until the cheese is mostly melted. Add the drained pasta shells to the skillet, toss thoroughly, season it with salt and pepper, and top it with the roasted peppers, sun-dried tomatoes, or sliced pancetta (optional). Serve it immediately.

Scramble Flavor Booster: Use the optional red pepper flakes, use the goat or feta cheese and the sun-dried tomatoes or pancetta, and sprinkle the finished dish with hot pepper sauce, such as Tabasco.

Tip: To add taste and texture to my salads, I often include a fruit (fresh or dried), a nut (such as pecans, pine nuts, pistachios or walnuts) and a cheese (such as feta, blue, or Parmesan).

Side Dish suggestion: In a large salad bowl, combine 6 to 8 cups lettuce, 1 pear, sliced, ¼ cup pecans, toasted, if desired, ¼ cup Gorgonzola or blue cheese, and 2 to 4 tablespoons salad dressing, to taste. Serve it with an extra sliced pear on the side for non-salad eaters.

get your kids in on the dinner act

Dinner doesn't need to be a one woman (or man) show. If each "actor" takes a "part," then the whole production will run more smoothly. Here are a few ways to get the whole cast involved:

- Young children can set the table, empty or load the dishwasher, and help with some basic cooking roles like cracking eggs, squeezing lemons, and basting (or "painting") meat or fish.

- Teenagers can step into the spotlight on occasion by grocery shopping, clearing the table, doing the dishes, and making basic meals for the family.

- Get the whole crew in on the menu planning—let each family member pick a meal from this cookbook. When old enough, each can even be in charge of cooking her or his selection.

- Keep the prop closet stocked: If every family member gets in the habit of updating your family grocery list when you run out of a staple ingredient, meal planning, cooking, and grocery shopping will go a whole lot more smoothly.

- Switch roles for a night: Let the kids cook, and the adults can clean up. This is always an enlightening role reversal and the whole family usually gets a kick out of the understudies' chance to shine and the leads staffing the stage crew.

This attractive dish is a great way to enjoy those cute little wagon wheel noodles (rotelle). Serve it with Roasted Portobello Mushrooms.

creamy wagon wheel pasta with cherry tomatoes

Prep + Cook = 30 minutes

8 servings

Nutritional Information per serving (% based upon daily values): Calories 310, Total Fat 8g, 12%, Saturated Fat 3g, 15%, Cholesterol 10mg, 3%, Sodium 198mg, 8%, Total Carbohydrate 47g, 16%, Dietary Fiber 2g, 8%, Sugar 4g, Protein 12g

Nutritional Information per serving with side dish (% based upon daily values) ⅙ of mushrooms: Calories: 400; Total Fat: 15g, 23%; Saturated Fat: 4g, 20%; Cholesterol: 10mg, 3%; Sodium: 253mg, 10%; Total Carbohydrate: 53g, 18%; Dietary Fiber: 3g, 12%; Sugar: 7g; Protein: 14g

1 package (16 ounces) wagon wheel pasta (rotelle)

2 tablespoons olive oil

1½ teaspoons minced garlic (about 3 cloves)

2 pints grape or cherry tomatoes, halved

½ cup grated Parmesan cheese

3–4 tablespoons herbed or plain goat cheese

2 tablespoons chopped fresh basil leaves or 1 teaspoon dried basil (optional)

¼ teaspoon salt, or to taste

¼ teaspoon black pepper, or to taste

Cook the pasta according to the package directions until it is al dente. Drain it (and prepare the mushrooms, if you are serving them).

While the pasta is cooking, heat the olive oil in a large heavy skillet over medium heat. Add the garlic and tomatoes and cook, stirring occasionally, until the tomatoes are slightly softened, 5 to 7 minutes. Reduce the heat and stir in the drained pasta, Parmesan cheese, goat cheese, and basil (optional).

Season it with the salt and black pepper, and serve it immediately.

Scramble Flavor Booster: Use herbed goat cheese and freshly grated aged Parmesan cheese. Serve it with crushed red pepper flakes.

Tip: To use fresh basil from a plant, pinch off the top leaves first, and make sure to cut off the flowers as soon as they appear, or the basil will stop producing new leaves.

Side Dish suggestion: To make Roasted Portobello Mushrooms, lightly rinse 4 portobello mushroom caps. Spray a baking dish just large enough to hold the mushrooms with nonstick cooking spray, and place the caps gills down in the baking dish. Preheat the oven to 450 degrees. In a large measuring cup, whisk together ¼ cup olive oil, ¼ cup balsamic vinegar, 2 teaspoons soy sauce, 1 teaspoon minced garlic (about 2 cloves), 1 teaspoon herbes de Provence or thyme, and ¼ teaspoon black pepper. Pour the marinade evenly over the mushrooms, and flip the mushrooms twice, so the gills remain down. Marinate the mushrooms for 10 to 60 minutes, if time allows. Sprinkle 1 coarsely chopped yellow onion around the mushrooms. Bake the mushrooms and onions for 15 minutes. Flip the mushrooms and bake them for 5 more minutes until they have shrunken slightly and are dark brown and tender. Slice the mushrooms into thick slices before serving.

This is a super-flavorful sauce that is a breeze to make. Scramble recipe tester Gina Jermakwowicz said, "Much to my surprise, even my five-year-old liked it!!!" Serve it with a green salad with carrots, red bell peppers, walnuts, and grated Parmesan cheese.

linguine with basil and clams

Prep + Cook = 25 minutes

8 servings

Nutritional Information per serving (% based upon daily values): Calories 300, Total Fat 5g, 8%, Saturated Fat .5g, 3%, Cholesterol 10mg, 3%, Sodium 690mg, 29%, Total Carbohydrate 53g, 18%, Dietary Fiber 4g, 16%, Sugar 6g, Protein 13g

Nutritional Information per serving with side dish (% based upon daily values) 1½ cups salad: Calories: 366; Total Fat: 11g, 16%; Saturated Fat: 2g, 6%; Cholesterol: 11mg, 3%; Sodium: 744mg, 31%; Total Carbohydrate: 57g, 19%; Dietary Fiber: 5g, 22%; Sugar: 8g; Protein: 15g

1 package (16 ounces) linguine or any long pasta

2 tablespoons olive oil

2–3 shallots (about 4 tablespoons minced shallots)

1 can (28 ounces) crushed tomatoes

¼ teaspoon black pepper

1 can or jar (14 ounces) hearts of palm or artichoke hearts, drained and chopped

1 can (10 ounces) baby clams, partially drained (or substitute canned or fresh sliced mushrooms)

1 tablespoon sugar

2 tablespoons chopped fresh basil or 2 teaspoons dried basil

¼ cup grated Parmesan cheese, for serving

Cook the pasta according to the package directions, and drain it.

Meanwhile, make the sauce. In a large saucepan or heavy skillet over medium heat, heat the oil. Add the shallots and sauté them for 3 to 4 minutes until they start to brown.

Add the tomatoes, pepper, hearts of palm, clams, and sugar (if using dried basil, add it now, too) and bring the mixture to a boil. Reduce the heat and simmer for 5 to 10 minutes. (Meanwhile, make the salad, if you are serving it.) Stir in the fresh basil and serve the sauce over the pasta. Top it with Parmesan cheese to taste.

Tip: I think of a shallot as a cross between a red onion and garlic. If you can't find shallots in your supermarket you can substitute ¼ cup minced onion and 1 clove minced garlic.

Scramble Flavor Booster: Use extra fresh basil and serve the linguine with freshly grated aged Parmesan cheese.

Side Dish suggestion: To make the salad, toss 6 to 8 cups lettuce, 1 cup shredded carrots or zucchini, ½ red bell pepper, diced, ¼ chopped walnuts, and ⅛ to ¼ cup grated Parmesan cheese with 2 to 4 tablespoons vinaigrette dressing.

Perfect risotto without having to stir it for 30 minutes straight! This is a wonderful version, inspired by a recipe from my friend Debbie Lehrich. Even my husband, who doesn't normally like risotto very much, had three helpings! If you prefer a meatier dish, use 2 cups diced cooked chicken or turkey sausage instead of the mushrooms. Serve it with Maple Butternut Squash.

baked risotto with spinach and cremini mushrooms

Prep (30 minutes) + Cook (30 minutes)

6 servings

Nutritional Information per serving (% based upon daily values): Calories 210, Total Fat 9g, 14%, Saturated Fat 3.5g, 18%, Cholesterol 10mg, 3%, Sodium 350mg, 15%, Total Carbohydrate 23g, 8%, Dietary Fiber 3g, 12%, Sugar 2g, Protein 10g

Nutritional Information per serving with side dish (% based upon daily values) ¼ of squash: Calories: 342; Total Fat: 15g, 23%; Saturated Fat 7g, 37%; Cholesterol: 25mg, 8%; Sodium: 358mg, 15%; Total Carbohydrate: 44g, 15%; Dietary Fiber: 5g, 19%; Sugar: 9g; Protein: 12g

2 tablespoons olive oil

1 medium yellow onion, finely chopped

1½ cups Arborio rice

6 ounces baby spinach

3 cups reduced-sodium chicken or vegetable broth

8 ounces sliced cremini or baby bella mushrooms

¼ teaspoon salt-free lemon-pepper seasoning

1 cup shredded or grated Parmesan cheese, plus extra for serving

1 tablespoon sherry (optional but great)

Preheat the oven to 400 degrees.

Heat the oil in a Dutch oven or large ovenproof stockpot over medium heat. Add the onions and cook them for about 5 minutes, or until they are tender. Add the rice and stir to coat it with the oil. Stir in the spinach, broth, mushrooms, and lemon-pepper seasoning. Bring it to a boil and simmer it for 7 minutes.

Stir in ¾ cup cheese, and then sprinkle the remaining ¼ cup cheese on top. Cover the pot and bake for 25 minutes. (Meanwhile, prepare the squash, if you are serving it.)

Remove the pot from the oven, stir in the sherry (optional), and return it to the oven for 5 more minutes, uncovered. Serve immediately, topped with additional Parmesan cheese, if desired.

Scramble Flavor Booster: Double the lemon-pepper seasoning, use freshly grated aged Parmesan cheese, and season the risotto with freshly ground black pepper.

Tip: Arborio rice is short-grain Italian rice used for making risotto. It is not to be confused with orzo, which is actually a rice-shaped pasta.

Side Dish suggestion: To make Maple Butternut Squash, cook 1 to 1½ pounds peeled and diced butternut squash (some markets sell it already peeled and chopped) plus ¼ cup of water on high power in the microwave for 10 minutes, or steam it on the stovetop until it is very tender, 15 to 20 minutes. Mash the cooked squash with 2 tablespoons butter, ¼ teaspoon salt, or to taste, and 1 tablespoon pure maple syrup (or more syrup, to taste). For a fluffier texture, whip the cooked squash in a mixer.

why i'm nuts about nuts

When I was growing up, my dad, who was a doctor and one of the original health "nuts," encouraged us to help ourselves to the bowl of nuts that sat on the kitchen table (the walnuts, pecans, almonds, hazelnuts, and Brazil nuts were still in their shells and we loved using the nutcrackers to break them open). We subscribed to his oft-repeated axiom, "An almond a day keeps the doctor away," though we usually had more than one. However, once I became a diet-conscious adult, I thought I knew better, and I usually avoided nuts as too fattening. Well, as with most things, it turns out my dad was right all along, and nuts are a superfood for our health—at least in moderation.

Nuts are now hailed in study after study as a healthy indulgence (unless, of course, you or someone in your family is allergic to them.) Most nuts have the kind of unsaturated fat that is heart healthy and can help lower cholesterol and reduce diabetes risk. They also contain natural fiber and other nutrients such as vitamin E, folic acid, magnesium, and copper.

As with most things, the key is moderation—while satisfying, nuts are calorie dense and are best enjoyed in small servings and in place of less healthy snacks. Most nutrition experts recommend eating just 1 or 2 ounces of satisfying nuts a day, or about 15 to 20 nuts. Here are a couple of good strategies to avoid overindulging in nuts from Lee Unangst, the Six O'Clock Scramble's registered dietician: "I think the idea of a bowl of nuts still in the shell is great because it helps keep you from overeating (and you get a bit of exercise, too.) I also suggest taking the time to pre-portion nuts into snack-size bags in order to help prevent overeating. Both of these ideas are great strategies for enjoying the health benefits of nuts without plowing through a whole bag."

My family sometimes keeps a bowl of nuts in the kitchen, and we enjoy nuts as snacks and in many of our meals. We opt for the low-salt or unsalted varieties and we add small amounts to dishes for added texture and flavor. For example, we add pistachios to yogurt and berries, walnuts or pecans to salads, pine nuts (we used to call these monkey nuts!) to pasta and vegetables, slivered almonds to rice salads or pilafs, and peanuts or cashews to stir-fries. We also enjoy a spoonful of peanut butter as an occasional after-school or late-night snack.

This is a surprising combination of flavors that really work together. Eating smoked trout is a great way to get healthy fish protein into your family's diet—my kids had no idea there was "fish" in the sauce until I let it slip, and by then it was too late for them to think it was weird because they had cleaned their plates! Serve it with a French Beet Salad (page 115).

fusilli with smoked trout and plum tomatoes

Prep + Cook =
25 minutes

8 servings

Nutritional Information per serving (% based upon daily values): Calories 340, Total Fat 7g, 11%, Saturated Fat 1g, 5%, Cholesterol 5mg, 2%, Sodium 440mg, 18%, Total Carbohydrate 55g, 18%, Dietary Fiber 9g, 36%, Sugar 13g, Protein 15g

Nutritional Information per serving with side dish (% based upon daily values) ¼ of salad: Calories: 376; Total Fat: 7g, 11%; Saturated Fat: 1g, 5%; Cholesterol: 5mg, 2%; Sodium: 523mg, 22%; Total Carbohydrate: 63g, 21%; Dietary Fiber: 11g, 42%; Sugar: 19g; Protein: 16g

1 package (16 ounces) whole wheat fusilli (spiral) pasta

2 tablespoons olive oil

1–2 pounds plum (or Roma) tomatoes, halved lengthwise, seeds scooped out, and cut into strips

1–2 teaspoons minced garlic (2–4 cloves), to taste

¼ teaspoon crushed red pepper flakes

1 jar (28 ounces) tomato-basil pasta sauce

4 ounces smoked trout, in a can or from the deli (or substitute anchovies, smoked salmon, or canned tuna), chopped

⅓ cup fresh parsley, chopped

¼–½ cup grated or shredded Parmesan cheese for serving (optional)

Cook the pasta in salted water according to the package directions, and drain it. (Meanwhile, start the salad, if you are serving it.)

While the pasta is cooking, in a large heavy skillet, heat the oil over medium to medium-high heat. Add the fresh tomatoes, garlic, and red pepper flakes and sauté them for 3 to 4 minutes until the tomatoes soften. Add the pasta sauce and smoked trout and simmer it for a few minutes. When the pasta is nearly done, stir the parsley into the sauce. Combine the pasta and sauce and serve hot, topped with the cheese, if desired.

Scramble Flavor Booster: Add extra crushed red pepper flakes (up to 1 teaspoon) to the sauce. Stir in extra parsley, if desired.

Tip: To scoop seeds out of the tomatoes, use a serrated grapefruit spoon.

I was a little skeptical about whether our kids would eat this, but I was delighted when they asked for seconds. Gnocchi (pronounced nyo-key), made from potatoes, is a great alternative to pasta, as it has more fiber. It also has a really rich mouth feel even though it is fat free. Serve it with Green Beans with Lemon and Garlic.

gnocchi dokey (gnocchi with greens)

Prep + Cook = 20 minutes

6 servings

Nutritional Information per serving (% based upon daily values): Calories 250, Total Fat 7g, 11%, Saturated Fat 2g, 10%, Cholesterol 20mg, 7%, Sodium 790mg, 33%, Total Carbohydrate 38g, 13%, Dietary Fiber 4g, 16%, Sugar 5g, Protein 9g

Nutritional Information per serving with side dish (% based upon daily values) 1 cup green beans: Calories: 295; Total Fat: 10g, 15%; Saturated Fat: 2g, 10%; Cholesterol: 20mg, 7%; Sodium: 790mg, 33%; Total Carbohydrate: 44g, 15%; Dietary Fiber: 7g, 28%; Sugar: 6g; Protein: 10g

1 package (16 ounces) gnocchi (potato dumplings, sold vacuum-packed or frozen)

2 tablespoons olive oil

2 teaspoons minced garlic (about 4 cloves)

1 head (10–12 ounces) Swiss chard (or use fresh spinach or kale), coarsely chopped

1 can (15 ounces) diced tomatoes, slightly drained

¼ teaspoon salt (optional)

½ cup shredded Parmesan cheese

Cook the gnocchi according to package directions and drain it.

Meanwhile, in a large heavy skillet over medium heat, heat the oil. Add the garlic and sauté it for about 1 minute until it is golden. Add the Swiss chard (or other greens) and sauté it, uncovered, for 1 to 2 minutes. Cover the pan and steam the greens for 5 to 8 minutes until the gnocchi goes in the boiling water. (If you are using spinach or other delicate greens, steam them for only 2 to 3 minutes.) (Meanwhile, prepare the green beans, if you are serving them.)

Add the tomatoes and salt (optional) to the greens and simmer them for several minutes. Add the cooked gnocchi to the skillet or combine everything in a large serving bowl and top it with the cheese. Serve it immediately.

Scramble Flavor Booster: Add ¼ to ½ teaspoon crushed red pepper flakes to the pan with the garlic, and add 1 teaspoon balsamic vinegar to the pan with the Swiss chard.

Tip: When using leafy greens, be sure to wash the stems thoroughly, soaking them if necessary, to remove any grit.

Side Dish suggestion: To make Green Beans with Lemon and Garlic, heat 1 tablespoon olive oil in a large skillet over medium heat. Add 1 teaspoon minced garlic (about 2 cloves) and stir it for 30 seconds until the garlic is fragrant. Stir in 1 pound fresh trimmed or frozen green beans. Cover the pan and steam the beans until they are tender (5 to 8 minutes). Add 1 teaspoon fresh lemon juice (about ⅛ lemon) for the last minute of cooking, and season it with salt and black pepper, if desired.

This is a light and healthy dinner with a fresh Greek flavor, suggested by our friend Mark Spindel. It's so simple, yet unbelievably delicious! Serve it with Greek olives.

greek rice bowl with spinach, feta, and pine nuts

Prep + Cook = 25 minutes

4 servings

Nutritional Information per serving (% based upon daily values): Calories 400, Total Fat 14g, 22%, Saturated Fat 6g, 28%, Cholesterol 25mg, 8%, Sodium 470mg, 20%, Total Carbohydrate 59g, 20%, Dietary Fiber 3g, 10%, Sugar 8g, Protein 9g

Nutritional Information per serving with side dish (% based upon daily values) 5 Greek olives: Calories: 475; Total Fat: 21g, 32%; Saturated Fat: 6g, 28%; Cholesterol: 25mg, 8%; Sodium: 870mg, 37%; Total Carbohydrate: 63g, 21%; Dietary Fiber: 5g 17%; Sugar: 8g; Protein: 9g

1½ cups dry white or quick-cooking brown rice

¼ cup pine nuts

1 tablespoon olive oil

½ teaspoon minced garlic (about 1 clove)

1–2 packages (12–18 ounces total) baby spinach

¼ lemon, juice only (about 1 tablespoon)

¼ cup raisins or currants (optional)

¼ teaspoon salt, or to taste

⅛ teaspoon black pepper, or to taste

1 cup crumbled feta cheese

Cook the rice according to the package directions. Meanwhile, lightly toast the pine nuts in a toaster oven or conventional oven (see Tip) and set them aside.

In a large skillet, heat the oil over medium heat and sauté the garlic for about 30 seconds (but don't let it brown). Stir in the spinach and cover the pan. Steam the spinach until it is just wilted, about 3 minutes. Reduce the heat to low.

To the spinach, add the lemon juice, pine nuts, and raisins or currants (optional), and stir it gently until it is warmed through. Season it with salt and black pepper.

Serve the rice in bowls, topped with the spinach and feta cheese.

Scramble Flavor Booster: Double the garlic, season the spinach and cheese with extra freshly ground black pepper, and/or stir a little fresh oregano into the wilted spinach.

Tip: To toast pine nuts, bake them in a preheated 350 degree toaster or conventional oven until they are golden, 3 to 5 minutes (watch them carefully so they don't burn).

My friend and first cookbook co-author, Lisa Flaxman, used to make this dish all the time for her family. It's so versatile, and even makes a great dip for tortilla chips! This is a good meal to save for the end of the week, when you have little fresh food in the house. (For more on weekly menu planning and shopping, visit www.thescramble.com). Serve it with home-made guacamole (page 151) and baby carrots.

cuban black beans and rice with sweet corn

Prep + Cook = 20 minutes

4 servings

Nutritional Information per serving (% based upon daily values): Calories 300, Total Fat 3.5g, 5% Saturated Fat 0g, 0%, Cholesterol 0mg, 0%, Sodium 1330mg, 55%, Total Carbohydrate 60g, 20%, Dietary Fiber 10g, 40%, Sugar 8g, Protein 11g

Nutritional Information per serving with side dish (% based upon daily values) ¼ cup guacamole and ½ cup carrot sticks: Calories: 370; Total Fat: 6g, 9%; Saturated Fat: 1g, 3%; Cholesterol: 0mg, 0%; Sodium: 1,057mg, 44%; Total Carbohydrate: 70g, 24%; Dietary Fiber: 14g, 55%; Sugar: 7g; Protein: 14g

¾ cup quick-cooking brown rice, yielding 2 cups cooked rice

1 can (15 ounces) black beans, drained and rinsed

1 teaspoon ground cumin

½ teaspoon garlic powder

1 can (15 ounces) corn kernels, drained

16 ounces chunky salsa

½ lime, juice only (about 1 tablespoon)

4 whole wheat, flour, or corn tortillas (optional)

1 cup shredded Cheddar cheese (optional)

Cook the brown rice according to the package directions. (Meanwhile, make the guacamole, if you are serving it.)

In a medium saucepan over medium heat, combine the beans, cumin, garlic powder, corn, salsa, lime juice, and the cooked rice. Stir to combine, and heat through.

Remove the rice mixture from the heat and serve it on its own or wrapped in warm tortillas, and sprinkled with Cheddar cheese, if desired. (You can refrigerate the beans and rice for up to 3 days before serving, if desired, or freeze it for up to 3 months.)

Scramble Flavor Booster: Use extra cumin and add ⅛ to ¼ teaspoon cayenne pepper for an extra kick.

Bulgur wheat is one of my favorite whole grains. This ancient Mediterranean grain cooks quickly and has a mild, nutty flavor that works well for casseroles, stews, and pilafs. In this flavorful recipe, the Middle East meets the Southwest, and it's a match made in heaven! The pilaf is also great wrapped in tortillas. Serve it with seedless grapes.

southwestern black bean pilaf

Prep + Cook =
20 minutes

6 servings

Nutritional
Information per
serving (with 1 tor-
tilla) (% based upon
daily values):
Calories 480, Fat
11.5g, 18%, Saturated
Fat 5g, 26%, Choles-
terol 20mg, 7%,
Sodium 780mg, 33%,
Total Carbohydrate
79g, 27%, Dietary
Fiber 14g, 56%,
Sugar 6g, Protein 20g

Nutritional
Information per
serving with side dish
(% based upon daily
values) ½ cup grapes:
Calories: 532; Total
Fat: 12g, 18%; Satu-
rated Fat: 5g, 26%;
Cholesterol: 20mg,
7%; Sodium: 782mg,
33%; Total Carbohy-
drate: 93g, 32%;
Dietary Fiber: 15g,
59%; Sugar: 18g;
Protein: 21g

1½ cups bulgur wheat (or use quick-cooking brown rice)

2 cans (15 ounces each) reduced-sodium chicken or vegetable broth

¼ teaspoon ground cinnamon

1 small green or red bell pepper, finely diced

1 can (15 ounces) black beans, drained and rinsed

1 can (14 ounces) unsweetened corn kernels, drained

¼ lemon, juice only (about 1 tablespoon)

1 cup (more or less to taste) shredded Cheddar or Monterey Jack cheese
    for serving (optional)

1 cup salsa for serving (optional)

6 small whole wheat tortillas (optional)

In a medium pot with a tight-fitting lid, bring the bulgur wheat (or brown rice) and broth to a boil over high heat. Stir in the cinnamon and diced bell pepper, cover the pot, reduce the heat, and simmer for 15 minutes. When the bulgur is cooked, add the beans, corn, and lemon juice and stir over low heat for 1 minute to warm through.

Serve the pilaf topped with the cheese and salsa, and wrap it in a tortilla, if desired.

Scramble Flavor Booster: Serve it with medium or spicy salsa and add 1 diced jalapeño pepper along with the bell pepper.

Side Dish suggestion: Serve it with fresh seedless purple or green grapes, or you can serve frozen grapes for a sweet and crunchy treat. Safety note: Young children (3 and younger) should eat only halved grapes to prevent choking.

This is a winning recipe from Scramble subscriber Diane Ray of Carroll-ton, Texas. It is unbelievably quick, delicious, and full of protein and fiber. This is a good recipe for the kids to help prepare, and they can embellish their own bowls of soup at the table to their tastes with the optional toppings listed below. Vegetarians can leave out the chicken altogether or use diced extra-firm tofu instead. Serve it with a plate of baby carrots, celery, and jicama sticks (a Mexican root vegetable) sprinkled with fresh lime juice, salt, and paprika.

chicken tortilla soup

Prep + Cook = 15 minutes

4 servings

Nutritional Information per serving (% based upon daily values): Calories 380, Total Fat 11g, 17%, Saturated Fat 4.5g, 23%, Cholesterol 60mg, 20%, Sodium 1,230mg, 51%, Total Carbohydrate 45g, 15%, Dietary Fiber 7g, 28%, Sugar 6g, Protein 30g

Nutritional Information per serving with side dish (% based upon daily values) 1/2 cup carrots and 1/2 cup celery: Calories: 412; Total Fat: 11g, 17%; Saturated Fat: 5g, 23%; Cholesterol: 60mg, 20%; Sodium: 1,312mg, 55%; Total Carbohydrate: 53g, 18%; Dietary Fiber: 10g, 38%; Sugar: 10g; Protein: 31g

1 can (10 ounces) mild or spicy enchilada sauce

1 can (15 ounces) reduced-sodium chicken or vegetable broth

1 can (15 ounces) corn kernels or creamed corn, with liquid

1 can (15 ounces) black beans, drained and rinsed

1 large or 2 medium tomatoes, diced (about 1½ cups total)

1½ cups diced, precooked chicken or extra-firm tofu (optional)*

½ cup shredded Cheddar cheese for serving

1 cup crumbled tortilla chips for serving (use the broken chips from the bottom of the bag)

Optional toppings: 1 diced avocado, ½ cup light sour cream, Tabasco or other hot pepper sauce, lime wedges, diced white onion, and fresh cilantro leaves

In a medium stockpot over medium heat, combine the enchilada sauce, broth, corn, beans, tomatoes, and chicken or tofu (optional). Stir to combine, and heat through to just below boiling.

Meanwhile, put the cheese, chips, and other optional toppings in small serving bowls at the table.

Serve the soup hot, stirring in whatever toppings you like from the list above.

*Note: To make your own seasoned chicken, cut 1 boneless, skinless chicken breast half (⅓ to ½ pound) into bite-size pieces and season the pieces with salt, pepper, and garlic powder. Heat 1 tablespoon olive oil in a nonstick skillet over medium heat and cook the chicken, flipping often, until it is no longer pink in the center, 5 to 7 minutes total. Remove it from the heat and add it to the soup.

Scramble Flavor Booster: Use hot enchilada sauce rather than mild, and use extra-sharp Cheddar cheese.

This belly-filling and bone-warming chili from Scramble subscriber Julia Blocksma is as healthy as can be. Serve it with Corny Cornbread and a green salad with dried cranberries and shredded Parmesan cheese.

chicken corn chili

Prep + Cook = 30 minutes

8 servings

Nutritional Information per serving (% based upon daily values): Calories 220, Total Fat 7g, 11%, Saturated Fat 1.5g, 8%, Cholesterol 35mg, 12%, Sodium 480mg, 20%, Total Carbohydrate 24g, 8%, Fiber 7g, 28%, Sugar 6g, Protein 17g

Nutritional Information per serving with side dish (% based upon daily values) 1 piece cornbread; 1½ cups salad: Calories: 384; Total Fat: 9g, 22%; Saturated Fat: 5g, 24%; Cholesterol: 81mg, 27%; Sodium: 844mg, 35%; Total Carbohydrate: 54g, 18%; Dietary Fiber: 9g, 36%; Sugar: 16g; Protein: 22g

1 tablespoon olive oil

1 yellow onion, chopped

1 red bell pepper, cored and diced

2 celery stalks, sliced

1½ teaspoons minced garlic (about 3 cloves)

1 pound ground chicken (or use turkey or meatless crumble)

2 tablespoons chili powder

1 can (28 ounces) crushed tomatoes

1 can (15 ounces) black beans with their liquid

1½–2 cups frozen corn

(If you are making cornbread, make the batter and put it in the oven first.) In a large heavy-duty stockpot over medium-high heat, heat the oil. Sauté the onions, bell peppers, celery, and garlic for 5 to 7 minutes until the vegetables start to soften. (You can add the vegetables as you chop them, to speed up the cooking). Add the chicken and continue cooking until it is no longer pink, about 5 minutes.

Stir in the chili powder, tomatoes, and beans and bring to a boil. Reduce the heat and simmer, partially covered, stirring it occasionally, for 15 to 20 minutes. (Meanwhile, prepare the salad.)

Stir in the corn and cook it for 1 more minute until heated through. Serve the chili hot.

Scramble Flavor Booster: Sprinkle the chili with hot pepper sauce (such as Tabasco), and top it with shredded Cheddar cheese.

Tip: Especially in the fall and winter, I love to serve my family soups and stews because they are so filling, nutritious, and easy to make ahead of time for busy nights. If there are leftovers, I pack them in single serving containers and save them for our lunches.

Side Dish suggestion: Prepare cornbread according to the package directions, mixing 1 cup of corn kernels into the batter, if desired.

Side Dish suggestion: In a large salad bowl, combine 6 to 8 cups lettuce, 2 to 3 tablespoons dried cranberries, ¼ cup shredded or grated Parmesan cheese, and 2 to 4 tablespoons vinaigrette dressing, to taste.

With this quick and colorful stew, all you need to do is make rice and you have your whole dinner in a bowl. So convenient and satisfying, and you'll feel a thousand times better about yourself than if you succumb to the lure of the drive-thru!

spicy seafood stew

Prep + Cook = 30 minutes

4 servings

Nutritional Information per serving (% based upon daily values): Calories 280, Total Fat 9g, 14%, Saturated Fat 1g, 5%, Cholesterol 155mg, 52%, Sodium 580mg, 24%, Total Carbohydrate 24g, 8%, Dietary Fiber 4g, 16%, Sugar 18g, Protein 23g

Nutritional Information per serving with side dish (% based upon daily values) ¾ cup white rice: Calories: 434; Total Fat: 9g, 15%; Saturated Fat: 1g, 5%; Cholesterol: 155mg, 52%; Sodium: 581mg, 24%; Total Carbohydrate: 57g, 19%; Dietary Fiber: 5g, 18%; Sugar: 18g; Protein: 26g

2 tablespoons olive oil

1 red bell pepper, chopped

1 yellow onion, chopped

3 celery stalks, thinly sliced (about 1 cup)

1 can (28 ounces) tomato sauce

1 can (15 ounces) diced tomatoes with green chiles, partially drained

¼ teaspoon crushed red pepper flakes (optional)

1 pound seafood blend (such as calamari, scallops, and peeled and deveined shrimp), often sold frozen

In a large heavy pot, heat the oil over medium heat. Add the bell peppers, onions, and celery, and cook, stirring occasionally, until the onions are translucent, 5 to 7 minutes. (Meanwhile, start the rice if you are making it.)

Meanwhile, in a saucepan, combine the tomato sauce, diced tomatoes, and crushed red pepper flakes (optional) and bring to a boil. Simmer for about 10 minutes.

Add the seafood to the pot with the vegetables, increase the heat, if necessary, and cook, stirring frequently, for 3 to 4 minutes until the shrimp are just pink and the scallops are opaque. Add the tomato sauce mixture, return to a boil, and simmer for about 2 minutes. Serve over rice.

Scramble Flavor Booster: Double the crushed red pepper and season the stew with freshly ground black pepper or use hot pepper sauce, such as Tabasco. You can also use a can of spicy V8 juice in place of some of the tomato sauce.

Tip: Bell peppers, onions, and celery are all good options for cooking in the cooler months, as they have long growing seasons and can be kept in cold storage for quite a while.

I know it's a departure for the Scramble, but once in a while it's fun to make a rich, slow-cooking stew. If weekdays are too hectic, you can make this easy recipe on the weekend and enjoy it during the busy week. Or, put it in your slow cooker in the morning and enjoy it when you get home in the evening (see slow cooker directions below). Serve it with whole grain bread.

hearty beef stew

Prep (25 minutes) +
Cook (90 minutes)

8 servings

Nutritional
Information per
serving (% based
upon daily values):
Calories 300, Total
Fat 20g, 31%, Satu-
rated Fat 7g, 35%,
Cholesterol 60mg,
20%, Sodium 250mg,
10%, Total Carbohy-
drate 9g, 3%, Dietary
Fiber 2g, 8%, Sugar
3g, Protein 18g

Nutritional
Information per
serving with side dish
(% based upon daily
values) 1 slice whole
grain bread:
Calories: 400; Total
Fat: 22g, 34%; Satu-
rated Fat: 7g, 35%;
Cholesterol: 60mg,
20%; Sodium: 430mg,
18%; Total Carbohy-
drate: 29g, 10%;
Dietary Fiber: 5g,
20%; Sugar: 6g;
Protein: 22g

1½ **pounds beef chuck, cut into 1-inch cubes**

½ **cup flour**

2 **tablespoons vegetable oil**

1 **yellow or white onion, diced**

1 **cup beef broth**

1 **cup tomato sauce or crushed tomatoes**

½ **cup red wine (or use tomato juice)**

1 **tablespoon Worcestershire sauce**

1 **teaspoon dried thyme**

3 **large carrots, peeled and sliced**

3 **red potatoes, cut into 1-inch pieces**

Dredge the meat in the flour and reserve 1 tablespoon of the flour. Heat the oil over medium heat in a large stockpot and brown the meat in a single layer, flipping it once or twice, until it is almost cooked through, 6 to 8 minutes. Reduce the heat if it is getting too brown.

Remove the meat from the pan and add the onions and the reserved 1 tablespoon flour. Sauté for about 5 minutes until the onions begin to brown. Return the meat to the pot and add the broth, tomato sauce, wine or juice, Worcestershire, and thyme. Bring it to a boil, reduce the heat, cover, and simmer for 45 minutes to 1 hour, stir-ring occasionally.

Add the carrots and potatoes and cover and simmer the stew for 45 minutes more, until the meat and vegetables are tender. Serve it right away or refrigerate it for up to 3 days.

Slow Cooker directions: Place the carrots and potatoes in the slow cooker. Dredge the meat in the flour and reserve 1 tablespoon of the flour. Heat the oil over medium heat in a large skillet and brown the meat in a single layer, flipping it once or twice. Remove the meat from the pan and add it to the slow cooker on top of the vegetables. Add the onions and the reserved 1 tablespoon flour to the skillet. Sauté for about 5 minutes until the onions start to brown. Remove the onions from the pan and add to the slow cooker on top of the meat and vegetables. Add 2 cups broth or 1 cup broth and 1 cup water (rather than 1 cup broth above), tomato sauce, wine, or juice, Worcestershire, and thyme to the skillet and warm through while scraping up the brown bits from the bottom of the pan. Pour the mixture over the meat and vegetables. Cover and cook for 8 to 10 hours on Low, or 4 to 5 hours on High. Add extra broth or water during cooking if it looks too thick.

Scramble Flavor Booster: Season the stew with salt and freshly ground black pepper and/or hot pepper sauce, such as Tabasco.

keep yourself on the cutting edge

Do you ever feel like you're trying to cut through a tomato with the back of a comb? If you're like us, you probably purchased a few knives soon after your wedding, before you knew much about slicing and chopping, let alone cooking. If you're like many home cooks, you've hardly sharpened them since.

If you are straining your muscles and patience trying to saw through a squash, you may not be using the right tool for the job. In my experience of daily cooking, I primarily use three knives for all my kitchen tasks—a large chef's knife, a medium-length serrated knife, and a long, serrated bread knife. I also find that a top-notch peeler and grater come in very handy.

For these core implements, it's worth investing in good quality, and protecting your investment by keeping the knives in great condition. Straight-edged knives should be sharpened every week or two—it makes a huge difference to slice, dice, and julienne with a well-honed knife. Sharper knives are actually safer because they do not slip off of vegetable skins or lurch unevenly through foods. Your knives should also be protected in a knife holder or a kitchen drawer that is not overcrowded, so their blades won't get bent or dinged (or nick the unwary hand).

With a few high-quality, well-cared-for kitchen knives, you will slice onion rings evenly (with a chef's knife), tomatoes smoothly (with a serrated knife), and bread effortlessly (with a bread knife, of course). That small investment can help make quick and easy cooking with the Scramble a pleasure!

This popular Scramble recipe is super for a time-pressed weeknight, and can easily be doubled for bigger families. Serve it with Italian bread and take advantage of those crisp and delicious fall apples by making a Carrot and Apple Salad (page 199).

tortellini soup with spinach and tomatoes

Prep + Cook = 20 minutes

5 servings

Nutritional Information per serving (% based upon daily values): Calories 254, Total Fat 10g, 16%, Saturated Fat 3g, 16%, Cholesterol 36mg, 12%, Sodium 431mg, 18%, Total Carbohydrate 27g, 9%, Dietary Fiber 7g, 27%, Sugar 4.5g, Protein 13g

Nutritional Information per serving with side dish (% based upon daily values) 1 slice bread; ½ cup salad: Calories: 385; Total Fat: 11g, 18%; Saturated Fat: 3g, 17%; Cholesterol: 36mg, 12%; Sodium: 636mg, 26%; Total Carbohydrate: 55g, 18%; Dietary Fiber: 10g, 38%; Sugar: 11g; Protein: 17g

1 tablespoon olive oil

1 teaspoon minced garlic (about 2 cloves)

1 box (32 ounces) reduced-sodium chicken or vegetable broth

1 package (9 ounces) whole wheat or regular cheese tortellini (sold refrigerated)

1 can (15 ounces) no-salt-added diced tomatoes, with their liquid

¼ teaspoon black pepper

½ teaspoon dried basil

½ teaspoon dried oregano

3 cups baby spinach

¼ cup shredded Parmesan cheese, or to taste

In a large saucepan, heat the olive oil over medium-high heat. Sauté the garlic for 1 minute, then stir in the broth. Bring it to a boil, then add the tortellini, tomatoes, pepper, basil, and oregano.

Reduce the heat to keep it at a low boil for 7 minutes, then add the spinach. (Meanwhile, prepare the salad, if you are serving it.) Simmer it for 2 more minutes, then remove it from the heat and serve it immediately, topped with Parmesan cheese.

Scramble Flavor Booster: Stir ¼ teaspoon crushed red pepper flakes into the soup with the other spices. Use freshly grated aged Parmesan cheese to top the soup.

This simple recipe is perfect for soothing colds and coughs that seem to plague us as soon as the kids are back in school. Making it isn't that much harder than warming a can of soup, but you'll probably feel better knowing that your family is eating your homemade elixir. Make sure to slice the vegetables thinly, which helps them cook faster. Serve it with Garlic Cheese Bread (page 187) and extra sliced carrots and celery.

simple chicken noodle soup

Prep + Cook =
30 minutes

6 servings

Nutritional
Information per
serving (% based
upon daily values):
Calories 240, Total
Fat 5g, 8%, Saturated
Fat 1.5g, 8%, Choles-
terol 105mg, 35%,
Sodium 290mg, 12%,
Total Carbohydrate
23g, 8%, Dietary
Fiber 1g, 4%, Protein
26g, Sugar 3g

Nutritional Informa-
tion per serving with
side dish (% based
upon daily values)
1 slice garlic cheese
bread ($\frac{1}{2}$ pita); $\frac{1}{2}$
cup carrots and $\frac{1}{2}$
cup celery:
Calories: 421; Total
Fat: 11g, 18%; Satu-
rated Fat: 4g, 17%;
Cholesterol: 113mg,
38%; Sodium: 613mg,
26%; Total Carbohy-
drate: 48g, 17%;
Dietary Fiber: 5g,
17%; Sugar: 7g;
Protein: 33g

1 pound boneless, skinless chicken breasts (or use diced shiitake mushrooms or extra-firm tofu)

6 cups reduced-sodium chicken or vegetable broth

2 carrots, thinly sliced

2 celery stalks, thinly sliced

$\frac{1}{2}$ red onion, finely diced

$\frac{1}{4}$ teaspoon herbes de Provence (or use $\frac{1}{4}$ teaspoon dried thyme)

2 cups fine egg noodles (or use 1 cup alphabet noodles)

3 tablespoons chopped fresh parsley

(Preheat the broiler or toaster oven if you are making Garlic Cheese Bread.) In a large stockpot over medium-high heat, combine the chicken, broth, carrots, celery, onions, and herbs. Bring, it to a boil, then lower the heat to medium and simmer until the chicken turns white, about 10 minutes. (For a meatless version, stir in diced shiitake mushrooms or tofu with the noodles.)

With a slotted spoon, remove the chicken from the pan and set it aside to cool, keeping the broth at a low boil. After the chicken cools slightly, shred or dice it into bite-size pieces.

While the chicken is cooling, add the noodles to the boiling broth. Cook them for 8 minutes, or until they are tender. (Meanwhile, prepare the Garlic Cheese Bread, if you are making it.)

Stir in the chicken and parsley and serve it immediately.

Scramble Flavor Booster: Season the soup with freshly ground black pepper.

Scramble subscriber Ilana Knab says she grew up eating soup nearly every day of the year, and it was one of her warmest (literally and figuratively) memories of childhood. She shared her family's recipe for classic potato-leek soup, which is smooth and creamy, though it is low in fat and high in vitamins and fiber. Serve it with a green salad with shredded carrots, diced avocado and feta cheese (page 123), and a loaf of sourdough bread.

creamy potato-leek soup

Prep + Cook =
30 minutes

6 servings

Nutritional Information per serving (% based upon daily values): Calories 130, Total Fat 5g, 8%, Saturated Fat 1.5g, 8%, Cholesterol 5mg, 2%, Sodium 125mg, 5%, Total Carbohydrate 18g, 6%, Dietary Fiber 2g, 8%, Sugar 3g, Protein 4g

Nutritional Information per serving with side dish (% based upon daily values) 1½ cups salad; 1 slice bread: Calories: 367; Total Fat: 14g, 21%; Saturated Fat: 3g, 16%; Cholesterol: 11mg, 4%; Sodium: 541mg, 22%; Total Carbohydrate: 53g, 17%; Dietary Fiber: 7g, 30%; Sugar: 6g; Protein: 44g

2 tablespoons butter or margarine

2 teaspoons minced garlic (about 4 cloves)

2 leeks, white parts and tender green parts only, chopped and thoroughly soaked to remove dirt

1 very large baking potato, peeled and diced (about 1 pound)

1 box (32 ounces) reduced-sodium chicken or vegetable broth

¼ teaspoon black pepper

2 slices turkey, pork or vegetarian bacon, chopped and browned (optional)

¼ cup minced chives or scallions (optional)

Old Bay, Cajun, or Goya seasoning, to taste, for serving (optional)

1 lemon, cut into wedges for serving (optional)

In a large stockpot, melt the butter or margarine over medium heat. Add the garlic and sauté it for about 30 seconds until it is fragrant. Add the leeks, potatoes, broth, and black pepper. Bring it to a boil, reduce the heat, and simmer it for about 15 minutes until the potatoes are tender. Meanwhile, cook the bacon (optional). (Make the salad, if you are serving it.).

Using a hand-held immersion or standing blender, blend the soup until it is smooth. Serve it hot, topped with the bacon (optional), chives (optional), seasonings (optional), and lemon wedges (optional).

Scramble Flavor Booster: Spice it up by sprinkling some fresh lemon juice on each bowl of soup, and some black pepper, Old Bay or Cajun seasoning, or Goya brand seasoning mix (found in the Latino section of many supermarkets).

Tip: Leeks, which look like giant scallions, are members of the onion family. They are milder and sweeter than onions, and can even be eaten raw or tossed in salads. They are generally available year-round, though they are usually harvested in the fall.

healthier halloween snacks and edible crafts

Halloween has always been my favorite holiday. In addition to my lifelong weakness for sweet treats, I love the wackiness and creativity that infuse the day and the element of fantasy as kids and adults get to dress up in outlandish costumes. But other than trying to resist it ourselves, what are we to do about the irresistible candy?!

As a parent, I believe that treats have their place at parties and special occasions, especially in the context of a healthy diet. Andrew and I usually let our kids binge for a night, then save the rest of the treats for special times. Sometimes, I think our kids care more about scoring and sorting the candy than they do about eating it, anyhow.

Over the past few years, I've collected and invented some ideas for healthy Halloween snacks. While we wouldn't miss trick-or-treating, these cute snacks can help you celebrate the holiday at home or at school parties with at least a little bit of good nutrition. I've found that the kids don't even mind the absence of frosting or candy with these hands-on treats:

Edible Spiders: Let kids spread peanut butter or cream cheese on a round cracker. Put another round cracker on top, leaving a little space between them. Insert eight pretzel sticks between the crackers for spider legs. Using a dab of the peanut butter or cream cheese, attach raisins or chocolate chips to the top of the crackers to make the spiders' eyes.

Ghost and Ghoul Sandwiches: Kids can use Halloween-shaped cookie cutters to turn sandwiches (on wheat bread, of course) or Cheddar cheese slices into a scary lunchtime treat or snack.

Spooky Fruit: Use small cookie cutters to cut autumn shapes out of thin wedges of cantaloupe, or carve funny mouths out of apple slices and put them on pumpkin-shaped slices of Cheddar cheese (see suggestion above) or rice cakes. Peeled grapes make great slimy eyeballs, too.

Spooks on a Stick: Cut a peeled banana in half crosswise. Let kids push the pointy ends of chocolate chips into the banana to make a ghost face (the pointy ends of the banana halves are the tops of the ghosts). Push a popsicle stick or chopstick into the flat end of the banana so the ghosts can float around before the kids eat them.

Pumpkin Faces: Use a few drops of food coloring to turn cream cheese orange. Spread the cream cheese on toasted English muffins. Make silly jack-o-lantern faces using raisins or chocolate chips.

Freaky Eyeballs: Slice hard-boiled eggs in half lengthwise. Replace the yolk with an olive with pimiento and sprinkle a little paprika on the whites to make them look bloodshot.

Monster Fingers: Put black olive "fingernails" on the ends of baby carrots or mini hot dogs. Or use cheese sticks with a piece of red pepper on the end.

Wormy Apples: Make homemade caramel apples by melting caramel and dipping crispy apples. While the caramel is still warm, let kids stick a gummy worm to the outside of each apple.

Witches' Tears: Finally, instead of soda or punch, serve apple cider at class Halloween parties for a healthier beverage.

Start the night of trick-or-treating off right with a healthy bowl of Great Pumpkin Tomato Soup (recipe follows).

From Scramble subscriber Kelly O'Rourke, this quick and delicious soup is perfect for filling your family's tummies with something healthy and warm before they hit the candy circuit on Halloween. Our junior testers really enjoyed this healthy soup. Serve with mini corn muffins and a green salad with shredded red cabbage, blue cheese, and walnuts (page 189).

the great pumpkin tomato soup

Prep + Cook = 30 minutes

4 servings

Nutritional Information per serving (% based upon daily values) (with nonfat milk): Calories 170, Total Fat 7g, 11%, Saturated Fat 4g, 20%, Cholesterol 20mg, 7%, Sodium 570mg, 24%, Total Carbohydrate 21g, 7%, Dietary Fiber 4g, 16%, Sugar 14g, Protein 7g

Nutritional Information per serving with side dish (% based upon daily values) 2 mini corn muffins; 1½ cups salad: Calories: 326; Total Fat: 14g, 19%; Saturated Fat: 6g, 26%; Cholesterol: 31mg, 11%; Sodium: 882mg, 37%; Total Carbohydrate: 43g, 14%; Dietary Fiber: 7g, 28%; Sugar: 19g; Protein: 11g

2 tablespoons butter

½ yellow onion, diced

1 can (14 ounces) diced tomatoes, with their liquid

1 can (14 ounces) pumpkin (or see fresh pumpkin directions below)

1 can (14 ounces) reduced-sodium chicken or vegetable broth

½ teaspoon salt

¼ teaspoon black pepper

1½ teaspoons dried tarragon or 1 tablespoon minced fresh

2 cups nonfat or low-fat milk (or 1 can [14 ounces] light coconut milk + 2 ounces water)

In a large stockpot, melt the butter over medium heat. Add the onions and sauté them for about 5 minutes, until they are softened. (Meanwhile, start the corn muffins, if you are serving them.)

In a blender or food processor, puree the cooked onions with the tomatoes. (If you have a hand-held immersion blender, you can puree the soup after you have added the pumpkin and broth.)

Return the mixture to the pot and add the remaining ingredients, except the milk. Simmer it for 5 to 10 minutes. (Meanwhile, prepare the salad, if you are serving it.) Add the milk (or coconut milk) and stir until heated through. Serve immediately or refrigerate it for up to 48 hours or freeze it for up to 3 months.

Scramble Flavor Booster: Sauté ¼ to ½ teaspoon cayenne pepper with the onions or serve the soup with hot pepper sauce, such as Tabasco. For a richer soup, stir ¼ cup of natural peanut butter into the soup with the milk.

Tip: If you prefer, you can use a small fresh pumpkin in this recipe: Cut it in half (if you can't cut the pumpkin in half, put it in the microwave first for 3 to 5 minutes to soften it), remove the seeds, brush the flesh with butter, sprinkle it with kosher salt, and bake it at 400 degrees for 30 to 45 minutes until it is tender. Use about 2 cups of the roasted pumpkin flesh in the soup.

Registered dietitian Carrie Zisman sent me her mom's popular recipe for a nourishing fall stew. The flavor is fabulous and the ingredients are wholesome, so you can feel great about serving it to your family. Serve it with couscous and Cheesy Broccoli.

sweet potato and peanut stew

Prep (15 minutes) +
Cook (25 minutes)

6 servings

Nutritional Information per serving (% based upon daily values): Calories 340, Total Fat 15g, 23%, Saturated Fat 2.5g, 13%, Cholesterol 5mg, 0%, Sodium 490mg, 20%, Total Carbohydrate 37g, 12%, Dietary Fiber 8g, 32%, Sugar 12g, Protein 13g

Nutritional Information per serving with side dish (% based upon daily values) 3/4 cup prepared couscous; 1 cup prepared broccoli: Calories: 554; Total Fat: 18g, 27%; Saturated Fat: 4g, 21%; Cholesterol: 12mg, 3%; Sodium: 602mg, 25%; Total Carbohydrate: 76g, 25%; Dietary Fiber: 15g, 60%; Sugar: 14g; Protein: 23g

1 tablespoon vegetable or peanut oil

1 large yellow onion, diced (about 2 cups)

2–3 medium sweet potatoes, peeled and diced into ½ -inch cubes (about 6 cups)

2 teaspoons ground cumin

½ teaspoon black pepper

1 can (15 ounces) chickpeas, drained and rinsed

1 can (28 ounces) diced tomatoes, with their liquid

1 box (32 ounces) reduced-sodium vegetable or chicken broth

½ cup chunky or smooth natural peanut butter

¼ cup chopped peanuts for garnish (optional)

In a large stockpot or Dutch oven, heat the oil over medium heat and sauté the onions for about 5 minutes until they are translucent. Add the sweet potatoes, cumin, and black pepper and sauté for another 1 or 2 minutes.

Add the chickpeas, tomatoes, broth, and peanut butter and bring it to a boil. Simmer, partially covered, for 15 to 25 minutes until the potatoes are very tender. (Meanwhile, prepare the couscous and the broccoli.) (For a less chunky stew, puree part of the soup with a hand-held immersion blender or in a standing blender.) Garnish the stew with the peanuts (optional), and serve it immediately, or let it cool and refrigerate or freeze it for later use.

Scramble Flavor Booster: For a spicier stew, stir in a little cayenne pepper or chipotles in adobo sauce for the last 5 minutes of cooking.

Side Dish suggestion: To make Cheesy Broccoli, steam 1 pound of broccoli spears for 8 to 10 minutes to desired tenderness. Drain, return to the pan, and top immediately with ¼ to ½ cup shredded Cheddar cheese (to taste) or a few slices of Cheddar, Colby, or Swiss cheese. Cover for 1 minute to let the cheese melt.

Tip: Peanuts are a power food! They contain important nutrients, including vitamin E, niacin, thiamin, riboflavin, vitamin B6, and minerals such as copper, phosphorous, potassium, zinc, and magnesium, and are a good source of fiber and protein.

This is a rich and hearty stew that is surprisingly quick to prepare. If you suspect that your kids won't eat this all mixed together, set aside some chickpeas and spinach for them to eat separately. Serve the stew with pita bread and hummus.

moroccan vegetable stew

Prep + Cook = 30 minutes

8 servings

Nutritional Information per serving (% based upon daily values): Calories 220, Total Fat 9g, 13%, Saturated Fat 1g, 6%, Cholesterol 0mg, 0%, Sodium 390mg, 16%, Total Carbohydrate 29g, 10%, Dietary Fiber 7g, 29%, Protein 7g, Sugar 9g

Nutritional Information per serving with side dish (% based upon daily values) ½ piece pita and ¼ cup hummus: Calories: 407; Total Fat: 16g, 23%; Saturated Fat: 2g, 10%; Cholesterol: 0mg, 0%; Sodium: 788mg, 33%; Total Carbohydrate: 55g, 19%; Dietary Fiber: 12g, 47%; Sugar: 10g; Protein: 15g

¼ cup olive oil

1 red onion, chopped

1 medium eggplant, peeled and chopped into 1-inch cubes

1 can (15 ounces) chickpeas (garbanzo beans), drained and rinsed

1 teaspoon minced garlic (about 2 cloves)

1 teaspoon ground cumin

handful of fresh mint leaves (about 15 leaves), coarsely chopped (or use fresh basil)

½ teaspoon kosher salt

1 can (28 ounces) crushed tomatoes

1 package (6 ounces) baby spinach (use 2–3 cups) or 1 box (10 ounces) chopped frozen spinach, thawed

Heat the oil in a large heavy skillet or saucepan over medium heat. Add the onions and sauté them until they are soft, about 5 minutes.

Add the eggplant and sauté it for a few more minutes, stirring it frequently, so the eggplant does not stick to the bottom of the pan.

Add the chickpeas, garlic, cumin, mint, and salt and sauté it, stirring, for 1 more minute. Add the tomatoes. Bring the stew to a boil, reduce the heat, and simmer it gently for about 15 minutes, until the eggplant is very tender. (Meanwhile, prepare the couscous.)

Add the spinach and stir it until the spinach is wilted, about 2 minutes (or about 5 minutes for frozen spinach). Serve the stew over couscous.

Scramble Flavor Booster: Double the garlic and cumin.

Tip: At the end of the week, I like to make a large dinner salad, omelet or frittata, or pasta sauce with any leftover meat and veggies from the week's meals. That way I can clean out the 'fridge to get ready for the next week's groceries.

This recipe from our friend Richard Brooks makes one giant flavorful omelet that your whole family can enjoy. You can substitute ham, sausage, or smoked salmon for the turkey, or for a meatless version, use sliced mushrooms. Serve the omelet with hash browns.

giant smoked turkey and cheddar omelet

Prep + Cook =
20 minutes

4 servings

Nutritional
Information per
serving (with the avo-
cado) (% based upon
daily values):
Calories 370, Total
Fat 22g, 34%, Satu-
rated Fat 8g, 40%,
Cholesterol 395mg,
132%, Sodium
1,260mg, 53%, Total
Carbohydrate 17g,
6%, Dietary Fiber 3g,
12%, Sugar 5g,
Protein 36g

Nutritional
Information per
serving with side dish
(% based upon daily
values) ⅙ of hash
browns:
Calories: 460; Total
Fat: 27g, 41%; Satu-
rated Fat: 9g, 43%;
Cholesterol: 395mg,
132%; Sodium:
1,360mg, 57%; Total
Carbohydrate: 29g,
10%; Dietary Fiber:
4g, 16%; Sugar: 8g;
Protein: 37g

½ tablespoon butter or margarine

½ yellow onion, finely diced (about 1 cup)

1 cup chopped smoked turkey slices (or use sliced mushrooms, ham, or sausage)

6 eggs, beaten

½ cup shredded reduced-fat Cheddar cheese

1 avocado, sliced (optional)

(If you are serving the hash browns, start them first.) In a large nonstick skillet, melt the butter or margarine over medium heat. Add the onions and turkey and sauté them until they are slightly browned, 5 to 7 minutes.

Add the eggs and scramble them gently for a couple of minutes until they start to get firm. Then smooth them out evenly across the whole pan with a spatula, trying to distribute the filling ingredients evenly. When the eggs are just firm, top them with the cheese and, using one or two spatulas, fold the omelet in half.

Remove the omelet to a serving dish, top it with the avocado slices (optional) and serve immediately.

Scramble Flavor Booster: Serve the omelet with hot pepper sauce, such as Tabasco, or salsa.

Tip: For a lower-fat meal, use egg whites or egg substitute in place of some or all of the eggs in this recipe.

Side Dish suggestion: To make hash browns, cut 2 to 3 russet potatoes into ¾-inch cubes. Boil or microwave them until they are slightly softened, about 5 to 7 minutes, and drain them. (Alternatively, you can grate the potatoes and cook them with the onions, flipping occasionally). Meanwhile, in a heavy skillet over medium heat, sauté 1 diced yellow onion in 2 tablespoons olive oil or butter until the onions are translucent, and just starting to brown, 5 to 7 minutes. Add the potatoes and sauté for 5 to 7 minutes, until they are browned. Season with ¼ to ½ teaspoon salt, ⅛ to ¼ teaspoon black pepper and ⅛ teaspoon garlic powder, or to taste. Serve hot with salsa or ketchup, or topped with shredded Cheddar cheese, if desired.

One of my oldest friends, Ann Callison, has become a gifted cook since our Santa Barbara High School pizza-scarfing days. She invented this delectable salad that is perfect to highlight those delicious autumn dates and apples. If you don't want to make your own dressing, buy raspberry vinaigrette instead. Serve it with warm French bread.

santa barbara salad with apples, dates, and goat cheese

Prep + Cook = 25 minutes

4 servings

Nutritional Information per serving (with chicken) (% based upon daily values): Calories 400, Total Fat 24g, 37%, Saturated Fat 4.5g, 23%, Cholesterol 50mg, 17%, Sodium 100mg, 4%, Total Carbohydrate 29g, 10%, Dietary Fiber 5g, 20%, Sugar 21g, Protein 21g

Nutritional Information per serving with side dish (% based upon daily values) 1 slice bread: Calories: 488; Total Fat: 35g, 38%; Saturated Fat: 5g, 24%; Cholesterol: 50mg, 17%; Sodium: 295mg, 12%; Total Carbohydrate: 46g, 16%; Dietary Fiber: 6g, 24%; Sugar: 21g; Protein: 24g

For the dressing (or use store-bought raspberry vinaigrette)

¼ cup olive oil

⅛ cup raspberry or balsamic vinegar

1 minced shallot

¼ teaspoon cinnamon

For the salad

1 package (6 ounces) baby salad greens, or ½ head soft-leafed lettuce (such as Boston or butter)

4 dates, pitted and chopped (or use ½ cup pre-chopped dried dates)

1 pint (8 to 10 ounces) grape or cherry tomatoes, halved

⅓ cup crumbled goat cheese

¼ cup pine nuts, toasted until light brown

1 red apple (use a crisp and good eating variety, such as gala or Fuji) or persimmon, diced

1½ cups cooked chicken strips, or use 1 can (15 ounces) chickpeas, drained and rinsed

In a measuring cup or salad dressing bottle, combine the oil, vinegar, shallot, and cinnamon. Refrigerate it until the salad is ready to be tossed.

In a large serving bowl, combine the salad ingredients. Toss it with the dressing (you probably won't need to use all of it) and serve it immediately. Reserve remaining dressing for future use.

Scramble Flavor Booster: Season the salad with freshly ground black pepper.

Tip: If you are crumbling your own goat cheese, put it in the freezer for about 10 minutes first so it crumbles more easily.

Side Dish suggestion: Serve it with a loaf of French bread.

This is the most delicious combination, especially if you are crazy about beets like I am. For this salad I used precooked and vacuum-packed lentils and beets from Trader Joe's, but it would also be terrific with freshly cooked lentils and fresh steamed beets.

lentil and beet salad
with honey-lemon dressing

Prep + Cook = 10 minutes

4 servings

Nutritional Information per serving (% based upon daily values): Calories 270, Total Fat 11g, 17%, Saturated Fat 3g, 15%, Cholesterol 10mg, 3%, Sodium 490mg, 20%, Total Carbohydrate 34g, 11% Dietary Fiber 11g, 44% Sugar 12g, Protein 13g

2 cups cooked lentils (if cooking your own, season them with some salt while cooking)

4 steamed beets, quartered and diced

½ cup crumbled goat or feta cheese

2 tablespoons lemon juice, or to taste

1 tablespoon honey

2 tablespoons olive oil

½ teaspoon dried dill or use 2 teaspoons chopped fresh dill

In a medium bowl, combine the lentils, beets, and cheese. In a small bowl or measuring cup, whisk together the lemon juice, honey, oil, and dill, and pour it over the salad. Toss gently, and serve immediately or chill it for up to 3 days.

Scramble Flavor Booster: Use the juice of a whole lemon to make the dressing

Tip: If you have a sunny space near a window, you can move many of your herbs indoors for the winter so you can enjoy fresh herbs all year long. If not, you can dry herbs such as rosemary yourself.

My sister-in-law, Soozy Miller, sent me this colorful and delicious recipe that's a family pleaser. Scramble recipe tester Nancy Bolen said her children loved it: "Scot (age ten) rated it a 10 and had two helpings, and Anna-Grace wanted to know how to write the number "Googol" (which is one followed by 100 zeroes). Serve it with a green salad with grapes, pistachio nuts, and maple-Dijon dressing.

mexican confetti casserole

Prep (20 minutes) + Cook (30 minutes)

6 servings

Nutritional Information per serving (% based upon daily values): Calories 250, Total Fat 10g, 15%, Saturated Fat 6g, 30%, Cholesterol 55mg, 18%, Sodium 740mg, 31%, Total Carbohydrate 15g, 5%, Dietary Fiber 3g, 12%, Sugar 8g, Protein 27g

Nutritional Information per serving with side dish (% based upon daily values) 1½ cups salad: Calories: 316; Total Fat: 14g, 20%; Saturated Fat: 6g, 31%; Cholesterol: 55mg, 18%; Sodium: 757mg, 32%; Total Carbohydrate: 24g, 8%; Dietary Fiber: 6g, 23%; Sugar: 13g; Protein: 28g

1 pound ground turkey, chicken, beef, or vegetarian ground "meat"

1 green bell pepper, diced

1 red bell pepper, diced

1 cup chunky salsa

½ teaspoon ground cumin

1 can (15 ounces) diced tomatoes, partially drained

1 can (15 ounces) corn kernels, drained, or 1½ cups fresh or frozen corn kernels

1½ cups shredded Cheddar or Monterey Jack cheese

Preheat the oven to 375 degrees. In a large skillet over medium heat, sauté the meat and bell peppers, stirring frequently, until the meat is almost cooked through, 6 to 8 minutes. If there is a lot of liquid from the meat, drain it, then add the salsa, cumin, tomatoes, and corn and bring it to a simmer. Remove the mixture from the heat.

Pour the meat mixture into a 9 × 13-inch baking dish. Top it with the cheese and bake for 25 to 30 minutes or until it is hot and bubbly. (Meanwhile, prepare the salad.)

Scramble Flavor Booster: Use Pepper Jack cheese and spicy salsa.

Tip: Is it your turn to drive the carpool home from after-school activities? You can make this casserole any time you have 20 minutes during the day, and keep it in the 'fridge until you are ready to bake it.

Side Dish suggestion: To make the salad, in a large bowl, combine 6 to 8 cups chopped lettuce, ½ cup halved grapes, and ¼ cup shelled pistachio nuts. To make your own maple-Dijon dressing, whisk together ¼ cup olive oil, ⅛ cup balsamic or red wine vinegar, 1 tablespoon pure maple syrup, 1 teaspoon Dijon mustard, and ¼ teaspoon herbes de Provence or thyme. Pour 2 to 4 tablespoons over the salad and toss it. Refrigerate any remaining dressing for future use.

Eggplant is a popular food in the Middle East, where it is often mixed with ground meat and tomatoes. Fearless Scramble recipe tester Debby Boltman said, "I didn't know I could like eggplant until I tried this dish!" If your kids won't eat the eggplant, they will likely enjoy the meat sauce scooped over the couscous. Serve it with Israeli (or regular) couscous.

israeli eggplant moussaka

Prep (30 minutes) +
Cook (45 minutes)

8 servings

Nutritional Information per serving (with turkey and hummus) (% based upon daily values):
Calories 200, Total Fat 7g, 11%, Saturated Fat 1g, 5%, Cholesterol 26mg, 8%, Sodium 820mg, 34%, Total Carbohydrate 20g, 7%, Dietary Fiber 5g, 20%, Sugar 7g, Protein 17g

Nutritional Information per serving with side dish (% based upon daily values) ³⁄₄ cup prepared couscous:
Calories: 282; Total Fat: 5g, 7%: Saturated Fat: 1g, 5%; Cholesterol: 25mg, 8%; Sodium: 746mg 31%; Total Carbohydrate: 40g, 13%; Dietary Fiber: 6g, 23%; Sugar: 7g; Protein: 20g

2 tablespoons olive oil

1 yellow onion, chopped

1 pound ground turkey, beef, lamb, or vegetarian ground "meat"

1 teaspoon minced garlic (about 2 cloves)

¼ teaspoon ground cinnamon

½ teaspoon salt

¼ teaspoon black pepper

1 large eggplant, sliced into ⅓-inch rounds

1 can (28 ounces) or 2 cans (15 ounces each) tomato sauce

8 ounces hummus or baba gannoush for serving (optional)

Preheat the oven to 375 degrees and spray a large round casserole dish with nonstick cooking spray.

In a large heavy skillet, heat the oil over medium heat. Cook the onions until they are lightly browned, 8 to 10 minutes. Add the meat and garlic and brown the meat, breaking it up with the spatula. Add the cinnamon, salt, and black pepper and cook it for several more minutes.

Lay half the eggplant slices in the bottom of the casserole dish. Put half of the onion-meat mixture on top of the eggplant, and then pour half the tomato sauce over everything.

Put the remaining eggplant slices on top of the sauce. Top it with the remaining meat mixture and the remaining tomato sauce. Cover the dish with aluminum foil and bake it for 45 minutes, until the eggplant is very soft. (Meanwhile, prepare the couscous, if you are serving it.) Uncover it and allow it to cool for a few minutes before serving. You can refrigerate it for up to 2 days or freeze it for up to 3 months. Top it with hummus or baba gannoush at the table, if desired.

Scramble Flavor Booster: Serve it with hot pepper sauce, such as Tabasco.

Tip: Look for eggplants that are firm, shiny, and free of blemishes. They are at their best in the late summer and fall.

When I first arrived at college in Philadelphia many years ago, someone had to explain to me what a cheese steak was. After four years of eating in the "City of Brotherly Love," I now know that a cheese steak is a hot sandwich with cooked beef, cheese, and often onions and other condiments. I don't know how to say this humbly, but I don't think Philly's favorite sandwich is as good as the version I now make myself (and my family, who has tried both versions, agrees). Try it for yourself and let me know what you think! Scramble recipe tester Jennifer Doig said, "The sandwiches were perfectly toasty and soft, warm, and delicious! And for the health-conscious, not at all greasy as I imagine a true Philly sandwich would be." Serve it with Tropical Smoothies (unless you can get your hands on some Philly cheese fries).

philadelphia cheese steaks

Prep + Cook = 25 minutes

6 servings

Nutritional Information per serving (% based upon daily values): Calories 610, Total Fat 21g, 33%, Saturated Fat 6g, 30%, Cholesterol 65mg, 22%, Sodium 1,100mg, 45%, Total Carbohydrate 66g, 22%, Dietary Fiber 5g, 20%, Sugar 11g, Protein 40g

Nutritional Information per serving with side dish (% based upon daily values) ⅙ of smoothie: Calories: 720; Total Fat: 21g, 33%; Saturated Fat: 6g, 30%; Cholesterol: 65mg, 22%; Sodium: 1,135mg, 46%; Total Carbohydrate: 92g, 31%; Dietary Fiber: 7g, 28%; Sugar: 31g; Protein: 43g

2½ tablespoons olive oil

2 yellow onions, thinly sliced

2 bell peppers, any color, thinly sliced

2 large soft baguettes or hero rolls

1½ pounds sliced roast beef (such as all-natural Applegate Farms)

6 slices provolone cheese (or you can always use Philly's favorite, Cheez Whiz!)

¼ cup ketchup, or to taste, for serving (optional)

2 teaspoons hot pepper sauce such as Tabasco, for serving (optional)

Preheat the oven to 300 degrees. Heat 2 tablespoons olive oil in a large heavy skillet over medium heat. Sauté the onions and bell peppers, stirring occasionally, until they are very soft and the onions are starting to brown, 8 to 10 minutes. After about 5 minutes, put the baguettes or rolls in the oven to warm them.

Transfer the onions and peppers to a bowl, cover them, and set them aside. In the same skillet, heat the remaining oil over medium heat. Cut the roast beef into thin strips and sauté it in the oil, stirring frequently, until it is heated through, about 5 minutes. (Meanwhile, make the smoothies, if you are serving them.)

Remove the baguettes from the oven and slice them lengthwise, cutting them most of the way through. Line the bottoms of the sandwiches with the cheese, and top it with the beef, onions, and bell peppers. Cut each baguette into 3 sandwiches, and serve them warm, topped with the ketchup and hot pepper sauce, if desired.

Scramble Flavor Booster: Serve the sandwiches with your favorite hot sauce or sliced hot peppers.

Tip: Compare labels: Look for lower-sodium versions of the meat, cheese, and bread for this recipe, as the combination of prepared ingredients make the sodium for this dish higher than most Scramble recipes. To help your body cope with salty meals, eat a banana (potassium balances sodium) and drink some water with lemon slices (lemon is a diuretic.)

Side Dish suggestion: To make a Tropical Smoothie, blend 2 cups frozen or fresh mango chunks, 1 cup orange juice, 2 ripe bananas, and 1 cup nonfat vanilla yogurt (or use plain if you don't want it as sweet) until smooth.

This versatile recipe is adapted from my friends Bettina Stern and Suzanne Simon of Loulies.com (a cool Web site for foodies). This salad can be eaten as a sandwich, on top of greens, or with crackers or pita chips as an appetizer. Serve it with celery sticks, which are also good for scooping the salad.

danish egg salad sandwiches with smoked salmon

Prep + Cook = 25 minutes

6 servings

Nutritional Information per serving (% based upon daily values): Calories 240, Total Fat 17g, 26%, Saturated Fat 4g, 20%, Cholesterol 330mg, 110%, Sodium 820mg, 34%, Total Carbohydrate 5g, 2%, Dietary Fiber 1g, 4%, Sugar 3g, Protein 16g

Nutritional Information par serving with side dish (% based upon daily values) 1 cup celery: Calories: 257; Total Fat: 17g, 26%; Saturated Fat: 4g, 20%; Cholesterol: 330mg, 110%; Sodium: 916mg, 38%; Total Carbohydrate: 9g, 3%; Dietary Fiber: 2g, 5%; Sugar: 5g; Protein: 17g

6 eggs (to save time, cook the eggs in advance and refrigerate them until ready to use)

2 celery stalks, finely chopped (about ½ cup)

½ small red onion, finely chopped (about ½ cup, or use extra celery instead)

4 ounces smoked salmon, finely chopped (about 1 cup)

1 tablespoon capers, drained (optional)

1 tablespoon chopped fresh dill or 1 teaspoon dried

3 tablespoons mayonnaise, any variety

¼ cup plain nonfat yogurt or sour cream

French or ciabatta rolls, rye bread, or lettuce

Lettuce for serving (optional)

Put the eggs in a small saucepan and cover them with cold water. Bring the water to a boil, cover the pot, turn off the heat, and let the eggs stand in the hot water for 12 to 14 minutes. Drain them and rinse them under cold running water until they are cool. Peel and chop the eggs.

In a medium bowl, combine the eggs, celery, onions, smoked salmon, capers (optional), and dill. Combine the mayonnaise and yogurt or sour cream and stir it into the egg mixture. Refrigerate it for up to 2 days, or serve it immediately on lightly toasted bread or over lettuce.

Scramble Flavor Booster: Add extra onions and capers and season the salad with freshly ground black pepper.

Tip: If you don't think your kids will eat these ingredients combined, serve extra hard-boiled eggs, celery, smoked salmon, and bread for them to eat separately.

These open-faced sandwiches make a simple dinner and are perfect for a busy night. You can top the melts with different cheeses, such as Swiss or Monterey Jack, or leave off the tomato or avocado, according to your family's tastes. Serve it with a Waldorf Salad, one of my favorite autumn side dishes.

tuna melts with sliced avocado and tomato

Prep + Cook = 15 minutes

4 servings

Nutritional Information per serving (% based upon daily values): Calories 360, Total Fat 18g, 28%, Saturated Fat 6g, 30%, Cholesterol 45mg, 15%, Sodium 660mg, 28%, Total Carbohydrate 31g, 10%, Dietary Fiber 5g, 20%, Protein 20g, Sugar 1g

Nutritional Information per serving with side dish (% based upon daily values) ¾ cup Waldorf Salad: Calories: 440; Total Fat: 23g, 36%; Saturated Fat: 6g, 30%; Cholesterol: 45mg, 15%; Sodium: 695mg, 29%; Total Carbohydrate: 40g, 13%; Dietary Fiber: 7g, 28%; Sugar: 7g; Protein: 22

2 cans or pouches (6 ounces each) chunk light tuna in water, drained

2 tablespoons reduced-fat mayonnaise

1 celery stalk, finely diced

4 slices sourdough bread

1 avocado, peeled, pitted, and thinly sliced (optional)

1 tomato, thinly sliced (optional)

4 slices Cheddar or Muenster cheese

Preheat the oven to 350 degrees and line a baking sheet with aluminum foil or spray it with nonstick cooking spray. (Prepare the Waldorf Salad now, if you are serving it.)

In a small bowl, combine the tuna, mayonnaise, and celery and mix it thoroughly.

Lightly toast the bread. Spread about one-fourth of the tuna on each piece of sourdough toast and top it with slices of avocado and tomato (optional), and a thin slice of cheese. Transfer the sandwiches to the baking sheet and bake them for about 5 minutes, or until the cheese is melted. Slice the sandwiches in half to serve them.

Scramble Flavor Booster: Add slivered almonds, sunflower seeds, black pepper, and/or fresh lemon juice to the tuna.

Tip: Most avocados are picked when they are green, and turn nearly black when they are ripe. Ripe avocados will yield to gentle pressure. To speed the ripening process, put them in a paper bag with an apple or banana for a day or two.

Side Dish suggestion: To make a Waldorf Salad, combine 2 diced tart apples, 4 diced celery stalks, ¼ cup walnuts, 2 teaspoons reduced-fat mayonnaise, and 1 tablespoon pineapple juice. (You can use the juice from a can of diced pineapple and serve the pineapple separately to the kids.)

This colorful and flavorful Indian curry is simple to make, and it's a very healthy and affordable meal. If these ingredients are unfamiliar to your kids, you may need to start them off with just a little bit of the mixture over rice until their taste buds mature. Serve it with steamed basmati rice and pomegranates.

curried chickpeas with spinach and potatoes

Prep + Cook = 30 minutes

4 servings

Nutritional Information per serving (% based upon daily values): Calories 260, Total Fat 6g, 9%, Saturated Fat 1g, 5%, Cholesterol 0mg, 0%, Sodium 380mg, 16%, Total Carbohydrate 47g, 16%, Dietary Fiber 9g, 36%, Sugar 14g, Protein 10g

Nutritional Information per serving with side dish (% based upon daily values) ¾ cup basmati rice; ½ pomegranate: Calories: 474; Total Fat: 7g, 11%; Saturated Fat: 2g, 9%; Cholesterol: 0mg, 0%; Sodium: 389mg, 17%; Total Carbohydrate: 94g, 27%; Dietary Fiber: 13g, 49%; Sugar: 28g; Protein: 15g

1 tablespoon vegetable oil

1 yellow onion, diced

1 Yukon Gold or white potato, peeled and diced into small pieces (about ½ inch)

1 package (10 ounces) frozen chopped spinach

1 red bell pepper, diced

1 teaspoon ground cumin

1 tablespoon curry powder, or to taste

1 can (15 ounces) chickpeas, with their liquid

¼ cup raisins

½ lemon, juice only (about 2 tablespoons juice)

¼ teaspoon salt, or to taste

⅛ teaspoon black pepper, or to taste

1 cup plain nonfat yogurt for serving (optional)

In a large heavy skillet, heat the oil over medium heat. Sauté the onions and potatoes, stirring occasionally, until the onions are softened, about 5 minutes. Meanwhile, defrost the spinach in the microwave or on the stovetop and drain it thoroughly (press it with a bowl or your hands to squeeze out the extra liquid). (Start the rice now, too, if you are making it.)

To the onions and potatoes in the skillet, add the bell peppers, cumin, and curry powder. Cover and continue to cook for about 5 more minutes. Stir in the chickpeas and the raisins, and cook for about 5 more minutes, until the potatoes are fork-tender. Add the defrosted spinach and the lemon juice and heat it through for a couple more minutes. Season it with salt and pepper to taste.

Serve the curry mixture over rice, and top with a spoonful of yogurt, if desired, or refrigerate it for a future meal.

Scramble Flavor Booster: Use all of the curry powder and serve it with chutney on the side.

Tip: Pomegranates are one of my very favorite fall foods. Eating them is like a culinary treasure hunt, and each little seed is like a precious jewel. Our kids love eating them, too, but I don't recommend anyone wear white for the occasion.

Side Dish suggestion: Serve the curry with 1 to 2 pomegranates. To cut the pomegranate, slice off the top of the fruit and use a paring knife to score the rind from top to bottom in several places. Tear the fruit into sections and eat the red seeds (called arils). Or, to remove the pomegranate seeds from the fruit, deeply score the pomegranate and place it in a bowl of water. Break it open underwater to free the seeds. Keep breaking and freeing seeds until they're released from the pomegranate's skin.

Rather than getting a pizza delivered, try making one to order using one of those prebaked pizza crusts—they're actually quite good, especially if you use fresh toppings. If your kids don't like these gourmet toppings, make theirs more traditional using shredded mozzarella cheese instead. Serve it with a green salad with apples, goat cheese, pecans, and light honey vinaigrette.

portobello mushroom, caramelized onion, and goat cheese pizza

Prep + Cook = 30 minutes

8 servings

Nutritional Information per serving (% based upon daily values): Calories 261, Total Fat 8g, 12%, Saturated Fat 3.5g, 17%, Cholesterol 5mg, 2%, Sodium 445mg, 18%, Total Carbohydrate 39g, 13%, Dietary Fiber 2g, 9%, Sugar 3g, Protein 9.5g

Nutritional Information per serving with side dish (% based upon daily values) 1½ cups salad: Calories: 372; Total Fat: 15g, 23%; Saturated Fat: 7g, 33%; Cholesterol: 16mg, 6%; Sodium: 538mg, 22%; Total Carbohydrate: 39g, 16%; Dietary Fiber: 5g, 20%; Sugar: 9g; Protein: 14g

1 tablespoon olive oil

1 small yellow onion, halved top to bottom and thinly sliced

6 ounces portobello mushroom caps, coarsely chopped

1 cup tomato sauce or red pasta sauce

2 whole wheat or white thin prebaked pizza crusts, such as Boboli (10 ounces each)

1 teaspoon dried basil

1 teaspoon dried oregano

2–4 ounces crumbled goat cheese, or fresh or shredded mozzarella cheese

Preheat the oven to 450 degrees. In a large heavy skillet, heat the oil over medium heat, and add the onions. Sauté them for 2 to 3 minutes, stirring occasionally, until they start to brown. Add the mushrooms and sauté for about 5 more minutes until the mushrooms begin to get dark and tender.

Spread ½ cup tomato sauce on each pizza crust, nearly to the edges. Top each with basil and oregano, followed by the mushrooms, onions, and cheese. Bake the pizzas directly on the oven rack for 10 minutes. (Prepare the salad, if you are making it). Allow the pizzas to cool for about 2 minutes before slicing them with a pizza cutter.

Scramble Flavor Booster: Top the pizzas with a little fresh basil or oregano just before baking them, and serve them with crushed red pepper flakes at the table.

Tip: If you still have fresh herbs growing in your garden, use them instead of the dried herbs recommended in the recipe.

Side Dish suggestion: To make light honey vinaigrette dressing, in a jar, combine ¼ cup red wine vinegar, ⅛ yellow or white onion, minced (about 2 tablespoons), ½ teaspoon minced garlic (about 1 clove), 2 tablespoons olive oil, 2 tablespoons honey, 1 tablespoon fresh lemon juice (about ¼ lemon), ¼ teaspoon salt, and ¼ teaspoon black pepper. Shake well before serving. Serve the dressing over a green salad with 6 to 8 cups of lettuce, 1 diced apple or pear, ¼ cup crumbled goat or feta cheese, and 2 tablespoons pecans.

Scramble subscriber Monica Smith gave me the idea for this delectable tofu dish that pumps flavor and texture into our humble bean curd. Recipe tester Alexandra Taylor said: "This was so-oooooo good. Only problem was I couldn't stop eating it. It was the perfect combination of sweet and sour." Serve it with Sesame Stir-Fried Broccoli and steamed brown or white rice.

delectable sweet-and-sour tofu

Prep + Cook =
30 minutes

4 servings

Nutritional Information per serving (% based upon daily values): Calories 170, Total Fat 9g, 14%, Saturated Fat 1.5g, 8%, Cholesterol 0mg, 0%, Sodium 190mg, 8%, Total Carbohydrate 9g, 3%, Dietary Fiber 2g, 8%, Sugar 5g, Protein 12g

Nutritional Information per serving with side dish (% based upon daily values) 1 cup broccoli; 3/4 cup brown rice: Calories: 412; Total Fat: 14g, 22%; Saturated Fat: 3g, 15%; Cholesterol: 0mg, 0%; Sodium: 387mg, 13%; Total Carbohydrate: 50g, 12%; Dietary Fiber: 9g, 35%; Sugar: 8g; Protein: 20g

1 pound extra-firm tofu in water

1 tablespoon vegetable or peanut oil

1 lime, juice and zest

1 juicing orange, squeezed (or use 1/4 cup orange juice)

1/2 teaspoon salt-free lemon-pepper seasoning

1 tablespoon reduced-sodium soy sauce

1 tablespoon Asian sweet chili sauce (or use 1 tablespoon orange marmalade and 1/8 teaspoon crushed red pepper flakes)

Drain the tofu and wrap it in a clean towel for at least 10 minutes and up to 2 hours to remove the water.

(Start the broccoli and rice first, if you are serving them.) When you are ready to begin cooking, cut the tofu crosswise into 3 equal rectangles and cut the rectangles into 4 long strips.

Heat the oil in a large nonstick skillet over medium to medium-high heat until the oil is very hot. Add the tofu in a single layer and cook for about 4 minutes per side until it is medium-brown on the top and bottom. Meanwhile, combine the remaining ingredients. When the tofu is browned, add the sauce and let it boil down for about 2 minutes until the sauce is thick. Remove it from the heat and serve it immediately.

Scramble Flavor Booster: Add 1/2 teaspoon of Asian chili-garlic sauce to the marinade.

Tip: Tofu, a heart-healthy food made from soybeans, is very high in protein and is a good source of iron, omega-3 fatty acids (the heart-healthy fats), phosphorus, copper, calcium, and magnesium. If you think you don't like tofu, you probably just haven't had it prepared the right way!

Side Dish suggestion: To make Sesame Stir-Fried Broccoli, heat 1 tablespoon sesame oil in a wok or frying pan over medium-high heat. Lightly brown 1 to 2 teaspoons minced garlic (2 to 4 cloves), about 30 seconds. Add 1 pound broccoli spears or florets and 2 tablespoons water. Cover and cook it for about 5 minutes over medium-high heat. Add 1 tablespoon reduced-sodium soy sauce, and stir-fry the broccoli for 1 more minute before serving.

At our house, you can never have enough variations of quesadillas. I love this recipe from our friend Sherry Ettleson because it uses nutritious and delicious sweet potatoes, which are a staple in my kitchen during the fall and winter. Serve them topped with salsa and sour cream or plain yogurt, and with red or orange bell peppers with light ranch dressing.

melted sweet potato quesadillas

Prep + Cook =
30 minutes

8 servings

Nutritional Information per serving (% based upon daily values): Calories 300, Total Fat 11.5g, 17%, Saturated Fat 4g, 20%, Cholesterol 25mg, 8%, Sodium 660mg, 28%, Total Carbohydrate 39g, 13%, Dietary Fiber 5g, 20%, Sugar 6g, Protein 11g

Nutritional Information per serving with side dish (% based upon daily values) ½ pepper and 4 tsp. dressing: Calories: 366; Total Fat: 16g, 23%; Saturated Fat: 4g, 22%; Cholesterol: 29mg, 10%; Sodium: 848mg, 36%; Total Carbohydrate: 37g, 17%; Dietary Fiber: 7g, 26%; Sugar: 10g; Protein: 12g

2 tablespoons vegetable oil

1 small yellow onion, diced

1 teaspoon minced garlic (about 2 cloves)

2 medium sweet potatoes, peeled and grated (about 4 cups)

1 teaspoon dried oregano or 1 tablespoon minced fresh

1 teaspoon chili powder

2 teaspoons ground cumin

¼ teaspoon salt, or to taste

8 medium (soft taco size) wheat or flour tortillas

1½ cups shredded Monterey Jack, Pepper Jack, or Cheddar cheese

1 cup salsa for serving (optional)

1 cup nonfat sour cream for serving (optional)

Preheat the oven to 375 degrees. In a large nonstick skillet over medium heat, heat the oil. Sauté the onions and garlic until the onions are soft, about 5 minutes. Stir in the grated sweet potatoes, oregano, chili powder, cumin, and salt. Cook, covered, for about 10 minutes, stirring frequently. (Meanwhile, prepare the bell peppers, if you are serving them.)

To assemble the quesadillas, spread ⅓ to ½ cup of the sweet potato filling on half of each tortilla and top it with about 2 tablespoons cheese. Fold the tortillas over to make semicircles. Bake the quesadillas on a baking sheet for 8 to 10 minutes until they are just starting to brown. (Alternatively you can cook them in a large skillet over medium heat, flipping once.) Serve the tortillas with a spoonful of sour cream and salsa on top of the filling (we pry them open to do this), if desired.

Scramble Flavor Booster: Use chipotle chili powder or hot Mexican chili powder instead of traditional chili powder, and serve the quesadillas with spicy salsa.

Tip: If your kids aren't very adventurous eaters, you may want to make a couple of quesadillas with only cheese, just in case.

Chimichangas, a specialty of Mexican restaurants in the southwestern U.S., are basically deep-fried burritos. Baking them, rather than frying, gives them a nice crunch without all the fat and calories that come from frying. Serve them with fruit kabobs (page 183).

baked green chile chimichangas

Prep (30 minutes) +
Cook (20 minutes)

8 servings

Nutritional
Information per
serving (% based
upon daily values):
Calories 490, Total
Fat 15g, 23%, Satu-
rated Fat 6g, 30%,
Cholesterol 20mg,
7%, Sodium 890mg,
37%, Total Carbohy-
drate 69g, 23%,
Dietary Fiber 9g,
36%, Sugar 3g,
Protein 19g

Nutritional informa-
tion per serving with
side dish (% based
upon daily values) 1
cup mixed fruit:
Calories: 567; Total
Fat: 16g, 23%; Satu-
rated Fat: 6g, 30%;
Cholesterol: 20mg,
7%; Sodium: 898mg,
37%; Total Carbohy-
drate: 88g, 29%;
Dietary Fiber: 12g,
47%; Sugar: 16g;
Protein: 20g

1 tablespoon olive oil

½ yellow onion, diced

½ cup quinoa, rinsed (if you can't find quinoa in your store, use quick-cooking brown rice)

½ cup tomato sauce

2 cans (15 ounces each) black beans, drained and rinsed (or use 1 can black beans and 1 pound ground turkey or beef)

1 can (7 ounces) mild diced green chiles, or green salsa (salsa verde)

1 pint grape tomatoes, halved

8 large (burrito-size) wheat or flour tortillas

1½ cups shredded Monterey Jack, Pepper Jack, or Cheddar cheese

1 cup salsa for serving

Preheat the oven to 375 degrees. Spray a 9 × 13-inch baking dish with nonstick cooking spray. In a large heavy skillet, heat the oil over medium heat. Add the onions and sauté them for several minutes, stirring occasionally, until they soften. (If you are using meat, add that now too, and brown it with the onions.)

Stir in the quinoa to coat it, and then add the tomato sauce, beans, and chiles or salsa. Bring it to a low boil, reduce the heat, and simmer it for 5 minutes, then add the tomatoes. Simmer the mixture for 10 more minutes, uncovered, stirring occasionally.

Remove the mixture from the heat, and spoon equal amounts of it into the center of each tortilla. Top it with a handful of cheese. Fold the tortillas burrito style (first fold in the ends, then roll it over), and lay them seam side down in the baking dish. (At this point, you can bake them or refrigerate them for up to 12 hours.) Bake the chimichangas for 15 to 20 minutes until they are lightly browned and heated through. (Meanwhile, prepare the fruit kabobs, if you are serving them.)

Serve the chimichangas hot, topped with the salsa.

Scramble Flavor Booster: Use Pepper Jack cheese for a spicy kick.

This is a terrific twist on Eggplant Parmesan. This version is a little creamier and the panko makes it crunchier, too. Serve it with sourdough bread and Green Beans Almondine.

three-cheese eggplant melt

Prep (20 minutes) + Cook (25 minutes)

4 servings

Nutritional Information per serving (% based upon daily values): Calories 320, Total Fat 12g, 18%, Saturated Fat 7g, 35%, Cholesterol 90mg, 30%, Sodium 360mg, 15%, Total Carbohydrate 31g, 10%, Dietary Fiber 6g, 24%, Sugar 8g, Protein 21g

Nutritional Information per serving with side dish (% based upon daily values) 1 slice bread; ¾ cup green beans: Calories: 524; Total Fat: 18g, 26%; Saturated Fat: 8g, 42%; Cholesterol: 95mg, 32%; Sodium: 565mg, 23%; Total Carbohydrate: 63g, 20%; Dietary Fiber: 10g, 41%; Sugar: 9g; Protein: 28g

1 egg

¼ cup flour

1 cup whole wheat or white panko or bread crumbs

1 medium to large eggplant, cut into ½ -inch-round slices

1–1½ cups nonfat or low-fat ricotta or cottage cheese

1 cup tomato sauce or tomato-basil pasta sauce

1 cup shredded part-skim mozzarella cheese

2 tablespoons grated or shredded Parmesan cheese

¼–½ teaspoon garlic powder, to taste

Preheat the broiler and place the rack about 5 inches from the heat source. Line a baking sheet with foil.

In a shallow bowl, beat the egg. Put the flour in a shallow bowl and the panko (or bread crumbs) in another shallow bowl.

Dip the eggplant slices first in the flour, then in the egg, letting the excess egg drip back into the bowl, then dip the slices in the panko or bread crumbs, coating both sides. Place the slices on the baking sheet.

Broil the eggplant slices on each side until they are medium-brown, 3 to 5 minutes per side. (Be sure to set a timer in case you get distracted—they burn easily!)

Preheat the oven to 375 degrees. Spray a 9 × 13-inch baking dish with nonstick cooking spray. Line the bottom of the pan with the eggplant slices. Cover each slice of eggplant with 1 to 2 tablespoons of ricotta or cottage cheese, and then top each eggplant slice with 1 tablespoon sauce. When all the eggplant is covered, top everything with the mozzarella, then with the Parmesan cheese, and finally the garlic powder.

Bake it for about 20 minutes, until the cheeses are melted and slightly browned. (Meanwhile, prepare the green beans, if you are serving them.) Allow the eggplant to cool for 5 minutes before serving it.

Scramble Flavor Booster: Top the dish with crushed red pepper flakes.

Tip: High-heat broiling allows foods to get crispy, so it is a healthier alternative to deep-frying.

Side Dish suggestion: To make Green Beans Almondine, trim and steam 1 pound green beans for about 5 minutes in the microwave or on the stovetop. Meanwhile, in a small skillet, heat 1 tablespoon butter or margarine over medium heat. Add ¼ cup sliced almonds and sauté them for 1 to 2 minutes until they start to toast. Drain and add the green beans and sauté them with the almonds for 1 to 2 minutes. Stir in the juice of ¼ lemon before serving, if desired.

ten tips to save money on your family food budget

Economic concerns are compelling Americans to cook at home more, which can be a healthy way to save hundreds of dollars every month. That makes grocery shopping strategies, meal planning, and organizing even more important. Below are my top ten tips on how to make home-cooked meals your biggest savings solution:

1. Plan for a week of meals so you don't waste food. An online meal planning service (like the Six O'Clock Scramble, www.thescramble.com) can save you time and help you stick to a schedule.

2. Before grocery shopping, try to use all of the food in your refrigerator, freezer, and pantry. Stretch your budget by making a meal at the end of the week out of ingredients you haven't finished. (Omelets, quesadillas, stir-fries, and pasta sauces are flexible options.)

3. Shop with a grocery list so you remember to get what you need, and you don't buy things you already have. Keep the list on or near the refrigerator so the whole family can update it. (Grocery lists for the twenty weekly menus in this cookbook are available at www.thescramble.com/SOS.)

4. Leverage the leftover idea. (Some people even put some away before serving the meal!) Use them for lunches the next day, or freeze half for a future dinner.

5. Defrost and use something from your freezer at least once a week. Many people sit on hundreds of dollars of food they've forgotten until it's freezer-burned beyond use.

6. Use less meat! Cooking with non-meat proteins like beans, tofu, and eggs is very economical and healthy.

7. Buy frozen vegetables like broccoli, green beans, and peas. Picked and frozen at their peak of fresh-ness, they are a healthy and economical alternative to fresh produce. (Consider freezing your own produce when it's in season.)

8. Buy in bulk. Find great deals on meat, chicken, fish, or cheese and repack into 1- or 2-pound pack-ages before freezing them. Choose large bags or containers of snack foods like applesauce, raisins, and chips, instead of single-serving sizes, and divide them up yourself.

9. Try buying store-brand products, which are often less expensive than name brands.

10. Buy food when it's on sale, especially nonperishables (see list of Scramble staples, page 5).

Armed with these suggestions, you should be able to shave hundreds of dollars off your family food bill each month, while enjoying delicious and healthy homemade food.

We enjoyed tiny wedges of this crustless quiche on slices of toasted bread at a lively tapas (little Spanish appetizers) bar called Txapela in Barcelona. It is so flavorful and can be eaten hot or cold. Serve it with Garlic Toast (page 105) and sliced oranges.

crustless spanish quiche

Prep (10 minutes) +
Cook (45 minutes)

4 servings

Nutritional
Information per
serving (% based
upon daily values):
Calories 230, Total
Fat 11g, 17%, Satu-
rated Fat 4.5g, 23%,
Cholesterol 220mg,
73%, Sodium 830mg,
35%, Total Carbohy-
drate 11g, 4%,
Dietary Fiber 2g, 8%,
Sugar 4g, Protein 19g

Nutritional
Information per
serving with side dish
(% based upon daily
values) 1 slice bread;
1 orange:
Calories: 391; Total
Fat: 19g, 29%; Satu-
rated Fat: 6g, 28%;
Cholesterol: 220mg,
73%; Sodium:
1,080mg, 45%; Total
Carbohydrate: 32g,
11%; Dietary Fiber:
5g, 18%; Sugar: 10g;
Protein: 22g

1 package (10 ounces) frozen chopped spinach

4 eggs

½ cup plain nonfat yogurt

1 cup shredded mozzarella or Swiss cheese

¼ cup flour

1 jar (5 ounces) Spanish olives with pimientos, chopped

Preheat the oven to 375 degrees. Spray a pie dish with nonstick cooking spray. Defrost the spinach and press out any extra liquid (if the spinach is too hot, I some-times put the spinach in a colander and use the bottom of a bowl to press the water out).

In a large bowl, beat together the eggs, yogurt, cheese, and flour. Stir in the spinach and olives.

Pour the mixture into the pie plate and smooth the top. Bake for 45 minutes until it is lightly browned and firm. (While the quiche is baking, prepare the Garlic Toast, if you are serving it.) Cut it into wedges to serve it hot or cold.

Scramble Flavor Booster: Add ½ to 1 teaspoon dried herbs or 1 to 2 tablespoons fresh herbs, such as basil, oregano, or dill, with the spinach and olives.

Tip: Buying frozen vegetables can be a great money saver, especially off season, as they often cost about half of the price of fresh vegetables, and are just as healthy.

winter

five weekly winter menus

To help you enjoy all the warm and comforting flavors of winter, here are five weekly menus. (You can also make your shopping a breeze by grabbing the accompanying organized grocery list for each of these menus at www.thescramble.com/SOS.)

week 1

Irresistible Honey-Curry Chicken
Savory Mustard Salmon
Miraculous Macaroni and Cheese
Chinese New Year Stir-Fry with Tofu or Pork
Soup-er Easy Black Bean and Corn Soup

week 2

Turkey Milanesa
Scrambalaya (Cajun Jambalaya with Smoked Ham)
Catfish in a Curried Tomato Sauce
Rigatoni with Roasted Red Peppers, Walnuts, and Basil
Nacho Average Nachos

week 3

Panko-Peanut Crusted Pork Chops (or Chicken or Tilapia)
Mahi Mahi with Garlic and Rosemary
Fearless Tomato and Winter Squash Soup with Sausage
Penne Puttanesca
Hot Eggplant (or Chicken) Parmesan Subs

week 4

Zesty Turkey and Black Bean Chili
French Cassoulet with White Beans and Sausage
Tilapia with Chinese Black Bean Sauce
Rotini with Sun-dried Tomatoes and Goat Cheese
French Bread Calzones

week 5

Sautéed Chicken with Lemon and Capers
Tropical Shrimp (or Chicken)
Rigatoni with Diced Tomatoes and Bacon
Rich and Creamy Potato, Leek, and Barley Stew
Orange-Cumin Black Beans over Rice

poultry, pork, and beef

fish

pastas, grains, soups, and stews

Key: (V) = Vegetarian or vegetarian optional;
     * = Scramble Express: 30 minutes or less total;
   (M) = Make-ahead, freeze, or slow-cooker option

sandwiches, wraps, salads, and other fare

Key: (V) = Vegetarian or vegetarian optional;
        * = Scramble Express: 30 minutes or less total;
      (M) = Make-ahead, freeze, or slow-cooker option

ten resolutions for scrambling families

THIS YEAR is going to be different—just like last year! Actually, I'm not usually one for making New Year's resolutions; the inspiration for change hits me at odd times, rather than at the dawn of a new year. But there are plenty of things I'd like to do better in the New Year, starting with working less at night and resisting urges for sweets (which, not coincidentally, hit hardest when I'm working the night shift!). I've written some resolutions that I am going to try to adhere to, and that may inspire you to make some changes in your own home:

We, Scrambling families, are already doing our best to work hard, nourish ourselves and our families, maintain some order in our homes, and shower our families with love and affection. But, we can strive to be a little better. In the new year, we hereby resolve to:

1. Finish the snacks in the cabinets before buying new ones (and reduce other waste!).

2. Eat more organic, locally grown, and fair-trade food (where workers and producers in developing nations are treated and paid fairly for their products).

3. Be more conscientious about reducing our use of and recycling cans, bottles, bags, and paper.

4. Serve more fruits and vegetables (even if they don't always get eaten).

5. Teach our kids how to cook.

6. Have the kids make their own breakfasts and lunches more often.

7. Eat only the food on our plates (not the leftovers from our kids' plates!).

8. Leave a dirty dish or two in the sink at night, on occasion, without freaking out.

9. Eat home-cooked dinners together more often as a family.

10. Be more appreciative of those we love.

Many New Year's goals are too abstract or out of reach. I prefer ideas like these that can be done on a daily basis. But taken together, over the course of a year, small changes can have big, long-term, habit-forming benefits for our bodies, our families, and the planet.

happy winter!

Celia requested a chicken stir-fry for dinner and I gladly obliged her with this quick version that includes some of her favorite ingredients. Serve it with steamed brown or white rice and the remaining pineapple slices.

pineapple chicken stir-fry

Prep + Cook =
15 minutes

4 servings

Nutritional Information per serving (% based upon daily values): Calories 280, Total Fat 5g, 8%, Saturated Fat 1g, 5%, Cholesterol 65mg, 22%, Sodium 570mg, 24%, Total Carbohydrate 29g, 10%, Dietary Fiber 3g, 12%, Sugar 22g, Protein 27g

Nutritional Information per serving with side dish (% based upon daily values) ¾ cup brown rice:
Calories: 442; Total Fat: 6.5g, 10%; Saturated Fat: 1.5g, 6%; Cholesterol: 65mg, 22%; Sodium: 577mg, 24%; Total Carbohydrate: 62.5g, 21%; Dietary Fiber: 5.5g, 23%; Sugar: 22.5g; Protein: 31g

1 can (20 ounces) pineapple slices in 100 percent juice, drained and juice reserved

3 tablespoons reduced-sodium soy sauce

1 tablespoon brown sugar

¼–½ teaspoon ground ginger

1 tablespoon cornstarch

1 tablespoon peanut oil

2 celery stalks, thinly sliced

2 large carrots, thinly sliced

1 pound boneless, skinless chicken breasts (or use vegetarian quorn or seitan), cut into bite-size pieces

¼ yellow or white onion, slivered

(Start the rice first, if you are making it.) In a small bowl, combine 3 tablespoons pineapple juice from the can of pineapple slices with the soy sauce, sugar, ginger, and cornstarch. Set it aside. (Use the remaining juice to drink or make popsicles or smoothies).

In a large nonstick skillet or wok, heat the oil over medium-high heat. Add the celery and carrots and stir-fry for about 3 minutes. Add the chicken, onions, and 2 pineapple rings, cut into small chunks (reserve the remaining 8 pineapple slices to serve on the side). Stir-fry for about 3 more minutes until the chicken is white on the outside and cooked about halfway through. Add the sauce and stir-fry everything for 1 to 2 more minutes until the chicken is just cooked through. Remove it from the heat and serve over the rice, if desired, or refrigerate it for up to 24 hours.

Scramble Flavor Booster: Add chili-garlic sauce or hot pepper flakes to taste with the vegetables.

Tip: Having seen how they are grown and harvested firsthand in Costa Rica, I try to buy organic pineapples rather than conventional whenever possible, because the organic farming practices are better for the native soil and the people where they are grown. You can even buy canned organic pineapple at many stores.

Long ago, I spent a summer working in Buenos Aires, Argentina, where I fell in love with all things Argentinean—especially the food. Argentina has strong European influences because of substantial immigrant populations from Germany, Italy, and Spain, so this dish resembles typical fried cutlets from those regions, too (like German wiener schnitzel). Milanesa, crispy breaded cutlets often made with veal in Argentina, is a typical food in the region. I've made my own low-fat version that is amazingly reminiscent of the dish I devoured years ago. Serve it with boiled new or red potatoes (see page 28) and a green salad with sliced pears, pecans, and Gorgonzola cheese (page 207).

turkey milanesa

Prep + Cook = 25 minutes

4 servings

Nutritional Information per serving (% based upon daily values): Calories 350, Total Fat 14g, 22%, Saturated Fat 4g, 20%, Cholesterol 160mg, 53%, Sodium 520mg, 22%, Total Carbohydrate 10g, 3%, Dietary Fiber <1g, 4%, Sugar <1g, Protein 43g

Nutritional Information per serving with side dish (% based upon daily values) 3 small potatoes; 1½ cups salad: Calories: 507; Total Fat: 22g, 33%; Saturated Fat: 5g, 26%; Cholesterol: 163mg, 54%; Sodium: 665mg, 28%; Total Carbohydrate: 36g, 12%; Dietary Fiber: 7g, 25%; Sugar: 17g; Protein: 65g

1 egg
½ teaspoon salt
½ cup bread crumbs or panko
1–1½ pounds turkey, chicken, or veal cutlets (thin cuts)
2 tablespoons olive oil
1 tablespoon butter
¾ lemon, cut into wedges for serving

(Start the potatoes first, if you are serving them.)

In a shallow bowl, beat the egg and stir in the salt. Put the bread crumbs in a separate shallow bowl or on a small plate. Dip each cutlet in the egg, allowing the excess to drip off, and then coat thoroughly with the bread crumbs. Set them aside on a plate.

In a heavy skillet or electric frying pan, heat the oil over medium-high heat and add the butter. When the butter starts to bubble, put the cutlets in the pan, press them down to flatten them, and cook for about 5 minutes per side until they are golden brown. (Meanwhile, make the salad.) Reduce the heat if the cutlets are getting too browned. Remove the cutlets from the heat, squeeze fresh lemon juice over them and serve them immediately (or serve them with ketchup for the kids).

Scramble Flavor Booster: Mix about ¼ teaspoon cayenne pepper or ½ teaspoon Old Bay seasoning into the bread crumbs.

This flavorful stovetop chicken, inspired by a recipe from my friend Ginny Maycock, works for all ages. The onion topping can be served on the side so picky eaters can have plain chicken, while adventurous eaters can combine the flavors. Serve it with whole wheat rolls and Greek-Style Green Beans (page 149).

lemony greek chicken

Prep + Cook =
30 minutes

4 servings

Nutritional Information per serving (% based upon daily values): Calories 310, Total Fat 11g, 17%, Saturated Fat 3g, 15%, Cholesterol 105mg, 35%, Sodium 220mg, 9%, Total Carbohydrate 10g, 3%, Dietary Fiber >1g, 4%, Sugar 2g, Protein 42g

Nutritional Information per serving with side dish (% based upon daily values) 1 roll; 1 cup prepared green beans: Calories: 482; Total Fat: 16g, 26%; Saturated Fat: 4g, 19%; Cholesterol: 108mg, 36%; Sodium: 579mg, 23%; Total Carbohydrate: 37g, 12%; Dietary Fiber: 8g, 32%; Sugar: 6g; Protein: 49g

1½–2 pounds boneless, skinless chicken breasts, or chicken cutlets

¼ cup flour

1 teaspoon dried oregano

2 tablespoons olive oil

1 medium yellow onion, halved and thinly sliced

½ lemon, juice only (about 2 tablespoons)

¼ cup crumbled feta cheese

Place the chicken between sheets of plastic wrap and flatten with a mallet or rolling pin (unless you are using cutlets, which are already thin).

In a shallow bowl, combine the flour and ½ teaspoon oregano. Dredge the chicken breasts in the flour mixture and shake off the excess.

In a large nonstick skillet, heat 1 tablespoon olive oil over medium heat. Add the chicken breasts and cook them for 4 to 5 minutes per side until they are browned and just cooked through. (Meanwhile, prepare the green beans, if you are serving them.) Remove them to a plate and cover to keep them warm.

Raise the temperature to medium-high and, without wiping out the pan, heat the remaining 1 tablespoon oil and add the onions. Cook the onions for several minutes until they start to brown. Stir in the lemon juice, the remaining oregano, and the cheese, and cook for about 1 more minute. Transfer the onion mixture to a small serving bowl. Serve the chicken immediately, topped with the onion mixture.

Scramble Flavor Booster: Season the chicken and onions with plenty of freshly ground black pepper.

Tip: If you use wooden cutting boards, which absorb flavors and odors, keep a separate cutting board to use just for onions, so your cut melon and berries don't have a faint onion flavor.

This chicken is so moist and tasty your family will love it! It's also great for company because you can prepare it in advance, and relax and enjoy your guests. Serve it with Roasted Portobello Mushrooms (page 208) (which are at their peak in the fall and winter) and steamed brown or white rice.

far-out chicken teriyaki

Prep (5 minutes) + Cook (35–40 minutes) + Marinate (30 minutes–24 hours)

6 servings

Nutritional Information per serving (without skin) (% based upon daily values):
Calories 250, Total Fat 8g, 12%, Saturated Fat 2g, 10%, Cholesterol 165mg, 55%, Sodium 250mg, 10%, Total Carbohydrate 1g, 0%, Dietary Fiber 0g, 0%, Sugar 0g, Protein 40g

Nutritional Information per serving with side dish (% based upon daily values) ¾ cup brown rice; ⅙ of mushrooms and onions:
Calories: 502; Total Fat: 16.5g, 25%; Saturated Fat: 3.5g, 16%; Cholesterol: 165mg, 55%; Sodium: 312mg, 12%; Total Carbohydrate: 40.5g, 13%; Dietary Fiber: 3.5g, 15%; Sugar: 3.5g; Protein: 46g

3 pounds chicken drumsticks and boneless or bone-in thighs, any combination, skin removed, if desired

¼ cup Soy Vay Veri Veri Teriyaki or other teriyaki sauce

2 tablespoons rice vinegar

2 tablespoons Chinese mustard (or use Dijon)

1 tablespoon Chinese duck sauce (or use apricot jam)

Put the chicken in a flat baking dish large enough to hold it in a single layer. In a large measuring cup, whisk together the remaining ingredients. Marinate the chicken for at least 30 minutes and up to 24 hours, if time allows, flipping it once.

Preheat the oven to 450 degrees. (Start the rice and mushrooms if you are making them.) Flip the chicken once more and bake it in the preheated oven for 35 to 40 minutes, flipping it once, until it is tender and a meat thermometer inserted into the meat registers 170 degrees.

Scramble Flavor Booster: Serve the chicken with Chinese mustard and duck sauce.

A great recipe from Scramble subscriber Janet Krolman, this chicken is quick to prepare and makes a nice light meal. The sauce is appealing to many kids, but if your kids are very picky eaters you can leave some chicken plain rather than topping it with the lemon-caper sauce. Serve it with Roasted Sweet Potato Slices and crispy breadsticks.

sautéed chicken
with lemon and capers

Prep + Cook =
20 minutes

4 servings

Nutritional
Information per
serving (% based
upon daily values):
Calories 270, Total
Fat 9g, 14%, Satu-
rated Fat 1.5g, 8%,
Cholesterol 100mg,
33%, Sodium 250mg,
10%, Total Carbohy-
drate 6g, 2%, Dietary
Fiber 0g, 0%, Protein
39g, Sugar 5g

Nutritional
Information per
serving with side dish
(% based upon daily
values) ¼ of a sweet
potato; 5 breadsticks:
Calories: 491; Total
Fat: 13g, 17%; Satu-
rated Fat: 2g, 9%;
Cholesterol: 100mg,
33%; Sodium: 461mg,
20%; Total Carbohy-
drate: 50g, 17%;
Dietary Fiber: 3g,
11%; Sugar: 9g;
Protein: 45g

2 tablespoons olive oil

1½ teaspoons minced garlic (about 3 cloves)

1½ pounds boneless, skinless chicken breasts, cut into 1-inch pieces

¼ teaspoon salt, or to taste

⅛ teaspoon black pepper, or to taste

1–2 lemons (squeeze ¼ cup juice and cut extra lemons into wedges for
    serving, if desired)

2 tablespoons capers

1 tablespoon honey (optional)

(Start the sweet potatoes first, if you are making them.) In a large skillet, heat the olive oil over medium heat. Add the garlic and sauté it for about 30 seconds. Add the chicken and cook it, tossing often, until just cooked through and no longer pink inside, about 5 minutes. Season the chicken with salt and pepper, transfer it to a plate, and cover it loosely with aluminum foil.

Add the lemon juice and capers to the pan and simmer the mixture for about 3 minutes until the sauce is slightly reduced. Stir in the honey (optional), remove it from the heat, and pour the sauce over the chicken. Serve immediately.

Scramble Flavor Booster: Serve the chicken with lemon wedges.

Side Dish suggestion: To make Roasted Sweet Potato Slices, preheat the oven to 400 degrees. Spray a baking sheet with nonstick cooking spray. Slice 2 large sweet potatoes crosswise into ½-inch-thick rounds. Put the sweet potatoes on the baking sheet, and brush the tops of the sweet potatoes with 1 tablespoon canola or olive oil. In a small bowl, combine ½ teaspoon ground cinnamon, ¼ teaspoon ground allspice or cloves, and 1 tablespoon brown sugar. Sprinkle the mixture evenly over the potatoes. Bake the potatoes for 30 minutes, until they are very soft and lightly browned. Serve them hot.

The house smells wonderful while this sweet chicken is baking. Scramble recipe tester Debbie Firestone said even "the toughest critics in my family gave it 10 out of 10." Serve it with Festive Wild Rice and Lemony-Garlic Spinach (page 33).

balsamic-rosemary baked chicken

Prep (10 minutes) + Cook (50 minutes) + optional Marinate (up to 12 hours)

6 servings

Nutritional Information per serving (% based upon daily values): Calories 380, Total Fat 23g, 35%, Saturated Fat 6g, 30%, Cholesterol 145mg, 48%, Sodium 140mg, 6%, Total Carbohydrate 2g, 1%, Dietary Fiber 0g, 0%, Sugar 1g, Protein 39g

Nutritional Information per serving with side dish (% based upon daily values) ⅙ of wild rice; ¼ of spinach: Calories: 580; Total Fat: 31g, 44%; Saturated Fat: 7g, 32%; Cholesterol: 145mg, 48%; Sodium: 225mg, 9%; Total Carbohydrate: 32g, 11%; Dietary Fiber: 9g, 36%; Sugar: 6g; Protein: 46g

¼ cup balsamic vinegar

2 tablespoons olive oil

1 tablespoon honey

2 tablespoons Dijon mustard

2 tablespoons Worcestershire sauce

1 teaspoon dried or chopped fresh rosemary

¾ teaspoon dried tarragon or 2 teaspoons chopped fresh tarragon

1 teaspoon minced garlic (about 2 cloves)

1 whole chicken, cut up

1 diced white or yellow onion (about 2 cups)

Preheat the oven to 400 degrees. In a large measuring cup, whisk together the vinegar, oil, honey, mustard, Worcestershire sauce, rosemary, tarragon, and garlic.

Spread the chicken pieces in a large roasting pan just large enough to hold it in a single layer. Pour the sauce evenly over the chicken, and sprinkle the onions over and around everything. Marinate the chicken for up to 12 hours or bake it immediately in the preheated oven for 50 minutes, basting it after 25 minutes. (Meanwhile, prepare the rice and spinach, if you are serving them.)

Serve it hot with the sauce spooned over the chicken and rice, or refrigerate it for up to 3 days, or freeze it for up to 3 months.

Scramble Flavor Booster: Double the garlic and add ¼ teaspoon black pepper to the sauce.

Tip: Dried herbs are an affordable and flavorful meal solution in the cooler months. I generally use one-third as much of the dry herb as I would fresh, and add them earlier in the cooking process to enhance their flavor.

Side Dish suggestion: To make Festive Wild Rice, toss 3 to 4 cups cooked wild rice or wild rice pilaf with ¼ cup toasted, coarsely chopped pecans, ¼ cup dried cranberries or cherries and ⅛ to ¼ cup of vinaigrette dressing. Serve it warm or cool.

This is one of my favorite ways to make chicken, from subscriber and recipe tester Nancy Bolen. Both Nancy's and my sometimes picky sons gobbled it up! Solomon, who rarely gives much thought to food, said, "What's this yummy sauce? You should put this sauce on chicken more often!" Serve it with basmati rice and Roasted Cauliflower Poppers (even people who think they don't like cauliflower have been known to devour these tasty morsels).

irresistible honey-curry chicken

Prep (10 minutes) + Cook (50 minutes)

6 servings

Nutritional Information per serving (skinless chicken) (% based upon daily values): Calories 220, Total Fat 6g, 9%, Saturated Fat 2.5g, 13%, Cholesterol 110mg, 37%, Sodium 230mg, 10%, Total Carbohydrate 5g, 2%, Dietary Fiber 0g, 0%, Sugar 4g, Protein 34g

Nutritional Information per serving with side dish (% based upon daily values) ¾ cup rice with broth; ⅙ cauliflower: Calories: 520; Total Fat: 11g, 16%; Saturated Fat: 4g, 21%; Cholesterol: 115mg, 39%; Sodium: 370mg, 18%; Total Carbohydrate: 63g, 21%; Dietary Fiber: 4g, 16%; Sugar: 8g; Protein: 54g

2 tablespoons butter or margarine

¼ cup orange juice

½ lemon, juice only (about 2 tablespoons)

3 tablespoons honey

1 tablespoon Dijon or yellow mustard

1 tablespoon curry powder

½ teaspoon salt

6–8 pieces of bone-in chicken, any variety (remove skin for a lower-fat version)

1 teaspoon cornstarch (optional)

⅓ cup cold water (optional)

Preheat the oven to 375 degrees. In a small saucepan, melt the butter or margarine over medium heat. Once it's melted, add the next six ingredients (orange juice through salt) to the pot and whisk them together. Remove the pan from the heat.

Place the chicken in a 9 × 13-inch baking pan. Pour the butter mixture evenly over the chicken, reserving the unwashed saucepan for later. Bake in the preheated oven for 45 to 50 minutes, basting it occasionally, until the chicken is cooked through. (Meanwhile, prepare the rice and cauliflower.)

When the chicken is fully cooked, remove it from the oven and put it on a serving plate. Pour the sauce from the bottom of the baking pan into a serving bowl. (For a richer sauce, whisk together the cornstarch and water in the saucepan. Add the sauce from the chicken to the cornstarch mixture and set it over medium-high heat. Bring it to a boil, and cook it, stirring often, until it thickens, about 2 minutes.) Serve the sauce on the side with the cooked chicken and rice.

Scramble Flavor Booster: Use a little extra curry powder or add 1 teaspoon ground cumin and ¼ teaspoon cayenne pepper.

Tip: Most of the fat in poultry resides in its skin. For easy skin-trimming, I use kitchen scissors.

Side Dish suggestion: To make Roasted Cauliflower Poppers, preheat the oven to 400 degrees. Cut 1 head of cauliflower into florets. Toss them with 1 tablespoon olive oil, ½ teaspoon chili powder, or more to taste, ¼ teaspoon ground cumin, or more to taste, and ¼ teaspoon salt. Roast for 20 to 30 minutes until the cauliflower is browned and soft, tossing once. (This delectable recipe was suggested by Scramble subscriber Rachel Scherr.)

holiday gifts without the guilt

I enjoy holiday time and I don't mean to sound like a Grinch, but each year I have a few quibbles with the usual holiday gift exchanges:

- When budgets are tight, I don't want to spend money on things my loved ones won't use (nor do I want them to waste money on me!).
- I'm trying to keep our house neater, so I just don't have room for any more "stuff."
- I think many gifts are a waste of environmental resources to manufacture, package, and ship and if unwanted, often end up in a landfill. (For more on this topic, I recommend watching *The Story of Stuff* at www.storyofstuff.com with your kids.)

With those thoughts in mind, here are some ideas the Scramble crew has come up with for affordable, clutter-free, and eco-friendly holiday gifts:

Homemade Treats: If you're longer on time and creativity than cash, make edible gifts such as chili and combread, homemade soup, molded chocolate (you can buy adorable reusable molds at baking-supply stores), and freshly baked breads, cookies, and cakes.

Consumable Gifts: I'm always glad to receive delicious fair-trade and eco-friendly coffee and chocolate (www.thanksgivingcoffee.com and www.divinechocolate.com), bath oils, fresh fruit baskets, fresh herb plants, or flowering plants such as orchids or African violets.

Great Reads: Books don't take up much space and can be savored and shared.

Active Gifts: It's exhilarating to receive something that will enrich our lives, such as a membership to a museum or a National Park, a gift certificate to a paint-your-own-pottery shop, an exercise class or something a little more indulgent like a pedicure or spa treatment.

Gifts That Change Lives: These are four unique organizations where your gift recipients can select exactly how they want to affect change with your gift donation:

- Micro-finance a business project: www.kiva.org
- Help a teacher: www.donorschoose.com
- Give sustenance: www.heifer.org
- Plant a tree in a Costa Rican rainforest: www.savebiogems.org/costarica/

Priceless Gifts: Give family and friends "priceless gifts," such as coupons for babysitting, rides to the airport, dog walks, back massages, and other valuable gestures of time and care.

Gift of Great Taste, Good Health, and Time: You can give a gift subscription to the Scramble's online meal planning service or a set of *Six O'Clock Scramble* cookbooks. The recipient will get a weekly menu plan with easy, healthy and delicious recipes and an automated grocery list. Go to thescramble.com and use the promotion code SOSCOOKBOOK for $3 off a six-month subscription. A generous portion of your purchase will be donated to the nonprofit Environmental Working Group, which works to keep our sources of food safe for human consumption.

I'm crazy about this topping, which can be used for pork, chicken, or fish. As long as you keep the proportions of dry and wet ingredients the same, you can experiment with it by using different nuts or no nuts, or honey or chutney instead of the apricot jam or hoisin sauce. Serve it with a loaf of whole grain bread and a green salad with dried cranberries and shredded Parmesan cheese (page 218).

panko-peanut crusted pork chops (or chicken or tilapia)

Prep + Cook =
20 minutes

4 servings

Nutritional
Information per
serving (% based
upon daily values):
Calories 340, Total
Fat 16g, 25%, Saturated Fat 4g, 20%,
Cholesterol 75mg,
25%, Sodium 190mg,
8%, Total Carbohydrate 19g, 6%,
Dietary Fiber 2g, 8%,
Sugar 11g, Protein
31g

Nutritional
Information per
serving with side dish
(% based upon daily
values) 1 slice bread;
1½ cups salad:
Calories: 500; Total
Fat: 20g, 31%; Saturated Fat: 5g, 24%;
Cholesterol: 76mg,
25%; Sodium: 485mg,
20%; Total Carbohydrate: 47g, 16%;
Dietary Fiber: 6g,
25%; Sugar: 21g;
Protein: 35g

4 thin-cut boneless pork chops, chicken cutlets, or tilapia fillets

3 tablespoons apricot jam (or use 2 tablespoons hoisin sauce and 1 tablespoon jam)

1 tablespoon Dijon mustard

1 tablespoon hot water

½ cup panko (Japanese-style bread crumbs, whole wheat, if available) or use bread crumbs

½ cup unsalted peanuts, smashed to about the same size crumbs as the panko

1 tablespoon butter, melted

Preheat the oven to 425 degrees. Place the pork (or other meat) on an aluminum foil–lined baking sheet.

In a small bowl, combine 2 tablespoons jam or hoisin sauce, the mustard, and the hot water. Using a pastry brush, brush the mixture on top of the pork (or chicken or fish).

In a medium bowl, combine the panko, peanuts, the remaining 1 tablespoon jam, and the melted butter, and stir until the liquid ingredients lightly coat the dry ingredients. Sprinkle and press the mixture evenly over the meat. Bake the pork (or chicken or tilapia) for 10 minutes, until it is cooked through and the topping is lightly browned. (Meanwhile, prepare the salad, if you are serving it.)

Tip: Panko is a Japanese-style bread crumb, which I've come to love because the grains are large and airy, and make for a crunchier coating than traditional bread crumbs.

Scramble Flavor Booster: Serve the pork with a dipping sauce made up of half Dijon mustard and half apricot jam.

My friend Kirsten Thistle shared this irresistible recipe for mini meat-loaves. Both of our families gobbled these little cuties right up, and when recipe tester (and Six O'Clock Scramble customer-service goddess) Betsy Goldstein asked her family "to rate it on a scale of 1 to 10, it got anywhere from a 9 to an 11 (and the 11 came from Danny, my really picky one)!" Another plus for these mini meatloaves is that they cook in half the time of a big meatloaf. Serve it with baked potatoes (page 183).

mini meatloaf muffins

Prep (15 minutes) +
Cook (30 minutes)

6 servings

Nutritional
Information per
serving (with lean
beef) (% based upon
daily values):
Calories 390, Total
Fat 21g, 32%, Satu-
rated Fat 8g, 40%,
Cholesterol 115mg,
38%, Sodium 260mg,
11%, Total Carbohy-
drate 23g, 8%,
Dietary Fiber 2g, 8%,
Sugar 5g, Protein 26g

Nutritional
Information per
serving with side dish
(% based upon daily
values) ½ potato, ½
tsp. butter, 1 tbsp.
sour cream, ½ tbsp.
salsa, 1 tsp. scallions,
1 tsp. cheese:
Calories: 492; Total
Fat: 23g, 35%; Satu-
rated Fat: 9g, 42%;
Cholesterol: 116mg,
38%; Sodium: 360mg,
15%; Total Carbohy-
drate: 43g, 15%;
Dietary Fiber: 4g,
14%; Sugar: 7g;
Protein: 28g

1 teaspoon olive oil

½ white or yellow onion, finely chopped (about 1 cup)

1–2 large carrots, finely chopped (about ½ cup)

1 teaspoon dried oregano

1 teaspoon minced garlic (1–2 cloves)

1½ pounds lean ground beef, ground turkey, or ground chicken

¾ cup ketchup or tomato sauce

1 cup Italian bread crumbs, or crushed crackers

2 tablespoons Dijon mustard

1 tablespoon Worcestershire sauce

1 egg

(If you are making baked potatoes in the oven, start them first.) Preheat the oven to 350 degrees. In a skillet, heat the oil over medium heat and sauté the onions, carrots, oregano, and garlic for 3 to 5 minutes until the vegetables are tender. Remove them from the heat and let them cool for about 5 minutes. Meanwhile, in a large mixing bowl, combine the remaining ingredients, then add the onion and carrot mixture, and stir thoroughly.

Spray the wells of a 12-cup muffin tin with nonstick cooking spray. Spoon the meat mixture into the wells, dividing it evenly—each mini meatloaf should completely fill a muffin well but won't go much over the top of it. Bake the meatloaf muffins in the preheated oven for 30 minutes.

Remove them from the oven and let them sit for 5 minutes before serving, or refrigerate them for up to 2 days before reheating and serving, or freeze them for up to 3 months.

Scramble Flavor Booster: Add up to ½ teaspoon black pepper to the meatloaf mixture, and serve the meatloaf with barbecue sauce.

Tip: You can make the meatloaf mixture in advance and bake the meatloaves just before dinner; or bake them up to 2 days in advance, as meatloaf gets even tastier after a day or two.

good nutrition *can* come out of cans, bags, and boxes

While buying fruits and vegetables directly from a farm is generally the best way to go if you're looking for food at its peak, fitting the task into your weekly routine can be tough for many of us, unless, of course, you can see the cornfield from Susie's soccer field.

Here's the skinny on fresh versus frozen versus canned:

Fresh: While buying your fruits and vegetables fresh is often preferable, unless we buy them straight from the farmer we can't always be sure how long some items have been sitting on display, or how far they have traveled to get to our store. If they look peppy and it's close to the season when they actually grow in your region, this is certainly a healthy way to go.

Frozen: Frozen fruits and vegetables are another good alternative to the produce section of your local store. Like canned goods, frozen produce is generally processed as soon as it is trucked off the field, thus preserving most of the nutrients. They are also very reasonably priced and easy to work with, saving time and money. Just be sure to buy frozen produce without additives.

Canned: Like frozen, generally, vegetables are canned immediately upon harvesting, before the nutrition content deteriorates. Choose canned veggies with little or no salt or additives. One recent concern with canned foods, however, is the presence of BPA (Bisphenol-A) in can linings. BPA is a chemical compound found in a variety of consumer products that has been linked to a range of health problems, including a higher risk of certain cancers, birth defects, and diabetes. While many companies are looking into BPA-free lining alternatives, the vast majority of cans still contain this chemical.

Cassoulet is a French bean stew that is usually made with meat, tomatoes, and spices. This version is amazing because it's so quick to prepare, yet tastes like it's been stewing for hours! Your family can build a fire and pretend you are in the French countryside on a cold winter night. Serve it with roasted Brussels sprouts (page 205), and spaetzle (a German dumpling, sold with pastas or international foods), to complete the European adventure.

french cassoulet
with white beans and sausage

Prep + Cook =
30 minutes

6 servings

Nutritional Information per serving (with turkey sausage):
Calories 300, Total Fat 14g, 22%, Saturated Fat 2.5g, 13%, Cholesterol 40mg, 13%, Sodium 740mg, 31%, Total Carbohydrate 27g, 9%, Dietary Fiber 5g, 20%, Sugar 3g, Protein 18g

Nutritional Information per serving with side dish (% based upon daily values) 1 cup Brussels sprouts; ¾ cup spaetzle:
Calories: 542; Total Fat: 22g, 34%; Saturated Fat: 4g, 18%; Cholesterol: 70mg, 23%; Sodium: 925mg, 39%; Total Carbohydrate: 64g, 21%; Dietary Fiber: 10g, 38%; Sugar: 7g; Protein: 27g

3 tablespoons olive oil

1 package (14 ounces) Gimme Lean (meatless) Sausage or
    1 pound uncooked pork or turkey sausage

1 yellow onion, diced

1 teaspoon minced garlic (about 2 cloves)

½ teaspoon dried oregano

½ teaspoon dried basil

¼ cup bread crumbs

1 can (15 ounces) diced tomatoes, with their liquid

1 can (15 or 19 ounces) white beans (also called cannellini beans or
    white kidney beans), drained and rinsed

Preheat the oven to 400 degrees. (If you are making the Brussels sprouts and spaetzle, start them first.)

In a large Dutch oven or deep ovenproof skillet, heat 2 tablespoons of the oil over medium heat. Add the sausage (if you are using real sausage, remove it from its casing), breaking it up with the edge of a spatula. Add the onions, garlic, oregano, and basil. Cook the sausage and onions, stirring frequently, for 6 to 8 minutes, until the sausage is browned. Meanwhile, in a small bowl, combine the bread crumbs and the remaining tablespoon of oil with your fingers or a fork and set it aside.

Add the tomatoes and beans to the sausage mixture, and bring it to a low boil. Simmer it for 4 to 5 minutes, then top it evenly with the bread crumb mixture and transfer it to the oven. Bake the stew for 10 minutes, uncovered. Remove it from the oven and serve it.

Tip: Gimme Lean is such a realistic substitute for sausage that my family doesn't know the difference unless I reveal my secret. It is fat-free and higher in fiber than traditional sausage. Look for it in your supermarket's refrigerated section with other meatless foods.

Scramble Flavor Booster: Double the oregano and basil and add ¼ teaspoon crushed red pepper flakes with the other spices.

Side Dish suggestion: Prepare 1 package (10 ounces) spaetzle (or use gnocchi or orzo) according to the package directions. Drain and toss it with 1 to 2 tablespoons butter or olive oil and ¼ teaspoon salt, or to taste.

On a visit to New Mexico, I fell in love with the green chili stew that is a staple on the menu of nearly every restaurant we visited. Serve it with roasted parsnips or carrots (page 195) and whole grain bread.

santa fe–style beef stew

Prep (20 minutes) + Cook (90 minutes)

8 servings

Nutritional Information per serving (% based upon daily values): Calories 360, Total Fat 24g, 37%, Saturated Fat 9g, 45%, Cholesterol 75mg, 25%, Sodium 160mg, 7%, Total Carbohydrate 11g, 4%, Dietary Fiber 1g, 4%, Sugar 2g, Protein 24g

Nutritional Information per serving with side dish (% based upon daily values) ⅙ of parsnips; 1 slice bread: Calories: 547; Total Fat: 29g, 44%; Saturated Fat: 10g, 47%; Cholesterol: 75mg, 25%; Sodium: 352mg, 20%; Total Carbohydrate: 45g, 16%; Dietary Fiber: 8g, 31%; Sugar: 9g; Protein: 29g

2 tablespoons canola or vegetable oil

2 pounds cubed beef (such as top sirloin or stewing meat) or boneless pork, cut into 1-inch pieces

1 large yellow onion, chopped

¾ teaspoon garlic powder

1 teaspoon ground cumin

½ teaspoon salt (optional)

1 can (10 ounces) diced tomatoes with green chiles (sold with Mexican foods), with their liquid

1 can (4 ounces) chopped green chiles with their liquid, or 2 fresh jalapeño peppers, finely diced

1 can (15 ounces) reduced-sodium beef broth

¼ cup water

2 large white potatoes, peeled and chopped into 1-inch pieces

In a large Dutch oven or stockpot over medium heat, heat the oil and brown the meat on all sides. Add the onions and cook them for about 5 minutes until they soften. Add the garlic powder, cumin, salt (optional), tomatoes, chiles, broth, and water. Bring to a boil, reduce the heat, and simmer it for 1 hour, partially covered, stirring occasionally. Add a little more broth or water if the liquid gets too low.

After 1 hour, stir in the potatoes and simmer, partially covered, stirring occasionally, for an additional 20 to 30 minutes, until the potatoes are fork-tender. (Meanwhile, prepare the roasted parsnips or carrots.)

Serve hot, or refrigerate it for up to 2 days and reheat it when you are ready to serve it.

Scramble Flavor Booster: Double the cumin and add 1 teaspoon chili powder with it.

Slow Cooker cooking directions: After browning the meat and onions, transfer them to the slow cooker and add the rest of the ingredients. Give it a good stir to combine everything. Cook it on Low for 10 to 12 hours or on High for 6 to 8 hours. (It is best to cook on Low for the longest time as it makes the meat more tender, but if time is short, 6 to 8 hours on High will work.)

Tip: Keep your Scramble grocery list tacked to your refrigerator, so you can add items as you run out.

six tips for making your grocery trips count

Because I don't like to grocery shop too often (what a waste of precious time and gas!), I have developed some strategies for making grocery trips count, so I can shop as infrequently as possible. Here are a few of my suggestions:

1. **Shop once a week:** Grocery trips are most efficient if you plan dinners for the week in advance and make a grocery list (or use ours at www.thescramble.com/SOS) with the ingredients for all of the meals, plus any staples your family uses for breakfast, lunch, and snacks.

2. **Trust the list:** Keep your grocery list handy so you can update it any time you run out of something you need to replenish. I stick mine to the side of the refrigerator so everyone in my family can add to it.

3. **Check your freezer:** Rather than buying more chicken or peas, go shopping first in your own freezer. By using what you have already purchased, you can save money and freezer space.

4. **Stock up on essentials:** There are few things that irk me more than having to stop at the store just to buy milk or bread. Be sure to buy plenty of the things your family uses daily, so they can last until your next trip. (See listed pantry essentials used most often in Scramble meals on page 5.)

5. **Resist the candy and potato chips:** If you don't want to eat it (or you don't want your family to), don't buy it! Especially when shopping with kids or when we're feeling hungry, it can be tough to avoid the displays of fabulous cupcakes or half-priced chips. Have a healthy snack before you shop and try to stick to your list, rather than getting thrown off course by foods you don't want to eat. For me, that means averting my eyes when I pass the marshmallows. (However, I do allow myself occasional treats such as the individually wrapped pieces of dark chocolate, low-fat ice cream [we love Skinny Cow], or crunchy pita chips.) Unless they throw your healthy diet off course, you may want to allow for a few planned indulgences when you shop.

6. **Shop sales wisely:** Is that sale item really going to save you money? In general, only buy sale items if they are nonperishable and are something you would otherwise buy. If it goes bad or sits in your pantry for two years, is it really a bargain? (I'm talking to you, four-year-old-unopened-box-of-Lipton-Vegetable-Soup-Mix in my cupboard). On the other hand, if you can stock up on expensive items when they are on sale, and shop in your freezer before you go to the store (see item #3), you could save a bundle.

P.S. Don't forget to keep your reusable shopping bags in your car to protect our precious planet (and to keep zillions of plastic and paper bags from cluttering up your kitchen space). Some towns are beginning to charge customers for disposable grocery bags, so this can be a money saver, too.

This is a great preparation for a weeknight dinner. Any leftover salmon can be served cold the next day over a salad. Serve it with Bulgur Wheat Pilaf with Grapes and Pecans (page 195) and steamed broccoli with lemon-pepper seasoning (page 46).

savory mustard salmon

Prep + Cook =
20 minutes

4 servings

Nutritional Information per serving (% based upon daily values): Calories 260, Total Fat 12g, 18%, Saturated Fat 2g, 10%, Cholesterol 95mg, 32%, Sodium 260mg, 11%, Total Carbohydrate 2g, 1%, Dietary Fiber 0g, 0%, Sugar 0g, Protein 35g

Nutritional Information per serving with side dish (% based upon daily values) ¾ cup cooked bulgur pilaf; 1 cup broccoli: Calories: 456; Total Fat: 17g, 25%; Saturated Fat: 3g, 13%; Cholesterol: 95mg, 32%; Sodium: 380mg, 17%; Total Carbohydrate: 36g, 13%; Dietary Fiber: 11g, 44%; Sugar: 3g; Protein: 44g

1½ tablespoons Dijon mustard

1½ tablespoons reduced-fat mayonnaise

1 teaspoon creamy horseradish sauce or Chinese mustard (optional)

1 tablespoon minced chives or scallions

1½ pounds salmon fillet (preferably wild Alaskan salmon)

Preheat the oven to 450 degrees. (Meanwhile, make the bulgur pilaf, if you are serving it.)

In a small bowl, combine the mustard, mayonnaise, horseradish (optional), and chives or scallions.

Line a baking sheet with aluminum foil and spray the foil with nonstick cooking spray. Put the salmon, skin side down, on the foil and, using a pastry brush or spoon, spread a thick layer of the sauce on top of it.

Bake the salmon for 10 to 15 minutes in the preheated oven until it flakes easily in the thickest part of the fish. (Meanwhile, make the broccoli, if you are serving it.) Serve the salmon immediately, or refrigerate it overnight and serve it over greens.

Scramble Flavor Booster: Use grainy Dijon mustard and the optional horseradish or mustard. Serve it with lemon-pepper seasoning or lemon wedges.

Tip: Did you know many appliances drain electricity even when you're not using them? Consider unplugging your cell phone charger, laptop, toaster, and other appliances from the wall when they are not in use.

This is a light and delectable preparation for any mild white fish. Serve it with Orange-Ginger Glazed Carrots (page 165) and a baguette.

lightning-quick cod with lemon and lime

Prep + Cook = 25 minutes

4 servings

Nutritional Information per serving (% based upon daily values): Calories 150, Total Fat 1g, 2%, Saturated Fat 0g, 0%, Cholesterol 75mg, 25%, Sodium 160mg, 7%, Total Carbohydrate 2g, 1%, Dietary Fiber 0g, 0%, Sugar 0g, Protein 30g

Nutritional Information per serving with side dish (% based upon daily values) ¾ cup carrots; ¼ of baguette: Calories: 397; Total Fat: 6g, 9%; Saturated Fat: 0g, 0%; Cholesterol: 81mg, 27%; Sodium: 616mg, 26%; Total Carbohydrate: 50g, 16%; Dietary Fiber: 3g, 13%; Sugar: 7g; Protein: 39g

1½ pounds cod, white roughy, tilapia, or other mild white fish fillets

½ teaspoon salt-free lemon-pepper seasoning

½ teaspoon paprika

½ teaspoon garlic powder

¼ teaspoon salt

1–2 limes, juice only (3–4 tablespoons)

Preheat the oven to 400 degrees. Lay the fillets flat in a baking dish large enough to hold them in one layer. In a small bowl, mix the lemon pepper, paprika, garlic powder, and salt. Pour the lime juice over the fish and top it evenly with the spices.

Bake the fish in the preheated oven for 15 to 20 minutes, until it is opaque throughout and flakes easily in the thickest part. (Meanwhile, prepare the carrots, if you are serving them.)

Scramble Flavor Booster: Sprinkle the fillets with ¼ to ½ teaspoon Old Bay seasoning or Goya seasoning (found in the Latin American section of stores) before baking it.

Tip: I like to use citrus fruits in the winter when they are at their best, and many other fruits are either unavailable or are being shipped from the other hemisphere.

Our friend Claudia Ades invented this delightfully sweet shrimp that makes your mouth feel like it's on a tropical vacation—you'll almost wish you had a straw to drink the sauce. Serve it with steamed peas.

tropical shrimp (or chicken)

Prep + Cook = 25 minutes

6 servings

Nutritional Information per serving (with shrimp and rice noodles) (% based upon daily values): Calories 370, Fat 8g, 12%, Saturated Fat 5g, 25%, Cholesterol 125mg, 42%, Sodium 150mg, 6%, Total Carbohydrate 55g, 18%, Dietary Fiber 2g, 12%, Sugar 2g, Protein 18g

Nutritional Information per serving with side dish (% based upon daily values) $\frac{1}{2}$ cup peas: Calories: 432; Total Fat: 8g, 12%; Saturated Fat: 5g, 25%; Cholesterol: 125mg, 42%; Sodium: 152mg, 6%; Total Carbohydrate: 67g, 22%; Dietary Fiber: 7g, 30%; Sugar: 6g; Protein: 22g

1 package (7–10 ounces) rice noodles or white or quick-cooking brown rice (need 3 cups cooked rice noodles or steamed rice)

2 tablespoons butter or margarine

1 medium yellow onion, finely diced

1 tablespoon minced garlic (about 6 cloves)

2 tomatoes, chopped

$\frac{1}{4}$ lemon, juice only (about 1 tablespoon)

1 pound large shrimp, peeled and deveined, or boneless chicken breasts (if using chicken, cut it into 1-inch pieces)

$\frac{1}{4}$ cup light unsweetened coconut milk

1 large juicing orange ($\frac{1}{2}$ cup fresh orange juice)

1 ounce tequila or rum (optional)

$\frac{1}{8}$ teaspoon crushed red pepper flakes (optional)

$\frac{1}{4}$–$\frac{1}{2}$ teaspoon salt, to taste

$\frac{1}{8}$ teaspoon black pepper, or to taste

Cook the rice noodles or rice according to the package directions. Meanwhile, in a large heavy skillet, melt the butter or margarine over medium heat. Add the onions and garlic and sauté them for 3 to 4 minutes until the onions soften and become fragrant.

Add the tomatoes, lemon juice, and shrimp (or chicken) to the skillet. Sauté them for about 5 minutes, until the shrimp turn pink (or the chicken is no longer pink in the center). (Meanwhile, prepare the peas, if you are serving them.)

Add the coconut milk, orange juice, tequila or rum (optional), and red pepper flakes (optional) to the skillet and stir until heated through. Season with salt and pepper to taste.

Serve the shrimp (or chicken) and sauce ladled over the noodles or rice.

Scramble Flavor Booster: Double the crushed red pepper flakes.

Tip: To save time on weeknights I buy frozen shrimp already peeled and deveined.

This is my favorite new fish recipe created by my friend Madhavi Naik. It looks so simple but you won't believe how complex and tantalizing the flavor is. Scramble recipe tester Catherine O'Leary said, "It was awesome. The kids loved it—I was really surprised!" Serve it with basmati rice and Lemony-Garlic Spinach (page 33) unless you prefer to bake the spinach with the fish.

catfish in a curried tomato sauce

Prep (15 minutes) +
Cook (25 minutes)

6 servings

Nutritional Information per serving (% based upon daily values): Calories 250, Total Fat 14g, 22%, Saturated Fat 3g, 15%, Cholesterol 70mg, 23%, Sodium 300mg, 13%, Total Carbohydrate 6g, 2%, Dietary Fiber 2g, 8%, Sugar 3g, Protein 24g

Nutritional Information per serving with side dish (% based upon daily values) ¾ cup rice with broth; ¼ of spinach:
Calories: 460; Total Fat: 19g, 27%; Saturated Fat: 4g, 20%; Cholesterol: 75mg, 25%; Sodium: 445mg, 19%; Total Carbohydrate: 41g, 13%; Dietary Fiber: 9g, 36%; Sugar: 4g; Protein: 31g

2 pounds catfish, or other thin white fish fillets

½ teaspoon salt

¼ teaspoon turmeric

1 tablespoon vegetable oil

1 medium yellow onion, finely chopped

1 teaspoon minced garlic (about 2 cloves)

¼ teaspoon cayenne pepper

2 teaspoons curry powder

1 can (15 ounces) diced tomatoes (preferably no-salt-added), with their liquid

1 package (6 ounces) baby spinach (optional)

Season the fillets with half of the salt and all of the turmeric, rubbing the spices gently into the fillets. Set them aside.

Preheat the oven to 350 degrees. Meanwhile, in a large heavy skillet, heat the oil over medium heat. Add the onions and sauté them until they are lightly browned, stirring occasionally. Add the garlic, the remaining ¼ teaspoon salt, the cayenne pepper, and the curry powder to the pan with the onions. Sauté for about 1 minute, then add the tomatoes and simmer everything for 3 to 5 minutes. (Start the rice, if you are making it.)

Meanwhile, spray a 9 × 13-inch baking dish with nonstick cooking spray, and put the fish in the dish. (Top the fish with the baby spinach, if desired.) Spread the tomato sauce evenly over the fillets, and bake in the preheated oven for 20 to 25 minutes until the fish flakes easily in the thickest part. (If you have added the spinach, stir the sauce once while the fish is baking to make sure the spinach wilts into the tomato sauce.) (If you are serving the spinach on the side, prepare it now.) Serve the fish immediately.

Scramble Flavor Booster: Double the cayenne pepper and the turmeric.

Tip: Adding baby spinach to the dish gives it additional color and increases its nutritional content. Whenever possible, buy organic spinach, as conventional spinach tends to have high pesticide residue.

Tilapia is a great fish to make at home—it is low-fat, low priced, and healthy for the earth and people. Its mild flavor takes well to flavorful sauces like this one. Serve it with the remaining pineapple, Israeli couscous (or any variety), and a crisp green salad with cashews and raisins.

tilapia with caribbean pineapple sauce

Prep + Cook = 20 minutes

4 servings

Nutritional Information per serving (% based upon daily values): Calories 310, Total Fat 15g, 23%, Saturated Fat 1.5g, 8%, Cholesterol 0mg, 0%, Sodium 340mg, 14%, Total Carbohydrate 15g, 5%, Dietary Fiber 1g, 4%, Sugar 8g, Protein 29g

Nutritional Information per serving with side dish (% based upon daily values) ¾ cup Israeli couscous; 1½ cups salad:
Calories: 531; Total Fat: 20g, 31%; Saturated Fat: 2g, 11%; Cholesterol: 0mg, 0%; Sodium: 487mg, 20%; Total Carbohydrate: 51.5g, 18%; Dietary Fiber: 4g, 17%; Sugar: 13g; Protein: 36g

3 tablespoons olive oil

½ yellow or red onion, slivered

1 can (20 ounces) pineapple tidbits or chunks in 100 percent juice, drained, juice reserved

1 tablespoon reduced-sodium soy sauce

¼ cup flour

¼ teaspoon salt, or to taste

⅛ teaspoon black pepper, or to taste

4 to 6 tilapia fillets (about 1½ pounds total)

In a small saucepan, heat 1 tablespoon oil over medium heat and add the onions. Cook them for about 3 minutes, stirring occasionally. Add 1 cup pineapple tidbits (if using chunks, chop them first) and sauté them for 2 more minutes. Add ¼ cup of the reserved pineapple juice and the soy sauce and continue cooking, stirring occasionally, until the liquid has reduced by about half, 5 to 7 more minutes. (Serve remaining pineapple with dinner.) (Meanwhile, make the couscous and salad.)

Put the flour on a shallow dish, season it to taste with salt and pepper, and lightly coat the tilapia with the flour. Heat the remaining 2 tablespoons oil in a large nonstick skillet over medium heat. Cook the fish for about 4 minutes per side, flipping it once, until it is opaque and cooked through. Serve the fish topped with the pineapple sauce.

Scramble Flavor Booster: Serve the fish with jerk seasoning sauce.

Side Dish Suggestion: To make the salad, combine 6 to 8 cups chopped lettuce, ¼ cup raisins, and ¼ cup cashews, and toss it with 2 to 4 tablespoons salad dressing.

This simple preparation of fish, suggested by our friend (and a fantastic cook) Jackie Cohen, appeals to kids and adults. Serve it with a White Bean and Red Onion Salad (page 76).

cod with cornflake crust

Prep + Cook =
20 minutes

4 servings

Nutritional Information per serving (% based upon daily values): Calories 250, Total Fat 7g, 11%, Saturated Fat 3.5g, 18%, Cholesterol 130mg, 43%, Sodium 280mg, 12%, Total Carbohydrate 10g, 3%, Dietary Fiber 0g, 0%, Sugar 1g, Protein 35g

Nutritional Information per serving with side dish (% based upon daily values) ¼ of salad: Calories: 400; Total Fat: 11g, 17%; Saturated Fat: 4g, 21%; Cholesterol: 130mg, 43%; Sodium: 790mg, 33%; Total Carbohydrate: 33g, 11%; Dietary Fiber: 6g, 24%; Sugar: 2g; Protein: 43g

¼ cup cornflakes or other flake cereal, smashed into coarse crumbs (kids can help smash them)

¼ cup grated Parmesan cheese

¼ cup bread crumbs or panko

1 egg

1½ pounds cod or other thick white fish fillets

1 tablespoon butter

1 lemon, cut into wedges for serving (optional)

Preheat the oven to 500 degrees. In a large resealable bag, combine the cornflake crumbs, Parmesan cheese, and bread crumbs. In a shallow bowl, beat the egg.

Dip the fillets in the egg, then add the fish to the bag and shake and press until each piece is well coated.

Spray a large ovenproof skillet with nonstick cooking spray and melt the butter in it over medium-high heat. Add the fish and cook it for 1 to 2 minutes per side, until it is lightly browned.

(Meanwhile, start the salad.) Transfer the pan to the oven and bake the cod for 5 to 7 minutes, depending on its thickness, or until it flakes easily. Serve it with lemon wedges, if desired.

Scramble Flavor Booster: Use aged Parmesan cheese for the coating and season the coating mixture with Old Bay seasoning or other fish seasoning blend.

Tip: To keep the cornflakes from spraying across the kitchen, smash them in the plastic bag with a mallet. You want them smashed but not pulverized, so they still have a crunchy texture.

This is a quick and easy preparation for a thick fish fillet such as mahi mahi or halibut. You can also use chicken or pork, if you prefer. Serve it with rice pilaf and apples dipped in honey.

mahi mahi with garlic and rosemary

Prep + Cook =
20 minutes

4 servings

Nutritional Information per serving (% based upon daily values): Calories 200, Total Fat 8g, 12%, Saturated Fat 1g, 5%, Cholesterol 125mg, 42%, Sodium 390mg, 16%, Total Carbohydrate 0g, 0%, Dietary Fiber 0g, 0%, Sugar 0g, Protein 32g

Nutritional Information per serving with side dish (% based upon daily values) ¾ cup prepared rice pilaf; ½ apple and 1 tbsp. honey: Calories: 441; Total Fat: 11g, 17%; Saturated Fat: 3g, 13%; Cholesterol: 133mg, 45%; Sodium: 999mg, 41%; Total Carbohydrate: 53g, 18%; Dietary Fiber: 4g, 14%; Sugar: 17g; Protein: 36g

1 teaspoon minced garlic (about 2 cloves)

½ teaspoon minced fresh or dried rosemary

2 tablespoons olive oil

½ teaspoon kosher salt

1–1½ pounds mahi mahi fillets (or other thick white fish)

½ lemon, cut into wedges for serving

Preheat the broiler with the rack about 4 inches from the heat source, or preheat the grill (and start the rice pilaf, if you are making it). In a small bowl, combine the garlic, rosemary, oil, and salt.

Place the fillets on an aluminum foil–lined baking sheet. Spoon half the garlic mixture over the fish and rub it in. Broil (or grill) the fish for 4 to 5 minutes on one side.

Remove the fish from the oven, flip it, and spoon and rub the remaining garlic mixture over the fish. Broil (or grill) it for 4 to 5 minutes more until the fish is opaque and flakes easily with a knife. Serve it with the lemon wedges.

Scramble Flavor Booster: Double the garlic and serve the fish with freshly ground black pepper.

Tip: Mahi mahi, also known as dolphinfish or dorado, is an excellent seafood choice for your family's health and the environment. In fact, mahi mahi is selected as an "Eco-best" choice for seafood by Environmental Defense (www.oceansalive.org). Mahi mahi is a delicious alternative to Chilean sea bass (an "Eco-worst" choice), which has a declining population and high mercury levels.

Side Dish suggestion: Dip sliced apples in honey for a delicious and healthy side dish or dessert.

This is my variation on the traditional Chinese dish—it's a sweet and savory Asian treat for all ages. As Scramble recipe tester Debby Boltman reports, "Wow! Talk about quick, easy, and yummy!" You can use chicken tenderloins or extra-firm tofu in place of the fish, if you prefer, cooking them for about the same length of time as you would the fish. Serve it with steamed brown or white rice and Sesame Stir-Fried Broccoli (page 241).

tilapia with chinese black bean sauce

Prep + Cook = 15 minutes

4 servings

Nutritional Information per serving (% based upon daily values): Calories 150, Total Fat 4g, 6%, Saturated Fat 2.6g, 13%, Cholesterol 95mg, 32%, Sodium 570mg, 24%, Total Carbohydrate 8g, 3%, Dietary Fiber <1g, 4%, Sugar 5g, Protein 19g

Nutritional Information per serving with side dish (% based upon daily values) ¾ cup brown rice; 1 cup broccoli: Calories: 392; Total Fat: 9g, 14%; Saturated Fat: 5g, 20%; Cholesterol: 95mg, 32%; Sodium: 767mg, 29%; Total Carbohydrate: 50g, 12%; Dietary Fiber: 8g, 31%; Sugar: 8g; Protein: 27g

1 tablespoon rice wine (or substitute sherry or apple juice)

2 tablespoons Chinese black bean sauce (or substitute soy sauce)

1 tablespoon honey

1 teaspoon sesame oil

1 teaspoon minced garlic (about 2 cloves)

1 teaspoon minced fresh ginger or ¼ teaspoon ground ginger

4 tilapia fillets (about 1 pound total), or other thin white fish fillets

4 scallions, green and most of the white parts, thinly sliced

(If you are making the rice and broccoli, start them first.) In a small bowl or measuring cup, combine the wine, black bean sauce, honey, oil, garlic, and ginger to make the sauce.

In a large nonstick skillet, bring the sauce to a low boil over medium heat. Add the fish fillets in one layer and cook them, partially covered, for about 4 minutes. Reduce the heat as necessary to keep the sauce at a simmer. (Meanwhile, start the broccoli.)

Flip the fish and add the scallions. Continue cooking the fish, partially covered, for 4 to 5 minutes until it is cooked through and flakes easily in the thickest part. Serve it hot.

Scramble Flavor Booster: Double the ginger and add ¼ teaspoon Asian chili sauce to the marinade.

Tip: If your family doesn't eat much fish, you can almost always substitute thinly cut or pounded boneless chicken breasts for white fish in Scramble recipes such as this one.

Scramble subscriber Jessica Tomback of Washington, D.C., sent me her mother's delectable recipe for spinach meatballs. Even though the green spinach mixed into the meatballs didn't fool our kids, they devoured the moist and flavorful meatballs anyway, while I serenaded them with Popeye's theme song (it was a little hard for them to eat with their hands covering their ears). Serve it with whole wheat rolls and a green salad with diced orange, walnuts, and Parmesan cheese (page 72).

spaghetti with power meatballs

Prep + Cook =
30 minutes

8 servings

Nutritional Information per serving (% based upon daily values): Calories 390, Total Fat 10g, 15%, Saturated Fat 2.5g, 13%, Cholesterol 70mg, 23%, Sodium 600mg, 25%, Total Carbohydrate 53g, 18%, Dietary Fiber 4g, 16%, Sugar 7g, Protein 21g

Nutritional Information per serving with side dish (% based upon daily values) 1 roll; 1½ cups salad: Calories: 556; Total Fat: 16g, 24%; Saturated Fat: 4g, 17%; Cholesterol: 72mg, 24%; Sodium: 832mg, 35%; Total Carbohydrate: 77g, 26%; Dietary Fiber: 9g, 37%; Sugar: 14g; Protein: 27g

1 package (16 ounces) spaghetti

1 package (10 ounces) frozen chopped spinach

1 pound ground turkey, chicken, or beef (or vegetarian meatballs)

1 egg, lightly beaten

1 jar (26 ounces) tomato-basil pasta sauce

¼ cup Italian-style bread crumbs

¼ cup grated Parmesan cheese for serving (optional)

Set a large pot of salted water to boil for the pasta. In the microwave or on the stovetop, defrost the spinach and drain it well by pressing out the water with another bowl or your hands.

Meanwhile, in a medium bowl, combine the turkey, egg, ½ cup of the pasta sauce, and the bread crumbs. In a very large skillet (use 2 if you don't have one that is at least 10 inches in diameter), bring the remaining marinara sauce to a low boil.

Add the spinach to the meat mixture and combine thoroughly. With wet hands, form the meat mixture into 1- to 2-inch meatballs and add them to the sauce in the skillet. Once all the meatballs (it should make 15 to 20) are in the pan, cover the pan almost completely, leaving room for a little air to escape, and simmer the sauce. After 10 minutes, carefully turn the meatballs and partially cover the pan again. (Meanwhile, make the salad, if you are serving it.) Cook the meatballs for 5 to 10 more minutes while the pasta cooks.

Meanwhile, cook the pasta until it is al dente and drain it. Top the spaghetti with the sauce and meatballs (cut a meatball first to make sure it is no longer pink in the middle) and serve it topped with Parmesan cheese, if desired.

Scramble Flavor Booster: Top the dish with freshly grated aged Parmesan cheese and pass around crushed red pepper flakes.

This is a sophisticated combination of Italian flavors that is especially well suited to adults, but our kids didn't mind the combination. Serve it with Roasted Baby Carrots (page 19).

rotini with sun-dried tomatoes and goat cheese

Prep + Cook = 20 minutes

6 servings

Nutritional Information per serving (% based upon daily values): Calories 380, Total Fat 8g, 12%, Saturated Fat 2g, 10%, Cholesterol 5mg, 2%, Sodium 160mg, 7%, Total Carbohydrate 64g, 21%, Dietary Fiber 4g, 16%, Sugar 6g, Protein 13g

Nutritional Information per serving with side dish (% based upon daily values) 1 cup roasted carrots: Calories: 465; Total Fat: 13g, 20%; Saturated Fat: 5g, 22%; Cholesterol: 5mg, 2%; Sodium: 383mg, 16%; Total Carbohydrate: 74g, 24%; Dietary Fiber: 8g, 30%; Sugar: 10g; Protein: 14g

1 package (16 ounces) rotini pasta

2 tablespoons olive oil

1 yellow onion, finely diced

½ cup julienne-cut sun-dried tomatoes

½–1 teaspoon fresh or dried rosemary, to taste

1 can (15 ounces) diced tomatoes, partially drained

2–3 ounces goat cheese, coarsely chopped

¼ teaspoon salt, or to taste

⅛ teaspoon black pepper, or to taste

Cook the pasta according to the package directions. (Meanwhile, start the carrots, if you are serving them.)

In a large heavy skillet, heat the oil over medium heat. Add the onions, sun-dried tomatoes, and rosemary and sauté, stirring often, until the onions start to brown, about 5 minutes. Add the diced tomatoes and simmer the sauce, stirring occasionally.

Drain the pasta briefly and transfer it to a large metal bowl or back to the pot. Add the goat cheese and stir until the cheese coats the pasta. Stir in the tomato mixture. Season with salt and pepper to taste, and serve.

Scramble Flavor Booster: Use 1 teaspoon fresh rosemary in the sauce.

Tip: Did you know that canned tomatoes are already cooked and peeled? They're a terrific solution for quick and healthy meals, especially when fresh and locally grown tomatoes aren't available. Whenever possible, I spring for organic canned produce to preserve my family's and the planet's health.

This is a quick and flavorful pasta sauce from my friend Sherry Ettleson. Don't be scared off by the anchovies. They add richness and protein to the sauce and no one will even know they are in there. The sauce can be made ahead of time and tastes even better the next day. It can also be used as a spread on crusty bread or crackers. Serve it with kale or other hearty greens with garlic and onions.

penne puttanesca

Prep + Cook = 30 minutes

8 servings

Nutritional Information per serving (% based upon daily values): Calories 300, Fat 6g, 9%, Saturated Fat 1g, 5%, Cholesterol: 5mg, 2%, Sodium 790mg, 33%, Total Carbohydrate 50g, 17%, Dietary Fiber 4g, 16%, Sugar 5g, Protein 11g

Nutritional Information per serving with side dish (% based upon daily values) ¾ cup kale: Calories: 380; Total Fat: 11g, 17%; Saturated Fat: 2g, 8%; Cholesterol: 5mg, 2%; Sodium: 825mg, 34%; Total Carbohydrate: 59g, 20%; Dietary Fiber: 6g, 24%; Sugar: 7g; Protein: 14g

1 package (16 ounces) penne pasta

1½ tablespoons olive oil

1 yellow onion, finely chopped

1 teaspoon minced garlic (about 2 cloves)

1 can (28 ounces) crushed tomatoes

2 ounces anchovies, drained and finely chopped
    (or 2 tablespoons anchovy paste or tomato paste)

1 cup pitted kalamata olives, coarsely chopped

2 tablespoons capers, drained

¼ teaspoon crushed red pepper flakes (optional)

¼ cup grated Parmesan cheese, or to taste

Cook the pasta according to the package directions.

In a heavy saucepan, heat the oil over medium heat. Sauté the onions and garlic until the onions are slightly browned, about 5 minutes. (Meanwhile, start the kale, if you are serving it.)

Stir in the tomatoes, anchovies, olives, capers, and red pepper flakes (optional). Simmer the sauce for 15 to 20 minutes.

Drain the penne and coat it with the sauce. (Remember to leave some of the pasta plain if your kids don't like flavorful sauces.) You can refrigerate the sauce for up to 2 days, freeze it for up to 3 months, or use it immediately. Top it at the table with Parmesan cheese.

Scramble Flavor Booster: Use the optional red pepper flakes and use freshly grated aged Parmesan cheese.

Tip: Scientific studies have shown that anchovies are among the fish that are high in omega-3 fatty acids, which help maintain cardiovascular health. Small fish like anchovies and sardines are also low in environmental contaminants because they are low on the food chain.

Side Dish suggestion: For the kale (or Swiss chard, collards, or other hearty greens) thoroughly wash and soak 1 bunch of kale or other greens to remove any dirt. In a large skillet, heat 2 tablespoons olive oil over medium heat and sauté 2 teaspoons minced garlic (3 to 4 cloves) until it starts to turn golden, about 1 minute. Add ½ medium yellow onion, finely diced, and continue to cook it for about 5 minutes until the onions start to brown. Coarsely chop the kale and add the kale and 1 cup of water to the skillet with the garlic and onions. Bring the water to a boil, cover, and steam the kale for about 10 minutes, until it is wilted. Drain, if necessary, sprinkle it with salt and pepper or a splash of balsamic vinegar for a sweeter taste, if desired, and serve.

the scramble diet?
for some, weight loss is only one of the healthy benefits of cooking with the scramble

Move over Slim-Fast. Look out South Beach. Here comes the Six O'Clock Scramble Diet! A number of subscribers have given me some unexpected feedback about the Scramble. By following the healthy, low-fat dinner recipes, some Scramblers have lost unwanted weight or improved their cholesterol levels. For example, Katie B. of Illinois said, "Since we started cooking with the Scramble, my husband's cholesterol has dropped 36 points into the healthy range!" And many subscribers have also reported that the Scramble works well with their Weight Watchers weight loss or maintenance plans, especially because our detailed nutritional information makes it easy to calculate Weight Watchers points.

What's more, by taking the title of this book to heart and eating at 6:00 P.M., 6:30 P.M., or as early as you reasonably can, rather than closer to bedtime, you will have more time to digest your healthy meal. Eating early can help you lose or maintain weight (and it's a terrible feeling to try to sleep when you feel like there's a brick of heavy food in your stomach!).

Recently, I received this encouraging e-mail from Dr. Marc Bingham of Boiling Spring, SC: "Dear Scramble, You did it! I am a family physician and my wife is an OB-GYN. We are busy, have four children, and feel strongly about doing as much of our own cooking as possible so we can be home and eating by 6:00 P.M. with our children. Your website and great quick recipes make it possible. And even better, we are eating low-fat, heart-healthy foods that I can recommend to my patients and friends!"

Of course, my main goal is to suggest quick, healthy, delicious meals that you can eat as a family. I strive to make the Scramble recipes balanced, incorporating a variety of in-season fruits, vegetables, whole grains, legumes, and other nutritious foods. Fresh ingredients rather than processed shortcuts also mean that Scramble meals are naturally lower in sodium and higher in fiber. But these fresh ingredients also mean better taste for you and yours.

This couscous is an easy one-pot dish to throw together on a busy night. Serve it with orange slices.

moroccan couscous
with chickpeas and spinach

Prep + Cook =
20 minutes

4 servings

Nutritional
Information per
serving (% based
upon daily values):
Calories 410, Total
Fat 10g, 15%, Satu-
rated Fat 2g, 10%,
Cholesterol 5mg, 2%,
Sodium 560mg, 23%,
Total Carbohydrate
61g, 20%, Dietary
Fiber 17g, 68%,
Sugar 4g, Protein
19g.

Nutritional
Information per
serving with side dish
(% based upon daily
values) 1 orange:
Calories: 441; Total
Fat: 10g, 15%; Satu-
rated Fat: 2g, 10%;
Cholesterol: 5mg,
2%; Sodium: 560mg,
23%; Total Carbohy-
drate: 69g, 23%;
Dietary Fiber: 19g,
74%; Sugar: 10g;
Protein: 20g

2 tablespoons olive oil

1 small red onion, diced

1 teaspoon minced garlic (about 2 cloves)

1 teaspoon ground cumin

1 teaspoon curry powder

1¼ cups Israeli (large-grain) couscous

3 cups reduced-sodium chicken or vegetable broth

12–16 ounces spinach, stems removed and coarsely chopped

1 can (15 ounces) chickpeas, drained and rinsed

½ lemon, juice only (about 2 tablespoons)

¼ teaspoon salt, or to taste

⅛ teaspoon black pepper, or to taste

In a stockpot, heat the oil over medium heat. Add the onions, garlic, cumin, and curry powder and cook for about 3 minutes, until the onions begin to get tender. Add the couscous and continue sautéing it, stirring frequently, until the onions are tender, 3 to 5 more minutes.

Add the broth, bring it to a boil, and cook it, covered, for 5 minutes, reducing the heat so that it doesn't boil over. Add the spinach and bring it back to a boil, and cook it covered for about 3 minutes, or until the couscous is fully cooked.

Gently stir in the chickpeas, lemon juice, and salt and pepper until it is heated through. Serve it immediately or refrigerate it for up to 2 days.

Scramble Flavor Booster: Add ⅛ teaspoon cayenne pepper with the cumin and curry powder, double the curry powder, and serve it topped with feta or goat cheese.

Tip: If you use baby spinach rather than conventional spinach, you do not need to chop it before adding it.

This flavorful sauce perks up weeknight pasta, but not so much that the kids will turn their noses up at it. Serve it with steamed broccoli tossed with olive oil and Parmesan cheese (page 35).

rigatoni with diced tomatoes and bacon

Prep + Cook =
25 minutes

8 servings

Nutritional
Information per
serving (% based
upon daily values):
Calories 300, Total
Fat 6g, 9%, Saturated
Fat 2g, 10%, Choles-
terol 10mg, 3%,
Sodium 710mg, 30%,
Total Carbohydrate
48g, 16%, Dietary
Fiber 2g, 8%, Sugar
5g, Protein 12g

Nutritional
Information per
serving with side dish
(% based upon daily
values) 1 cup pre-
pared broccoli:
Calories: 393; Total
Fat: 10g, 15%; Satu-
rated Fat: 3g, 17%;
Cholesterol: 14mg,
4%; Sodium: 837mg,
36%; Total Carbohy-
drate: 59g, 20%;
Dietary Fiber: 7g,
29%; Sugar: 7g;
Protein: 17g

1 tablespoon olive oil

4 ounces bacon (about 4 slices, turkey, pork, or meatless), diced

¼ yellow onion, finely diced (about ½ cup)

1 package (16 ounces) rigatoni

1 can (28 ounces) or 2 cans (15 ounces) diced tomatoes with Italian seasoning (or 2 pounds diced fresh tomatoes plus ½ teaspoon dried oregano and ½ teaspoon dried basil)

¾ cup grated Parmesan cheese

In a large heavy skillet, heat the oil over medium heat, and cook the bacon and onions until they are browned, 5 to 7 minutes.

Meanwhile, cook the rigatoni according to the package directions (and prepare the broccoli, if you are making it.)

Add the tomatoes to the bacon-onion mixture. Bring it to a boil, lower the heat, cover, and simmer it until the pasta is cooked.

Drain the rigatoni and immediately transfer it to a large metal serving bowl. Top it with the tomato sauce and Parmesan cheese and toss thoroughly. Serve it immediately or refrigerate it for up to 24 hours.

Scramble Flavor Booster: To give it a little more spice, stir ¼ teaspoon crushed red pepper flakes into the sauce.

Tip: As kids get a little older, in addition to clearing their plates after dinner, consider asking them to clear at least two more things and/or help you load or empty the dishwasher. Kids can also be a big help with setting the table, wiping off the table, and even helping to make dinner!

My cousin, Deborah Goldsholl, makes this dish when she needs a hearty and easy meal for company. You can get creative with it by making your own sauce or adding chopped spinach or broccoli with or instead of the meat, but it is such a crowd-pleaser as is. You can also split the ingredients into two 9-inch pie dishes, if you prefer, and freeze one after cooking. Serve it with a green salad with mushrooms, onions, and Parmesan cheese.

cheesy spaghetti bake

Prep (25 minutes) + Cook (30 minutes)

8 servings

Nutritional Information per serving (% based upon daily values): Calories 340, Total Fat 8g, 12%, Saturated Fat 4g, 20%, Cholesterol 95mg, 32%, Sodium 560mg, 23%, Total Carbohydrate 41g, 14%, Dietary Fiber 2g, 8%, Protein 31g, Sugar 8g

Nutritional Information per serving with side dish (% based upon daily values) 1½ cups salad: Calories: 404; Total Fat: 11g, 16%; Saturated Fat: 5g, 22%; Cholesterol: 97mg, 32%; Sodium: 798mg, 33%; Total Carbohydrate: 48g, 16%; Dietary Fiber: 5g, 18%; Sugar: 12g; Protein: 35g

12 ounces whole wheat or regular spaghetti

2 tablespoons butter or margarine

⅓ cup grated Parmesan cheese

2 eggs, beaten

1 pound ground turkey, beef, or vegetarian ground "meat"

1 jar (26 ounces) pasta sauce with mushrooms and garlic

1½ cups nonfat ricotta or cottage cheese

½ cup shredded part-skim mozzarella cheese

Preheat the oven to 350 degrees. Coat a 9 × 13-inch baking dish with nonstick cooking spray.

Break the spaghetti into thirds and cook it according to package directions until it is al dente. Drain the spaghetti. (You can make a 16-ounce package and reserve one-fourth of it to serve plain to picky eaters) Return the drained pasta to the pot, and toss it with the butter, Parmesan cheese, and eggs. Using a spatula, press the cooked spaghetti into the bottom of the prepared baking dish.

Meanwhile, brown the meat in a large skillet over medium heat. (If you are using vegetarian ground "meat," no need to brown it first.) Mix in the pasta sauce and remove the skillet from the heat.

Spread the ricotta or cottage cheese evenly over the spaghetti in the baking dish. Top it with the meat mixture and bake it, uncovered, for 25 minutes. (Prepare the salad, if you are making it, while the spaghetti is in the oven.) Remove the casserole from the oven, sprinkle it with mozzarella cheese, and bake it for 5 more minutes. Cut into squares to serve.

Scramble Flavor Booster: Add ¼ to ½ teaspoon each of dried basil and oregano to the skillet with the meat and sauce. Season the finished dish with crushed red pepper flakes or hot pepper sauce.

Tip: Whole wheat pasta has much more fiber than refined pasta, plus extra vitamins and minerals. If you use it in recipes like this one with lots of sauce and flavor, your family will probably not notice the difference in texture and taste.

Side Dish suggestion: To make the salad, combine 6 to 8 cups lettuce, 1 cup sliced mushrooms, ¼ to ½ red or yellow onion, sliced, and ¼ cup shredded or grated Parmesan cheese, and toss it thoroughly with 2 to 4 tablespoons of the dressing of your choice.

my kids ate brussels sprouts (and other strange but true stories)

Our kids, Solomon and Celia, ages twelve and ten, are pretty good eaters. They aren't fazed anymore by eating something different nearly every night, and they take my recipe disasters in stride. They even like giving me suggestions to improve the recipes I'm testing (and I'm always testing). But they used to be picky eaters, especially Solomon, who from the first day of his life didn't seem interested in eating much at all.

Since our kids were small, Andrew and I have tried to gently nudge Solomon and Celia to expand their palates. We don't make separate dinners for the kids, we sit down to dinner together whenever possible, and we put new foods on their plates and encourage them to try a bite or two before deciding if they like it. We praise the kids if they try something new, especially if they like it, and we refrain from criticizing them if they don't like it. I usually say something cheerful such as, "Well, you were adventurous to try it, and maybe you'll like it when you are older."

One vegetable our kids had never taken to was Brussels sprouts. Since I don't often let the kids' tastes dictate what I make for dinner, one week I roasted some cute little sprouts that I picked up at the farmers market (see page 205 for the recipe). I put one little green guy on each child's plate and encouraged Solomon and Celia to try it with an open mind. Celia popped the whole thing in her mouth and for the first time, didn't make a face! Then, to my shock, she said, "not bad," and took a few more from the bowl. Not to be outdone, Solomon downed his sprout with nary a grimace and said. "Mmmm, kind of tastes like broccoli." He proceeded to eat a few more, dipping them in barbecue sauce.

Now some of you may get a lift when your child brings home a great report card, or when your favorite team wins the World Series. But me? I get a little crazy when my kids eat a new healthy food, let alone a vegetable maligned by kids (and a lot of grownups) as icky. (I doubt those misguided souls have tried my Roasted, or Caramelized, Brussels Sprouts, though.)

Moral of the story? Don't give up on trying to expand your kids' palates. Just because they've rejected a food in the past (or nearly every food, as the case may be!), my advice is to keep it low key, keep it positive, and keep trying. One day you'll be as surprised as we were.

P.S. You could try my friend Holly's approach to feeding her three children. She tells them that they don't get to vote on whether or not they like a food until they've have had three or four bites.

I am so excited about this recipe for macaroni and cheese (can we ever have enough?) inspired by a recipe from Scramble subscriber Katie Ellis. Besides the creamy texture and rich taste, the best thing about this recipe is that you don't have to cook the macaroni in advance—it cooks perfectly in the oven. Serve it with a salad of baby greens with sliced pears and pecans (page 109).

miraculous macaroni and cheese

Prep (10 minutes) + Cook (60 minutes)

8 servings

Nutritional Information per serving (with sausage) (% based upon daily values): Calories 340, Total Fat 15g, 23%, Saturated Fat 7.5g, 38%, Cholesterol 40mg, 13%, Sodium 421mg, 18%, Total Carbohydrate 33g, 11%, Dietary Fiber 1g, 4%, Sugar 7g, Protein 18g

Nutritional Information per serving with side dish (% based upon daily values) 1½ cups salad: Calories: 406; Total Fat: 19g, 28%; Saturated Fat: 8g, 39%; Cholesterol: 40mg, 13%; Sodium: 438mg, 19%; Total Carbohydrate: 42g, 14%; Dietary Fiber: 4g, 15%; Sugar: 12g; Protein: 19g

2 tablespoons butter or margarine

2½ cups uncooked elbow macaroni

¼–½ teaspoon salt, to taste

¼ teaspoon dry mustard powder

¼ teaspoon ground nutmeg

2 cups shredded Cheddar cheese

3 ounces precooked andouille or turkey sausage, diced (about 1 cup) (optional)

3¾ cups skim milk (or whatever milk you have)

Preheat the oven to 350 degrees. Put the butter or margarine in a 2-quart casserole dish and melt it in the oven. Remove it from the oven, add the macaroni to the dish, and stir to coat the macaroni. Stir in the salt, mustard, nutmeg, cheese, and sausage (optional). Pour the milk over everything and stir gently.

Bake it for 1 hour, uncovered (be sure not to stir it while it's cooking). (Meanwhile, prepare the salad, if you are serving it.) Let the casserole cool for 5 to 10 minutes before serving it.

Scramble Flavor Booster: Double the dry mustard and use sharp Cheddar cheese.

Tip: Each serving of this casserole fulfills nearly one-third of your daily calcium requirement.

The key to fabulous flavor for this pasta sauce is buying good-quality roasted peppers so they have a fresh Italian flavor. Look for brands with all natural ingredients and without a lot of preservatives, sugar, and salt. Serve it with steamed broccoli (page 196).

rigatoni with roasted red peppers, walnuts, and basil

Prep + Cook = 25 minutes

8 servings

Nutritional Information per serving (% based upon daily values): Calories 310, Total Fat 9g, 14%, Saturated Fat 1.5g, 8%, Cholesterol 5mg, 0%, Sodium 45mg, 2%, Total Carbohydrate 47g, 16%, Dietary Fiber 3g, 12%, Sugar 3g, Protein 10g

Nutritional Information per serving with side dish (% based upon daily values) 1 cup steamed broccoli: Calories: 365; Total Fat: 10g, 15%; Saturated Fat: 2g, 9%; Cholesterol: 5mg, 0%; Sodium: 109mg, 5%; Total Carbohydrate: 58g, 20%; Dietary Fiber: 8g, 33%; Sugar: 5g; Protein: 14g

1 package (16 ounces) rigatoni pasta

3 tablespoons olive oil

½ white or yellow onion, finely diced

1 teaspoon minced garlic (about 2 cloves)

¼ cup walnuts, coarsely chopped

1 jar (12 ounces) roasted red peppers, drained and thinly sliced

1 cup fresh basil, cut into thin strips

¼ cup grated Parmesan cheese, or to taste

Cook the pasta according to the package directions. (Start the broccoli, if you are serving it.)

Meanwhile, in a large heavy skillet, heat 2 tablespoons of the oil over medium heat, and sauté the onions and garlic for about 3 minutes until the onions start to get tender. Add the walnuts and cook for about 2 more minutes, or until the onions are translucent. Add the red peppers and simmer, stirring occasionally, for about 5 more minutes. Add the basil and cook for about 2 more minutes.

Drain the pasta and combine it with the sauce, and stir in the remaining 1 tablespoon oil. Serve with Parmesan cheese at the table. (You may want to stir some Parmesan cheese into the finished dish before you serve it.)

Scramble Flavor Booster: Add an extra clove of garlic to the sauce and use feta cheese instead of the Parmesan.

Tip: Take this to heart: Walnuts are an excellent source of omega-3 essential fatty acids and monounsaturated fats, which can have a great effect on your cardiovascular health.

This fabulous casserole from my friend Kathryn Schwartz is great for company. You can prepare it ahead of time and bake it just before friends arrive. For a lower-fat version, eliminate the pesto, or just serve smaller servings with healthy side dishes like steamed green beans (page 101).

baked pesto penne with italian sausage

Prep (25 minutes) +
Cook (30 minutes)

10 servings

Nutritional
Information per
serving (% based
upon daily values):
Calories 400, Total
Fat 17g, 26%, Satu-
rated Fat 6g, 30%,
Cholesterol 40mg,
13%, Sodium 960mg,
40%, Total Carbohy-
drate 37g, 12%,
Dietary Fiber 3g,
12%, Protein 23g,
Sugar 5g

Nutritional
Information per
serving with side dish
(% based upon daily
values) 1 cup green
beans:
Calories: 434; Total
Fat: 17g, 26%; Satu-
rated Fat: 6g, 30%;
Cholesterol: 40mg,
13%; Sodium: 967mg,
40%; Total Carbohy-
drate: 45g, 15%;
Dietary Fiber: 7g,
27%; Sugar: 7g;
Protein: 25g

12 ounces penne pasta (or any medium tube-shaped pasta)

1 pound spicy Italian sausage (turkey, pork, or meatless)

1 yellow onion, chopped

1½ teaspoons minced garlic (about 3 cloves)

1 can (28 ounces) diced tomatoes, with their liquid

1 tablespoon (7 ounces) pesto sauce (refrigerated, not shelved)

¼ teaspoon crushed red pepper flakes (optional)

1 package (6–9 ounces) baby spinach

1 package (8 ounces) shredded part-skim mozzarella cheese

½ cup grated Parmesan cheese

Cook the penne according to the package directions until al dente. (If you use a 16-ounce box of pasta, make the whole package and reserve one-fourth to serve plain to picky eaters). Preheat the oven to 375 degrees. Coat a 9 × 13-inch baking dish with nonstick cooking spray.

Meanwhile, heat a large heavy saucepan over medium-high heat. Add the sausage, onions, and garlic, and sauté them, using a wooden spoon to break up the sausage, until it is cooked through, about 10 minutes. Add the tomatoes to the pan. Simmer it until the sauce thickens slightly, stirring occasionally, about 10 minutes. Stir in the pesto and red pepper flakes (optional).

In the baking dish, combine the pasta, spinach, mozzarella, and ¼ cup Parmesan cheese. Gently stir in the tomato mixture. Sprinkle the remaining ¼ cup Parmesan cheese on top. Bake the casserole until the sauce is bubbling and the cheeses melt, about 30 minutes. (Meanwhile, prepare the green beans.) This casserole can be frozen for up to 3 months and reheated in the oven or microwave.

Scramble Flavor Booster: Use spicy sausage and double the amount of crushed red pepper flakes.

Tip: To make delicious fresh pesto: In a blender or food processor, combine 2 cups (tightly packed) fresh basil leaves, 1 teaspoon minced garlic, 2 tablespoons pine nuts, ½ cup olive oil, and ½ cup grated Parmesan cheese. Process or blend until coarsely chopped.

This is a sweet and easy stir-fry that is very kid friendly, and has gotten fabulous reviews from Scramble subscribers. The Asian vegetable mix makes it so easy to have variety for low cost and effort. Serve it with steamed rice and Asian dumplings or egg rolls (sold frozen) for a super-easy meal.

chinese new year stir-fry with tofu or pork

Prep + Cook =
25 minutes

6 servings

Nutritional
Information per
serving (% based
upon daily values):
Calories 140, Total
Fat 6g, 9%, Saturated
Fat 1g, 5%, Choles-
terol 0mg, 0%,
Sodium 460mg, 19%,
Total Carbohydrate
12g, 4%, Dietary
Fiber 3g, 12%, Sugar
5g, Protein 8g

Nutritional
Information per
serving with side dish
(% based upon daily
values) ¾ cup white
rice; 2 dumplings:
Calories: 444; Total
Fat: 12g, 19%; Satu-
rated Fat: 3g, 12%;
Cholesterol: 9mg,
3%; Sodium: 848mg,
36%; Total Carbohy-
drate: 61g, 20%;
Dietary Fiber: 7g,
23%; Sugar: 10g;
Protein: 20g

1 pound extra-firm tofu packed in water (or use boneless pork, beef, or chicken)

1 tablespoon plus 1 teaspoon sesame or vegetable oil

¼ cup reduced-sodium soy sauce

2 tablespoons rice vinegar

1 tablespoon sugar

1 tablespoon black bean or hoisin sauce

1 tablespoon cornstarch

1 teaspoon minced garlic (about 2 cloves)

1 package (16 ounces) frozen mixed oriental vegetables

Drain the tofu and wrap it in a clean towel to absorb the moisture. (If you are using meat, skip this step.) Remove the mixed vegetables from the freezer and set them aside. (Meanwhile, prepare the rice and dumplings or egg rolls, if you are serving them.)

Dice the tofu (or meat) into ½-inch cubes. Heat 1 tablespoon of the oil in a large nonstick or heavy skillet over medium heat and sauté the tofu (or meat) for 5 to 8 minutes, flipping it occasionally, until it starts to turn golden (or until the meat is cooked through). Remove the tofu (or meat) from the pan and set it aside.

In a measuring cup, whisk together the soy sauce, vinegar, sugar, black bean or hoisin sauce, and cornstarch.

Heat the remaining oil in the same skillet over medium heat. Add the garlic and stir-fry it for 30 seconds, then add the vegetables. Cook until the vegetables are heated through and slightly softened, about 4 minutes. Add the tofu (or meat) and soy sauce mixture and cook it for 2 more minutes. Remove it from the heat and serve it immediately.

Scramble Flavor Booster: For an additional kick, add a few crushed red pepper flakes or red chili paste to the sauce.

Tip: The best oils to use in cooking are the ones that have the least amount of saturated fats. These include: canola, olive, peanut, safflower, sesame, sunflower, and avocado oils.

This nutritious and flavorful meal, suggested by subscriber Jennifer Gross, is perfect when paired with lightly buttered corn kernels.

orange-cumin black beans over rice

Prep + Cook = 20 minutes

4 servings

Nutritional Information per serving (% based upon daily values): Calories 440, Total Fat 10g, 15%, Saturated Fat 1.5g, 8%, Cholesterol 0mg, 0%, Sodium 630mg, 26%, Total Carbohydrate 74g, 25%, Dietary Fiber 12g, 48%, Sugar 6g, Protein 15g

Nutritional Information per serving with side dish (% based upon daily values) ½ cup corn kernels: Calories: 498; Total Fat: 11g, 17%; Saturated Fat: 2g, 10%; Cholesterol: 1mg, 1%; Sodium: 633mg, 27%; Total Carbohydrate: 87g, 29%; Dietary Fiber: 13g, 53%; Sugar: 8g; Protein: 17g

1 tablespoon olive oil

1 shallot, or ½ small yellow onion, finely diced

2 celery stalks, thinly sliced

1–1½ cups white or quick-cooking brown rice

2 cans (15 ounces each) black beans, drained and rinsed

1 tablespoon brown sugar (optional)

½ cup orange juice

½ cup reduced-sodium chicken or vegetable broth

1 teaspoon chili powder

1 teaspoon ground cumin

In a large skillet, heat the oil over medium heat. Add the shallot or onions and celery and sauté them for 5 to 7 minutes until they are tender. Meanwhile, start the rice.

Add the remaining ingredients except the rice, and bring it to a boil. Simmer it for 15 minutes, stirring occasionally, until most of the liquid is absorbed. (Make the corn, if you are serving it.)

Serve the beans over the cooked rice. (If you want to make it in advance, you can refrigerate the cooked beans for up to 2 days before serving them, or freeze them for up to 3 months. Prepare the rice when you are ready to serve the meal, or freeze the rice separately.)

Scramble Flavor Booster: Double the chili powder or use chipotle chili powder and sprinkle the beans with hot pepper sauce, such as Tabasco, to taste.

Tip: If you want this dish to be a little less sweet, omit or reduce the amount of brown sugar.

Side Dish suggestion: Cook 1 pound frozen corn kernels in the microwave or on the stovetop for 3 to 5 minutes (we like it a little undercooked so it doesn't get chewy). Toss the hot corn with 1 teaspoon butter or margarine and a squeeze of fresh lime juice (about ¼ lime), if desired. Season with salt, if desired.

My friend and recipe co-conspirator Lisa Flaxman called this dish Polenta Mash. It's not a beautiful dish to look at, but it's so tasty that you probably won't mind. (I prefer to dice, rather than mash, the polenta, but you may prefer it Lisa's way). This would also make a great side dish for chicken or fish. Serve it with crinkle-cut or baby carrots and guacamole (page 151).

polenta mash with roasted tomato salsa

Prep + Cook = 20 minutes

6 servings

Nutritional Information per serving (% based upon daily values): Calories 380, Total Fat 6g, 9% Saturated Fat 0.5g, 3%, Cholesterol 0mg, 0%, Sodium 630mg, 26%, Total Carbohydrate 70g, 23%, Dietary Fiber 7g, 28%, Sugar 4g, Protein 11g

Nutritional Information per serving with side dish (% based upon daily values) ¼ cup guacamole and ½ cup carrot sticks: Calories: 450; Total Fat: 10g, 15%; Saturated Fat: 1g, 6%; Cholesterol: 0mg, 0%; Sodium: 747mg, 31%; Total Carbohydrate: 78g, 26%; Dietary Fiber: 11g, 43%; Sugar: 7g; Protein: 13g

2 tablespoons olive oil

1 yellow onion, diced (about 2 cups)

1 roll (18–24 ounces) prepared polenta (sold in a tube with grains), diced into ¾-inch cubes

1 can (15 ounces) cannellini beans, drained and rinsed

½ cup roasted tomato salsa (or any variety)

½ cup nonfat or low-fat sour cream

2 tablespoons chopped fresh cilantro (optional)

In a large nonstick skillet, heat the oil over medium heat. Add the onions and cook, stirring occasionally, until they are lightly browned, 5 to 7 minutes. (Meanwhile, prepare the guacamole, if you are serving it.)

Add the polenta and beans and cook them, flipping gently and occasionally, until the polenta is softened, about 5 minutes. (At this point you can mash the polenta with the spatula or a potato masher, if desired, or keep it diced.)

In a measuring cup, combine the salsa and sour cream, and add it to the polenta mixture. Reduce the heat to medium-low so the sour cream won't curdle. Stir it gently until it is warm throughout. Top the polenta with the cilantro, if desired, and serve it immediately.

Scramble Flavor Booster: Use spicy instead of mild salsa.

Tip: As a fun alternative to her morning glass of juice, our daughter, Celia, sometimes likes to have a homemade juice popsicle. She feels like she's savoring a treat in the morning!

This is a simple but satisfying weeknight dish packed with healthy proteins and fiber. Scramble recipe tester, Maria Mullen, said that this is her husband's "new favorite chili!" Serve it with a Caesar salad (page 78).

zesty turkey and black bean chili

Prep + Cook =
25 minutes

6 servings

Nutritional
Information per
serving (% based
upon daily values):
Calories 270, Total
Fat 9g, 14%, Saturated Fat 2g, 10%,
Cholesterol 45mg,
15%, Sodium 960mg,
40%, Total Carbohydrate 28g, 9%,
Dietary Fiber 6g,
24%, Sugar 7g,
Protein 21g

Nutritional
Information per
serving with side dish
(% based upon daily
values) ¼ of the
salad:
Calories: 410; Total
Fat: 19g, 29%; Saturated Fat: 4g, 20%;
Cholesterol: 50mg,
17%; Sodium:
1,210mg, 50%; Total
Carbohydrate: 38g,
12%; Dietary Fiber:
9g, 36%; Sugar: 9g;
Protein: 25g

1 tablespoon olive oil

½ medium yellow onion, diced (1 cup)

1 teaspoon minced garlic (about 2 cloves)

1 pound ground turkey, beef, or vegetarian ground "meat"

1 tablespoon chili powder

1 can (15 ounces) diced tomatoes with green chilies

1 can (6 ounces) tomato paste

1 can (9 ounces) corn kernels, drained

1 can (15 ounces) black beans, drained and rinsed

hot pepper sauce such as Tabasco for serving

In a stockpot, heat the oil over medium heat. Cook the onions until they are tender, about 3 minutes. Add the garlic and stir for about 30 seconds, then add the turkey and chili powder, and brown the turkey for about 5 minutes until it is mostly cooked through. (If you are using vegetarian "meat," add it to the pot along with the tomatoes and chili powder, as there is no need to brown it.) Add the diced tomatoes and the tomato paste, the corn, and the beans, and bring to a simmer. Simmer it for 10 to 15 minutes, stirring occasionally. (Meanwhile, prepare the salad, if you are serving it.)

Slow Cooker directions: Prepare as above, up to the point of bringing it to a simmer. At that point, cook the chili in the slow cooker on Low for 6 to 8 hours or on High for 3 to 4 hours.

Scramble Flavor Booster: Use chipotle chili powder or add ¼ teaspoon cayenne pepper to the chili, and serve it at the table with hot pepper sauce, such as Tabasco.

Tip: Using canned beans makes it so quick and easy to get these healthy legumes into your family's diet. Beans are in the vegetable and protein group of the food pyramid. They are high in protein, fiber, iron, and other essential nutrients. I look for canned beans that are organic and low in sodium.

This vegetarian chili is sweet, chunky, and just a little spicy. If your kids won't eat these foods mixed together, remove a couple of spoonfuls of the beans and corn and set some extra carrots aside for them, but encourage them to have a taste of the chili, too. The chili can be made ahead and frozen for up to 3 months. Serve it alone or over rice, with baby carrots and ranch dressing.

chili non carne

Prep + Cook =
30 minutes

8 servings

Nutritional Information per serving (% based upon daily values): Calories 230, Total Fat 3g, 5%, Saturated Fat 0g, 0%, Cholesterol 0mg, 0%, Sodium 1,100mg, 46%, Total Carbohydrate 41g, 14%, Dietary Fiber 12g, 48%, Sugar 13g, Protein 10g

Nutritional Information per serving with side dish (% based upon daily values) ¾ cup white rice; ½ cup carrots; 1 tbsp. dressing: Calories: 490; Total Fat: 12g, 19%; Saturated Fat: 0g, 1%; Cholesterol: 5mg, 2%; Sodium: 1,281mg, 53%; Total Carbohydrate: 81g, 27%; Dietary Fiber: 16g, 66%; Sugar: 17g; Protein 15g

1 tablespoon olive oil

1 yellow onion, diced

1 red bell pepper, diced

1 cup diced baby carrots (about 20 baby carrots)

1 can (15 ounces) red kidney beans, with their liquid (preferably without added sugar)

1 can (15 ounces) black beans, with their liquid

1 cup mild salsa

1 can (28 ounces) crushed tomatoes

1 tablespoon chili powder, or more to taste

1 can (15 ounces) unsweetened corn kernels, drained

1 cup nonfat plain Greek yogurt or sour cream for serving (optional)

In a large heavy saucepan or stockpot, heat the olive oil over medium heat. Add the onions and bell peppers and sauté them until the onions start to brown, about 5 minutes.

Add the carrots, both types of beans, salsa, tomatoes, and chili powder. Bring it to a boil, lower the heat, and simmer it, uncovered, for 20 minutes or up to 40 minutes, stirring occasionally. (Meanwhile, prepare the rice, if you are making it.) About 10 minutes before serving, stir in the corn.

Serve the chili in bowls alone or over rice, topped with a dollop of the sour cream or yogurt, if desired.

Scramble Flavor Booster: Double the chili powder and serve the chili with hot pepper sauce, such as Tabasco. Top the chili with shredded Cheddar or mozzarella cheese.

Tip: The quality of the salsa can make all the difference in the flavor of this meal. Try a few varieties to learn your family's favorite and stock up. Read the labels, too, as some have too much added salt and sugar.

My friend and colleague Jeanne Rossomme used to live in New Orleans, where she learned to make this zesty jambalaya—she calls it "Poor Man's Jambalaya" because it's not as meaty as some versions. (Jeanne is famous in our neighborhood for making and selling 80 batches of her jambalaya to raise money for victims of Hurricane Katrina.) Serve it with a green salad with carrots, red bell peppers, walnuts, and Parmesan cheese (page 209).

scrambalaya
(cajun jambalaya with smoked ham)

Prep (25 minutes) +
Cook (20 minutes)

8 servings

Nutritional
Information per
serving (% based
upon daily values):
Calories 300, Total
Fat 9g, 14%, Satu-
rated Fat 2.5g, 13%,
Cholesterol 25mg,
8%, Sodium 420mg,
18%, Total Carbohy-
drate 42g, 14%,
Dietary Fiber 1g, 4%,
Sugar 2g, Protein 13g

Nutritional
Information per
serving with side dish
(% based upon daily
values) 1½ cups
salad:
Calories: 366; Total
Fat: 15g, 22%; Satu-
rated Fat: 4g, 16%;
Cholesterol: 26mg,
8%; Sodium: 474mg,
20%; Total Carbohy-
drate: 46g, 15%;
Dietary Fiber: 2g,
10%; Sugar: 4g;
Protein: 15g

2 tablespoons olive oil

12 ounces smoked ham, sausage, or turkey kielbasa, or vegetarian sausage, diced into ¼-inch pieces

3–4 bay leaves

½–1 teaspoon black pepper, to taste (it will make it a little spicy)

1 teaspoon dry mustard

½ teaspoon ground cumin

½ teaspoon dried thyme

1 medium yellow onion, chopped

3–4 celery stalks, chopped (about 1½ cups)

1 green bell pepper, chopped

2 cups white rice, uncooked

1 box (32 ounces) reduced-sodium chicken or vegetable broth

In a large stockpot, heat the oil over medium-high heat. Add the ham or sausage and cook it for about 5 minutes until it is nicely browned. (If you have picky eaters, remove some of the ham/sausage to serve to them before proceeding with the recipe.)

Add the remaining ingredients except the rice and broth, and sauté it for about 10 more minutes until the vegetables soften, stirring occasionally. Add the rice and stir it frequently for about 3 minutes to coat it. Add the broth and simmer it, uncovered, for about 20 minutes until the rice is tender to the bite, stirring occasionally and making sure to scrape the bottom of the pot so the rice doesn't stick. (Meanwhile, make the salad if you are serving it.)

Turn off the heat, cover the pot and let the flavors meld until you are ready to dig in. You can make this up to 2 days in advance, or freeze it for a future meal.

Scramble Flavor Booster: Use 1 teaspoon black pepper and serve it with hot pepper sauce, such as Tabasco.

Tip: If you want a meatier or more traditional version of jambalaya, use even more sausage, or stir in shrimp or crawfish with the rice.

tips for freezing meals

Many of you have asked for tips on freezing Scramble meals, either to save leftovers for another day or as a way to prepare meals in advance for those days when you don't even have 30 minutes to invest in dinner. Freezing is a great way to store food. The freezing process itself does not destroy nutrients and most meals retain their quality for two to three months after freezing. Knowing a few "freezer facts," however, will ensure that your Scramble meals are just as tasty when you reheat or cook them later:

- Most meals freeze well with the exception of those that contain mayonnaise, potatoes, cream, or coconut milk, which separate or change consistency when frozen.

- Ideally, your Scramble meal should be slightly undercooked or even uncooked (depending on what the meal is) when frozen. This ensures that it does not dry out when you cook or reheat it later.

- To prevent "freezer burn" (which does not make food unsafe, merely dry), make sure foods are airtight by using tight covers, heavy-duty aluminum foil, plastic wrap, freezer paper, or place the package inside a plastic freezer bag. (Make sure to reuse or recycle these later.)

- To ensure less waste, package your meals in sizes you are most likely to use—either family meals or individual portions. Also, be sure to label and date each container. You might even want to keep a list on the side of your freezer of what you put in there and when, as my clever mom does.

- There are several safe ways to defrost food. Some meals, such as casseroles, can go directly from the freezer to the oven—just increase the baking time if they are uncooked. If they are cooked, reheat them in the oven at the same temperature you used to cook them, or in the microwave. Food often needs 1 to 2 days to completely thaw in the refrigerator. For faster defrosting (1 to 2 hours), place food in a leak-proof plastic bag and immerse it in cold water. The fastest method is to use your microwave, but watch it carefully as you can easily go beyond thawing to cooking (or overcooking) your meal.

- Don't forget to use the foods you freeze. Try to incorporate frozen foods into your weekly menus so they don't go to waste, and rotate foods so that the foods that need to be used soonest aren't buried in the back of the freezer.

- Many Scramblers use freezing as a way of adjusting meal portions. For example, small families can freeze leftovers in individual-size containers for ready-to-go healthy lunches or single dinner servings.

Making good use of the freezer is another way we Scrambling families can make homemade meals (rather than unhealthy and expensive takeout or fast food) a reality, even on the busiest of days.

You can throw together this soup faster than you can order Chinese (or Japanese) takeout, and it only costs about $10 to make the entire meal. You can, of course, substitute your favorite vegetables in this soup. Serve it with orange slices and a green salad with avocado, carrots, raisins, and sunflower seeds.

japanese vegetable noodle soup

Prep + Cook = 10 minutes

6 servings

Nutritional Information per serving (% based upon daily values): Calories 170, Total Fat 7g, 11%, Saturated Fat 1.5g, 8%, Cholesterol 10mg, 3%, Sodium 590mg, 25%, Total Carbohydrate 16g, 5%, Dietary Fiber 2g, 8%, Sugar 7g, Protein 13g

Nutritional Information per serving with side dish (% based upon daily values) 1 orange: Calories: 277; Total Fat: 12g, 17%; Saturated Fat: 3g, 11%; Cholesterol: 10mg, 3%; Sodium: 608mg, 26%; Total Carbohydrate: 31g, 10%; Dietary Fiber: 7g, 23%; Sugar: 16g; Protein: 17g

2 boxes (32 ounces each) reduced-sodium chicken or vegetable broth

3 tablespoons reduced-sodium soy sauce

1 small piece fresh peeled ginger, cut in 3 quarter-size slices

2 cups bok choy or Napa cabbage, sliced

2 cups sliced cremini or other mushrooms

2 medium carrots, sliced on the diagonal

½–1 package (8–16 ounces) extra-firm or firm tofu, packed in water, cubed

2 packages (3 ounces each) ramen noodle soup, any variety

4 scallions, thinly sliced

2 tablespoons rice wine or mirin (or use juice of ½ lime)

(Make the salad first, if you are serving it.) In a stockpot, bring the broth, soy sauce, and ginger to a boil over medium-high heat.

Add the bok choy or cabbage, mushrooms, carrots, and tofu and cook for about 2 minutes, then add the ramen noodles (discard the flavor packets), stirring with each addition. Reduce the heat, if necessary, to keep the soup at a low boil.

Cook the noodles for 3 minutes, and then add the scallions and rice wine. Cook for 1 more minute until everything is heated through, and serve immediately.

Scramble Flavor Booster: Add a few drops of sesame oil or hot chili sesame oil into each bowl at the table, or stir a handful of fresh cilantro, mint, or basil into the soup before serving.

Tip: Bok choy and Napa cabbage are usually interchangeable in Asian recipes calling for one or the other.

Side Dish suggestion: Toss 6 to 8 cups of chopped lettuce with 1 large sliced carrot, 1 peeled and diced avocado, 2 tablespoons raisins, 2 tablespoons sunflower seeds or soy nuts, and 2 to 4 tablespoons vinaigrette or spicy peanut dressing.

I just love the combined flavors of broccoli and Cheddar cheese. This soup is most satisfying when eaten very hot. Serve it with baked potatoes (page 183).

broccoli and cheddar soup

Prep + Cook =
25 minutes

6 servings

Nutritional Information per serving (% based upon daily values): Calories 170, Total Fat 12g, 18%, Saturated Fat 7g, 35%, Cholesterol 35mg, 12%, Sodium 450mg, 19%, Total Carbohydrate 9g, 3%, Dietary Fiber 3g, 12%, Sugar 4g, Protein 8g

Nutritional Information per serving with side dish (% based upon daily values) 1/2 potato, 1/2 tsp. butter, 1 tbsp. sour cream, 1/2 tbsp. salsa, 1 tsp. scallions, 1 tsp. cheese: Calories: 272; Total Fat: 14g, 21%; Saturated Fat: 8g, 37%; Cholesterol: 36mg, 12%; Sodium: 550mg, 23%; Total Carbohydrate: 29g, 10%; Dietary Fiber: 5g, 18%; Sugar: 6g; Protein: 10g

2 tablespoons butter or olive oil

1 small yellow onion, chopped

1 teaspoon minced garlic (about 2 cloves)

1 package (16 ounces) frozen broccoli florets

1 box (32 ounces) reduced-sodium chicken or vegetable broth

1/2 teaspoon dried thyme or 1 1/2 teaspoons fresh

1 cup sharp shredded Cheddar cheese, or more to taste

(If you are making the potatoes, start them first.) In a large stockpot, melt the butter or heat the olive oil over medium heat. Add the onions and garlic and sauté them until the onions are translucent and soft, about 5 minutes. Add the broccoli, broth, and thyme and bring to a boil. Simmer it for about 5 minutes until the broccoli is very tender.

Using a hand-held immersion blender or a standing blender, puree the soup. Return it to the pot to reheat, if necessary, and stir in the cheese until it is fully melted, about 1 minute. Remove it from the heat and serve immediately.

Scramble Flavor Booster: Double the garlic and serve it with freshly ground black pepper and/or hot pepper sauce, such as Tabasco.

My college roommate, Vicki Botnick, has been making this hearty stew for her family for years (which amazes me, because when we were in school together, she was the master of macaroni and cheese from a box!). Serve it with an Ambrosia Fruit Salad (page 54) and whole wheat rolls.

rich and creamy potato, leek, and barley stew

Prep (30 minutes) +
Cook (30 minutes)

8 servings

Nutritional Information per serving (% based upon daily values): Calories 260, Total Fat 8g, 12%, Saturated Fat 4.5g, 23%, Cholesterol 20mg, 7%, Sodium 400mg, 17%, Total Carbohydrate 37g, 12%, Dietary Fiber 7g, 28%, Sugar 5g, Protein 9g

Nutritional Information per serving with side dish (% based upon daily values) 1 cup fruit salad; 1 roll: Calories: 450; Total Fat: 11g, 17%; Saturated Fat: 5g, 23%; Cholesterol: 20mg, 7%; Sodium: 585mg, 25%; Total Carbohydrate: 78g, 26%; Dietary Fiber: 13g, 52%; Sugar: 25g; Protein: 15g

1 cup quick-cooking or regular barley (if using regular barley, soak in water overnight, if time allows)

2 tablespoons butter

3 leeks, white parts only, sliced and soaked in water to clean them

3 medium white potatoes, diced

2 carrots, sliced

½ teaspoon fresh or dried rosemary

6 cups reduced-sodium vegetable or chicken broth plus extra water or broth to taste

1 cup shredded Swiss cheese

⅛ teaspoon black pepper, or to taste

Soak the barley while you are preparing the stew (unless you are using quick-cooking barley) and set it aside. (Soak it overnight, if possible, for quicker cooking.)

In a large saucepan, preferably nonstick, melt the butter over medium heat. Add the leeks, potatoes, carrots, and rosemary, and sauté them until they are slightly softened, 6 to 8 minutes. Add the broth and bring it to a boil. Reduce the heat and simmer it, uncovered, for 10 minutes.

Puree the soup carefully in a blender or use a hand-held immersion blender (add up to 1 cup of water or broth for a thinner soup) and return it to the pot over medium heat. Add the cheese and drained barley. Allow the barley to cook until it is tender, about 30 minutes, stirring it occasionally. (Check the barley after 10 minutes if you used quick-cooking barley or soaked it overnight.) (Meanwhile, prepare the fruit salad, if you are serving it.) Stir in the black pepper, and serve immediately.

Scramble Flavor Booster: Double the rosemary and add ½ teaspoon thyme. Season the soup with freshly ground black pepper.

Scramble subscriber Michele Houghton shared her favorite quick and easy "pantry meal" with me. Serve it with homemade tortilla chips (page 171) and diced pineapple.

soup-er easy black bean and corn soup

Prep + Cook = 10 minutes

6 servings

Nutritional Information per serving (% based upon daily values): Calories 280, Total Fat 2.5g, 4%, Saturated Fat 0g, 0%, Cholesterol 5mg, 2%, Sodium 1,170mg, 49%, Total Carbohydrate 50g, 17%, Dietary Fiber 12g, 48%, Sugar 8g, Protein 13g

Nutritional Information per serving with side dish (% based upon daily values) ¼ of chips; 1 cup pineapple: Calories: 500; Total Fat: 7g, 11%; Saturated Fat: 1g, 3%; Cholesterol: 5mg, 2%; Sodium: 1,372mg, 55%; Total Carbohydrate: 94g, 32%; Dietary Fiber: 17g, 69%; Sugar: 23g; Protein: 17g

3 cans (15 ounces each) black beans (reduced salt, if possible)
1 cup chunky salsa or any variety
1 cup water
½ teaspoon ground cumin, or more to taste
1 can (14 ounces) corn kernels, with their liquid
1 cup nonfat Greek yogurt or sour cream for serving (optional)

(If you are serving the tortilla chips, start them first.) In a medium stockpot over medium heat, combine the beans, salsa, water, and cumin and bring it to a boil. While it is heating, use a hand-held immersion blender to puree about half the mixture, so it is still chunky. Add the corn and its liquid, and continue to heat it for about 5 minutes, stirring occasionally. (For a smoother soup, add the corn before pureeing the soup.)

Serve the soup with a dollop of Greek yogurt or sour cream, if desired. Alternatively, you can refrigerate the soup for up to 3 days, or freeze it for up to 3 months.

Scramble Flavor Booster: Serve it with hot pepper sauce, and stir in chopped fresh cilantro and thinly sliced scallions at the table.

Tip: The canned beans and salsa make this dish higher in sodium than most Scramble meals. Occasionally eating meals that are high in sodium isn't a problem for most people, but if you are concerned, you can either use low-sodium canned products instead, or, to counteract the sodium, drink lots of water with lemon and/or eat bananas, as potassium balances out sodium in our systems.

If you are turned off by the idea of squash soup, have no fear. The squash disappears into the tomato-based broth so you (and your kids!) won't even know it's in there. This soup, suggested by subscriber Jody Gan, is not only unusually delicious, but actually tastes so nourishing that I had a burst of energy after eating a bowl of it. Scramble recipe tester Sara Sheldon said, "The soup was AWESOME! We really liked how the squash melted into the broth, so as Devin (almost two) was drinking the broth through a straw, he didn't even know he was eating veggies!" Serve it with crispy bread sticks.

fearless tomato and
winter squash soup with sausage

Prep + Cook =
25 minutes

6 servings

Nutritional Information per serving (% based upon daily values): Calories 310, Total Fat 14g, 22%, Saturated Fat 4g, 20%, Cholesterol 45mg, 15%, Sodium 770mg, 32%, Total Carbohydrate 32g, 11%, Dietary Fiber 4g, 16%, Sugar 13g, Protein 15g

Nutritional Information per serving with side dish (% based upon daily values) 5 breadsticks: Calories: 430; Total Fat: 16g, 22%; Saturated Fat: 5g, 20%; Cholesterol: 45mg, 15%; Sodium: 980mg, 41%; Total Carbohydrate: 56g, 19%; Dietary Fiber: 6g, 23%; Sugar: 14g; Protein: 19g

12–16 ounces cooked chicken or turkey chorizo (spicy sausage) or other flavored sausage (or use meatless sausage or portobello or cremini mushrooms for a vegetarian version)

1 tablespoon olive oil

1 yellow onion, diced

2 packages (12 ounces each) frozen winter squash

1 box (32 ounces) reduced-sodium chicken or vegetable broth

1 can (28 ounces) pureed or crushed tomatoes

2 tablespoons pure maple syrup

Quarter the sausage links lengthwise and dice them into small pieces (or dice the mushrooms). In a large Dutch oven or soup pot, heat the oil over medium heat and brown the sausage (or mushrooms) and onions, stirring occasionally, about 5 minutes. Meanwhile defrost the squash in the microwave or on the stovetop.

Add the broth, tomatoes, squash, and maple syrup to the pot with the sausage and onions. Simmer it for 10 to 15 minutes and serve it hot.

Scramble Flavor Booster: Use spicy sausage, such as chorizo.

Tip: Our kids love dipping bread, crispy bread sticks, or dropping soup crackers, such as reduced-sodium Goldfish, into their soup and then fishing them out with a spoon to eat them.

In many places, including the American South, black-eyed peas are eaten for good luck on New Year's Day (some people even hide a coin in the stew, but I wouldn't recommend that!). Our friend Sara Emley, who lives in Durham, North Carolina, created this black-eyed pea gumbo (a Southern spicy stew) for her family and friends to enjoy on the first day of the year. You can enjoy it any day you need a healthy and comforting supper. Serve it with grapes, which are linked to good luck in Spain and Peru (some people there eat 12 grapes at midnight on New Year's Eve for good luck every month of the year).

new year's good luck gumbo

Prep + Cook = 30 minutes

6 servings

Nutritional Information per serving (% based upon daily values): Calories 240, Total Fat 3.5g, 5%, Saturated Fat 0.5g, 3%, Cholesterol 0mg, 0%, Sodium 320mg, 16%, Total Carbohydrate 41g, 14%, Dietary Fiber 6g, 24%, Sugar 5g, Protein 11g

Nutritional Information per serving with side dish (% based upon daily values) 1/2 cup grapes: Calories: 292; Total Fat: 3.5g, 5%; Saturated Fat: 0.5g, 3%; Cholesterol: 0mg, 0%; Sodium: 322mg, 16%; Total Carbohydrate: 54.5g, 19%; Dietary Fiber: 7g, 27%; Sugar: 17g; Protein: 11.5g

1 tablespoon olive oil
1 yellow onion, chopped
1 green bell pepper, chopped
3 celery stalks, chopped
1 teaspoon minced garlic (about 2 cloves)
1 cup quick-cooking brown rice
1 teaspoon ground cumin
1/4 teaspoon black pepper
1 bay leaf
1 can (15 ounces) reduced-sodium chicken or vegetable broth
2 cans (15 ounces each) black-eyed peas with their liquid
1 can (15 ounces) diced tomatoes, with their liquid
1 can (4 ounces) chopped green chiles, with their liquid

Heat the olive oil in a large saucepan over medium heat. Add the onions, bell peppers, celery, and garlic and cook, stirring occasionally, until the vegetables are tender, 8 to 10 minutes.

Add the rice, cumin, black pepper, and the bay leaf and stir it for about 1 minute until the rice is glistening. Add the broth, peas, tomatoes, and chiles. Bring the mixture to a boil, reduce the heat, and simmer, uncovered, for 15 to 20 minutes until the rice is tender and much of the liquid is absorbed. Remove the bay leaf before serving.

Scramble Flavor Booster: Serve it with hot pepper sauce, such as Tabasco.

Tip: For a meatier meal, brown 1/2 pound sausage with the vegetables, or stir cooked shrimp into the finished dish.

Ever since watching Kramer and Elaine rave about it on the "Soup Nazi" episode of *Seinfeld*, I've been intrigued by mulligatawny stew. Now, after making a batch, I can see what all the fuss was about. This Indian stew is rich, aromatic, and delicious. Serve it with Roasted Cauliflower Poppers (page 259).

mulligatawny stew (indian lentil stew)

Prep (20 minutes) + Cook (30 minutes)

6 servings

Nutritional Information per serving (% based upon daily values): Calories 230, Total Fat 10g, 15%, Saturated Fat 4.5g, 23%, Cholesterol <5mg, 2%, Sodium 105mg, 4%, Total Carbohydrate 28g, 9%, Dietary Fiber 10g, 40%, Sugar 8g, Protein 11g

Nutritional Information per serving with side dish (% based upon daily values) ⅙ of cauliflower poppers: Calories: 360; Total Fat: 13g, 20%; Saturated Fat: 6g, 28%; Cholesterol: 5mg, 2%; Sodium: 175mg, 9%; Total Carbohydrate: 52g, 17%; Dietary Fiber: 13g, 52%; Sugar: 11g; Protein: 26g

2 tablespoons vegetable oil

2 yellow onions, chopped (about 3 cups)

2 teaspoons minced garlic (about 4 cloves)

1 tablespoon fresh ginger, peeled and minced, or 1 teaspoon ground ginger

1 teaspoon curry powder

1 teaspoon garam masala

¾ cup dried yellow or green lentils, soaked in water overnight, if possible

1 can (15 ounces) diced tomatoes, with their liquid

1 box (32 ounces) reduced-sodium chicken or vegetable broth

1½ cups basmati or long-grain rice, uncooked

½ cup light coconut milk

1 lemon, cut into wedges for serving (optional)

1 cup fresh cilantro, chopped for serving (optional)

(If you have soaked the lentils for faster cooking, drain them before proceeding with the recipe.) Heat the oil in a stockpot over medium-high heat. Add the onions, garlic, ginger, curry powder, and garam masala and sauté it, stirring occasionally, until the onions are lightly browned, 6 to 8 minutes.

Stir in the lentils to coat them and add the tomatoes and broth (if you presoaked the lentils, you may only want to use 3 cups of the broth because the lentils will have absorbed extra water). Bring the soup to a boil and simmer, stirring occasionally, until the lentils are tender, 25 to 30 minutes (or 10 to 15 minutes for presoaked lentils). Meanwhile, cook the rice according to the package directions (and prepare the cauliflower, if you are making it).

Puree the soup to desired thickness in a blender or right in the pot using a handheld immersion blender—it can be smooth or chunky, depending on your preference. Stir in the coconut milk until it is heated through, and ladle it over the rice, squeezing fresh lemon juice over it, if desired, and garnishing with fresh cilantro (optional).

Scramble Flavor Booster: Double the curry powder and garam masala and serve it with the optional lemon and cilantro.

Tip: If you can't find the Indian spice mixture, garam masala, at your store, use extra curry powder or make your own by mixing ground coriander, cumin, cinnamon, black pepper, cardamom, and cloves.

feeding kids a quick and healthy breakfast before the school bus arrives

Early start times for middle and high school students don't leave much time for breakfast, let alone a relaxed one. When thinking about filling breakfasts for your active kids, look for foods with protein and whole grains to keep them full until lunch, and without too much sugar or artificial colors, which can rev them up temporarily, then slow them down. Don't rule out traditional lunch and dinner foods, such as a turkey sandwich, cold pizza, chicken, or quesadillas, or even healthy varieties of protein bars and muffins in a pinch. Below are some breakfast ideas that can fuel growing (and groggy) children during those hectic mornings on the go:

- A sandwich of rice cakes (or a whole wheat bagel or tortilla) with a thick layer of peanut butter, and all-fruit jelly or sliced bananas in the middle.

- A bagel with cream cheese and smoked salmon, or a whole grain English muffin with melted Cheddar cheese (add a slice of tomato or avocado for the more sophisticated teenage palate.)

- Hard-boiled eggs alone, or diced and mixed with cubed and buttered toast or cheese.

- Yogurt with dry cereal or granola, and/or fruit, or even instant oatmeal mixed in.

- Bags of homemade trail mix with nuts, raisins (or other dried fruit), sunflower seeds, whole grain cereal or popcorn, and even semi-sweet chocolate chips.

- Breakfast smoothies: Store the unblended smoothie (made with yogurt, fresh or frozen fruit, and juice, or peanut butter, banana, milk, and chocolate syrup) in the refrigerator overnight, and blend it in the morning.

Once you know your child is fortified with a nutritious breakfast, you can breathe a sigh of relief as the school bus pulls away, knowing that though your nest is emptier, your child's stomach is fuller . . . just do yourself a favor and don't look at their room!

My favorite deli sandwich is also a quick and satisfying treat for dinner. If you can't find corned beef in your supermarket's deli section, substitute sliced roast beef, ham, or turkey, or even vegetarian deli slices. If you like a sweeter taste, you can substitute coleslaw for the sauerkraut. Serve it with Baked Potato Chips (page 33).

hot reuben melts

Prep + Cook =
20 minutes

4 servings

Nutritional Information per serving (% based upon daily values): Calories 430, Total Fat 16g, 25%, Saturated Fat 6g, 30%, Cholesterol 85mg, 28%, Sodium 1,790mg, 75%, Total Carbohydrate 37g, 12%, Dietary Fiber 5g, 20%, Sugar 4g, Protein 31g

Nutritional Information per serving with side dish (% based upon daily values) 1/2 cup baked potato chips: Calories: 520; Total Fat: 20g, 30%; Saturated Fat: 6g, 30%; Cholesterol: 85mg, 28%; Sodium: 2,030mg, 85%; Total Carbohydrate: 50g, 16%; Dietary Fiber: 7g, 28%; Sugar: 5g; Protein: 33g

¼ cup ketchup

2 tablespoons light mayonnaise

8 slices rye or pumpernickel bread

1 tablespoon margarine or butter, softened

1 pound sliced corned beef (or use sliced roast beef, turkey, ham, or vegetarian deli slices)

4 slices Swiss cheese

1 cup sauerkraut or coleslaw

(If you are serving homemade baked potato chips, start those first.) In a small bowl or measuring cup, combine the ketchup and mayonnaise to make Russian dressing.

On one side of each piece of bread, spread a thin layer of margarine or butter. On the non-buttered side of 4 slices of the bread, layer about 6 slices of corned beef, 1 slice of cheese, 1 large spoonful of sauerkraut or coleslaw, and about 1 tablespoon of the dressing. Press the top half of each sandwich on so the buttered sides of both pieces of bread are on the outside.

Heat a large nonstick skillet over medium heat. Cook the sandwiches on both sides, pressing them down with a spatula, until the outsides are nicely browned, 3 to 5 minutes per side. Remove them from the pan and slice the sandwiches on the diagonal to serve.

Scramble Flavor Booster: Substitute pastrami (which has a peppery taste) for the corned beef.

Tip: Corned beef is a cured variety of beef often sold at delicatessens. Sliced corned beef makes a flavorful sandwich filling, but any sliced deli meat can be substituted for corned beef in this recipe.

I knew this recipe was a hit when our kids went back for third helpings! This is a great recipe to experiment with and adapt to your taste or diet, and would be a terrific option to serve during the Super Bowl or any casual gathering. Serve it with sliced oranges and grapefruit.

nacho average nachos

Prep + Cook =
30 minutes

6 servings

Nutritional Information per serving (with ground turkey) (% based upon daily values): Calories 410, Total Fat 18g, 28%, Saturated Fat 6g, 30%, Cholesterol 50mg, 17%, Sodium 840mg, 35%, Total Carbohydrate 34g, 11%, Dietary Fiber 6g, 24%, Sugar 3g, Protein 28g

Nutritional Information per serving with side dish (% based upon daily values) 1 orange: Calories: 441; Total Fat: 18g, 28%; Saturated Fat: 6g, 30%; Cholesterol: 50mg, 17%; Sodium: 840mg, 35%; Total Carbohydrate: 42g, 14%; Dietary Fiber: 8g, 30%; Sugar: 9g; Protein: 29g

1 tablespoon olive oil

1 small yellow onion, diced

1 pound ground turkey or beef (or use 1 extra can of black beans, tuna, or refried beans)

1 tablespoon chili powder, or more to taste

¼ teaspoon garlic powder, or more to taste

½ teaspoon salt

6–8 cups (about 1 medium bag) tortilla chips (baked, whole grain, or any variety)

1 can (15 ounces) black beans, drained and rinsed, or vegetarian refried beans

1 can (14 ounces) petite diced tomatoes, drained, or 1½ –2 cups mild chunky salsa

¼–½ cup sliced jalapeños or sliced olives (optional)

1 cup shredded Cheddar cheese, or more to taste

1 cup guacamole or diced avocado, nonfat or low-fat sour cream, and extra salsa for serving (optional)

Preheat the oven to 375 degrees. In a large heavy skillet, heat the oil over medium heat. Brown the onions and meat, stirring occasionally, and season them with the chili powder, garlic powder, and salt. When the meat is cooked and the onions are softened, 6 to 8 minutes, remove the pan from the heat.

Meanwhile, spread the chips in the bottom of a large flat baking dish with sides (a metal roasting pan is ideal.) Top the chips evenly with the meat mixture, then the beans, tomatoes or salsa, jalapeños or olives (optional), and cheese.

Bake the nachos for 8 to 10 minutes until everything is hot and the cheese is melted, but before the edges of the chips get browned. Serve it immediately, scooping the chips and toppings onto each plate, and topping it with guacamole or diced avocado, sour cream, and extra salsa, if desired.

Scramble Flavor Booster: Use chipotle or hot Mexican chili powder and the optional jalapeños.

Tip: Vegetarian refried beans are very flavorful and are lower in fat and calories than traditional refried beans.

simple ways to reduce our environmental impact at home

Recently, the county in which my family lives expanded its recycling program to include nearly all plastic and paper products. I was overjoyed when, for the first time, I tossed our yogurt containers and plastic cups into the bright blue recycling bin (along with the other cans and bottles) instead of into the dreary green trash can, which is downright roomy at the end of the week these days. In the California town where my mom and sister live, they can toss anything made of plastic into their bins, even sandwich bags and shrink wrap, further reducing their family's trash output.

The Scramble's most recent poll showed that most of you are already doing a great job of recycling at home (86 percent), while a small margin of you (14 percent) are trying to do better at reducing your impact or don't consider it a priority.

Of course, one of the best ways to reduce our environmental impact is to use less stuff and reuse what we can. Scrambling families go a long way toward these goals by shopping once a week with a master plan, and using nearly everything we buy, rather than throwing away unwanted food and its packaging. In addition to reducing and reusing what we can, here are some additional ways that my family has been able to cut back on our waste:

- **Recycle it:** Though we try not to use it very often, when we do, we rinse and recycle aluminum foil, along with our other cans, bottles, and plastic containers.

- **Reuse it:** When we send the kids off to school or camp, we pack their lunches and snacks in reusable containers—we even wash and reuse their plastic utensils and baggies (we keep a special multi-pronged drying rack for plastic baggies next to our sink).

- **Unplug it:** We recently realized that we can live without the extra refrigerator in the basement. We still have it down there just in case, but it's unplugged so it's no longer draining energy. We also unplug our laptops and phone chargers at night to conserve energy.

- **Say no to plastic or paper:** I am proud to report that I have now converted to bringing my own bags to the grocery store, farmers' market, and other errands nearly 100 percent of the time. I keep the bags in the car so I don't have to challenge my faulty memory by remembering to bring them when I shop. Some stores even give incentives for bringing your own bags, and some cities are mandating that stores charge consumers for plastic bags, so we may as well adopt the habit early.

- **Bundle errands to save on gas and reduce traffic and pollution:** When we have an errand to do, we try to think of every other routine errand that's in the same direction so we can make them all in one trip.

Every bag, plastic container, or foil wrapper that doesn't get unnecessarily manufactured, incinerated, or thrown in landfills because of our efforts helps preserve the health of our planet.

Longtime Scramble subscriber Colleen Masse sent me the recipe for her family's favorite end-of-the-week dinner. She unrolls and fills Pillsbury French bread dough with whatever is left in the fridge at the end of the week, such as meats, sauces, vegetables, and cheese, and bakes it in a pocket. Scramble recipe tester Kimberly Wilcox said she customized the calzones to her teenagers' tastes and they "both wolfed them down and loved them!" They can also make a great party appetizer, sliced into 8 smaller rectangles. Serve this with a spinach salad with mushrooms, sliced onions, and shredded Parmesan cheese.

french bread calzones

Prep + Cook =
30 minutes

4 servings

Nutritional
Information per
serving (% based
upon daily values):
Calories 520, Total
Fat 14g, 22%, Satu-
rated Fat 7g, 35%,
Cholesterol 20mg,
7%, Sodium 1,650mg,
69%, Total Carbohy-
drate 74g, 25%,
Dietary Fiber 5g,
20%, Sugar 8g,
Protein 24g

Nutritional
Information per
serving with side dish
(% based upon daily
values) ¼ of salad:
Calories: 589; Total
Fat: 17g, 26%; Satu-
rated Fat: 7g, 36%;
Cholesterol: 20mg,
7%; Sodium: 1,715mg,
72%; Total Carbohy-
drate: 79g, 26%;
Dietary Fiber: 7g,
26%; Sugar: 10g;
Protein: 26g

2 loaves (11 ounces each) Pillsbury Low Fat Crusty French Roll or Pizza Dough

1 cup red pasta sauce, any variety

1 cup shredded mozzarella cheese

4–8 slices salami (1–2 ounces) (optional)

¾–1 cup sliced mushrooms

1 cup baby spinach

Preheat the oven to 350 degrees, and spray a large baking sheet with nonstick cook-ing spray.

On the baking sheet, unroll the loaves, one at a time, so you have two large flat rec-tangles. On one half of each dough, spread half the sauce and half the cheese. Top it with desired toppings (such as salami, mushrooms, spinach) and fold the other half of the dough over, forming a rectangular pocket. Press the edges of the dough together with your fingers to seal the calzones.

Bake the calzones for 20 to 25 minutes until they are golden brown. (Meanwhile, prepare the salad.) Remove the calzones from the oven, slice them into quarters, let them cool for a few minutes, and serve.

Scramble Flavor Booster: Shake some crushed red pepper flakes or black pepper over the calzone fillings before you close and bake them. Use a more flavorful cheese, such as feta.

Side Dish suggestion: To make the salad, combine 1 bag (6 to 9 ounces) baby spinach (minus the 1 cup used to make the calzones) 1 cup sliced mushrooms, ¼ to ½ red or yellow onion, sliced, ¼ cup shredded or grated Parmesan cheese, and toss it thoroughly with 2 to 4 tablespoons of the dressing of your choice.

This variation of Huevos Rancheros (or ranch eggs) is inspired by my family's annual trip to the Tanque Verde Guest Ranch in Tucson, Arizona. Dude ranch owner Bob Coates serves his ranch eggs with blueberry pancakes and hash browns at a breakfast cookout. Since my family rarely has time for a cookout, let alone a hot breakfast, I like to serve these eggs for a weeknight dinner or a weekend breakfast with crisp turkey bacon and warm whole wheat tortillas.

huevos rancheros with crispy potatoes

Prep (15 minutes) + Cook (30 minutes)

6 servings

Nutritional Information per serving (% based upon daily values): Calories 350, Total Fat 20g, 31%, Saturated Fat 7g, 35%, Cholesterol 305mg, 102%, Sodium 280mg, 12%, Total Carbohydrate 25g, 8%, Dietary Fiber 3g, 12%, Sugar 4g, Protein 17g

Nutritional Information per serving with side dish (% based upon daily values) 2 slices turkey bacon; 1 whole wheat tortilla: Calories: 560; Total Fat: 27g, 42%; Saturated Fat: 10g, 50%; Cholesterol: 335mg, 112%; Sodium: 1,020mg, 43%; Total Carbohydrate: 51g, 17%; Dietary Fiber: 5g, 20%; Sugar: 7g; Protein: 25g

3 medium yellow or red potatoes, cut into ½ -inch cubes

1 large sweet potato, cut into ½ -inch cubes

3 tablespoons olive oil

1 large yellow onion, diced

8 eggs

½ cup nonfat or low-fat cottage cheese

¾ cup shredded Cheddar cheese

2 to 4 tablespoons canned chopped green chiles, or substitute salsa to taste

1 tablespoon butter or margarine

¼ – ½ teaspoon salt, or to taste

⅛ teaspoon black pepper, or to taste

1–2 cups salsa or ketchup for serving (optional)

6 whole wheat tortillas, for serving (optional)

First, start the hash browns: In a microwave-safe dish with a loose-fitting lid, microwave all of the potatoes on high with a few tablespoons of water for 5 to 8 minutes (depending on your microwave) until they are slightly tender when pierced with a fork, or boil them for 5 minutes. You want them fork-tender but not mushy. Drain the potatoes thoroughly.

In a large nonstick skillet or a heavy skillet coated with nonstick cooking spray, heat the oil over medium to medium-high heat. Sauté the onions and potatoes, stirring occasionally, until the potatoes are nicely browned and crispy in some spots, 20 to 30 minutes. (After the potatoes have cooked for about 10 minutes, start the bacon, if you are making it.) Season them with salt and black pepper to taste.

Meanwhile, in a large bowl, beat together the eggs, cottage cheese, Cheddar cheese, and green chiles. In a medium nonstick skillet, heat the butter or margarine over medium heat. When the butter is melted, add the egg mixture and reduce the heat to medium-low. Cook, stirring frequently, until the eggs are just firm, and season them with salt (optional) and black pepper. Remove them from the heat and cover them. Serve the eggs and potatoes with salsa or ketchup, if desired.

Scramble Flavor Booster: Sauté 1 jalapeño pepper with the potatoes and onions. Season the eggs with freshly ground black pepper.

Tip: The trick to browning the potatoes is not to stir them too often, only every 5 minutes or so.

Side Dish suggestion: Prepare 1 package (8 ounces) turkey bacon according to the package directions.

Our whole family likes these sandwiches made with the eggplant, but if you prefer, you can make them with chicken cutlets instead. Serve it with sliced red bell peppers and carrots with ranch or other dip.

hot eggplant (or chicken) parmesan subs

Prep (15 minutes) + Cook (25 minutes)

4 servings

Nutritional Information per serving (% based upon daily values): Calories 390, Total Fat 13g, 20%, Saturated Fat 6g, 30%, Cholesterol 75mg, 25%, Sodium 1,000mg, 42%, Total Carbohydrate 52g, 17%, Dietary Fiber 10g, 40%, Sugar 18g, Protein 22g

Nutritional Information per serving with side dish (% based upon daily values) $\frac{1}{4}$ bell pepper, 1 carrot, 1 tbsp. ranch dressing: Calories: 496; Total Fat: 21g, 32%; Saturated Fat: 7g, 36%; Cholesterol: 30mg, 77%; Sodium: 1,165mg, 49%; Total Carbohydrate: 61g, 20%; Dietary Fiber: 13g, 49%; Sugar: 23g; Protein: 23g

1 egg

$\frac{1}{8}$ cup nonfat or low-fat milk

$\frac{3}{4}$ cup crushed stoned wheat crackers, panko (Japanese bread crumbs), or bread crumbs

$\frac{1}{4}$ cup plus 1 tablespoon grated Parmesan cheese

1 medium eggplant, sliced into $\frac{1}{2}$-inch-thick rounds, or 1 pound chicken cutlets

2 (8–10-inch) loaves of soft whole grain bread

1 cup red pasta sauce or tomato sauce

4 ounces sliced or shredded part-skim mozzarella cheese

Preheat the oven to 475 degrees. In a shallow bowl, beat the egg with the milk. In a second shallow bowl, combine the crackers or bread crumbs and $\frac{1}{4}$ cup Parmesan cheese.

Spray two large baking sheets with nonstick cooking spray. Dip each eggplant slice (or chicken cutlet) in the egg mixture, allowing the excess to drip back into the bowl, and then dip them in the bread crumb mixture, turning them to coat them completely. Lay the slices on the first baking sheet and bake them without flipping them until they are golden brown, 15 to 20 minutes.

Meanwhile, split the loaves in half (try not to cut all the way through) and lay the halves on the second baking sheet, cut side up. Once the eggplant (or chicken) is browned, spread the pasta sauce on all cut sides of the bread, then top one-half of each loaf with the eggplant slices and top the eggplant with a thin layer of mozzarella and Parmesan cheese. Bake them until the cheese is melted and slightly browned, but remove them before the edges of the bread are too brown, 5 to 7 minutes. Close the sandwiches and slice them in half crosswise to serve.

Scramble Flavor Booster: Use spicy pasta sauce or add $\frac{1}{4}$ teaspoon crushed red pepper flakes to the sauce.

Tip: Making the bread (or cracker) crumbs is a great way to finish a box of wheat crackers. Just put the crackers in a bag and pound them with the flat side of a mallet.

index

special offer for SOS! cookbook owners

free trial subscription to the six o'clock scramble

Make weekly shopping and meal planning even faster and easier with the Six O'Clock Scramble Online Menu Planner

WANT TO MAKE YOUR LIFE even easier day in and day out as 6:00 looms and dinner has to be on the table pronto? Organize your weekly meal planning and shopping in seconds with the Six O'Clock Scramble online menu planner. The whole process is as easy as 1-2-3:

1. **Receive the weekly menu plan by e-mail.** Each week you will get a suggested meal plan of 5 seasonal Scramble dinner recipes and side dishes delivered to your e-mail inbox. Use all 5 recipes or customize the menu to fit the tastes and schedules of your family. *As an online subscriber, you will have access to all of the recipes in this cookbook as well as hundreds more in the Scramble database.* And you can search recipes by ingredient, by meal type, or by nutritional requirements to accommodate food allergies, diets, and picky eaters. (To save paper you can print only those recipes not included in this book.)

2. **Print your organized shopping list.** Once you have decided on your Scramble meals for the week, print your customized grocery list that is organized by section of the store. You'll buy only what you need and avoid making extra trips to the store for forgotten ingredients. Subscribers report saving hundreds of dollars each month by wasting less food and gas.

3. **Relax and enjoy with easy, healthy, and delicious seasonal meals.** Since most Scramble recipes take 30 minutes or less to prepare, and you know you have all ingredients on hand, you can come home knowing that the Six O'Clock Scramble has been tamed to a relaxing rhythm.

As a SOS! cookbook owner you are entitled to a free month trial (with absolutely no obligation) so you can see for yourself just how easy the Scramble system can be.

Get your FREE one-month trial subscription today at www.thescramble.com/SOS/freetrial and enter the free trial code "soscookbooktrial."

Offer will expire *no earlier* than 12/31/10.